Management and Cost Accounting

Student's Manual

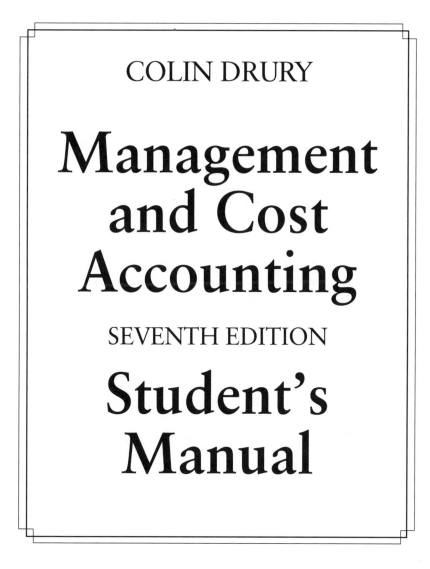

COLIN DRURY

Management and Cost Accounting

SEVENTH EDITION

Student's Manual

SOUTH-WESTERN
CENGAGE Learning

Australia • Brazil • Japan • Korea • Mexico • Singapore • Spain • United Kingdom • United States

SOUTH-WESTERN
CENGAGE Learning

**Management and Cost Accounting
Student's Manual, 7th Edition**

Colin Drury

Publishing Director: Linden Harris

Publisher: Pat Bond

Development Editor: James Clark

Content Project Editor: Alissa Chappell

Production Controller: Paul Herbert

Marketing Manager: Amanda Cheung

Typesetter: Saxon Graphics

Cover design: Jackie Wrout

For product information and technology assistance, contact **emea.info@cengage.com**.
For permission to use material from this text or product, and for permission queries, email **clsuk.permissions@cengage.com.**

The Author has asserted the right under the Copyright, Designs and Patents Act 1988 to be identified as Author of this Work.

British Library Cataloguing-in-Publication Data
A catalogue record for this book is available from the British Library.

ISBN: 978-1-84480-568-6

Cengage Learning EMEA
Cheriton House, North Way, Andover, Hampshire, SP10 5BE, United Kingdom

Cengage Learning products are represented in Canada by Nelson Education Ltd.

For your lifelong learning solutions, visit **www.cengage.co.uk**

Purchase your next print book, e-book or e-chapter at **www.CengageBrain.com**

Printed by RR Donnelley, China
5 6 7 8 9 10 – 12 11 10

Contents

Preface

This manual is complementary to the main text, *Management and Cost Accounting.* Throughout the main text the illustrations have been kept simple to enable the reader to understand the principles involved in designing and evaluating management and cost accounting systems. It is essential that students work through a wide range of problems to gain experience on the application of principles but there is insufficient classroom time for tutorial guidance to meet this requirement. The Students' Manual provides this guidance by enabling students to work independently on a wide range of problems and compare their answers with the suggested solutions.

The solutions given in this manual are my own and not the approved solutions of the professional body setting the question. Where an essay question is asked and a full answer requires undue repetition of the book, either references are made to the appropriate sections of the main book, or an answer guide or outline is provided. You should note that there will be no 'ideal' answer to questions which are not strictly numerical. Answers are provided which, it is felt, would be generally acceptable in most contexts.

Where possible the questions are arranged in ascending order of difficulty. The reader should select questions which are appropriate to the course which is being pursued. As a general rule questions titled 'Intermediate' and are appropriate for a first year course. These questions are mainly concerned with cost accounting which is covered in Part II of the main text. Questions titled 'Advanced' are appropriate for a second year course.

Finally I would like to thank, once again, the Association of Accounting Technicians, the Institute of Chartered Accountants in England and Wales, the Chartered Association of Certified Accountants and the Chartered Institute of Management Accountants for permission to reproduce questions which have appeared in past examinations.

Part I
Questions

An introduction to cost terms and concepts

Questions to Chapter 2

Advanced

Question 2.1

(i) Costs may be classified in a number of ways including classification by behaviour, by function, by expense type, by controllability and by relevance.

(ii) Management accounting should assist in EACH of the planning, control and decision making processes in an organisation.

Discuss the ways in which relationships between statements (i) and (ii) are relevant in the design of an effective management accounting system.

(15 marks)
ACCA Paper 9 Information for Control and Decision Making

Intermediate

Question 2.2

(a) 'Discretionary costs are troublesome because managers usually find it difficult to separate and quantify the results of their use in the business, as compared with variable and other fixed costs.'

You are required to discuss the above statement and include in your answer the meaning of discretionary costs, variable costs and fixed costs; give two illustrations of each of these three named costs.

(12 marks)

(b) A drug company has initiated a research project which is intended to develop a new product. Expenditures to date on this particular research total £500 000 but it is now estimated that a further £200 000 will need to be spent before the product can be marketed. Over the estimated life of the product the profit potential has a net present value of £350 000.

You are required to advise management whether they should continue or abandon the project. Support your conclusion with a numerate statement and state what kind of cost is the £500 000.

(5 marks)

(c) Opportunity costs and notional costs are not recognized by financial accounting systems but need to be considered in many decisions taken by management.

You are required to explain briefly the meanings of opportunity costs and notional costs; give two examples of each to illustrate the meanings you have attached to them.

(8 marks)
(Total 25 marks)
CIMA Stage 2 Cost Accounting

Intermediate: Relevant costs and cost behaviour

Question 2.3

(a) Distinguish between 'opportunity cost' and 'out of pocket cost' giving a numerical example of each using your own figures to support your answer.

(6 marks)

(b) Jason travels to work by train to his 5-day week job. Instead of buying daily tickets he finds it cheaper to buy a quarterly season ticket which costs £188 for 13 weeks.

Debbie, an acquaintance, who also makes the same journey, suggests that they both travel in Jason's car and offers to give him £120 each quarter towards his car expenses. Except for weekend travelling and using it for local college attendance near his home on three evenings each week to study for his CIMA Stage 2, the car remains in Jason's garage.

Jason estimates that using his car for work would involve him, each quarter, in the following expenses:

	(£)
Depreciation (proportion of annual figure)	200
Petrol and oil	128
Tyres and miscellaneous	52

You are required to state whether Jason should accept Debbie's offer and to draft a statement to show clearly the monetary effect of your conclusion.

(5 marks)

(c) A company with a financial year 1 September to 31 August prepared a sales budget which resulted in the following cost structure:

		% of sales
Direct materials		32
Direct wages		18
Production overhead:	variable	6
	fixed	24
Administrative and selling costs:	variable	3
	fixed	7
Profit		10

After ten weeks, however, it became obvious that the sales budget was too optimistic and it has now been estimated that because of a reduction in sales volume, for the full year, sales will total £2 560 000 which is only 80% of the previously budgeted figure.

You are required to present a statement for management showing the amended sales and cost structure in £s and percentages, in a marginal costing format.

(4 marks)
(Total 15 marks)
CIMA Stage 2 Cost Accounting

Cost assignment

Questions to Chapter 3

Intermediate: Overhead analysis, calculation of overhead rates and a product cost

Question 3.1

Knowing that you are studying for the CIMA qualification, a friend who manages a small business has sought your advice about how to produce quotations in response to the enquiries which her business receives. Her business is sheet metal fabrication – supplying ducting for dust extraction and air conditioning installations. She believes that she has lost orders recently through the use of a job cost estimating system which was introduced, on the advice of her auditors, seven years ago. You are invited to review this system.

Upon investigation, you find that a plant-wide percentage of 125% is added to prime costs in order to arrive at a selling price. The percentage added is intended to cover all overheads for the three production departments (Departments P, Q and R), all the selling, distribution and administration costs, and the profit.

You also discover that the selling, distribution and administration costs equate to roughly 20% of total production costs, and that to achieve the desired return on capital employed, a margin of 20% of sales value is necessary.

You recommend an analysis of overhead cost items be undertaken with the objective of determining a direct labour hour rate of overhead absorption for each of the three departments work passes through. (You think about activity-based costing but feel this would be too sophisticated and difficult to introduce at the present time.)

There are 50 direct workers in the business plus 5 indirect production people.

From the books, records and some measuring, you ascertain the following information which will enable you to compile an overhead analysis spreadsheet, and to determine overhead absorption rates per direct labour hour for departmental overhead purposes:

Cost/expense	Annual amount	Basis for apportionment where allocation not given
	£	
Repairs and maintenance	62 000	Technical assessment: P £42 000, Q £10 000, R £10 000
Depreciation	40 000	Cost of plant and equipment
Consumable supplies	9 000	Direct labour hours
Wage-related costs	87 000	12½% of direct wages costs
Indirect labour	90 000	Direct labour hours
Canteen/rest/smoke room	30 000	Number of direct workers
Business rates and insurance	26 000	Floor area

COST ASSIGNMENT ▬▬▬▬▬▬▬▬▬▬▬▬▬▬▬▬▬▬▬▬▬▬▬▬▬▬▬▬▬▬▬ 5

Other estimates/information

	Department P	Department Q	Department R
Estimated direct labour hours	50 000	30 000	20 000
Direct wages costs	£386 000	£210 000	£100 000
Number of direct workers	25	15	10
Floor area in square metres	5 000	4 000	1 000
Plant and equipment, at cost	£170 000	£140 000	£90 000

Required:

(a) Calculate the overhead absorption rates for each department, based on direct labour hours.

(9 marks)

(b) Prepare a sample quotation for Job 976, utilizing information given in the question, your answer to (a) above, and the following additional information:

Estimated direct material cost: £800
Estimated direct labour hours: 30 in Department P
  10 in Department Q
  5 in Department R

(3 marks)

(c) Calculate what would have been quoted for Job 976 under the 'auditors' system' and comment on whether your friend's suspicions about lost business could be correct.

(3 marks)
(Total 15 marks)
CIMA Stage 2 Cost Accounting

Question 3.2

Intermediate: Calculation of overhead rates and a product cost

DC Limited is an engineering company which uses job costing to attribute costs to individual products and services provided to its customers. It has commenced the preparation of its fixed production overhead cost budget for 2001 and has identified the following costs:

	(£000)
Machining	600
Assembly	250
Finishing	150
Stores	100
Maintenance	80
	1 180

The stores and maintenance departments are production service departments. An analysis of the services they provide indicates that their costs should be apportioned accordingly:

	Machining	Assembly	Finishing	Stores	Maintenance
Stores	40%	30%	20%	—	10%
Maintenance	55%	20%	20%	5%	—

The number of machine and labour hours budgeted for 2001 is:

	Machining	Assembly	Finishing
Machine hours	50 000	4 000	5 000
Labour hours	10 000	30 000	20 000

Requirements:

(a) Calculate appropriate overhead absorption rates for each production department for 2001.

(9 marks)

(b) Prepare a quotation for job number XX34, which is to be commenced early in 2001, assuming that it has:

Direct materials   costing £2400
Direct labour   costing £1500
and requires:

	machine hours	labour hours
Machining department	45	10
Assembly department	5	15
Finishing department	4	12

and that profit is 20% of selling price.

(5 marks)

(c) Assume that in 2001 the actual fixed overhead cost of the assembly department totals £300 000 and that the actual machine hours were 4200 and actual labour hours were 30 700.

Prepare the fixed production overhead control account for the assembly department, showing clearly the causes of any over-/under-absorption.

(5 marks)

(d) Explain how activity based costing would be used in organisations like DC Limited.

(6 marks)
(Total marks 25)
CIMA Stage 2 Operational Cost Accounting

Intermediate: Calculation of overhead absorption rates and under/over recovery of overheads

Question 3.3

A manufacturing company has two production cost centres (Departments A and B) and one service cost centre (Department C) in its factory.

A predetermined overhead absorption rate (to two decimal places of £) is established for each of the production cost centres on the basis of budgeted overheads and budgeted machine hours.

The overheads of each production cost centre comprise directly allocated costs and a share of the costs of the service cost centre.

Budgeted production overhead data for a period is as follows:

	Department A	Department B	Department C
Allocated costs	£217 860	£374 450	£103 970
Apportioned costs	£45 150	£58 820	(£103 970)
Machine hours	13 730	16 110	
Direct labour hours	16 360	27 390	

Actual production overhead costs and activity for the same period are:

	Department A	Department B	Department C
Allocated costs	£219 917	£387 181	£103 254
Machine hours	13 672	16 953	
Direct labour hours	16 402	27 568	

70% of the actual costs of Department C are to be apportioned to production cost centres on the basis of actual machine hours worked and the remainder on the basis of actual direct labour hours.

Required:

(a) Establish the production overhead absorption rates for the period.

(3 marks)

(b) Determine the under- or over-absorption of production overhead for the period in each production cost centre. (Show workings clearly.)

(12 marks)

(c) Explain when, and how, the repeated distribution method may be applied in the overhead apportionment process.

(5 marks)
(Total 20 marks)
ACCA Management Information – Paper 3

Question 3.4

Intermediate: Analysis of under/over recovery of overheads and a discussion of blanket versus department overheads

(a) One of the factories in the XYZ Group of companies absorbs fixed production overheads into product cost using a pre-determined machine hour rate.

In Year 1, machine hours budgeted were 132 500 and the absorption rate for fixed production overheads was £18.20 per machine hour. Overheads absorbed and incurred were £2 442 440 and £2 317 461 respectively.

In Year 2, machine hours were budgeted to be 5% higher than those actually worked in Year 1. Budgeted and actual fixed production overhead expenditure were £2 620 926 and £2 695 721 respectively, and actual machine hours were 139 260.

Required:

Analyse, in as much detail as possible, the under-/over-absorption of fixed production overhead occurring in Years 1 and 2, and the change in absorption rate between the two years.

(15 marks)

(b) Contrast the use of

(i) blanket as opposed to departmental overhead absorption rates;
(ii) predetermined overhead absorption rates as opposed to rates calculated from actual activity and expenditure.

(10 marks)
(Total 25 marks)
ACCA Cost and Management Accounting 1

Question 5

Intermediate: Calculation of fixed and variable overhead rates, normal activity level and under/over recovery of overheads

(a) C Ltd is a manufacturing company. In one of the production departments in its main factory a machine hour rate is used for absorbing production overhead. This is established as a predetermined rate, based on normal activity. The rate that will be used for the period which is just commencing is £15.00 per machine hour. Overhead expenditure anticipated, at a range of activity levels, is as follows:

Activity level (machine hours)	(£)
1500	25 650
1650	26 325
2000	27 900

Required:

Calculate:

(i) the variable overhead rate per machine hour;

(ii) the total budgeted fixed overhead;

(iii) the normal activity level of the department; and

(iv) the extent of over-/under-absorption if actual machine hours are 1700 and expenditure is as budgeted.

(10 marks)

(b) In another of its factories, C Ltd carries out jobs to customers' specifications. A particular job requires the following machine hours and direct labour hours in the two production departments:

	Machining Department	Finishing Department
Direct labour hours	25	28
Machine hours	46	8

Direct labour in both departments is paid at a basic rate of £4.00 per hour. 10% of the direct labour hours in the finishing department are overtime hours, paid at 125% of basic rate. Overtime premiums are charged to production overhead.

The job requires the manufacture of 189 components. Each component requires 1.1 kilos of prepared material. Loss on preparation is 10% of unprepared material, which costs £2.35 per kilo.

Overhead absorption rates are to be established from the following data:

	Machining Department	Finishing Department
Production overhead	£35 280	£12 480
Direct labour hours	3 500	7 800
Machine hours	11 200	2 100

Required:

(i) Calculate the overhead absorption rate for each department and justify the absorption method used.

(ii) Calculate the cost of the job.

(15 marks)
(Total 25 marks)
ACCA Level 1

Question 3.6

Intermediate: Calculation of overhead rates and under/over-recovery
(This question relates to material covered in Learning Note 3.1)

A factory with three departments uses a single production overhead absorption rate, expressed as a percentage of direct wages cost. It has been suggested that departmental overhead absorption rates would result in more accurate job costs. Set out below are budgeted and actual data for the previous period, together with information relating to job no. 657.

		Direct wages (000s)	Direct labour hours	Machine hours	Production overheads (000s)
Budget:					
Department:	A	25	10 000	40 000	120
	B	100	50 000	10 000	30
	C	25	25 000	—	75
Total:		150	85 000	50 000	225
Actual:					
Department:	A	30	12 000	45 000	130
	B	80	45 000	14 000	28
	C	30	30 000	—	80
Total:		140	87 000	59 000	238

During this period job no. 657 incurred the actual costs and actual times in the departments as shown below:

		Direct material (£)	Direct wages (£)	Direct labour hours	Machine hours
Department:	A	120	100	20 000	40 000
	B	60	60	40 000	10 000
	C	10	10	10 000	—

After adding production overhead to prime cost, one-third is added to production cost for gross profit. This assumes that a reasonable profit is earned after deducting administration, selling and distribution costs. You are required to:

(a) calculate the current overhead absorption rate;

(b) using the rate obtained in (a) above, calculate the production overhead charged to job no. 657, and state the production cost and expected gross profit on this job;

(c) (i) comment on the suggestion that departmental overhead absorption rates would result in more accurate job costs; and

   (ii) compute such rates, briefly explaining your reason for each rate;

(d) using the rates calculated in (c) (ii) above, show the overhead, by department and in total, that would apply to job no. 657;

(e) show the over-/under-absorption, by department and in total, for the period, using:

   (i) the current rate in your answer to (a) above; and

   (ii) your suggested rates in your answers to (c) (ii) above.

(20 marks)
CIMA Cost Accounting 1

Reapportionment of service department costs

A business operates with two production centres and three service centres. Costs have been allocated and apportioned to these centres as follows:

Production centres		Service centres		
1	**2**	**A**	**B**	**C**
£2000	£3500	£300	£500	£700

Information regarding how the service centres work for each other and for the production centres is given as:

Work done for:

	Production centres		Service centres		
	1	**2**	**A**	**B**	**C**
By A	45%	45%	—	10%	—
By B	50%	20%	20%	—	10%
By C	60%	40%	—	—	—

Information concerning production requirements in the two production centres is as follows:

	Centre 1	Centre 2
Units produced	1500 units	2000 units
Machine hours	3000 hours	4500 hours
Labour hours	2000 hourws	6000 hours

Required

(a) Using the reciprocal method calculate the total overloads in production centres 1 and 2 after reapportionment of the service centre costs.

(7 marks)

(b) Using the most appropriate basis establish the overhead absorption rate for production centre 1. Briefly explain the reason for your chosen absorption basis.

(3 marks)
(Total 10 marks)
ACCA Paper 1.2 – Financial Information for Management

Advanced: Reapportionment of service department costs and a discussion of how fully allocated costs can be useful

Megalith Manufacturing divides its plant into two main production departments, Processing and Assembly. It also has three main service-providing departments, Heat, Maintenance and Steam, which provide services to the production departments and to each other. The costs of providing these services are allocated to departments on the bases indicated below:

	Total cost	Basis of allocation
Heat	£90 000	Floor area
Maintenance	£300 000	Hours worked
Steam	£240 000	Units consumed

During the last year, the services provided were:

To	Heat	Maintenance	Steam	Processing	Assembly
From Heat (m²)		5 000	5 000	40 000	50 000
Maintenance (hrs)	3 000		4 500	7 500	15 000
Steam (units)	192 000	48 000		480 000	240 000

Requirements:

(a) Allocate the costs of service departments to production departments, using each of the following methods:

    (i)   direct

(3 marks)

    (ii) step-down

(4 marks)

    (iii) reciprocal

(6 marks)

(b) What is the main problem likely to be encountered in using the information generated by any of the above systems of allocation, given that a substantial proportion of the costs incurred in each service department are fixed for the year? How would you attempt to overcome this problem?

(5 marks)

(c) Given that cost allocation is an essentially arbitrary process, explain how total costs which include substantial amounts of allocated costs can be useful.

(7 marks)
(Total 25 marks)
ICAEW P2 Management Accounting

Question 3.9

Intermediate: Explanation of a product cost calculation

In order to identify the costs incurred in carrying out a range of work to customer specification in its factory, a company has a job costing system. This system identifies costs directly with a job where this is possible and reasonable. In addition, production overhead costs are absorbed into the cost of jobs at the end of each month, at an actual rate per direct labour hour for each of the two production departments.

One of the jobs carried out in the factory during the month just ended was Job No. 123. The following information has been collected relating specifically to this job:

400 kilos of Material Y were issued from stores to Department A. 76 direct labour hours were worked in Department A at a basic wage of £4.50 per hour. 6 of these hours were classified as overtime at a premium of 50%.

300 kilos of Material Z were issued from stores to Department B. Department B returned 30 kilos of Material Z to the storeroom being excess to requirements for the job.

110 direct labour hours were worked in Department B at a basic wage of £4.00 per hour. 30 of these hours were classified as overtime at a premium of 40%. *All* overtime worked in Department B in the month is a result of the request of a customer for early completion of another job, which had been originally scheduled for completion in the month following.

Department B discovered defects in some of the work, which was returned to Department A for rectification. 3 labour hours were worked in Department A on rectification (these are additional to the 76 direct labour hours in Department A noted above). Such rectification is regarded as a normal part of the work carried out generally in the department.

Department B damaged 5 kilos of Material Z which then had to be disposed of. Such losses of material are not expected to occur.

	Department A (£)	Department B (£)
Direct materials issued from stores*	6 500	13 730
Direct materials returned to stores	135	275
Direct labour, at basic wage rate†	9 090	11 200
Indirect labour, at basic wage rate	2 420	2 960
Overtime premium	450	120
Lubricants and cleaning compounds	520	680
Maintenance	720	510
Other	1 200	2 150

Materials are priced at the end of each month on a weighted average basis. Relevant information of material stock movements during the month, for materials Y and Z, is as follows:

	Material Y	Material Z
Opening stock	1050 kilos (value £529.75)	6970 kilos (value £9946.50)
Purchases	600 kilos at £0.50 per kilo 500 kilos at £0.50 per kilo 400 kilos at £0.52 per kilo	16 000 kilos at £1.46 per kilo
Issues from stores	1430 kilos	8100 kilos
Returns to stores	—	30 kilos

*This includes, in Department B, the scrapped Material Z. This was the only material scrapped in the month.
†All direct labour in Department A is paid a basic wage of £4.50 per hour, and in Department B £4.00 per hour. Department A direct labour includes a total of 20 hours spent on rectification work.

Required:

(a) Prepare a list of the costs that should be assigned to Job No. 123. Provide an explanation of your treatment of each item.

(17 marks)

(b) Discuss briefly how information concerning the cost of individual jobs can be used.

(5 marks)
(Total 22 marks)
ACCA Level 1 Costing

Accounting entries for a job costing system

Questions to Chapter 4

Question 4.1

Intermediate: Interlocking accounts

CD Ltd, a company engaged in the manufacture of specialist marine engines, operates a historic job cost accounting system that is not integrated with the financial accounts.

At the beginning of May 2000 the opening balances in the cost ledger were as follows:

	(£)
Stores ledger control account	85 400
Work in progress control account	167 350
Finished goods control account	49 250
Cost ledger control account	302 000

During the month, the following transactions took place:

	(£)
Materials:	
Purchases	42 700
Issues to production	63 400
to general maintenance	1 450
to construction of manufacturing equipment	7 650
Factory wages:	
Total gross wages paid	124 000

£12 500 of the above gross wages were incurred on the construction of manufacturing equipment, £35 750 were indirect wages and the balance was direct.

Production overheads: the actual amount incurred, excluding items shown above, was £152 350; £30 000 was absorbed by the manufacturing equipment under construction and under absorbed overhead written off at the end of the month amounted to £7550.

Royalty payments: one of the engines produced is manufactured under licence. £2150 is the amount that will be paid to the inventor for the month's production of that particular engine.

Selling overheads: £22 000.

Sales: £410 000.

The company's gross profit margin is 25% on factory cost.

At the end of May stocks of work in progress had increased by £12 000. The manufacturing equipment under construction was completed within the month, and transferred out of the cost ledger at the end of the month.

Required:

Prepare the relevant control accounts, costing profit and loss account, and any other accounts you consider necessary to record the above transactions in the cost ledger for May 2000.

(22 marks)
ACCA Foundation Costing

Intermediate: Reconciliation of cost and financial accounts

K Limited operates separate cost accounting and financial accounting systems. The following manufacturing and trading statement has been prepared from the financial accounts for the *quarter* ended 31 March:

	(£)	(£)
Raw materials:		
Opening stock	48 800	
Purchases	108 000	
	156 800	
Closing stock	52 000	
Raw materials consumed		104 800
Direct wages		40 200
Production overhead		60 900
Production cost incurred		205 900
Work in progress:		
Opening stock	64 000	
Closing stock	58 000	6 000
Cost of goods produced		211 900
Sales		440 000
Finishing goods:		
Opening stock	120 000	
Cost of goods produced	211 900	
	331 900	
Closing stock	121 900	
Cost of goods sold		210 000
Gross profit		230 000

From the cost accounts, the following information has been extracted:

Control account balances at 1 January	(£)
Raw material stores	49 500
Work in progress	60 100
Finished goods	115 400

Transactions for the quarter:	(£)
Raw materials issued	104 800
Cost of goods produced	222 500
Cost of goods sold	212 100
Loss of materials damaged by flood (insurance claim pending)	2 400

A notional rent of £4000 *per month* has been charged in the cost accounts. Production overhead was absorbed at the rate of 185% of direct wages.

You are required to:

(a) prepare the following control accounts in the cost ledger:
    raw materials stores;
    work in process;
    finished goods;
    production overhead;

(10 marks)

(b) prepare a statement reconciling the gross profits as per the cost accounts and the financial accounts;

(11 marks)

(c) comment on the possible accounting treatment(s) of the under or over absorption of production overhead, assuming that the financial year of the company is 1 January to 31 December.

(4 marks)
CIMA Cost Accounting 1

Question 4.3

Integrated accounts and computation of the net profit

Set out below are incomplete cost accounts for a period for a manufacturing business:

Stores Ledger Control Account

Opening Balance	£60 140		
Cost Ledger Control A/c	£93 106		
	£153 246		£153 246

Production Wages Control Account

Cost Ledger Control A/c		Finished Goods A/c	£87 480
		Production O'hd Control A/c	

Production Overhead Control Account

Cost Ledger Control A/c	£116 202		
Prod. Wages Control A/c			

Finished Goods Control Account

Opening Balance	£147 890	Prod. Cost of Sales (variable)	
		Closing Balance	£150 187

Notes:

1. *Raw materials:*

   Issues of materials from stores for the period:

   Material Y: 1164 kg (issued at a periodic weighted average price, calculated to two decimal places of £). Other materials: £78 520.

   No indirect materials are held on the Stores ledger.

   Transactions for Material Y in the period:

   Opening stock: 540 kg, £7663
   Purchases: 1100 kg purchased at £14.40 per kg

2. *Payroll:*

	Direct workers	Indirect workers
Hours worked:		
Basic time	11 140	4 250
Overtime	1 075	405
Productive time – direct workers	11 664	
Basic hourly rate (£)	7.50	5.70

Overtime, which is paid at basic rate plus one third, is regularly worked to meet production targets.

3. *Production overheads:*

   The business uses a marginal costing system. 60% of production overheads are fixed costs. Variable production overhead costs are absorbed at a rate of 70% of actual direct labour.

4. *Finished goods:*

   There is no work in progress at the beginning or end of the period, and a Work in Progress Account is not kept. Direct materials issued, direct labour and production overheads absorbed are transferred to the Finished Goods Control Account.

   Required:

   (a) Complete the above four accounts for the period, by listing the missing amounts and descriptions.

   (13 marks)

   (b) Provide an analysis of the indirect labour for the period.

   (3 marks)

   (c) Calculate the contribution and the net profit for the period, based on the cost accounts prepared in (a) and using the following additional information:

Sales	£479 462
Selling and administration overheads:	
variable	£38 575
fixed	£74 360

   (4 marks)
   (Total 20 marks)
   ACCA Management Information – Paper 3

Intermediate: Stores pricing and preparation of relevant ledger accounts

Question 4.4

V Ltd operates interlocking financial and cost accounts. The following balances were in the cost ledger at the beginning of a month, the last month (Month 12) of the financial year:

	Dr	Cr
Raw material stock control a/c	£28 944	
Finished goods stock control a/c	£77 168	
Financial ledger control a/c		£106 112

There is no work in progress at the end of each month.

21 600 kilos of the single raw material were in stock at the beginning of Month 12. Purchases and issues during the month were as follows:
Purchases:
   7th, 17 400 kilos at £1.35 per kilo
   29th, 19 800 kilos at £1.35 per kilo

Issues:
   1st, 7270 kilos
   8th, 8120 kilos
   15th, 8080 kilos
   22nd, 9115 kilos

A weighted average price per kilo (to four decimal places of a £) is used to value issues of raw material to production. A new average price is determined after each material purchase, and issues are charged out in total to the nearest £.
Costs of labour and overhead incurred during Month 12 were £35 407. Production of the company's single product was 17 150 units.

Stocks of finished goods were:

Beginning of Month 12,	16 960 units.
End of Month 12,	17 080 units.

Transfers from finished goods stocks on sale of the product are made on a FIFO basis.

Required:

(a) Prepare the raw material stock control account, and the finished goods stock control account, for Month 12. (Show detailed workings to justify the summary entries made in the accounts.)

(12 marks)

(b) Explain the purpose of the financial ledger control account.

(4 marks)

(c) Prepare the raw material usage and the raw material purchases budgets for the year ahead (in kilos) using the following information where relevant:

Sales budget, 206 000 units.

Closing stock of finished goods at the end of the budget year should be sufficient to meet 20 days sales demand in the year following that, when sales are expected to be 10% higher in volume than in the budget year.

Closing stock of raw materials should be sufficient to produce 11 700 units.

(NB You should assume that production efficiency will be maintained at the same level, and that there are 250 working days in each year.)

(9 marks)
(Total 25 marks)
ACCA Level 1 Costing

Question 4.5

Integrated accounts, profits computation and reconciliation relating to absorption and marginal costing

A company manufactures two products (A and B). In the period just ended production and sales of the two products were:

	Product A (000 units)	Product B (000 units)
Production	41	27
Sales	38	28

The selling prices of the products were £35 and £39 per unit for A and B respectively.

Opening stocks were:

Raw materials	£72 460
Finished goods:	
Product A	£80 640 (3200 units)
Product B	£102 920 (3100 units)

Raw material purchases (on credit) during the period totalled £631 220. Raw material costs per unit are £7.20 for Product A and £11.60 for Product B.

Direct labour hours worked during the period totalled 73 400 (1 hour per unit of Product A and 1.2 hours per unit of Product B), paid at a basic rate of £8.00 per hour.

3250 overtime hours were worked by direct workers, paid at a premium of 25% over the basic rate. Overtime premiums are treated as indirect production costs. Other indirect labour costs during the period totalled £186 470 and production overhead costs (other than indirect labour) were £549 630. Production overheads are absorbed at a rate of £10.00 per direct labour hour (including £6.80 per hour for fixed production overheads). Any over-/under- absorbed balances are transferred to the Profit and Loss Account in the period in which they arise. Non-production over-heads totalled £394 700 in the period.

Required:

(a) Prepare the following accounts for the period in the company's integrated accounting system:
   (i)   Raw material stock control;
   (ii) Production overhead control;
   (iii) Finished goods stock control (showing the details of the valuation of closing stocks as a note).

(12 marks)

(b) Prepare the Profit and Loss Account for the period, clearly showing sales, production cost of sales and gross profit for each product.

(4 marks)

(c) Calculate, and explain, the difference in the net profit (loss) for the period if the marginal costing method is employed.

(4 marks)
(Total 20 marks)
ACCA Management Information – Paper 3

Intermediate: Labour cost accounting

Question 4.6

(a) Describe briefly the purpose of the 'wages control account'.

(3 marks)

(b) A manufacturing company has approximately 600 weekly paid direct and indirect production workers. It incurred the following costs and deductions relating to the payroll for the week ended 2 May:

	(£)	(£)
Gross wages		180 460
Deductions:		
Employees' National Insurance	14 120	
Employees' pension fund contributions	7 200	
Income tax (PAYE)	27 800	
Court order retentions	1 840	
Trade union subscriptions	1 200	
Private health care contributions	6 000	
Total deductions		58 160
Net wages paid		122 300

The employer's National Insurance contribution for the week was £18 770.

From the wages analysis the following information was extracted:

	Direct workers £	Indirect workers £
Paid for ordinary time	77 460	38 400
Overtime wages at normal hourly rates	16 800	10 200
Overtime premium (treat as overhead)	5 600	3 400
Shift premiums/allowances	8 500	4 500
Capital work in progress expenditure*	—	2 300*

Statutory sick pay	5 700	3 300
Paid for idle time	4 300	—
	118 360	62 100

*Work done by building maintenance workers concreting floor area for a warehouse extension.

You are required to show journal entries to indicate clearly how each item should be posted into the accounts
(i) from the payroll, and
(ii) from the Wages Control Account to other accounts, based on the wages analysis.

Note: Narrations for the journal entries are not required.

(12 marks)
(Total 15 marks)
CIMA Stage 2 Cost Accounting

Question 4.7

Intermediate: Calculation as analysis of gross wages and preparation of wages and overhead control accounts

The finishing department in a factory has the following payroll data for the month just ended:

	Direct workers	Indirect workers
Total attendance time (including overtime)	2640 hours	940 hours
Productive time	2515 hours	—
Non-productive time:		
Machine breakdown	85 hours	—
Waiting for work	40 hours	—
Overtime	180 hours	75 hours
Basic hourly rate	£5.00	£4.00
Group bonuses	£2840	£710
Employers' National Insurance contributions	£1460	£405

Overtime, which is paid at 140% of basic rate, is usually worked in order to meet the factory's general requirements. However, 40% of the overtime hours of both direct and indirect workers in the month were worked to meet the urgent request of a particular customer.
Required:

(a) Calculate the gross wages paid to direct workers and to indirect workers in the month.

(4 marks)

(b) Using the above information, record the relevant entries for the month in the finishing department's wages control account and production overhead control account. (You should clearly indicate the account in which the corresponding entry would be made in the company's separate cost accounting system. Workings must be shown.)

(10 marks)
(Total 14 marks)
ACCA Foundation Paper 3

Process costing

Questions to Chapter 5

Intermediate: Preparation of process accounts with all output fully completed   **Question 5.1**

A chemical compound is made by raw material being processed through two processes. The output of Process A is passed to Process B where further material is added to the mix. The details of the process costs for the financial period number 10 were as shown below:

Process A

Direct material	2000 kilograms at 5 per kg
Direct labour	£7200
Process plant time	140 hours at £60 per hour

Process B

Direct material	1400 kilograms at £12 per kg
Direct labour	£4200
Process plant time	80 hours at £72.50 per hour

The departmental overhead for Period 10 was £6840 and is absorbed into the costs of each process on direct labour cost.

	Process A	Process B
Expected output was	80% of input	90% of input
Actual output was	1400 kg	2620 kg

Assume no finished stock at the beginning of the period and no work in progress at either the beginning or the end of the period.
Normal loss is contaminated material which is sold as scrap for £0.50 per kg from Process A and £1.825 per kg from Process B, for both of which immediate payment is received.
You are required to prepare the accounts for Period 10, for
- (i) Process A,
- (ii) Process B,
- (iii) Normal loss/gain,
- (iv) Abnormal loss/gain,
- (v) Finished goods,
- (vi) Profit and loss (extract).

(15 marks)
CIMA Stage 2 Cost Accounting

Intermediate: Equivalent production and no losses   **Question 5.2**

A firm operates a process, the details of which for the period were as follows. There was no opening work-in-progress. During the period 8250 units were received from the previous process at a value of £453 750, labour and overheads were £350 060 and material introduced was £24 750. At the end of the period the closing work-in-progress was 1600 units, which were 100% complete in respect of materials, and

60% complete in respect of labour and overheads. The balance of units were transferred to finished goods.

Requirements:

(a) Calculate the number of equivalent units produced.

(3 marks)

(b) Calculate the cost per equivalent unit.

(2 marks)

(c) Prepare the process account.

(7 marks)

(d) Distinguish between joint products and by-products, and briefly explain the difference in accounting treatment between them.

(3 marks)

(Total 15 marks)

CIMA Stage 1 Cost Accounting and Quantitative Methods

Question 5.3   **Intermediate: Losses in process (weighted average)**

A company manufactures a product that requires two separate processes for its completion. Output from Process 1 is immediately input to Process 2.

The following information is available for Process 2 for a period:

(i) Opening work-in-progress units:
12 000 units: 90% complete as to materials, 50% complete as to conversion costs.

(ii) Opening work-in-progress value:
Process 1 output: £13 440
Process 2 materials added: £4970
Conversion costs: £3120.

(iii) Costs incurred during the period:
Process 1 output: £107 790 (95 000 units)
Process 2 materials added: £44 000
Conversion costs: £51 480.

(iv) Closing work-in-progress units
10 000 units: 90% complete as to materials, 70% complete as to conversion costs.

(v) The product is inspected when it is complete. 200 units of finished product were rejected during the period, in line with the normal allowance. Units rejected have no disposal value.

Required:

(a) Calculate the unit cost of production for the period in Process 2 (to three decimal places of £), using the periodic weighted average method.

(7 marks)

(b) Prepare the Process 2 Account for the period using the unit cost of production calculated in (a) above.

(5 marks)

(c) Explain why, and how, the Process 2 Account would be different if there was no normal allowance for rejects. NB The process account should not be reworked.

(5 marks)

(d) Explain how the process account workings, required in (a) above to calculate the unit cost, would differ if the FIFO valuation method was used instead.

(3 marks)

(Total 20 marks)

ACCA Management Information – Paper 3

Intermediate: Equivalent production with no losses (FIFO method)

A company operates a manufacturing process where six people work as a team and are paid a weekly group bonus based upon the actual output of the team compared with output expected.

A basic 37 hour week is worked during which the expected output from the process is 4000 equivalent units of product. Basic pay is £5.00 per hour and the bonus for the group, shared equally, is £0.80 per unit in excess of expected output.

In the week just ended, basic hours were worked on the process. The following additional information is provided for the week:

Opening work in process (1000 units):
   Materials £540 (100% complete)
   Labour and overheads £355 (50% complete).
During the week:
   Materials used £2255
   Overheads incurred £1748
   Completed production 3800 units
Closing work in process (1300 units)
   Materials (100% complete)
   Labour and overheads (75% complete).
There are no process losses.
The FIFO method is used to apportion costs.

Required:

(a) Prepare the process account for the week just ended.

(*10 marks*)

(b) Explain the purpose of the following documents which are used in the control of, and accounting for, the materials used in the process described in part (a)
   (i)   purchase requisition
   (ii) materials (stores) requisition.

(*4 marks*)
(*14 marks*)
ACCA Foundation Stage Paper 3

Intermediate: Equivalent production and losses in process

A concentrated liquid fertilizer is manufactured by passing chemicals through two consecutive processes. Stores record cards for the chemical ingredients used exclusively by the first process show the following data for May 2000:

Opening stock	4 000 litres	£10 800
Closing stock	8 000 litres	£24 200
Receipts into store	20 000 litres	£61 000

Other process data for May is tabulated below:

	Process 1	Process 2
Direct labour	£4880	£6000
Direct expenses	£4270	—
Overhead absorption rates	250% of direct labour	100% of direct labour
Output	8000 litres	7500 litres
Opening stock of work in process	—	—
Closing stock of work in process	5600 litres	—
Normal yield	85% of input	90% of input
Scrap value of loss	—	—

In process 1 the closing stock of work in process has just passed through inspection, which is at the stage where materials and conversion costs are 100% and 75% completed respectively.
In process 2 inspection is the final operation.

Required:

(a) Prepare the relevant accounts to show the results of the processes for May 2000 and present a detailed working paper showing your calculations and any assumptions in arriving at the data shown in those accounts.

(18 marks)

(b) If supplies of the required chemicals are severely restricted and all production can be sold immediately, briefly explain how you would calculate the total loss to the company if, at the beginning of June, 100 litres of the correct mix of chemicals were spilt on issue to process 1.

(4 marks)
(Total 22 marks)
ACCA Foundation Costing

Question 5.6   **Intermediate: Preparation of process accounts with output fully completed and a discussion of FIFO and average methods of WIP valuation**

(a) Z Ltd manufactures metal cans for use in the food processing industry. The metal is introduced in sheet form at the start of the process. Normal wastage in the form of offcuts is 2% of input. The offcuts can be sold for £0.26 per kilo. Each metal sheet weighs 2 kilos and is expected to yield 80 cans. In addition to wastage through offcuts, 1% of cans manufactured are expected to be rejected. These rejects can also be sold at £0.26 per kilo.

Production, and costs incurred, in the month just completed, were as follows:

Production:	3 100 760 cans
Costs incurred:	
Direct materials:	39 300 metal sheets at £2.50 per sheet
Direct labour and overhead:	£33 087

There was no opening or closing work in process.

Required:

Prepare the process accounts for the can manufacturing operation for the month just completed.

(15 marks)

(b) Another of the manufacturing operations of Z Ltd involves the continuous processing of raw materials with the result that, at the end of any period, there are partly completed units of product remaining.

Required:

With reference to the general situation outlined above
(i) explain the concept of equivalent units

(3 marks)

(ii) describe, and contrast, the FIFO and average methods of work in process valuation.

(7 marks)
(Total 25 marks)
ACCA Level 1 Costing

Equivalent production with losses (FIFO method)

Adam, the management accountant of Mark Limited, has on file the costs per equivalent unit for the company's process for the last month but the input costs and quantities appear to have been mislaid.

Information that is available to Adam for last month is as follows:

Opening work in progress	100 units, 30% complete
Closing work in progress	200 units, 40% complete
Normal loss	10% of input valued at £2 per unit
Output	1250 units

The losses were as expected and Adam has a record of there being 150 units scrapped during the month. All materials are input at the start of the process. The cost per equivalent unit for materials was £2.60 and for conversion costs was £1.50. Mark Limited uses the FIFO method of stock valuation in its process account.

Required:

(a) Calculate the units input into the process   *(2 marks)*

(b) Calculate the equivalent units for materials and conversion costs.   *(4 marks)*

(c) Using your answer from (b) calculate the input costs.   *(4 marks)*
                                                              (10 marks)

Intermediate: FIFO method and losses in process

The manufacture of one of the products of A Ltd requires three separate processes. In the last of the three processes, costs, production and stock for the month just ended were:

(1) Transfers from Process 2: 180 000 units at a cost of £394 200.

(2) Process 3 costs: materials £110 520, conversion costs £76 506.

(3) Work in process at the beginning of the month: 20 000 units at a cost of £55 160 (based on FIFO pricing method). Units were 70% complete for materials, and 40% complete for conversion costs.

(4) Work in process at the end of the month: 18 000 units which were 90% complete for materials, and 70% complete for conversion costs.

(5) Product is inspected when it is complete. Normally no losses are expected but during the month 60 units were rejected and sold for £1.50 per unit.

Required:

(a) Prepare the Process 3 account for the month just ended.
                                                              (15 marks)

(b) Explain how, and why, your calculations would be affected if the 60 units lost were treated as normal losses.
                                                              (5 marks)

(c) Explain how your calculations would be affected by the use of weighted average pricing instead of FIFO.
                                                              (5 marks)
                                                        (Total 25 marks)
                          ACCA Cost and Management Accounting 1

Advanced: FIFO stock valuation, standard costing and cost-plus pricing

Campex Ltd uses a dyeing and waterproofing process for its fabrics which are later made up into tents and other outdoor pursuit items, or sold to other manufacturers. Each roll of fabric is subject to the same process, with dyeing and waterproofing materials being added at specific times in the process. The direct labour costs are incurred uniformly throughout the process.

Inspection of the fabric for spoilage can take place only at the end of the process when it can be determined whether or not there has been any spoilage. Amounts of up to 10% of good output are acceptable as normal spoilage. Any abnormal spoilage is treated as a period loss. Some spoiled fabric can be reworked and it is saved up until a batch of 500 rolls can be reprocessed.

The reworking costs are charged to process overheads, and any reworked goods will not usually need the full cost of conversion spent on them. The work in progress is valued using the FIFO method.

At the beginning of the month of June the work in progress in the dyeing and waterproofing department was 1000 rolls which were valued at £12 000 direct materials and £4620 direct labour. The work in progress has had all the direct materials added, but was only 60% complete as far as the direct labour was concerned. During the month 5650 rolls were started from new, and 500 rolls were reworked. The rolls being reworked require 60% of direct materials and 50% of direct labour to bring them up to standard. By the end of the month 550 rolls had been found to be spoiled. The work in progress at the end of the month amounted to 800 rolls of which 80% were complete for direct materials and 40% were complete for direct labour. All other rolls were completed satisfactorily and transferred to stores to await further processing. The costs for June were direct materials £72 085, direct labour £11 718. The departmental overhead recovered was £3.5 for every £1 direct labour, whilst actual overhead expenditure amounted to £34 110 for the month (excluding the reworking costs).

Requirements:

(a) Prepare a schedule showing the actual equivalent units processed for each cost element in the processing department for the month of June and the costs per roll for the direct material used and the direct labour and applied overheads.

(7 marks)

(b) Prepare a schedule showing the allocation of the costs of production to the various cost headings for the month of June, including the value of closing work in progress using the FIFO method.

(6 marks)

(c) Discuss the usefulness of converting the system used above to a standard cost based system.

(4 marks)

(d) Comment on the use of the actual costs you have computed above in (a) and (b) for product pricing.

(4 marks)

(e) Comment briefly on the implications of using replacement costs in a process costing system including valuation of month end work in progress.

(4 marks)
(Total 25 marks)
ICAEW Paper 2/Management Accounting

Joint and by-product costing

Questions to Chapter 6

Intermediate: Preparation of joint product account and a decision of further processing

Question 6.1

PQR Limited produces two joint products – P and Q – together with a by-product R, from a single main process (process 1). Product P is sold at the point of separation for £5 per kg, whereas product Q is sold for £7 per kg after further processing into product Q2. By-product R is sold without further processing for £1.75 per kg.

Process 1 is closely monitored by a team of chemists, who planned the output per 1000 kg of input materials to be as follows:

Product P	500 kg
Product Q	350 kg
Product R	100 kg
Toxic waste	50 kg

The toxic waste is disposed of at a cost of £1.50 per kg, and arises at the end of processing.

Process 2, which is used for further processing of product Q into product Q2, has the following cost structure:

Fixed costs	£6000 per week
Variable costs	£1.50 per kg processed

The following actual data relate to the first week of accounting period 10:

Process 1

Opening work in process	Nil
Materials input 10 000 kg costing	£15 000
Direct labour	£10 000
Variable overhead	£4 000
Fixed overhead	£6 000

Outputs:

Product P	4800 kg
Product Q	3600 kg
Product R	1000 kg
Toxic waste	600 kg
Closing work in progress	nil

Process 2

Opening work in process	nil
Input of product Q	3600 kg
Output of product Q2	3300 kg
Closing work in progress	300 kg, 50% converted

Conversion costs were incurred in accordance with the planned cost structure.

Required:

(a) Prepare the main process account for the first week of period 10 using the final sales value method to attribute pre-separation costs to joint products.

(12 marks)

(b) Prepare the toxic waste accounts and process 2 account for the first week of period 10.

(9 marks)

(c) Comment on the method used by PQR Limited to attribute pre-separation costs to its joint products.

(4 marks)

(d) Advise the management of PQR Limited whether or not, on purely financial grounds, it should continue to process product Q into product Q2:

   (i) if product Q could be sold at the point of separation for £4.30 per kg; *and*

   (ii) if 60% of the weekly fixed costs of process 2 were avoided by not processing product Q further.

(5 marks)
(Total 30 marks)
CIMA Stage 2 Operational Cost Accounting

Question 6.2

Intermediate: Flow chart and calculation of cost per unit for joint products

A distillation plant, which works continuously, processes 1000 tonnes of raw material each day. The raw material costs £4 per tonne and the plant operating costs per day are £2600. From the input of raw material the following output is produced:

	(%)
Distillate X	40
Distillate Y	30
Distillate Z	20
By-product B	10

From the initial distillation process, Distillate X passes through a heat process which costs £1500 per day and becomes product X which requires blending before sale.

Distillate Y goes through a second distillation process costing £3300 per day and produces 75% of product Y and 25% of product X1.

Distillate Z has a second distillation process costing £2400 per day and produces 60% of product Z and 40% of product X2. The three streams of products X, X1 and X2 are blended, at a cost of £1555 per day to become the saleable final product XXX.

There is no loss of material from any of the processes.

By-product B is sold for £3 per tonne and such proceeds are credited to the process from which the by-product is derived.

Joint costs are apportioned on a physical unit basis.

You are required to:

(a) draw a flow chart, flowing from left to right, to show for one day of production the flow of material and the build up of the operating costs for each product;

(18 marks)

(b) present a statement for management showing for *each* of the products XXX, Y and Z, the output for *one* day, the total cost and the unit cost per tonne;

(*5 marks*)

(c) suggest an alternative method for the treatment of the income receivable for by-product B than that followed in this question (figures are not required).

(*2 marks*)
(*Total 25 marks*)
CIMA Stage 2 Cost Accounting

Intermediate: Calculation of cost per unit and decision on further processing   **Question 6.3**

A chemical company carries on production operations in two processes. Materials first pass through process I, where a compound is produced. A loss in weight takes place at the start of processing. The following data, which can be assumed to be representative, relates to the month just ended:

Quantities (kg):

Material input	200 000
Opening work in process (half processed)	40 000
Work completed	160 000
Closing work in process (two-thirds processed)	30 000

Costs (£):

Material input	75 000
Processing costs	96 000
Opening work in process:	
Materials	20 000
Processing costs	12 000

Any quantity of the compound can be sold for £1.60 per kg. Alternatively, it can be transferred to process II for further processing and packing to be sold as Starcomp for £2.00 per kg. Further materials are added in process II such that for every kg of compound used, 2 kg of Starcomp result.

Of the 160 000 kg per month of work completed in process I, 40 000 kg are sold as compound and 120 000 kg are passed through process II for sale as Starcomp. Process II has facilities to handle up to 160 000 kg of compound per month if required. The monthly costs incurred in process II (other than the cost of the compound) are:

	120 000 kg of compound input	160 000 kg of compound input
Materials (£)	120 000	160 000
Processing costs (£)	120 000	140 000

Required:

(a) Determine, using the average method, the cost per kg of compound in process I, and the value of both work completed and closing work in process for the month just ended.

(*11 marks*)

(b) Demonstrate that it is worth while further processing 120 000 kg of compound.

(*5 marks*)

(c) Calculate the minimum acceptable selling price per kg, if a potential buyer could be found for the additional output of Starcomp that could be produced with the remaining compound.

(6 marks)
(Total 22 marks)
ACCA Level 1 Costing

Question 6.4

Intermediate: Joint cost apportionment and decisions on further processing

A process costing £200 000 produces 3 products – A, B and C. Output details are as follows:

Product A	6 000 litres
Product B	10 000 litres
Product C	20 000 tonnes

Each product may be sold at the completion of the process as follows:

	Sales value at the end of the first process
Product A	£10 per litre
Product B	£4 per litre
Product C	£10 per tonne

Alternatively, further processing of each individual product can be undertaken to produce an enhanced product thus:

	Subsequent processing costs	Sales value after final process
Enhanced Product A	£14 per litre	£20 per litre
Enhanced Product B	£2 per litre	£8 per litre
Enhanced Product C	£6 per tonne	£16 per tonne

Required:

(a) Explain the following terms:
 (i) normal process loss;
 (ii) joint product;
 (iii) by-product;

 and state the appropriate costing treatments for normal process loss and for by-products.

(10 marks)

(b) Calculate the apportionment of joint process costs to products A, B and C above.
(8 marks)

(c) Explain whether the initial process should be undertaken and which, if any, of the enhanced products should be produced.

(7 marks)
(Total 25 marks)
AAT

Question 6.5

Intermediate: Profitability analysis and a decision on further processing

C Ltd operates a process which produces three joint products. In the period just ended costs of production totalled £509 640. Output from the process during the period was:

Product W	276 000 kilos
Product X	334 000 kilos
Product Y	134 000 kilos

There were no opening stocks of the three products. Products W and X are sold in this state. Product Y is subjected to further processing. Sales of Products W and X during the period were:

Product W 255 000 kilos at £0.945 per kilo
Product X 312 000 kilos at £0.890 per kilo

128 000 kilos of Product Y were further processed during the period. The balance of the period production of the three products W, X and Y remained in stock at the end of the period. The value of closing stock of individual products is calculated by apportioning costs according to weight of output.

The additional costs in the period of further processing Product Y, which is converted into Product Z, were:

Direct labour £10 850
Production overhead £7 070

96 000 kilos of Product Z were produced from the 128 000 kilos of Product Y. A by-product BP is also produced which can be sold for £0.12 per kilo. 8000 kilos of BP were produced and sold in the period.

Sales of Product Z during the period were 94 000 kilos, with a total revenue of £100 110. Opening stock of Product Z was 8000 kilos, valued at £8640. The FIFO method is used for pricing transfers of Product Z to cost of sales.

Selling and administration costs are charged to all main products when sold, at 10% of revenue.

Required:

(a) Prepare a profit and loss account for the period, identifying separately the profitability of each of the three main products.

(14 marks)

(b) C Ltd has now received an offer from another company to purchase the total output of Product Y (i.e. before further processing) for £0.62 per kilo. Calculate the viability of this alternative.

(5 marks)

(c) Discuss briefly the methods of, and rationale for, joint cost apportionment.

(6 marks)
(Total 25 marks)
ACCA Level 1 Cost and Management Accounting 1

Advanced: Preparation of profit statements and decision on further processing

Question 6.6

A fish processing company has a contract to purchase all the fish caught by a fishing vessel. The processor removes the head and skeleton which are waste (Process 1) and is then able to sell the fish fillets which remain. The waste is estimated to be 40% by weight of the fish bought and is sold at 30p per kilo for animal food.

The fish fillets are inspected for quality and three categories are identified (standard, special and superior). Half the catch is expected to be of standard quality. Of the remainder there is twice as much special as superior.

For one contract period, the vessel contains a total of 36 000 kilos of whole fish and the contract price is £1.50 per kilo, irrespective of quality. The labour cost for Process 1 is £28 000 for this quantity.

As an alternative to sale as fresh produce, the fillets of fish may be cooked and coated in breadcrumbs (Process 2). The process of cooking the fillets and coating them in breadcrumbs cost 10p per kilo for material and 60p per kilo for labour. Current market prices of fresh fillets and the breadcrumbed alternatives are:

Category	£ per kilo	
	Fresh	Breadcrumbed
Superior	7.50	8.70
Special	6.80	7.50
Standard	4.00	5.20

In Process 1 the overhead costs are recovered based on 120% of labour costs; one third of these overheads are variable. In Process 2 the overhead rate set is 180% of labour costs, one quarter being variable.

Required:

(a) An often quoted phrase used in management accounting is 'different costs for different purposes'. To demonstrate the appropriateness of this phrase list and briefly describe three purposes of preparing product costs in a manufacturing organization.

(5 marks)

(b) Prepare statements of total net profit or loss per period for each category of fish if all sales are in the fresh state (i.e. after Process 1) and on the assumption that the total net cost is shared between the three categories based on:
(i) weight;
(ii) market value.

(6 marks)

(c) If a loss was revealed for a category under either (b) (i) or (ii) above, explain how the management should react.

(4 marks)

(d) Determine for each category whether it is profitable for the company to further process the fillets, and make brief comments.

(5 marks)
(Total 20 marks)
ACCA Paper 8 Managerial Finance

Question 6.7

Advanced: Joint cost apportionment and decision-making

Hawkins Ltd produces two joint products, Boddie and Soull. A further product, Threekeys, is also made as a by-product of one of the processes for making Soull. Each product is sold in bottles of one litre capacity.

It is now January 2001. You are a cost accountant for Hawkins Ltd. You have been instructed to allocate the company's joint costs for 2000 between Boddie and Soull, but not to the by-product Threekeys.

During 2000, 2 000 000 litres of a raw material, Necktar, costing £3 000 000, were processed in Department Alpha with no wastage. The processing costs were £1 657 000.

50% of the output of Department Alpha was unfinished Boddie, for which there was no external market. It was transferred to Department Beta, where it was further processed at an additional cost of £8 100 000. Normal wastage by evaporation was 16% of the input of unfinished Boddie. The remaining good output of finished Boddie was sold for £10 per litre in the outside market.

The other 50% of the output from the joint process in Department Alpha was in the form of processed Necktar. It was all transferred to Department Gamma, as there was no outside market for processed Necktar. In Department Gamma it was further processed, with no wastage, at a cost of £30 900 000.

72% of the output of Department Gamma was in the form of unfinished Soull, for which there was no external market. It was transferred to Department Delta, where it was subjected to a finishing process at a further cost of £719 000. Normal spoilage of $16^2\backslash 3\%$ of the input to the finishing process was experienced. The spoiled material was disposed of without charge, as effluent. The remaining finished Soull was sold in the outside market for £60 per litre.

The remaining 28% of the output of Department Gamma was in the form of finished Threekeys, the by-product. It was sold in the outside market for £8 per litre, but due to its dangerous nature special delivery costs of £70 000 were incurred in respect of it.

You are required:

(a) to allocate the appropriate joint costs between Boddie and Soull on the basis of relative sales value, treating the net realizable value of Threekeys as an addition to the sales value of Soull,

(6 marks)

(b) to prepare a statement showing the profit or loss attributed to each of the three products and the total profit or loss, for 2000, on the basis of the information above and allocating joint costs as in (a) above,

(4 marks)

(c) to show with reasons whether Hawkins Ltd should continue to produce all three products in 2001, assuming that input/output relationships, prices and sales volumes do not change.

(3 marks)
(Total 13 marks)
ICAEW Management Accounting

Advanced: Profitability analysis including an apportionment of joint costs and identification of relevant costs/revenues for a price/output decision

Question 6.8

A company manufactures two joint products in a single process. One is sold as a garden fertilizer, the other is a synthetic fuel which is sold to external customers but which can also be used to heat greenhouses in which the company grows fruit and vegetables all year round as a subsidiary market venture. Information relating to the previous 12 month period is as follows:

(i) 1 600 000 kilos of garden fertilizer were produced and then sold at £3.00 per kilo. Joint costs are apportioned between the garden fertilizer and the synthetic fuel on a physical units (weight) basis. The fertilizer has a contribution to sales ratio of 40% after such apportionment. There are no direct costs of fertilizer sales or production.

(ii) The synthetic fuel represents 20% of the total weight of output from the manufacturing process. A wholesaler bought 160 000 kilos at £1.40 per kilo under a long-term contract which stipulates that its availability to him will not be reduced below 100 000 kilos per annum. There is no other external market for the fuel. Fixed administrative, selling and distribution costs incurred specifically as a result of the fuel sales to the wholesaler totalled £40 000. That part of the fuel production which was sold to the wholesaler, incurred additional variable costs for packaging of £1.20 per kilo.

(iii) The remaining synthetic fuel was used to heat the company greenhouses. The greenhouses produced 5 kilos of fruit and vegetables per kilo of fuel. The fruit and vegetables were sold at an average price of £0.50 per kilo. Total direct costs of fruit and vegetable production were £520 000. Direct costs included a fixed labour cost of £100 000 which is avoidable if fruit and vegetable production ceases, the remainder being variable with the quantity produced.

A notional fuel charge of £1.40 per kilo of fuel is made to fruit and vegetable production. This notional charge is in addition to the direct costs detailed above.

(iv) Further company fixed costs were apportioned to the products as follows:

	(£)
Garden fertilizer	720 000
Synthetic fuel	18 000
Fruit and vegetables	90 000

The above data were used to produce a profit and loss analysis for the 12 month period for each of three areas of operation viz.

1. Garden fertilizer.

2. Synthetic fuel (including external sales and transfers to the greenhouses at £1.40 per kilo).

3. Fruit and vegetables (incorporating the deduction of any notional charges).

Required:

(a) Prepare a summary statement showing the profit or loss reported in each of the three areas of operation detailed above.

(8 marks)

(b) Calculate the percentage reduction in the fixed costs of £40 000 which would have been required before the synthetic fuel sales for the previous 12 month period would have resulted in a net benefit to the company.

(3 marks)

(c) Calculate the net benefit or loss which sales of fruit and vegetables caused the company in the previous 12 month period.

(3 marks)

(d) Advise management on the fruit and vegetable price strategy for the coming year if fruit and vegetable production/sales could be expanded according to the following price/demand pattern:

Sales (000 kilos)	1200	1300	1400	1500	1600
Average selling price/kilo (£)	0.50	0.495	0.485	0.475	0.465

All other costs, prices and quantities will remain unchanged during the coming year. The wholesaler will continue to purchase all available synthetic fuel not used in the greenhouses.

(8 marks)
(Total 22 marks)
ACCA Level 2 Management Accounting

Question 6.9

Advanced: Calculation of cost per unit, break-even point and recommended selling price

Amongst its products a chemical company markets two concentrated liquid fertilizers – type P for flowers and type Q for vegetables. In 2001 total sales are expected to be restricted by forecast sales of type Q which are limited to 570 000 litres for the year. At this level the plant capacity will be under-utilized by 20%.

The fertilizers are manufactured jointly as follows:

Mixing: Raw materials A and B are mixed together in equal amounts and filtered. After filtering there is a saleable residue, X, amounting to 5% of the input materials.

Distillation: The mixed materials are heated and there is an evaporation loss of 10%. The remaining liquid distils into one-third each of an extract P, an extract Q and a by-product Y.

Blending: Two parts of raw material C are blended with one part of extract P to form the fertilizer type P. One part of raw material D is blended with one part of extract Q to form the fertilizer type Q.

Fertilizer type P is filled into 3-litre cans and labelled. Fertilizer type Q is filled into 6-litre preprinted cans. Both are then ready for sale.

The costs involved are as under:

Raw material	Cost per 100 litres (£)
A	25
B	12
C	20
D	55

Cans	Cost each (£)
3-litre	0.32
6-litre	0.50

Labels	Cost per 1000 (£)
For 3-litre cans	3.33

Manufacturing costs:

	Direct wages (£)	Variable overhead (£)	Fixed overhead per year (£)
	per 100 litres of input processed		
Mixing	2.75	1.00	6 000
Distilling	3.00	2.00	20 000
Blending	5.00	2.00	33 250

The residue X and by-product Y are both sold to local companies at £0.03 and £0.04 per litre respectively. Supplies are collected in bulk by the buyers using their own transport. The sales revenue is credited to the process at which the material arises.

Product costs are apportioned entirely to the two main products on the basis of their output from each process.

No inventories of part-finished materials are held at any time.

The fertilizers are sold through agents on the basis of list price less 25%. Of the net selling price, selling and distribution costs amount to $13^{1}/_{3}$% and profit to 20%. Of the selling and distribution costs 70% are variable and the remainder fixed.

You are required to:

(a) calculate separately for the fertilizers type P and type Q for the year 2001:
   (i)   total manufacturing cost,
   (ii) manufacturing cost per litre,
   (iii) list price per litre,
   (iv) profit for the year

(*18 marks*)

(b) calculate the break-even price per litre to manufacture and supply an extra 50 000 litres of fertilizer type Q for export and which would incur variable selling and distribution costs of £2000;

(8 marks)

(c) state the price you would recommend the company should quote per litre for this export business, with a brief explanation for your decision.

(4 marks)
(Total 30 marks)
CIMA P3 Management Accounting

Income effects of alternative cost accumulation systems

Questions to Chapter 7

Intermediate: Preparation of variable and absorption costing profit statements
and an explanation of the change in profits

Question 7.1

A company sells a single product at a price of £14 per unit. Variable manufacturing
costs of the product are £6.40 per unit. Fixed manufacturing overheads, which are
absorbed into the cost of production at a unit rate (based on normal activity of 20
000 units per period), are £92 000 per period. Any over- or under-absorbed fixed
manufacturing overhead balances are transferred to the profit and loss account at the
end of each period, in order to establish the manufacturing profit.

Sales and production (in units) for two periods are as follows:

	Period 1	Period 2
Sales	15 000	22 000
Production	18 000	21 000

The manufacturing profit in Period 1 was reported as £35 800.

Required:

(a) Prepare a trading statement to identify the manufacturing profit for Period 2
using the existing absorption costing method.

(7 marks)

(b) Determine the manufacturing profit that would be reported in Period 2 if
marginal costing was used.

(4 marks)

(c) Explain, with supporting calculations:

(i) the reasons for the change in manufacturing profit between Periods 1 and 2
where absorption costing is used in each period;

(5 marks)

(ii) why the manufacturing profit in (a) and (b) differs.

(4 marks)
(Total 20 marks)
ACCA Management Information – Paper 3

Intermediate: Preparation of variable and absorption costing profit statements and
CVP analysis

Question 7.2

R Limited is considering its plans for the year ending 31 December 2001. It makes
and sells a single product, which has budgeted costs and selling price as follows:

	£ per unit
Selling price	45
Direct materials	11
Direct labour	8

Production overhead:

variable	4
fixed	3

Selling overhead:

variable	5
fixed	2

Administration overhead:

fixed	3

Fixed overhead costs per unit are based on a normal annual activity level of 96 000 units. These costs are expected to be incurred at a constant rate throughout the year.

Activity levels during January and February 2001 are expected to be:

	January units	February units
Sales	7000	8750
Production	8500	7750

Assume that there will be no stocks held on 1 January 2001.

Required:

(a) Prepare, in columnar format, profit statements for each of the two months of January and February 2001 using:
(i) absorption costing;
(ii) marginal costing.

(12 marks)

(b) Reconcile and explain the reasons for any differences between the marginal and absorption profits for each month which you have calculated in your answer to (a) above.

(3 marks)

(c) Based upon marginal costing, calculate:
(i) the annual breakeven sales value; and
(ii) the activity level, in units, which will yield an annual profit of £122 800.

(6 marks)

(d) Explain 3 fundamental assumptions underpinning single product breakeven analysis.

(6 marks)
(Total 27 marks)
CIMA Stage 2 – Operational Cost Accounting

Question 7.3

Intermediate: Preparation of variable and absorption costing statements as a reconciliation of the profits

The following budgeted profit statement has been prepared using absorption costing principles:

	January to June (£000)	(£000)	July to December (£000)	(£000)
Sales		540		360
Opening stock	100		160	
Production costs:				
Direct materials	108		36	
Direct labour	162		54	

Overhead	90		30	
	460		280	
Closing stock	160		80	
		300		200
GROSS PROFIT		240		160
Production overhead:				
(Over)/Under absorption	(12)		12	
Selling costs	50		50	
Distribution costs	45		40	
Administration costs	80		80	
		163		182
NET PROFIT/(LOSS)		77		(22)
Sales units	15 000		10 000	
Production units	18 000		6 000	

The members of the management team are concerned by the significant change in profitability between the two six-month periods. As management accountant, you have analysed the data upon which the above budget statement has been produced, with the following results:

1. The production overhead cost comprises both a fixed and a variable element, the latter appears to be dependent on the number of units produced. The fixed element of the cost is expected to be incurred at a constant rate throughout the year.

2. The selling costs are fixed.

3. The distribution cost comprises both fixed and variable elements, the latter appears to be dependent on the number of units sold. The fixed element of the cost is expected to be incurred at a constant rate throughout the year.

4. The administration costs are fixed.

Required:

(a) Present the above budgeted profit statement in marginal costing format.

(10 marks)

(b) Reconcile EACH of the six-monthly profit/loss values reported respectively under marginal and absorption costing.

(4 marks)

(c) Reconcile the six-monthly profit for January to June from the absorption costing statement with the six-monthly loss for July to December from the absorption costing statement.

(4 marks)

(d) Calculate the annual number of units required to break even.

(3 marks)

(e) Explain briefly the advantages of using marginal costing as the basis of providing managers with information for decision making.

(4 marks)
(Total 25 marks)
CIMA Stage 2 Operational Cost Accounting

Question 7.4

Intermediate: Preparation of variable and absorption costing profit statements for FIFO and AVECO methods

The following information relates to product J, for quarter 3, which has just ended:

	Production (units)	Sales (units)	Fixed overheads (£000)	Variable costs (£000)
Budget	40 000	38 000	300	1800
Actual	46 000	42 000	318	2070

The selling price of product J was £72 per unit.

The fixed overheads were absorbed at a predetermined rate per unit.

At the beginning of quarter 3 there was an opening stock of product J of 2000 units, valued at £25 per unit variable costs and £5 per unit fixed overheads.

Required:

(a) (i) Calculate the fixed overhead absorption rate per unit for the last quarter, and present profit statements using FIFO (first in, first out) using:

(ii) absorption costing;

(iii) marginal costing; and

(iv) reconcile and explain the difference between the profits or losses.

(12 marks)

(b) Using the same data, present similar statements to those required in part (a). Using the AVECO (average cost) method of valuation, reconcile the profit or loss figures, and comment briefly on the variations between the profits or losses in (a) and (b).

(8 marks)
(Total 20 marks)
ACCA Paper 8 Managerial Finance

Question 7.5

Advanced: Explanation of absorption costing changes in profits and preparation of variable costing profit statements

The Miozip Company operates an absorption costing system which incorporates a factory-wide overhead absorption rate per direct labour hour. For 1999 and 2000 this rate was £2.10 per hour. The fixed factory overhead for 2000 was £600 000 and this would have been fully absorbed if the company had operated at full capacity, which is estimated at 400 000 direct labour hours. Unfortunately, only 200 000 hours were worked in that year so that the overhead was seriously underabsorbed. Fixed factory overheads are expected to be unchanged in 2001 and 2002.

The outcome for 2000 was a loss of £70 000 and the management believed that a major cause of this loss was the low overhead absorption rate which had led the company to quote selling prices which were uneconomic.

For 2001 the overhead absorption rate was increased to £3.60 per direct labour hour and selling prices were raised in line with the established pricing procedures which involve adding a profit mark-up of 50% onto the full factory cost of the company's products. The new selling prices were also charged on the stock of finished goods held at the beginning of 2001.

In December 2001 the company's accountant prepares an estimated Profit and Loss Account for 2001 and a budgeted Profit and Loss Account for 2002. Although sales were considered to be depressed in 2000, they were even lower in 2001 but, nevertheless, it seems that the company will make a profit for that year. A worrying feature of the estimated accounts is the high level of finished goods stock held and the 2002 budget provides for a reduction in the stock level at 31 December 2002 to the (physical) level existing in January 2000. Budgeted sales for 2002 are set at the 2001 sales level.

The summarized profit statements for the three years to 31 December 2002 are as follows:

Summarized Profit and Loss Accounts

	Actual 2000		Estimated 2001		Budgeted 2002	
	(£)	(£)	(£)	(£)	(£)	(£)
Sales Revenue		1 350 000		1 316 250		1 316 250
Opening Stock of Finished Goods	100 000		200 000		357 500	
Factory Cost of Production	1 000 000		975 000		650 000	
	1 100 000		1 175 000		1 007 500	
Less: Closing Stock of Finished Goods	200 000		357 500		130 000	
Factory Cost of Goods Sold		900 000		817 500		877 500
		450 000		498 750		438 750
Less: Factory Overhead Under-Absorbed		300 000		150 000		300 000
		150 000		348 750		138 750
Administrative and Financial Costs		220 000		220 000		220 000
	Loss	(£70 000)		£128 750	Loss	(£81 250)

(a) You are required to write a short report to the board of Miozip explaining why the budgeted outcome for 2002 is so different from that of 2001 when the sales revenue is the same for both years.

(6 marks)

(b) Restate the Profit and Loss Account for 2000, the estimated Profit and Loss Account for 2001 and the Budgeted Profit and Loss Account for 2002 using marginal factory cost for stock valuation purposes.

(8 marks)

(c) Comment on the problems which *may* follow from a decision to increase the overhead absorption rate in conditions when cost plus pricing is used and overhead is currently underabsorbed.

(3 marks)

(d) Explain why the majority of businesses use full costing systems whilst most management accounting theorists favour marginal costing.

(5 marks)

NB Assume in your answers to this question that the value of the £ and the efficiency of the company have been constant over the period under review.

(Total 22 marks)
ACCA Level 2 Management Accounting

Question 7.6

Advanced: Explanation of absorption costing changes in profits and preparation of variable costing profit statements

Mahler Products has two manufacturing departments each producing a single standardized product. The data for unit cost and selling price of these products are as follows:

	Department A (£)	Department B (£)
Direct material cost	4	6
Direct labour cost	2	4
Variable manufacturing overheads	2	4
Fixed manufacturing overheads	12	16
Factory cost	20	30
Profit mark-up	50% 10	25% 7.50
Selling price	30	37.50

The factory cost figures are used in the departmental accounts for the valuation of finished goods stock.

The departmental profit and loss accounts have been prepared for the year to 30 June. These are given below separately for the two halves of the year.

Departmental profit and loss accounts – year to 30 June

	1 July–31 December		1 January–30 June	
	Department A (£000)	Department B (000)	Department A (£000)	Department B (£000)
Sales revenue	300	750	375	675
Manufacturing costs:				
Direct material	52	114	30	132
Direct labour	26	76	15	88
Variable overheads	26	76	15	88
Fixed overheads	132	304	132	304
Factory cost of production	236	570	192	612
Add Opening stock of finished goods	60	210	120	180
	296	780	312	792
Less Closing stock of finished goods	120	180	20	300
Factory cost of goods sold	176	600	292	492
Administrative and selling costs	30	100	30	100
	206	700	322	592
Net profit	94	50	53	83

The total sales revenue was the same in each six monthly period but in the second half of the year the company increased the sales of department A (which has the higher profit mark-up) and reduced the sales of department B (which has the lower profit mark-up). An increase in company profits for the second six months was anticipated but the profit achieved was £8000 lower for the second half of the year than for the first half. The profit for department A fell by £41 000 while the profit for department B rose by £33 000. There has been no change in prices of inputs or outputs.

You are required:

(a) to explain the situation described in the last paragraph – illustrate your answer with appropriate supporting calculations,

(14 marks)

(b) to redraft the departmental profit and loss accounts using marginal cost to value unsold stock.

(8 marks)
(Total 22 marks)
ACCA Level 2 Management Accounting

Cost–volume–profit analysis

Questions to Chapter 8

Question 8.1

Intermediate: Break-even, contribution and profit–volume graph

(a) From the following information you are required to construct:
   (i) a break-even chart, showing the break-even point and the margin of safety;
   (ii) a chart displaying the contribution level and the profit level;
   (iii) a profit–volume chart.

Sales	6000 units at	
	£12 per unit	= £72 000
Variable costs	6000 units at	
	£7 per unit	= £42 000
Fixed costs		= £20 000

(9 marks)

(b) State the purposes of each of the three charts in (a) above.

(6 marks)

(c) Outline the limitations of break-even analysis.

(5 marks)

(d) What are the advantages of graphical presentation of financial data to executives?

(2 marks)
(Total 22 marks)
AAT

Question 8.2

Intermediate: Profit–volume graph and changes in sales mix

A company produces and sells two products with the following costs:

	Product X	Product Y
Variable costs (per £ of sales)	£0.45	£0.6
Fixed costs	£1 212 000	£1 212 000
	per period	

Total sales revenue is currently generated by the two products in the following proportions:

Product X	70%
Product Y	30%

Required:

(a) Calculate the break-even sales revenue per period, based on the sales mix assumed above.

(6 marks)

(b) Prepare a profit–volume chart of the above situation for sales revenue up to £4 000 000. Show on the same chart the effect of a change in the sales mix to product X 50%, product Y 50%. Clearly indicate on the chart the break-even point for each situation.

(*11 marks*)

(c) Of the fixed costs £455 000 are attributable to product X. Calculate the sales revenue required on product X in order to recover the attributable fixed costs and provide a net contribution of £700 000 towards general fixed costs and profit.

(*5 marks*)
(*Total 22 marks*)
ACCA Level 1 Costing

Intermediate: Break-even chart with an increase in fixed costs and incorporating expected values

Question 8.3

A manufacturer is considering a new product which could be produced in one of two qualities – Standard or De Luxe. The following estimates have been made:

	Standard (£)	De Luxe (£)
Unit labour cost	2.00	2.50
Unit material cost	1.50	2.00
Unit packaging cost	1.00	2.00
Proposed selling price per unit	7.00	10.00
Budgeted fixed costs per period:		
0–99 999 units	200 000	250 000
100 000 and above	350 000	400 000

At the proposed selling prices, market research indicates the following demand:

Standard

Quantity	Probability
172 000	0.1
160 000	0.7
148 000	0.2

De Luxe

Quantity	Probability
195 500	0.3
156 500	0.5
109 500	0.2

You are required

(a) to draw separate break-even charts for *each* quality, showing the break-even points;

(*7 marks*)

(b) to comment on the position shown by the charts and what guidance they provide for management;

(*3 marks*)

(c) to calculate, for *each* quality, the expected unit sales, expected profits and the margin of safety;

(*3 marks*)

(d) using an appropriate measure of risk, to advise management which quality
should be launched.

(9 marks)
(Total 22 marks)
CIMA Stage 3 Management Accounting Techniques

Question 8.4

**Intermediate: Calculation of break-even points based on different sales mix
assumptions and a product abandonment decision**

M Ltd manufactures three products which have the following revenue and costs
(£ per unit).

	Product 1	2	3
Selling price	2.92	1.35	2.83
Variable costs	1.61	0.72	0.96
Fixed costs:			
Product specific	0.49	0.35	0.62
General	0.46	0.46	0.46

Unit fixed costs are based upon the following annual sales and production volumes
(thousand units):

Product 1	2	3
98.2	42.1	111.8

Required:

(a) Calculate:

(i) the break-even point sales (to the nearest £ hundred) of M Ltd based on the
current product mix;

(9 marks)

(ii) the number of units of Product 2 (to the nearest hundred) at the break-even
point determined in (i) above;

(3 marks)

(b) Comment upon the viability of Product 2.

(8 marks)
(Total 20 marks)
ACCA Cost and Management Accounting 1

Question 8.5

Intermediate: Calculation of break-even points and limiting factor decision-making

You are employed as an accounting technician by Smith, Williams and Jones, a small
firm of accountants and registered auditors. One of your clients is Winter plc, a large
department store. Judith Howarth, the purchasing director for Winter plc, has
gained considerable knowledge about bedding and soft furnishings and is considering
acquiring her own business.

She has recently written to you requesting a meeting to discuss the possible purchase
of Brita Beds Ltd. Brita Beds has one outlet in Mytown, a small town 100 miles from
where Judith works. Enclosed with her letter was Brita Beds' latest profit and loss
account. This is reproduced below.

Brita Beds Ltd
Profit and loss account – year to 31 May

Sales	(units)	(£)
Model A	1 620	336 960
Model B	2 160	758 160

Model C	1 620	1 010 880
Turnover		2 106 000
Expenses	(£)	
Cost of beds	1 620 000	
Commission	210 600	
Transport	216 000	
Rates and insurance	8 450	
Light heat and power	10 000	
Assistants' salaries	40 000	
Manager's salary	40 000	2 145 050
Loss for year		39 050

Also included in the letter was the following information:

1 Brita Beds sells three types of bed, models A to C inclusive.

2 Selling prices are determined by adding 30% to the cost of beds.

3 Sales assistants receive a commission of 10% of the selling price for each bed sold.

4 The beds are delivered in consignments of 10 beds at a cost of £400 per delivery. This expense is shown as 'Transport' in the profit and loss account.

5 All other expenses are annual amounts.

6 The mix of models sold is likely to remain constant irrespective of overall sales volume.

Task 1

In preparation for your meeting with Judith Howarth, you are asked to calculate:

(a) the minimum number of beds to be sold if Brita Beds is to avoid making a loss;

(b) the minimum turnover required if Brita Beds is to avoid making a loss.

At the meeting, Judith Howarth provides you with further information:

1 The purchase price of the business is £300 000.

2 Judith has savings of £300 000 currently earning 5% interest per annum, which she can use to acquire Beta Beds.

3 Her current salary is £36 550.

To reduce costs, Judith suggests that she should take over the role of manager as the current one is about to retire. However, she does not want to take a reduction in income. Judith also tells you that she has been carrying out some market research. The results of this are as follows:

1 The number of households in Mytown is currently 44 880.

2 Brita Beds Ltd is the only outlet selling beds in Mytown.

3 According to a recent survey, 10% of households change their beds every 9 years, 60% every 10 years and 30% every 11 years.

4 The survey also suggested that there is an average of 2.1 beds per household.

Task 2

Write a letter to Judith Howarth. Your letter should:

(a) identify the profit required to compensate for the loss of salary and interest;

(b) show the number of beds to be sold to achieve that profit;

(c) calculate the likely maximum number of beds that Brita Beds would sell in a year;

(d) use your answers in (a) to (c) to justify whether or not Judith Howarth should purchase the company and become its manager;

(e) give *two* possible reasons why your estimate of the maximum annual sales volume may prove inaccurate.

On receiving your letter, Judith Howarth decides she would prefer to remain as the purchasing director for Winter plc rather than acquire Brita Beds Ltd. Shortly afterwards, you receive a telephone call from her. Judith explains that Winter plc is redeveloping its premises and that she is concerned about the appropriate sales policy for Winter's bed department while the redevelopment takes place. Although she has a statement of unit profitability, this had been prepared before the start of the redevelopment and had assumed that there would be in excess of 800 square metres of storage space available to the bed department. Storage space is critical as customers demand immediate delivery and are not prepared to wait until the new stock arrives.

The next day, Judith Howarth sends you a letter containing a copy of the original statement of profitability. This is reproduced below:

Model	A	B	C
Monthly demand (beds)	35	45	20
	(£)	(£)	(£)
Unit selling price	240.00	448.00	672.00
Unit cost per bed	130.00	310.00	550.00
Carriage inwards	20.00	20.00	20.00
Staff costs	21.60	40.32	60.48
Department fixed overheads	20.00	20.00	20.00
General fixed overheads	25.20	25.20	25.20
Unit profit	23.20	32.48	(3.68)
Storage required per bed (square metres)	3	4	5

In her letter she asks for your help in preparing a marketing plan which will maximize the profitability of Winter's bed department while the redevelopment takes place. To help you, she has provided you with the following additional information:

1 Currently storage space available totals 300 square metres.

2 Staff costs represent the salaries of the sales staff in the bed department. Their total cost of £3780 per month is apportioned to units on the basis of planned turnover.

3 Departmental fixed overhead of £2000 per month is directly attributable to the department and is apportioned on the number of beds planned to be sold.

4 General fixed overheads of £2520 are also apportioned on the number of beds planned to be sold. The directors of Winter plc believe this to be a fair apportionment of the store's central fixed overheads.

5 The cost of carriage inwards and the cost of beds vary directly with the number of beds purchased.

Task 3

(a) Prepare a recommended monthly sales schedule in units which will maximize the profitability of Winter plc's bed department.

(b) Calculate the profit that will be reported per month if your recommendation is implemented.

AAT Technician's Stage

Question 8.6

Fosterjohn Press Ltd is considering launching a new monthly magazine at a selling price of £1 per copy. Sales of the magazine are expected to be 500 000 copies per month, but it is possible that the actual sales could differ quite significantly from this estimate.

Two different methods of producing the magazine are being considered and neither would involve any additional capital expenditure. The estimated production costs for each of the two methods of manufacture, together with the additional marketing and distribution costs of selling the new magazine, are summarized below:

	Method A	Method B
Variable costs	0.55 per copy	0.50 per copy
Specific fixed costs	£80 000	£120 000
	per month	per month

Semi-variable costs:

The following estimates have been obtained:

350 000 copies	£55 000 per month	£47 500 per month
450 000 copies	£65 000 per month	£52 500 per month
650 000 copies	£85 000 per month	£62 500 per month

It may be assumed that the fixed cost content of the semi-variable costs will remain constant throughout the range of activity shown.

The company currently sells a magazine covering related topics to those that will be included in the new publication and consequently it is anticipated that sales of this existing magazine will be adversely affected. It is estimated that for every ten copies sold of the new publication, sales of the existing magazine will be reduced by one copy.

Sales and cost data of the existing magazine are shown below:

Sales	220 000 copies per month
Selling price	0.85 per copy
Variable costs	0.35 per copy
Specific fixed costs	£80 000 per month

Required:

(a) Calculate, for each production method, the net increase in company profits which will result from the introduction of the new magazine, at each of the following levels of activity:

       500 000 copies per month
       400 000 copies per month
       600 000 copies per month

                                                      (12 marks)

(b) Calculate, for each production method, the amount by which sales volume of the new magazine could decline from the anticipated 500 000 copies per month, before the company makes no additional profit from the introduction of the new publication.

                                                      (6 marks)

(c) Briefly identify any conclusions which may be drawn from your calculations.

                                                      (4 marks)
                                         (Total 22 marks)
                                 ACCA Foundation Costing

Question 8.7

Intermediate: Decision-making and non-graphical CVP analysis

Mr Belle has recently developed a new improved video cassette and shown below is a summary of a report by a firm of management consultants on the sales potential and production costs of the new cassette.

Sales potential: The sales volume is difficult to predict and will vary with the price, but it is reasonable to assume that at a selling price of £10 per cassette, sales would be between 7500 and 10 000 units per month. Alternatively, if the selling price was reduced to £9 per cassette, sales would be between 12 000 and 18 000 units per month.

Production costs: If production is maintained at or below 10 000 units per month, then variable manufacturing costs would be approximately £8.25 per cassette and fixed costs £12 125 per month. However, if production is planned to exceed 10 000 units per month, then variable costs would be reduced to £7.75 per cassette, but the fixed costs would increase to £16 125 per month.

Mr Belle has been charged £2000 for the report by the management consultants and, in addition, he has incurred £3000 development costs on the new cassette.

If Mr Belle decides to produce and sell the new cassette it will be necessary for him to use factory premises which he owns, but are leased to a colleague for a rental of £400 per month. Also he will resign from his current post in an electronics firm where he is earning a salary of £1000 per month.

Required:

(a) Identify in the question an example of
  (i) an opportunity cost,
  (ii) a sunk cost.

(3 marks)

(b) Making whatever calculations you consider appropriate, analyse the report from the consultants and advise Mr Belle of the potential profitability of the alternatives shown in the report.

Any assumptions considered necessary or matters which may require further investigation or comment should be clearly stated.

(19 marks)
(Total 22 marks)
ACCA Level 1 Costing

Question 8.8

Advanced: Decision-making and CVP analysis

Bruno Ltd is considering proposals for design changes in one of a range of soft toys. The proposals are as follows:

(a) Eliminate some of the decorative stitching from the toy.

(b) Use plastic eyes instead of glass eyes in the toys (two eyes per toy).

(c) Change the filling material used. It is proposed that scrap fabric left over from the body manufacture be used instead of the synthetic material which is currently used.

The design change proposals have been considered by the management team and the following information has been gathered:

(i) Plastic eyes will cost £15 per hundred whereas the existing glass eyes cost £20 per hundred. The plastic eyes will be more liable to damage on insertion into the toy. It is estimated that scrap plastic eyes will be 10% of the quantity issued from stores as compared to 5% of issues of glass eyes at present.

(ii) The synthetic filling material costs £80 per tonne. One tonne of filling is sufficient for 2000 soft toys.

(iii) Scrap fabric to be used as filling material will need to be cut into smaller pieces before use and this will cost £0.05 per soft toy. There is sufficient scrap fabric for the purpose.

(iv) The elimination of the decorative stitching is expected to reduce the appeal of the product, with an estimated fall in sales by 10% from the current level. It is not felt that the change in eyes or filling material will adversely affect sales volume. The elimination of the stitching will reduce production costs by £0.60 per soft toy.

(v) The current sales level of the soft toy is 300 000 units per annum. Apportioned fixed costs per annum are £450 000. The net profit per soft toy at the current sales level is £3.

Required:

(a) Using the information given in the question, prepare an analysis which shows the estimated effect on annual profit if all three proposals are implemented, and which enables management to check whether each proposal will achieve an annual target profit increase of £25 000. The proposals for plastic eyes and the use of scrap fabric should be evaluated after the stitching elimination proposal has been evaluated.

(12 marks)

(b) Calculate the percentage reduction in sales due to the stitching elimination at which the implementation of all three design change proposals would result in the same total profit from the toy as that earned before the implementation of the changes in design.

(8 marks)

(c) Prepare a report which indicates additional information which should be obtained before a final decision is taken with regard to the implementation of the proposals.

(10 marks)
(Total 30 marks)
ACCA Level 2 Cost and Management Accounting II

Advanced: Cost–volume–profit analysis in a hospital

Question 8.9

A private hospital is organised into separate medical units which offer specialised nursing care (e.g. maternity unit, paediatric unit). Figures for the paediatric unit for the year to 31 May 2001 have just become available. For the year in question the paediatric unit charged patients £200 per patient day for nursing care and £4.4m in revenue was earned.

Costs of running the unit consist of variable costs, direct staffing costs and allocated fixed costs. The charges for variable costs such as catering and laundry are based on the number of patient days spent in hospital. Staffing costs are established from the personnel requirements applicable to particular levels of patient days. Charges for fixed costs such as security, administration etc. are based on bed capacity, currently 80 beds.

The number of beds available to be occupied is regarded as bed capacity and this is agreed and held constant for the whole year. There was an agreement that a bed capacity of 80 beds would apply to the paediatric unit for the 365 days of the year to 31 May 2001.

The tables below show the variable, staffing and fixed costs applicable to the paediatric unit for the year to 31 May 2001.

Variable costs (based on patient days)	£
Catering	450 000
Laundry	150 000
Pharmacy	500 000
	1 100 000

Staffing costs

Each speciality recruits its own nurses, supervisors and assistants. The staffing requirements for the paediatric unit are based on the actual patient days, see the following table:

Patient Days per annum	Supervisors	Nurses	Assistants
up to 20 500	4	10	20
20 500 to 23 000	4	13	24
Over 23 000	4	15	28

The annual costs of employment are: supervisors £22 000 each, nurses £16 000 each and assistants £12 000 each.

Fixed costs (based on bed capacity)	£
Administration	850 000
Security	80 000
Rent and property	720 000
	1 650 000

During the year to 31 May 2001 the paediatric unit operated a 100% occupancy (i.e. all 80 beds occupied) for 100 days of the year. In fact, the demand on these days was for a least 20 beds more.

As a consequence of this, in the budget for the following year to 31 May 2002, an increase in the bed capacity has been agreed. 20 extra beds will be contracted for the whole of the year. It is assumed that the 100 beds will be fully occupied for 100 days, rather than being restricted to 80 beds on those days. An increase of 10% in employment costs for the year to 31 May 2002, due to wage rate rises, will occur for all personnel. The revenue per patient day, all other cost factors and the remaining occupancy will be the same as the year to 31 May 2001.

Required:

(a) Determine, for the year to 31 May 2001, the actual number of patient-days, the bed occupancy percentage, the net profit/loss and the break-even number(s) of patient days for the paediatric unit.

(6 marks)

(b) Determine the budget for the year to 31 May 2002 showing the revised number of patient-days, the bed occupancy percentage, the net profit/loss and the number of patient-days required to achieve the same profit/loss as computed in (a) above.

(5 marks)

(c) Comment on your findings from (a) and (b) offering advice to the management of the unit.

(6 marks)

(d) A business or operating unit can have both financial and social objectives and at times these can be in conflict. Briefly explain and give an example.

(3 marks)
(20 marks)
ACCA Paper 8 Managerial Finance

In the last quarter it is estimated that YNQ will have produced and sold 20 000 units of their main product by the end of the year. At this level of activity it is estimated that the average unit cost will be:

	(£)
Direct material	30
Direct labour	10
Overhead: Fixed	10
Variable	10
	60

This is in line with the standards set at the start of the year. The management accountant of YNQ is now preparing the budget for the next year. He has incorporated into his preliminary calculations the following expected cost increases:

Raw material:	price increase of 20%
Direct labour:	wage rate increase of 5%
Variable overhead:	increase of 5%
Fixed overhead:	increase of 25%

The production manager believes that if a cheaper grade of raw material were to be used, this would enable the direct material cost per unit to be kept to £31.25 for the next year. The cheaper material would, however, lead to a reject rate estimated at 5% of the completed output and it would be necessary to introduce an inspection stage at the end of the manufacturing process to identify the faulty items. The cost of this inspection process would be £40 000 per year (including £10 000 allocation of existing factory overhead).

Established practice has been to reconsider the product's selling price at the time the budget is being prepared. The selling price is normally determined by adding a mark-up of 50% to unit cost. On this basis the product's selling price for last year has been £90 but the sales manager is worried about the implications of continuing the cost-plus 50% rule for next year. He estimates that demand for the product varies with price as follows:

Price:	£80	£84	£88	£90	£92	£96	£100
Demand (000)	25	23	21	20	19	17	15

(a) You are required to decide whether YNQ should use the regular or the cheaper grade of material and to calculate the best price for the product, the optimal level of production and the profit that this should yield. Comment briefly on the sensitivity of the solution to possible errors in the estimates.

(14 marks)

(b) Indicate how one might obtain the answer to part (a) from an appropriately designed cost–volume–profit graph. You should design such a graph as part of your answer but the graph need not be drawn to scale providing that it demonstrates the main features of the approach that you would use.

(8 marks)
(Total 22 marks)
ACCA Level 2 Management Accounting

Question 8.11   Advanced: CVP analysis and changes in product mix

Dingbat Ltd is considering renting additional factory space to make two products, Thingone and Thingtwo. You are the company's management accountant and have prepared the following monthly budget:

Sales (units)	Thingone 4000 (£)	Thingtwo 2000 (£)	Total 6000 (£)
Sales revenue	80 000	100 000	180 000
Variable material and labour costs	(60 000)	(62 000)	(122 000)
Fixed production overheads (allocated on direct labour hours)	(9 900)	(18 000)	(27 900)
Fixed administration overheads (allocated on sales value)	(1 600)	(2 000)	(3 600)
Profit	8 500	18 000	26 500

The fixed overheads in the budget can only be avoided if neither product is manufactured. Facilities are fully interchangeable between products.

As an alternative to the manual production process assumed in the budget, Dingbat Ltd has the option of adopting a computer-aided process. This process would cut variable costs of production by 15% and increase fixed costs by £12 000 per month.

The management of Dingbat Ltd is confident about the cost forecasts, but there is considerable uncertainty over demand for the new products.

The management believes the company will have to depart from its usual cash sales policy in order to sell Thingtwo. An average of three months' credit would be given and bad debts and administration costs would probably amount to 4% of sales revenue for this product.

Both products will be sold at the prices assumed in the budget. Dingbat Ltd has a cost of capital of 2% per month. No stocks will be held.

Requirements:

(a) Calculate the sales revenues at which operations will break-even for each process (manual and computer-aided) and calculate the sales revenues at which Dingbat Ltd will be indifferent between the two processes:
  (i) if Thingone alone is sold;

(4 marks)

  (ii) if Thingone and Thingtwo units are sold in the ratio 4:1, with Thingtwo being sold on credit.

(6 marks)

(b) Explain the implications of your results with regard to the financial viability of Thingone and Thingtwo.

(5 marks)

(c) Discuss the major factors to be considered in the pricing and sales forecasting for new productions.

(10 marks)
(Total 25 marks)
ICAEW P2 Management Accounting

Measuring relevant costs and revenues of decision-making

Questions to Chapter 9

Intermediate: Acceptance of a special order

Question 9.1

The production manager of your organization has approached you for some costing advice on project X, a one-off order from overseas that he intends to tender for. The costs associated with the project are as follows:

	(£)
Material A	4 000
Material B	8 000
Direct labour	6 000
Supervision	2 000
Overheads	12 000
	32 000

You ascertain the following:

(i) Material A is in stock and the above was the cost. There is now no other use for material A, other than the above project, within the factory and it would cost £1750 to dispose of. Material B would have to be ordered at the cost shown above.

(ii) Direct labour costs of £6000 relate to workers that will be transferred to this project from another project. Extra labour will need to be recruited to the other project at a cost of £7000.

(iii) Supervision costs have been charged to the project on the basis of $33^{1}/_{3}\%$ of labour costs and will be carried out by existing staff within their normal duties.

(iv) Overheads have been charged to the project at the rate of 200% on direct labour.

(v) The company is currently operating at a point above break-even.

(vi) The project will need the utilization of machinery that will have no other use to the company after the project has finished. The machinery will have to be purchased at a cost of £10 000 and then disposed of for £5250 at the end of the project.

The production manager tells you that the overseas customer is prepared to pay up to a maximum of £30 000 for the project and a competitor is prepared to accept the order at that price. He also informs you the minimum that he can charge is £40 000 as the above costs show £32 000, and this does not take into consideration the cost of the machine and profit to be taken on the project.

Required:

(a) Cost the project for the production manager, clearly stating how you have arrived at your figures and giving reasons for the exclusion of other figures.

(12 marks)

MEASURING RELEVANT COSTS AND REVENUES OF DECISION-MAKING ━━━━━━━━━━ 55

(b) Write a report to the production manager stating whether the organization should go ahead with the tender for the project, the reasons why and the price, bearing in mind that the competitor is prepared to undertake the project for £30 000.

(8 marks)

Note: The project should only be undertaken if it shows a profit.

(c) State four non-monetary factors that should be taken into account before tendering for this project.

(2 marks)

(d) What would be your advice if you were told that the organization was operating below break-even point? Give reasons for your advice.

(3 marks)
(Total 25 marks)
AAT Cost Accounting and Budgeting

Question 9.2

Intermediate: Make or buy decision

The management of Springer plc is considering next year's production and purchase budgets.

One of the components produced by the company, which is incorporated into another product before being sold, has a budgeted manufacturing cost as follows:

	(£)
Direct material	14
Direct labour (4 hours at £3 per hour)	12
Variable overhead (4 hours at £2 per hour)	8
Fixed overhead (4 hours at £5 per hour)	20
Total cost	54 per unit

Trigger plc has offered to supply the above component at a guaranteed price of £50 per unit.

Required:

(a) Considering cost criteria only, advise management whether the above component should be purchased from Trigger plc. Any calculations should be shown and assumptions made, or aspects which may require further investigation should be clearly stated.

(6 marks)

(b) Explain how your above advice would be affected by each of the two *separate* situations shown below.

(i) As a result of recent government legislation if Springer plc continues to manufacture this component the company will incur additional inspection and testing expenses of £56 000 per annum, which are not included in the above budgeted manufacturing costs.

(3 marks)

(ii) Additional labour cannot be recruited and if the above component is not manufactured by Springer plc the direct labour released will be employed in increasing the production of an existing product which is sold for £90 and which has a budgeted manufacturing cost as follows:

	(£)
Direct material	10
Direct labour (8 hours at £3 per hour)	24

Variable overhead (8 hours at £2 per hour)   16
Fixed overhead (8 hours at £5 per hour)   <u>40</u>
                                               <u>90</u> per unit

All calculations should be shown.

(4 marks)

(c) The production director of Springer plc recently said:

'We must continue to manufacture the component as only one year ago we purchased some special grinding equipment to be used exclusively by this component. The equipment cost £100 000, it cannot be resold or used elsewhere and if we cease production of this component we will have to write off the written down book value which is £80 000.'

Draft a brief reply to the production director commenting on his statement.

(4 marks)
(Total 17 marks)
ACCA Level 1 Costing

Intermediate: Calculation of minimum selling price

Question 9.3

You have received a request from EXE plc to provide a quotation for the manufacture of a specialized piece of equipment. This would be a one-off order, in excess of normal budgeted production. The following cost estimate has already been prepared:

		Note	(£)
Direct materials:			
Steel	10 m² at £5.00 per sq. metre	1	50
Brass fittings		2	20
Direct labour			
Skilled	25 hours at £8.00 per hour	3	200
Semi-skilled	10 hours at £5.00 per hour	4	50
Overhead	35 hours at £10.00 per hour	5	350
Estimating time		6	<u>100</u>
			770
Administrative overhead at 20% of production cost		7	<u>154</u>
			924
Profit at 25% of total cost		8	<u>231</u>
Selling price			<u>1155</u>

Notes:

1. The steel is regularly used, and has a current stock value of £5.00 per sq. metre. There are currently 100 sq. metres in stock. The steel is readily available at a price of £5.50 per sq. metre.

2. The brass fittings would have to be bought specifically for this job: a supplier has quoted the price of £20 for the fittings required.

3. The skilled labour is currently employed by your company and paid at a rate of £8.00 per hour. If this job were undertaken it would be necessary either to work

25 hours overtime which would be paid at time plus one half *or* to reduce production of another product which earns a contribution of £13.00 per hour.

4. The semi-skilled labour currently has sufficient paid idle time to be able to complete this work.

5. The overhead absorption rate includes power costs which are directly related to machine usage. If this job were undertaken, it is estimated that the machine time required would be ten hours. The machines incur power costs of £0.75 per hour. There are no other overhead costs which can be specifically identified with this job.

6. The cost of the estimating time is that attributed to the four hours taken by the engineers to analyse the drawings and determine the cost estimate given above.

7. It is company policy to add 20% on to the production cost as an allowance against administration costs associated with the jobs accepted.

8. This is the standard profit added by your company as part of its pricing policy.

Required:

(a) Prepare, on a relevant cost basis, the lowest cost estimate that could be used as the basis for a quotation. Explain briefly your reasons for using *each* of the values in your estimate.

(*12 marks*)

(b) There may be a possibility of repeat orders from EXE plc which would occupy part of normal production capacity. What factors need to be considered before quoting for this order?

(*7 marks*)

(c) When an organisation identifies that it has a single production resource which is in short supply, but is used by more than one product, the optimum production plan is determined by ranking the products according to their contribution per unit of the scarce resource.

Using a numerical example of your own, reconcile this approach with the opportunity cost approach used in (a) above.

(*6 marks*)
(*Total 25 marks*)
CIMA Stage Operational Cost Accounting

Question 9.4   Intermediate: Impact of a product abandonment decision and CVP analysis

(a) Budgeted information for A Ltd for the following period, analysed by product, is shown below:

	Product I	Product II	Product III
Sales units (000s)	225	376	190
Selling price (£ per unit)	11.00	10.50	8.00
Variable costs (£ per unit)	5.80	6.00	5.20
Attributable fixed costs (£000s)	275	337	296

General fixed costs, which are apportioned to products as a percentage of sales, are budgeted at £1 668 000.

Required:

(i) Calculate the budgeted profit of A Ltd, and of each of its products.

(*5 marks*)

MEASURING RELEVANT COSTS AND REVENUES OF DECISION-MAKING

(ii) Recalculate the budgeted profit of A Ltd on the assumption that Product III is discontinued, with no effect on sales of the other two products. State and justify other assumptions made.

(5 marks)

(iii) Additional advertising, to that included in the budget for Product I, is being considered.

Calculate the minimum extra sales units required of Product I to cover additional advertising expenditure of £80 000. Assume that all other existing fixed costs would remain unchanged.

(3 marks)

(iv) Calculate the increase in sales volume of Product II that is necessary in order to compensate for the effect on profit of a 10% reduction in the selling price of the product. State clearly any assumptions made.

(5 marks)

(b) Discuss the factors which influence cost behaviour in response to changes in activity.

(7 marks)
(Total 25 marks)
ACCA Cost and Management Accounting 1

Intermediate Price/output and key factor decisions

Question 9.5

You work as a trainee for a small management consultancy which has been asked to advise a company, Rane Limited, which manufactures and sells a single product. Rane is currently operating at full capacity producing and selling 25 000 units of its product each year. The cost and selling price structure for this level of activity is as follows:

	At 25 000 units output (£ per unit)	(£ per unit)
Production costs		
Direct material	14	
Direct labour	13	
Variable production overhead	4	
Fixed production overhead	8	
Total production cost		39
Selling and distribution overhead:		
Sales commission – 10% of sales value	6	
Fixed	3	
		9
Administration overhead:		
Fixed		2
Total cost		50
Mark up – 20%		10
Selling price		60

A new managing director has recently joined the company and he has engaged your organization to advise on his company's selling price policy. The sales price of £60 has been derived as above from a cost-plus pricing policy. The price was viewed as satisfactory because the resulting demand enabled full capacity operation.

You have been asked to investigate the effect on costs and profit of an increase in the selling price. The marketing department has provided you with the following estimates of sales volumes which could be achieved at the three alternative sales prices under consideration.

Selling price per unit	£70	£80	£90
Annual sales volume (units)	20 000	16 000	11 000

You have spent some time estimating the effect that changes in output volume will have on cost behaviour patterns and you have now collected the following information.

Direct material: The loss of bulk discounts means that the direct material cost per unit will increase by 15% for all units produced in the year if activity reduces below 15 000 units per annum.

Direct labour: Savings in bonus payments will reduce labour costs by 10% for all units produced in the year if activity reduces below 20 000 units per annum.

Sales commission: This would continue to be paid at the rate of 10% of sales price.

Fixed production overhead: If annual output volume was below 20 000 units, then a machine rental cost of £10 000 per annum could be saved. This will be the only change in the total expenditure on fixed production overhead.

Fixed selling overhead: A reduction in the part-time sales force would result in a £5000 per annum saving if annual sales volume falls below 24 000 units. This will be the only change in the total expenditure on fixed selling and distribution overhead.

Variable production overhead: There would be no change in the unit cost for variable production overhead.

Administration overhead: The total expenditure on administration overhead would remain unaltered within this range of activity.

Stocks: Rane's product is highly perishable, therefore no stocks are held.

Task 1

(a) Calculate the annual profit which is earned with the current selling price of £60 per unit.

(b) Prepare a schedule to show the annual profit which would be earned with each of the three alternative selling prices.

Task 2

Prepare a brief memorandum to your boss, Chris Jones. The memorandum should cover the following points:

(a) Your recommendation as to the selling price which should be charged to maximize Rane Limited's annual profits.

(b) *Two* non-financial factors which the management of Rane Limited should consider before planning to operate below full capacity.

Another of your consultancy's clients is a manufacturing company, Shortage Limited, which is experiencing problems in obtaining supplies of a major component. The component is used in all of its four products and there is a labour dispute at the supplier's factory, which is restricting the component's availability.

Supplies will be restricted to 22 400 components for the next period and the company wishes to ensure that the best use is made of the available components. This is the only component used in the four products, and there are no alternatives and no other suppliers.

The components cost £2 each and are used in varying amounts in each of the four products.

Shortage Limited's fixed costs amount to £8000 per period. No stocks are held of finished goods or work in progress.

The following information is available concerning the products.

Maximum demand per period	Product A 4000 units (£ per unit)	Product B 2500 units (£ per unit)	Product C 3600 units (£ per unit)	Product D 2750 units (£ per unit)
Selling price	14	12	16	17
Component costs	4	2	6	8
Other variable costs	7	9	6	4

Task 3

(a) Prepare a recommended production schedule for next period which will maximize Shortage Limited's profit.

(b) Calculate the profit that will be earned in the next period if your recommended production schedule is followed.

AAT Technicians Stage

Intermediate: Limiting factor optimum production and the use of simultaneous equations where more than one scarce factor exists

Question 9.6

A company manufactures two products (X and Y) in one of its factories. Production capacity is limited to 85 000 machine hours per period. There is no restriction on direct labour hours.

The following information is provided concerning the two products:

	Product X	Product Y
Estimated demand (000 units)	315	135
Selling price (per unit)	£11.20	£15.70
Variable costs (per unit)	£6.30	£8.70
Fixed costs (per unit)	£4.00	£7.00
Machine hours (per 000 units)	160	280
Direct labour hours (per 000 units)	120	140

Fixed costs are absorbed into unit costs at a rate per machine hour based upon full capacity.

Required:

(a) Calculate the production quantities of Products X and Y which are required per period in order to maximize profit in the situation described above.

(5 marks)

(b) Prepare a marginal costing statement in order to establish the total contribution of each product, and the net profit per period, based on selling the quantities calculated in (a) above.

(4 marks)

(c) Calculate the production quantities of Products X and Y per period which would fully utilize both machine capacity and direct labour hours, where the available direct labour hours are restricted to 55 000 per period. (The limit of 85 000 machine hours remains.)

(5 marks)
(Total 14 marks)
ACCA Foundation Paper 3

Question 9.7

Advanced: Assessing a number of options using relevant costs

MOV plc produces custom-built sensors. Each sensor has a standard circuit board (SCB) in it. The current average contribution from a sensor is £400. MOV plc's business is steadily expanding and in the year just ending (2001/2002), the company will have produced 55 000 sensors. The demand for MOV plc's sensors is predicted to grow over the next three years:

Year	Units
2002/03	58 000
2003/04	62 000
2004/05	65 000

The production of sensors is limited by the number of SCBs the company can produce. The present production level of 55 000 SCBs is the maximum that can be produced without overtime working. Overtime could increase annual output to 60 500, allowing production of sensors to also increase to 60 500. However, the variable cost of SCBs produced in overtime would increase by £75 per unit.

Because of the pressure on capacity, the company is considering having the SCBs manufactured by another company, CIR plc. This company is very reliable and produces products of good quality. CIR plc has quoted a price of £116 per SCB, for orders greater than 50 000 units a year.

MOV plc's own costs per SCB are predicted to be:

	£	
Direct material	28	
Direct labour	40	
Variable overhead	20	(based on labour cost)
Fixed overhead	24	(based on labour cost and output of 55 000 units)
Total cost	112	

The fixed overheads directly attributable to SCBs are £250 000 a year; these costs will be avoided if SCBs are not produced. If more than 59 000 units are produced, SCBs' fixed overheads will increase by £130 000.

In addition to the above overheads, MOV plc's fixed overheads are predicted to be:

Sensor production, in units:	54 001 to 59 000	59 001 to 64 000	64 001 to 70 000
Fixed overhead:	£2 600 000	£2 900 000	£3 100 000

MOV plc currently holds a stock of 3500 SCBs but the production manager feels that a stock of 8000 should be held if they are bought-in; this would increase stock-holding costs by £10 000 a year. A purchasing officer, who is paid £20 000 a year, spends 50% of her time on SCB duties. If the SCBs are bought-in, a liaison officer will have to be employed at a salary of £30 000 in order to liaise with CIR plc and monitor the quality and supply of SCBs. At present, 88 staff are involved in the production of SCBs at an average salary of £25 000 a year: if the SCBs were purchased, 72 of these staff would be made redundant at an average cost of £4000 per employee.

The SCB department, which occupies an area of 240 × 120 square metres at the far end of the factory, could be rented out, at a rent of £45 per square metre a year. However, if the SCBs were to be bought-in, for the first year only MOV plc would need the space to store the increased stock caused by outsourcing, until the main stockroom had been reorganized and refurbished. From 2003/04, the space could be rented out; this would limit the annual production of sensors to 60 500 units.

Alternatively, the space could be used for the production of sensors, allowing annual output to increase to 70 000 units if required.

Required:

(a) Critically discuss the validity of the following statement. It was produced by Jim Elliott, the company's accountant, to show the gain for the coming year (2002/2003) if the SCBs were to be bought-in.

Saving in:	£
Manufacturing staff – salaries saved: 72 staff × £25 000	1 800 000
Purchasing officer – time saved	10 000
Placing orders for SCB materials: 1000 orders × £20 per order	20 000
Transport costs for raw materials for SCBs	45 000
Cost saved	1 875 000
Additional cost per SCB: (£116 – £112) × 58 000 units	232 000
Net gain if SCBs purchased	1 643 000

(10 marks)

(b) (i) Produce detailed calculations that show which course of action is the best financial option for the three years under consideration. (Ignore the time value of money.)

(12 marks)

  (ii) Advise the company of the long-term advantages and disadvantages of buying-in SCBs.

(3 marks)
(Total 25 marks)
CIMA Management Accounting – Decision Making

Advanced: Optimal production programme, shadow prices and relevant costs for pricing decisions

Question 9.8

Rosehip has spare capacity in two of its manufacturing departments – Department 4 and Department 5. A five day week of 40 hours is worked but there is only enough internal work for three days per week so that two days per week (16 hours) could be available in each department. In recent months Rosehip has sold this time to another manufacturer but there is some concern about the profitability of this work.

The accountant has prepared a table giving the hourly operating costs in each department. The summarized figures are as follows:

	Department 4 (£)	Department 5 (£)
Power costs	40	60
Labour costs	40	20
Overhead costs	40	40
	120	120

The labour force is paid on a time basis and there is no change in the weekly wage bill whether or not the plant is working at full capacity. The overhead figures are taken from the firm's current overhead absorption rates. These rates are designed to absorb all budgeted overhead (fixed and variable) when the departments are operating at 90% of full capacity (assume a 50 week year). The budgeted fixed overhead attributed to Department 4 is £36 000 p.a. and that for Department 5 is £50 400 p.a.

As a short term expedient the company has been selling processing time to another manufacturer who has been paying £70 per hour for time in either department. This customer is very willing to continue this arrangement and to purchase any spare time available but Rosehip is considering the introduction of a new product on a minor scale to absorb the spare capacity.

Each unit of the new product would require 45 minutes in Department 4 and 20 minutes in Department 5. The variable cost of the required input material is £10 per unit. It is considered that:

with a selling price of £100 the demand would be 1500 units p.a.;
with a selling price of £110 the demand would be 1000 units p.a.; and
with a selling price of £120 the demand would be 500 units p.a.

(a) You are required to calculate the best weekly programme for the slack time in the two manufacturing departments, to determine the best price to charge for the new product and to quantify the weekly gain that this programme and this price should yield.

(12 marks)

(b) Assume that the new product has been introduced successfully but that the demand for the established main products has now increased so that all available time could now be absorbed by Rosehip's main-line products. An optimal production plan for the main products has been obtained by linear programming and the optimal LP. tableau shows a shadow price of £76 per hour in Department 4 and of £27 per hour in Department 5. The new product was not considered in this exercise. Discuss the viability of the new product under the new circumstances.

(5 marks)

(c) Comment on the relationship between shadow prices and opportunity costs.

(5 marks)
(Total 22 marks)
ACCA Level 2 Management Accounting

Question 9.9

Advanced: Decision relating to the timing of the conversion of a production process

A company extracts exhaust gases from process ovens as part of the manufacturing process. The exhaust gas extraction is implemented by machinery which cost £100 000 when bought five years ago. The machinery is being depreciated at 10% per annum. The extraction of the exhaust gases enhances production output by 10 000 units per annum. This production can be sold at £8 per unit and has variable costs of £3 per unit. The exhaust gas extraction machinery has directly attributable fixed operating costs of £16 000 per annum.

The company is considering the use of the exhaust gases for space heating. The existing space heating is provided by ducted hot air which is heated by equipment with running costs of £10 000 per annum. This equipment could be sold now for £20 000 but would incur dismantling costs of £3000. If retained for one year the equipment could be sold for £18 000 with dismantling costs of £3500.

The conversion to the use of the exhaust gases for space heating would involve the following:

(i) The removal of the existing gas extraction machinery. This could be implemented now at a dismantling cost of £5000 with sale of the machinery for £40 000. Alternatively it could be sold in one year's time for £30 000 with dismantling costs of £5500.

(ii) The leasing of alternative gas extraction equipment at a cost of £4000 per annum with annual fixed running costs of £12 000.

(iii) The conversion would mean the loss of 30% of the production enhancement which the exhaust gas extraction provides for a period of one year only, until the new system is 'run-in'.

(iv) The company has a spare electric motor in store which could be sold to company X for £3500 in one year's time. It could be fitted to the proposed leased gas extraction equipment in order to reduce the impact of the production losses during the running-in period. This course of action would reduce its sales value to company X in one year's time to £2000 and would incur £2500 of fitting and dismantling costs. It would, however, reduce the production enhancement loss from 30% to 10% during the coming year (year 1). This would not be relevant in year 2 because of an anticipated fall in the demand for the product. The electric motor originally cost £5000. If replaced today it would cost £8000. It was purchased for another process which has now been discontinued. It could also be used in a cooling process for one year if modified at a cost of £1000, instead of the company hiring cooling equipment at a cost of £3000 per annum. Because of its modification, the electric motor would have to be disposed of in one year's time at a cost of £250.

Ignore the time value of money.

Required:

(a) Prepare an analysis indicating all the options available for the use of the spare electric motor and the financial implications of each. State which option should be chosen on financial grounds.

(8 marks)

(b) Prepare an analysis on an incremental opportunity cost basis in order to decide on financial grounds whether to convert immediately to the use of exhaust gases for space heating or to delay the conversion for one year.

(18 marks)
(Total 26 marks)
ACCA Paper 9 Information for Control and Decision Making

Advanced: Decision on whether to subcontract an appliance repair service or do own maintenance

Question 9.10

A company producing and selling a range of consumer durable appliances has its after-sales service work done by local approved sub-contractors.

The company is now considering carrying out all or some of the work itself and it has chosen one area in which to experiment with the new routine.

Some of the appliances are so large and bulky that repair/service work can only be done at the customers' homes. Others are small enough for sub-contractors to take them back to their local repair workshops, repair them, and re-deliver them to the customer. If the company does its own after-sales service, it proposes that customers would bring these smaller items for repair to a local company service centre which would be located and organized to deal with visitors.

There is a *list price* to customers for the labour content of any work done and for materials used. However, the majority of the after-sales service work is done under an annual maintenance contract taken out by customers on purchasing the product; this covers the labour content of any service work to be done, but customers pay for materials used.

Any labour or materials needed in the first six months are provided to the customer free of charge under the company's product guarantee and *sub-contractors* are allowed *by the company a fixed sum of 3.5% of the selling price* for each appliance to cover this work. These sums allowed have proved closely in line with the work needed over the past few years. The price structure is:

For materials:

Price to sub-contractor:	Company cost plus 10%
Price to customer:	Sub-contractor's price plus 25%

For labour: Price to sub-contractor:

Work done under maintenance contract:	90% of list price
Ad hoc work (i.e. work NOT done under maintenance contract):	85% of list price

Records show that 60% by value of the work has to be carried out at customers' homes, whilst the remainder can be done anywhere appropriate.

The annual income that the company currently receives from sub-contractors for the area in which the experiment is to take place is:

		(£)
Labour	– under maintenance contract	30 000
	– ad hoc	12 000
Materials	– under maintenance contract	18 000
	– ad hoc	6 000
		£66 000

The company expects the volume of after-sales work to remain the same as last year for the period of the experiment.

The company is considering the following options:

1. Set up a local service centre at which it can service small appliances only.

   Work at customers' houses would continue to be done under sub-contract.

2. Set up a local service centre to act only as a base for its own employees who would only service appliances at customers' homes.

   Servicing of small appliances would continue to be done under sub-contract.

3. Set up a local combined service centre plus base for all work. No work would be sub-contracted.

   If the company were to do service work, annual fixed costs are budgeted to be:

	Option 1 (£000)	Option 2 (£000)	Option 3 (£000)
Establishment costs (rent, rates, light, etc.)	40	15	45
Management costs	20	15	30
Storage staff costs	10	10	15
Transport costs (all vans/cars hired)	8	65	70
Repair/service staff	70	180	225

You are required

(a) to recommend which of the three options the company should adopt from a financial viewpoint;

(18 marks)

(b) in relation to the data provided in order to make the recommendation required in (a) above, to comment critically in respect of non-financial features that might favourably or adversely affect the customer.

(7 marks)
(Total 25 marks)
CIMA Stage 4 Management Accounting Decision Making

Advanced: Throughput accounting

Question 9.11

(a) Flopro plc make and sell two products A and B, each of which passes through the same automated production operations. The following estimated information is available for period 1:

(i) Product unit data:

	A	B
Direct material cost (£)	2	40
Variable production overhead cost (£)	28	4
Overall hours per product unit (hours)	0.25	0.15

(ii) Production/sales of products A and B are 120 000 units and 45 000 units respectively. The selling prices per unit for A and B are £60 and £70 respectively.

(iii) Maximum demand for each product is 20% above the estimated sales levels.

(iv) Total fixed production overhead cost is £1 470 000. This is absorbed by products A and B at an average rate per hour based on the estimated production levels.

Required:

Using net profit as the decision measure, show why the management of Flopro plc argues that it is indifferent on financial grounds as to the mix of products A and B which should be produced and sold, and calculate the total net profit for period 1.

(6 marks)

(b) One of the production operations has a maximum capacity of 3075 hours which has been identified as a bottleneck which limits the overall production/sales of products A and B. The bottleneck hours required per product unit for products A and B are 0.02 and 0.015 respectively.

All other information detailed in (a) still applies.

Required:

Calculate the mix (units) of products A and B which will maximize net profit and the value (£) of the maximum net profit.

(8 marks)

(c) The bottleneck situation detailed in (b) still applies. Flopro plc has decided to determine the profit maximizing mix of products A and B based on the Throughput Accounting principle of maximizing the throughput return per production hour of the bottleneck resource. This may be measured as:

$$\textit{Throughput return per production hour} = \frac{\textit{(selling price – material cost)}}{\textit{bottleneck hours per unit}}$$

All other information detailed in (a) and (b) still applies, except that the variable overhead cost as per (a) is now considered to be fixed for the short/intermediate term, based on the value (£) which applied to the product mix in (a).

Required:

(i) Calculate the mix (units) of products A and B which will maximize net profit and the value of that net profit.

(8 marks)

(ii) Calculate the throughput accounting ratio for product B which is calculated as:

(3 marks)

$$\frac{throughput\ return\ per\ hour\ of\ bottleneck\ resource\ for\ product\ B}{overall\ total\ overhead\ cost\ per\ hour\ of\ bottleneck\ resource.}$$

(iii) Comment on the interpretation of throughput accounting ratios and their use as a control device. You should refer to the ratio for product B in your answer.

(6 marks)

(iv) It is estimated that the direct material cost per unit of product B may increase by 20% due to shortage of supply.

Calculate the revised throughput accounting ratio for product B and comment on it.

(4 marks)
(35 marks)
ACCA Paper 9 Information for Control and Decision Making

Activity-based costing

Questions to Chapter 10

ABC and traditional costing customer profitability analysis

ZP plc is a marketing consultancy that provides marketing advice and support to small and medium-sized enterprises. ZP plc employs four full-time marketing consultants who each expect to deliver 1,500 chargeable hours per year and each receive a salary of £60 000 per year. In addition the company employs six marketing support-administration staff whose combined total salary cost is £120 000 per year.

ZP plc has estimated its other costs for the coming year as follows:

	£000
Office premises, rent, rates, heating	50
Advertising	5
Travel to clients	15
Accommodation whilst visiting clients	11
Telephone, fax, communications	10

ZP plc has been attributing costs to each client (and to the projects undertaken for them) by recording the chargeable hours spent on each client and using a single cost rate of £75 per chargeable hour. The same basis has been used to estimate the costs of a project when preparing a quotation for new work.

ZP plc has reviewed its existing client database and determined the following three average profiles of typical clients.

Client profile	*D*	*E*	*F*
Chargeable hours per client	100	700	300
Distance (miles) to client	50	70	100
Number of visits per client	3	8	3
Number of clients in each profile	10	5	5

The senior consultant has been reviewing the company's costing and pricing procedures. He suggests that the use of a single cost rate should be abandoned and, where possible, activities should be costed individually. With this in mind he has obtained the following further information.

- It is ZP plc's policy that where a visit is made to a client and the distance to the client is more than 50 miles, the consultant will travel the day before the visit and stay in local accommodation so that the maximum time is available for meeting the client the following day.

- The cost of travel to the client is dependent on the number of miles travelled to visit the client.

- Other costs are facility costs – at present the senior consultant cannot identify an alternative basis to that currently being used to attribute costs to each client.

Required

(a) Prepare calculations to show the cost attributed to each client group using an activity-based system of attributing costs. *(7 marks)*

(b) Discuss the differences between the costs attributed using activity-based costing and those attributed by the current system and advise whether the senior consultant's suggestion should be adopted. (9 *marks*)

(c) In a manufacturing environment activity-based costing often classifies activities into those that are: unit; batch; producit sustaining; and facility sustaining. Discuss, giving examples, how similar classifications may be applied to the use of the technique in consultancy organizations such as ZP plc. (9 *marks*)

CIMA P2 Management Accounting: Decision Management

Question 10.2

Intermediate: Preparation of conventional costing and ABC profit statements

The following budgeted information relates to Brunti plc for the forthcoming period:

	Products		
	XYI (000)	YZT (000)	ABW (000)
Sales and production (units)	50	40	30
	(£)	(£)	(£)
Selling price (per unit)	45	95	73
Prime cost (per unit)	32	84	65
	Hours	Hours	Hours
Machine department (machine hours per unit)	2	5	4
Assembly department (direct labour hours per unit)	7	3	2

Overheads allocated and apportioned to production departments (including service cost centre costs) were to be recovered in product costs as follows:

Machine department at
£1.20 per machine hour
Assembly department at
£0.825 per direct labour hour

You ascertain that the above overheads could be re-analysed into 'cost pools' as follows:

Cost pool	£000	Cost driver	Quantity for the period
Machining services	357	Machine hours	420 000
Assembly services	318	Direct labour hours	530 000
Set-up costs	26	Set-ups	520
Order processing	156	Customer orders	32 000
Purchasing	84	Suppliers orders	11 200
	941		

You have also been provided with the following estimates for the period:

	Products		
	XYI	**YZT**	**ABW**
Number of set-ups	120	200	200
Customer orders	8000	8000	16 000
Suppliers' orders	3000	4000	4 200

Required:

(a) Prepare and present profit statements using:
   (i) conventional absorption costing;

(5 marks)

   (ii) activity-based costing;

(10 marks)

(b) Comment on why activity-based costing is considered to present a fairer valuation of the product cost per unit.

(5 marks)
(Total 20 marks)
ACCA Paper 8 Managerial Finance

Advanced: Computation of ABC and traditional product costs plus a discussion of ABC

Question 10.3

Repak Ltd is a warehousing and distribution company which receives products from customers, stores the products and then re-packs them for distribution as required. There are three customers for whom the service is provided – John Ltd, George Ltd and Paul Ltd. The products from all three customers are similar in nature but of varying degrees of fragility. Basic budget information has been gathered for the year to 30 June and is shown in the following table:

	Products handled (cubic metres)
John Ltd	30 000
George Ltd	45 000
Paul Ltd	25 000
	Costs (£000)
Packaging materials (see note 1)	1 950
Labour – basic	350
– overtime	30
Occupancy	500
Administration and management	60

Note 1: Packaging materials are used in re-packing each cubic metre of product for John Ltd, George Ltd and Paul Ltd in the ratio 1:2:3 respectively. This ratio is linked to the relative fragility of the goods for each customer.

Additional information has been obtained in order to enable unit costs to be prepared for each of the three customers using an activity-based costing approach. The additional information for the year to 30 June has been estimated as follows:

(i) Labour and overhead costs have been identified as attributable to each of three work centres – receipt and inspection, storage and packing as follows:

	Cost allocation proportions		
	Receipt and inspection %	Storage %	Packing %
Labour – basic	15	10	75
– overtime	50	15	35
Occupancy	20	60	20
Administration and management	40	10	50

(ii) Studies have revealed that the fragility of different goods affects the receipt and inspection time needed for the products for each customer. Storage required is related to the average size of the basic incoming product units from each customer. The re-packing of goods for distribution is related to the complexity of packaging required by each customer. The relevant requirements per cubic metre of product for each customer have been evaluated as follows:

	John Ltd	George Ltd	Paul Ltd
Receipt and inspection (minutes)	5	9	15
Storage (square metres)	0·3	0·3	0·2
Packing (minutes)	36	45	60

Required:

(a) Calculate the budgeted average cost per cubic metre of packaged products for each customer for each of the following two circumstances:
  (i) where only the basic budget information is to be used,

(6 marks)

  (ii) where the additional information enables an activity-based costing approach to be applied.

(14 marks)

(b) Comment on the activities and cost drivers which have been identified as relevant for the implementation of activity-based costing by Repak Ltd and discuss ways in which activity-based costing might improve product costing and cost control in Repak Ltd. Make reference to your answer to part (a) of the question, as appropriate.

(10 marks)
(Total 30 marks)
ACCA Level 2

Question 10.4

Advanced: Comparison of ABC with traditional product costing

(a) In the context of activity-based costing (ABC), it was stated in *Management Accounting – Evolution not Revolution* by Bromwich and Bhimani, that 'Cost drivers attempt to link costs to the scope of output rather than the scale of output thereby generating less arbitrary product costs for decision making.' You are required to explain the terms 'activity-based costing' and 'cost drivers'.

(13 marks)

(b) XYZ plc manufactures four products, namely A, B, C and D, using the same plant and processes. The following information relates to a production period:

Product	Volume	Material cost per unit	Direct labour per unit	Machine time cost per unit	Labour
A	500	£5	½ hour	¼ hour	£3
B	5000	£5	½ hour	¼ hour	£3
C	600	£16	2 hours	1 hour	£12
D	7000	£17	1½ hours	1½ hours	£9

Total production overhead recorded by the cost accounting system is analysed under the following headings:

Factory overhead applicable to machine-oriented activity is £37 424
   Set-up costs are £4355

   The cost of ordering materials is £1920
   Handling materials – £7580
   Administration for spare parts – £8600.

These overhead costs are absorbed by products on a machine hour rate of £4.80 per hour, giving an overhead cost per product of:

   A   £1.20   B   £1.20   C   £4.80   D   £7.20

However, investigation into the production overhead activities for the period reveals the following totals:

Product	Number of set-ups	Number of material orders	Number of times material was handled	Number of spare parts
A	1	1	2	2
B	6	4	10	5
C	2	1	3	1
D	8	4	12	4

You are required:

(i) to compute an overhead cost per product using activity-based costing, tracing overheads to production units by means of cost drivers.

(6 *marks*)

(ii) to comment briefly on the differences disclosed between overheads traced by the present system and those traced by activity-based costing.

(6 *marks*)
(*Total 25 marks*)
CIMA Stage 4 Management Accounting – Control and Audit

Intermediate

Question 10.5

In a marginal costing system only variable costs would be assigned to products or services, in which case management may rely on a *contribution approach to decisions*.

Required:

(a) Explain and discuss the contribution approach to decisions giving brief examples and drawing attention to any limitations.

(6 *marks*)

A full absorption costing system would involve the assignment of both variable and fixed overhead costs to products. A traditional full absorption costing system typically uses a *single volume related allocation base* (*or cost driver*) to assign overheads to products. An activity based costing (ABC) system would use *multiple allocation bases* (*or cost drivers*), taking account of *different categories of activities and related overhead costs* such as unit, batch, product sustaining and facility sustaining.

Required:

(b) Describe the likely stages involved in the design and operation of an ABC system.

(4 marks)

(c) Explain and discuss volume related allocation bases (or cost drivers), giving an example of one within a traditional costing system. Contrast this with the multiple allocation bases (or cost drivers) of an ABC system.

(6 marks)

(d) Briefly elaborate on the different categories of activities and related overhead costs, such as unit, batch, product sustaining and facility sustaining, which may be used in an ABC system.

(4 marks)
(Total 20 marks)
ACCA Paper 8 Managerial Finance

Question 10.6   **Advanced: ABC product cost computation and discussion relating to ABC, JIT and TQM**

During the last 20 years, KL's manufacturing operation has become increasingly automated with computer-controlled robots replacing operatives. KL currently manufactures over 100 products of varying levels of design complexity. A single, plant-wide overhead absorption rate (OAR), based on direct labour hours, is used to absorb overhead costs.

In the quarter ended March, KL's manufacturing overhead costs were:

	(£000)
Equipment operation expenses	125
Equipment maintenance expenses	25
Wages paid to technicians	85
Wages paid to storemen	35
Wages paid to dispatch staff	40
	310

During the quarter, RAPIER Management Consultants were engaged to conduct a review of KLs cost accounting systems. RAPIERs report includes the following statement:

In KL's circumstances, absorbing overhead costs in individual products on a labour hour absorption basis is meaningless. Overhead costs should be attributed to products using an activity based costing (ABC) system. We have identified the following as being the most significant activities:

(1)   receiving component consignments from suppliers
(2)   setting up equipment for production runs
(3)   quality inspections
(4)   dispatching goods orders to customers.

Our research has indicated that, in the short term, KL's overheads are 40% fixed and 60% variable. Approximately half the variable overheads vary in relation to direct labour hours worked and half vary in relation to the number of quality inspections. This model applies only to relatively small changes in the level of output during a period of two years or less.

Equipment operation and maintenance expenses are apportionable as follows:

- component stores (15%), manufacturing (70%) and goods dispatch (15%).

Technician wages are apportionable as follows:

- equipment maintenance (30%), setting up equipment for production runs (40%) and quality inspections (30%).

During the quarter

- a total of 2000 direct labour hours were worked (paid at £12 per hour),
- 980 component consignments were received from suppliers,
- 1020 production runs were set up,
- 640 quality inspections were carried out, and
- 420 goods orders were dispatched to customers.

Part One

KL's production during the quarter included components r, s and t. The following information is available:

	Component r	Component s	Component t
Direct labour hours worked	25	480	50
Direct material costs	£1 200	£2 900	£1 800
Component consignments received	42	24	28
Production runs	16	18	12
Quality inspections	10	8	18
Goods orders dispatched	22	85	46
Quantity produced	560	12 800	2 400

In April 2001 a potential customer asked KL to quote for the supply of a new component (z) to a given specification. 1000 units of z are to be supplied each quarter for a two-year period. They will be paid for in equal instalments on the last day of each quarter. The job will involve an initial design cost of £40 000 and production will involve 80 direct labour hours, £2000 materials, 20 component consignments, 15 production runs, 30 quality inspections and 4 goods dispatches per quarter.

KL's Sales Director comments:

Now we have a modern ABC system, we can quote selling prices with confidence. The quarterly charge we quote should be the forecast ABC production cost of the units plus the design cost of the z depreciated on a straight-line basis over the two years of the job – to which we should add a 25% mark-up for profit. We can base our forecast on costs experienced in the quarter ended March.

Requirements:

(a) Calculate the unit cost of components r, s and t, using KLs existing cost accounting system (single factory labour hour OAR).

(5 marks)

(b) Explain how an ABC system would be developed using the information given. Calculate the unit cost of components r, s and t, using this ABC system.

(11 marks)

(c) Calculate the charge per quarter that should be quoted for supply of component *z* in a manner consistent with the Sales Directors comments. Advise KL's management on the merits of this selling price, having regard to factors you consider relevant.

Note: KL's cost of capital is 3% per quarter.

(9 marks)
(Total 25 marks)

Part Two

It is often claimed that ABC provides better information concerning product costs than traditional management accounting techniques. It is also sometimes claimed that ABC provides better information as a guide to decision-making. However, one should treat these claims with caution. ABC may give a different impression of product costs but it is not necessarily a better impression. It may be wiser to try improving the use of traditional techniques before moving to ABC.

Comment by KL's management accountant on the RAPIER report

Requirements:

(a) Explain the ideas concerning cost behaviour which underpin ABC. Explain why ABC may be better attuned to the modern manufacturing environment than traditional techniques. Explain why KL might or might not obtain a more meaningful impression of product costs through the use of ABC.

(10 marks)

(b) Explain how the traditional cost accounting system being used by KL might be improved to provide more meaningful product costs.

(6 marks)

(c) Critically appraise the reported claim that ABC gives better information as a guide to decision-making than do traditional product costing techniques.

(9 marks)
(Total 25 marks)

Part Three

The lean enterprise [characterised by just-in-time (JIT), total quality management (TQM) and supportive supplier relations] is widely considered a better approach to manufacturing. Some have suggested, however, that ABC hinders the spread of the lean enterprise by making apparent the cost of small batch sizes.

Comment by an academic accountant

Requirements:

(a) Explain the roles that JIT, TQM and supportive supplier relations play in a modern manufacturing management. How might the adoption of such practices improve KLs performance?

(10 marks)

(b) Explain what the writer of the above statement means by 'the cost of small batch sizes'. Critically appraise the manner in which this cost is treated by KLs existing (single OAR-based) cost accounting system. Explain the benefits that KL might obtain through a full knowledge and understanding of this cost.

(10 marks)

(c) Explain and discuss the extent to which academic research in the area of management accounting is likely to influence the practice of management accounting.

(5 marks)
(Total 25 marks)
CIMA Stage 3 Management Accounting Applications

Pricing decisions and profitability analysis

Questions to Chapter 11

Advanced: Calculation of cost-plus selling price and an evaluation of pricing decisions

A firm manufactures two products EXE and WYE in departments dedicated exclusively to them. There are also three service departments, stores, maintenance and administration. No stocks are held as the products deteriorate rapidly.

Direct costs of the products, which are variable in the context of the whole business, are identified to each department. The step-wise apportionment of service department costs to the manufacturing departments is based on estimates of the usage of the service provided. These are expressed as percentages and assumed to be reliable over the current capacity range. The general factory overheads of £3.6m, which are fixed, are apportioned based on floor space occupied. The company establishes product costs based on budgeted volume and marks up these costs by 25% in order to set target selling prices.

Extracts from the budgets for the forthcoming year are provided below:

	Annual volume (units)	
	EXE	WYE
Max capacity	200 000	100 000
Budget	150 000	70 000

	EXE	WYE	Stores	Maintenance	Admin
Costs (£m)					
Material	1.8	0.7	0.1	0.1	
Other variable	0.8	0.5	0.1	0.2	0.2
Departmental usage (%)					
Maintenance	50	25	25		
Administration	40	30	20	10	
Stores	60	40			
Floor space (sq m)					
	640	480	240	80	160

Required:

Workings may be £000 with unit prices to the nearest penny.

(a) Calculate the budgeted selling price of one unit of EXE and WYE based on the usual mark up.

(5 marks)

(b) Discuss how the company may respond to each of the following independent events, which represent additional business opportunities.

  (i) an enquiry from an overseas customer for 3000 units only of WYE where a price of £35 per unit is offered

(ii) an enquiry for 50 000 units of WYE to be supplied in full at regular intervals during the forthcoming year at a price which is equivalent to full cost plus 10%

In both cases support your discussion with calculations and comment on any assumptions or matters on which you would seek clarification.

(11 marks)

(c) Explain the implications of preparing product full costs based on maximum capacity rather than annual budget volume.

(4 marks)
(Total 20 marks)
ACCA Paper 8 Managerial Finance

Question 11.2

Advanced: Preparation of full cost and marginal cost information

A small company is engaged in the production of plastic tools for the garden.

Sub-totals on the spreadsheet of budgeted overheads for a year reveal:

	Moulding Department	Finishing Department	General Factory Overhead
Variable overhead (£000)	1600	500	1050
Fixed overhead (£000)	2500	850	1750
Budgeted activity			
Machine hours (000)	800	600	
Practical capacity			
Machine hours (000)	1200	800	

For the purposes of reallocation of general factory overhead it is agreed that the variable overheads accrue in line with the machine hours worked in each department. General factory fixed overhead is to be reallocated on the basis of the practical machine hour capacity of the two departments.

It has been a long-standing company practice to establish selling prices by applying a mark-up on full manufacturing cost of between 25% and 35%.

A possible price is sought for one new product which is in a final development stage. The total market for this product is estimated at 200 000 units per annum. Market research indicates that the company could expect to obtain and hold about 10% of the market. It is hoped the product will offer some improvement over competitors' products, which are currently marketed at between £90 and £100 each.

The product development department have determined that the direct material content is £9 per unit. Each unit of the product will take two labour hours (four machine hours) in the moulding department and three labour hours (three machine hours) in finishing. Hourly labour rates are £5.00 and £5.50 respectively.

Management estimate that the annual fixed costs which would be specifically incurred in relation to the product are: supervision £20 000, depreciation of a recently acquired machine £120 000 and advertising £27 000. It may be assumed that these costs are included in the budget given above. Given the state of development of this new product, management do not consider it necessary to make revisions, to the budgeted activity levels given above, for any possible extra machine hours involved in its manufacture.

Required:

(a) Briefly explain the role of costs in pricing.

(6 marks)

(b) Prepare full cost and marginal cost information which may help with the pricing decision.

(9 marks)

(c) Comment on the cost information and suggest a price range which should be considered.

(5 marks)
(Total 20 marks)
ACCA Paper 8 Managerial Finance

Advanced: Impact of a change in selling price on profits based on a given elasticity of demand

Question 11.3

You are the management accountant of a medium-sized company. You have been asked to provide budgetary information and advice to the board of directors for a meeting where they will decide the pricing of an important product for the next period.

The following information is available from the records:

Sales	Previous period (£000)		Current period (£000)
(100 000 units at £13 each)	1300	(106 000 units at £13 each)	1378.0
Costs	1000		1077.4
Profit	300		300.6

You find that between the previous and current periods there was 4% general cost inflation and it is forecast that costs will rise a further 6% in the next period. As a matter of policy, the firm did not increase the selling price in the current period although competitors raised their prices by 4% to allow for the increased costs. A survey by economic consultants was commissioned and has found that the demand for the product is elastic with an estimated price elasticity of demand of 1.5. This means that volume would fall by 1½ times the rate of real price increase.

Various options are to be considered by the board and you are required

(a) to show the budgeted position if the firm maintains the £13 selling price for the next period (when it is expected that competitors will increase their prices by 6%);

(10 marks)

(b) to show the budgeted position if the firm also raises its price by 6%;

(6 marks)

(c) to write a short report to the board, with appropriate figures, recommending whether the firm should maintain the £13 selling price or raise it by 6%;

(3 marks)

(d) to state what assumptions you have used in your answers.

(3 marks)
(Total 22 marks)
CIMA Stage 3 Management Accounting Techniques

Advanced: Recommendation of which market segment to enter and selling price to charge

Question 11.4

AB Ltd is a well-established company producing high quality, technically advanced, electronic equipment.

In an endeavour to diversify, it has identified opportunities in the hi-fi industry. After some preliminary market research it has decided to market a new product that incorporates some of the most advanced techniques available together with a very distinctive design.

AB Ltd's special skill is that it can apply these techniques economically to medium-sized quantities and offer a product of excellent design with an advanced degree of technology.

The new product faces three categories of competition:

Category	Technology	Design	Quantities sold per annum	Number of models	Retail selling price range (£)
1	Good	Standard	22 000	4	600–1050
2	Good	Good	6 000	5	1450–1900
3	Advanced	Good	750	2	2500–3000

The product will be distributed through a range of specialist retailers who have undertaken not to discount prices. Their commission will be 25% on retail selling price. AB Ltd has also acquired the rights to sell the product under the name of a prestigious hi-fi manufacturer who does not offer this type of product. For this it will pay a royalty of 5% of the retail selling price.

AB Ltd assesses that its direct cost per product will be £670 (excluding the royalty and the retailers' commission) and the annual fixed costs relevant to the project are budgeted at:

	(£)
Production	250 000
Research and development	50 000
Marketing	200 000
Finance and administration	50 000

You are required, from the data provided and making such assumptions as you consider reasonable,

(a) to suggest a range of retail prices (i.e. to the consumer) from which AB Ltd should choose the eventual price for its product. Explain briefly why you have suggested that range of prices;

(10 marks)

(b) to select *one* particular price from the range in (a) above that you would recommend AB Ltd to choose. Explain, with any relevant calculations, why you have recommended that price. Mention any assumptions that you have made.

(15 marks)

Note: The prices suggested should be rounded to the nearest £100.

Ignore VAT (or sales taxes), taxation and inflation.

(Total 25 marks)
CIMA Stage 4 Management Accounting – Decision Making

Question 11.5

Advanced: Pricing strategies and calculation of optimum selling price

Just over two years ago, R Ltd was the first company to produce a specific 'off-the-shelf' accounting software packages. The pricing strategy, decided on by the Managing Director, for the packages was to add a 50% mark-up to the budgeted full cost of the packages. The company achieved and maintained a significant market share and high profits for the first two years.

Budgeted information for the current year (Year 3) was as follows:

Production and sales	15 000 packages
Full cost	£400 per package

At a recent Board meeting, the Finance Director reported that although costs were in line with the budget for the current year, profits were declining. He explained that the full cost included £80 for fixed overheads. The figure had been calculated by using an overhead absorption rate based on labour hours and the budgeted level of production which, he pointed out, was much lower than the current capacity of 25 000 packages.

The Marketing Director stated that competitors were beginning to increase their market share. He also reported the results of a recent competitor analysis which showed that when R Ltd announced its prices for the current year, the competitors responded by undercutting them by 15%. Consequently, he commissioned an investigation of the market. He informed the Board that the market research showed that at a price of £750 there would be no demand for the packages but for every £10 reduction in price the demand would increase by 1000 packages.

The Managing Director appeared to be unconcerned about the loss of market share and argued that profits could be restored to their former level by increasing the mark-up.

$$\text{Note:} \quad \text{If price} \quad = \quad a - bx$$
$$\text{then marginal revenue} = \quad a - 2bx$$

Required:

(a) Discuss the Managing Director's pricing strategy in the circumstances described above. Your appraisal must include a discussion of the alternative strategies that could have been implemented at the launch of the packages.

(10 marks)

(b) (i) Based on the data supplied by the market research, calculate the maximum annual profit that can be earned from the sale of the packages from year 3 onwards.

(6 marks)

(ii) A German computer software distribution company, L, which is interested in becoming the sole distributor of the accounting software packages, has now approached R Ltd. It has offered to purchase 25 000 accounting packages per annum at a fixed price of R930 per package. If R Ltd were to sell the packages to L, then the variable costs would be £300 per package.

The current exchange rate is €1 = £0.60.

Required:

Draw a diagram to illustrate the sensitivity of the proposal from the German company to changes in the exchange rate and then state and comment on the minimum exchange rate needed for the proposal to be worthwhile.

(7 marks)

(c) R Ltd has signed a contract with L to supply the accounting packages. However, there has been a fire in one of the software manufacturing departments and a machine has been seriously damaged and requires urgent replacement.

The replacement machine will cost £1 million and R Ltd is considering whether to lease or buy the machine. A lease could be arranged under which R Ltd would pay £300 000 per annum for four years with each payment being made annually in advance. The lease payments would be an allowable expense for taxation purposes.

Corporation tax is payable at the rate of 30% per annum in two equal instalments: one in the year that profits are earned and the other in the following year. Writing-down allowances are allowed at 25% each year on a reducing balance basis. It is anticipated that the machine will have a useful economic life of four years, at the end of which there will be no residual value.

The after-tax cost of capital is 12%.

Required:

Evaluate the acquisition of the new machine from a financial viewpoint.

(7 marks)
(Total 30 marks)
CIMA Management Accounting – Decision Making

Question 11.6

Advanced: Calculation of optimum selling prices using differential calculus

Alvis Taylor has budgeted that output and sales of his single product, flonal, will be 100 000 for the forthcoming year. At this level of activity his unit variable costs are budgeted to be £50 and his unit fixed costs £25. His sales manager estimates that the demand for flonal would increase by 1000 units for every decrease of £1 in unit selling price (and vice-versa), and that at a unit selling price of £200 demand would be nil.

Information about two price increases has just been received from suppliers. One is for materials (which are included in Alvis Taylor's variable costs), and one is for fuel (which is included in his fixed costs). Their effect will be to increase both the variable costs and the fixed costs by 20% in total over the budgeted figures.

Alvis Taylor aims to maximize profits from his business.

You are required, in respect of Alvis Taylor's business:

(a) to calculate, *before the cost increases*:
   (i) the budgeted contribution and profit at the budgeted level of sales of 100 000 units, and
   (ii) the level of sales at which profits would be maximized, and the amount of those maximum profits,

(7 marks)

(b) to show whether and by how much Alvis Taylor should adjust his selling price, in respect of the increases in, respectively:

(i) fuel costs

(ii) materials costs,

(6 marks)

(c) to show whether and by how much it is worthwhile for Alvis Taylor, following the increases in costs, to spend £1 000 000 on a TV advertising campaign if this were confidently expected to have the effect during the next year (but not beyond then) that demand would still fall by 1000 units for every increase of £1 in unit selling price (and vice-versa), but that it would not fall to nil until the unit selling price was £210,

(5 marks)

(d) to comment on the results which you have obtained in (a)–(c) above and on the assumptions underlying them.

(7 marks)
(Total 25 marks)
ICAEW Management Accounting

Question 11.7

Discuss the extent to which cost data is useful in the determination of pricing policy. Explain the advantages and disadvantages of presenting cost data for possible utilization in pricing policy determination using an absorption, rather than a direct, costing basis.

(14 marks)
ACCA P2 Management Accounting

Advanced

Question 11.8

'In providing information to the product manager, the accountant must recognize that decision-making is essentially a process of choosing between competing alternatives, each with its own combination of income and costs; and that the relevant concepts to employ are future incremental costs and revenues and opportunity cost, not full cost which includes past or sunk costs.' (Sizer)

Descriptive studies of pricing decisions taken in practice have, on the other hand, suggested that the inclusion of overhead and joint cost allocations in unit product costs is widespread in connection with the provision of information for this class of decision. Furthermore, these costs are essentially historic costs.

You are required to:

(a) explain the reasoning underlying the above quotation;

(10 marks)

(b) suggest reasons why overhead and joint cost allocation is nevertheless widely used in practice in connection with information for pricing decisions;

(10 marks)

(c) set out your own views as to the balance of these arguments.

(5 marks)
(Total 25 marks)
ICAEW Management Accounting

Decision-making under conditions of risk and uncertainty

Questions to Chapter 12

Question 12.1

Intermediate: Expected value requiring a decision tree

Firlands Limited, a retail outlet, is faced with a decision regarding whether or not to expand and build small or large premises at a prime location. Small premises would cost £300 000 to build and large premises would cost £550 000.

Regardless of the type of premises built, if high demand exists then the net income is expected to be £1 500 000. Alternatively, if low demand exists, then net income is expected to be £600 000.

If large premises are built then the probability of high demand is 0.75. If the smaller premises are built then the probability of high demand falls to 0.6.

Firlands has the option of undertaking a survey costing £50 000. The survey predicts whether there is likely to be a good or bad response to the size of the premises. The likelihood of there being a good response, from previous surveys, has been estimated at 0.8.

If the survey indicates a good response then the company will build the large premises. If the survey does give a good result then the probability that there will be high demand from the large premises increases to 0.95.

If the survey indicates a bad response then the company will abandon all expansion plans.
Required:

Using decision tree analysis, establish the best course of action for Firlands Limited.

(10 marks)
ACCA Paper 1.2 – Financial Information for Management

Question 12.2

Advanced: Calculation of expected value and the presentation of a probability distribution

The Dunburgh Bus Company operated during the year ended 31 May 2000 with the following results:

(i)   Average variable costs were £0.75 per bus mile.

(ii) Total fixed costs were £1 750 000.

(iii) The fare structure per journey was as follows:

Adults 0 to 3 miles	£0.20
4 to 5 miles	£0.30
over 5 miles	£0.50
Juveniles (any distance)	£0.15
Senior citizens (any distance)	£0.10

(iv) Total passenger journeys paid for were 24 000 000 which represented 60% capacity utilization. The capacity utilized comprised 60% adult, 20% juvenile and 20% senior citizen journeys. The adult journeys were broken down into 0–3 miles: 50%, 4–5 miles: 30%, over 5 miles: 20%.

(v) Twenty routes were operated with four buses per route, each bus covering 150 miles per day for 330 days of the year. The remaining days were taken up with maintenance work on the buses.

(vi) Advertising revenue from displays inside and outside the buses totalled £250 000 for the year. This is a fixed sum from contracts which will apply to each year up to 31 May 2002.

It is anticipated that all costs will increase by 10% due to inflation during the year to 31 May 2001 and that fares will be increased by 5% during the year. Whilst the fare increase of 5% has already been agreed and cannot be altered, it is possible that inflation might differ from the 10% rate anticipated.

Required:

(a) Prepare a statement showing the calculation of the net profit or loss for the year ended 31 May 2000.

(5 marks)

(b) Calculate the average percentage capacity utilization at which the company will break even during the forthcoming year to 31 May 2001 if all fares are increased by 5%, cost inflation is 10% as anticipated and the passenger mix and bus operating activity are the same as for the year to 31 May 2000.

(5 marks)

(c) Now assume that management have some doubts about the level of capacity utilization and rate of cost inflation which will apply in the year to 31 May 2001. Other factors are as previously forecast. Revised estimates of the likely levels of capacity utilization and inflation are as follows:

Capacity utilization	Probability	Inflation	Probability
70%	0.1	8%	0.3
60%	0.5	10%	0.6
50%	0.4	12%	0.1

(Capacity utilization rates and inflation rates are independent of each other.)

(i) Calculate the expected value of net profit or loss for the year to 31 May 2001 and show the range of profits or losses which may occur.

(9 marks)

(ii) Draw up a table of the possible profits and losses and their probabilities as calculated in (i) for the year ended 31 May 2001 in a way which brings to the attention of management the risks and opportunities which are implied and comment briefly on the figures.

(5 marks)

(d) Comment on factors which have not been incorporated into the model used in (c) above which may affect its usefulness to management in profit forecasting.

(6 marks)
(Total 30 marks)
ACCA Level 2 Cost Accounting II

Advanced: Pricing decision and the calculation of expected profit and margin of safety

Question 12.3

E Ltd manufactures a hedge-trimming device which has been sold at £16 per unit for a number of years. The selling price is to be reviewed and the following information is available on costs and likely demand.

The standard variable cost of manufacture is £10 per unit and an analysis of the cost variances for the past 20 months show the following pattern which the production manager expects to continue in the future.

Adverse variances of +10% of standard variable cost occurred in ten of the months.

Nil variances occurred in six of the months.

Favourable variances of –5% of standard variable cost occurred in four of the months.

Monthly data

Fixed costs have been £4 per unit on an average sales level of 20 000 units but these costs are expected to rise in the future and the following estimates have been made for the total fixed cost:

	(£)
Optimistic estimate (Probability 0.3)	82 000
Most likely estimate (Probability 0.5)	85 000
Pessimistic estimate (Probability 0.2)	90 000

The demand estimates at the two new selling prices being considered are as follows:

If the selling price/unit is demand would be:	£17	£18
Optimistic estimate (Probability 0.2)	21 000 units	19 000 units
Most likely estimate (Probability 0.5)	19 000 units	17 500 units
Pessimistic estimate (Probability 0.3)	16 500 units	15 500 units

It can be assumed that all estimates and probabilities are independent.

You are required to

(a) advise management, based only on the information given above, whether they should alter the selling price and, if so, the price you would recommend;

(6 marks)

(b) calculate the expected profit at the price you recommend and the resulting margin of safety, expressed as a percentage of expected sales;

(6 marks)

(c) criticise the method of analysis you have used to deal with the probabilities given in the question;

(4 marks)

(d) describe briefly how computer assistance might improve the analysis.

(4 marks)
(Total 20 marks)
CIMA Stage 3 Management Accounting Techniques

Question 12.4

Advanced: Machine hire decision based on uncertain demand and calculation of maximum price to pay for perfect information

Siteraze Ltd is a company which engages in site clearance and site preparation work. Information concerning its operations is as follows:

(i) It is company policy to hire all plant and machinery required for the implementation of all orders obtained, rather than to purchase its own plant and machinery.

(ii) Siteraze Ltd will enter into an advance hire agreement contract for the coming year at one of three levels – high, medium or low, which correspond to the requirements of a high, medium or low level of orders obtained.

(iii) The level of orders obtained will not be known when the advance hire agreement contract is entered into. A set of probabilities have been estimated by management as to the likelihood of the orders being at a high, medium or low level.

(iv) Where the advance hire agreement entered into is lower than that required for the level of orders actually obtained, a premium rate must be paid to obtain the additional plant and machinery required.

(v) No refund is obtainable where the advance hire agreement for plant and machinery is at a level in excess of that required to satisfy the site clearance and preparation orders actually obtained.

A summary of the information relating to the above points is as follows:

Level of orders	Turnover (£000)	Probability	Plant and machinery hire costs Advance hire (£000)	Plant and machinery hire costs Conversion premium (£000)
High	15 000	0.25	2300	
Medium	8 500	0.45	1500	
Low	4 000	0.30	1000	
Low to medium				850
Medium to high				1300
Low to high				2150

Variable cost (as percentage of turnover) 70%

Required: Using the information given above:

(a) Prepare a summary which shows the forecast net margin earned by Siteraze Ltd for the coming year for each possible outcome.

(6 marks)

(b) On the basis of maximizing expected value, advise Siteraze whether the advance contract for the hire of plant and machinery should be at the low, medium or high level.

(5 marks)

(c) Explain how the risk preferences of the management members responsible for the choice of advance plant and machinery hire contract may alter the decision reached in (b) above.

(6 marks)

(d) Siteraze Ltd are considering employing a market research consultant who will be able to say with certainty in advance of the placing of the plant and machinery hire contract, which level of site clearance and preparation orders will be obtained. On the basis of expected value, determine the maximum sum which Siteraze Ltd should be willing to pay the consultant for this information.

(5 marks)
(Total 22 marks)
ACCA Level 2: Cost and Management Accounting 11

Question 12.5

Advanced: Pricing decisions under conditions of uncertainty

(a) Allegro Finishes Ltd is about to launch an improved version of its major product – a pocket size chess computer – onto the market. Sales of the original model (at £65 per unit) have been at the rate of 50 000 per annum but it is now planned to withdraw this model and the company is now deciding on its production plans and pricing policy.

The standard variable cost of the new model will be £50 which is the same as that of the old, but the company intends to increase the selling price 'to recover the research and development expenditure that has been incurred'. The research and development costs of the improved model are estimated at £750 000 and the intention is that these should be written off over 3 years. Additionally there are annual fixed overheads of approximately £800 000 allocated to this product line.

The sales director has estimated the maximum annual demand figures that would obtain at three alternative selling prices. These are as follows:

Selling price (£)	Estimated maximum annual demand (physical units)
70	75 000
80	60 000
90	40 000

You are required to prepare a cost–volume–profit chart that would assist the management to choose a selling price and the level of output at which to operate. Identify the best price and the best level of output. Outline briefly any reservations that you have with this approach.

(5 marks)

(b) With the facts as stated for part (a), now assume the sales director is considering a more sophisticated approach to the problem. He has estimated, for each selling price, an optimistic, a pessimistic and a most likely demand figure and associated probabilities for each of these. For the £90 price the estimates are:

	Annual demand	Probability of demand
Pessimistic	20 000	0.2
Most likely	35 000	0.7
Optimistic	40 000	0.1
		1.0

On the cost side, it is clear that the standard unit variable cost of £50 is an 'ideal' which has rarely been achieved in practice. An analysis of the past 20 months shows that the following pattern of variable cost variances (per unit of output) has arisen:

an adverse variance of around £10 arose on 4 occasions,

an adverse variance of around £5 arose on 14 occasions

and a variance of around 0 arose on 2 occasions.

There is no reason to think that the pattern for the improved model will differ significantly from this or that these variances are dependent upon the actual demand level.

From the above, calculate the expected annual profit for a selling price of £90.

(6 marks)

(c) A tabular summary of the result of an analysis of the data for the other two selling prices (£70 and £80) is as follows:

	£70	£80
Probability of a loss of £500 000 or more	0.02	0
Probability of a loss of £300 000 or more	0.07	0.05
Probability of a loss of £100 000 or more	0.61	0.08
Probability of break-even or worse	0.61	0.10
Probability of break-even or better	0.39	0.91
Probability of a profit of £100 000 or more	0.33	0.52
Probability of a profit of £300 000 or more	0.03	0.04
Probability of a profit of £500 000 or more	0	0.01
Expected value of profit (loss)	55 750	68 500

You are required to compare your calculations in part (b) with the above figures and to write a short memo to the sales director outlining your advice and commenting on the use of subjective discrete probability distributions in problems of this type.

(9 marks)

(d) Assume that there is a 10% increase in the fixed overheads allocated to this product line and a decision to write off the research and development costs in one year instead of over 3 years. Indicate the general effect that this would have on your analysis of the problem.

(2 marks)
(Total 22 marks)
ACCA Level 2 Management Accounting

Advanced: Expected value comparison of low and high price alternatives

Question 12.6

The research and development department of Shale White has produced specifications for two new products for consideration by the company's production director. The director has received detailed costings which can be summarized as follows:

	Product newone (£)	Product newtwo (£)
Direct costs:		
Material	64	38
Labour (£3 per hour)	18	6
	82	44
Factory overheads		
(£3 per machine hour)	18	6
Total estimated unit cost	100	50

The sales department has provided estimates of the probabilities of various levels of demand for two possible selling prices for each product. The details are as follows:

	Product newone	Product newtwo
Low price alternative		
Selling price	£120	£60
Demand estimates:		
Pessimistic – probability 0.2	1000	3000
Most likely – probability 0.5	2000	4000
Optimistic – probability 0.3	3000	5000

High price alternative

Selling price	£130	£70
Demand estimates:		
Pessimistic – probability 0.2	500	1500
Most likely – probability 0.5	1000	2500
Optimistic – probability 0.3	1500	3500

It would be possible to adopt the low price alternative for product newone together with the high price alternative for newtwo, or the high price alternative for product newone with the low price alternative for newtwo (demand estimates are independent for the two products).

The factory has 60 000 machine hours available during the year. For some years past it has been working at 90% of practical capacity making a standardized product. This product is very profitable and it is only the availability of 6000 hours of spare machine capacity that has made it necessary to search for additional product lines to use the machines fully. The actual level of demand will be known at the time of production.

A statistical study of the behaviour of the factory overhead over the past year has indicated that it can be regarded as a linear function of factory machine time worked. The monthly fixed cost is estimated at £10 000 and the variable cost at £1 per machine hour with a coefficient of correlation of 0.8.

You are required:

(a) to identify the best plan for the utilization of the 6000 machine hours, to comment on the rational selling price alternatives that exist for this plan and to calculate the expected increase in annual profit which would arise for each alternative,

(17 marks)

(b) to discuss the relevance of regression analysis for problems of this type.

(5 marks)
(Total 22 marks)
ACCA Level 2 Management Accounting

Question 12.7

Advanced: Pricing decision based on competitor's response

In the market for one of its products, MD and its two major competitors (CN and KL) together account for 95% of total sales.

The quality of MD's products is viewed by customers as being somewhat better than that of its competitors and therefore at similar prices it has an advantage.

During the past year, however, when MD raised its price to £1.2 per litre, competitors kept their prices at £1.0 per litre and MD's sales declined even though the total market grew in volume.

MD is now considering whether to retain or reduce its price for the coming year. Its expectations about its likely volume at various prices charged by itself and its competitors are as follows:

Prices per litre			
MD (£)	CN (£)	KL (£)	MD's expected sales million litres
1.2	1.2	1.2	2.7
1.2	1.2	1.1	2.3
1.2	1.2	1.0	2.2
1.2	1.1	1.1	2.4
1.2	1.1	1.0	2.2

1.2	1.1	1.0	2.1
1.1	1.1	1.1	2.8
1.1	1.0	1.0	2.4
1.1	1.0	1.0	2.3
1.0	1.0	1.0	2.9

Experience has shown that CN tends to react to MD's price level and KL tends to react to CN's price level. MD therefore assesses the following probabilities:

If MD's price per litre is (£)	there is a probability of	that CN's price per litre will be (£)
1.2	0.2	1.2
	0.4	1.1
	0.4	1.0
	1.0	
1.1	0.3	1.1
	0.7	1.0
	1.0	
1.0	1.0	1.0

If CN's price per litre is (£)	there is a probability of	that KL's price per litre will be (£)
1.2	0.1	1.2
	0.6	1.1
	0.3	1.0
	1.0	
1.1	0.3	1.1
	0.7	1.0
	1.0	
1.0	1.0	1.0

Costs per litre of the product are as follows:

Direct wages	£0.24
Direct materials	£0.12
Departmental expenses:	
Indirect wages, maintenance and supplies	$16^2/_3$% of direct wages
Supervision and depreciation	£540 000 per annum
General works expenses (allocated)	$16^2/_3$% of prime cost
Selling and administration expenses (allocated)	50% of manufacturing cost

You are required to state whether, on the basis of the data given above, it would be most advantageous for MD to fix its price per litre for the coming year at £1.2, £1.1 or £1.0.

Support your answer with relevant calculations.

(20 marks)
CIMA P3 Management Accounting

Advanced: Expected value, maximin and regret criterion

Question 12.8

Stow Health Centre specialises in the provision of sports/exercise and medical/dietary advice to clients. The service is provided on a residential basis and clients stay for whatever number of days suits their needs.

Budgeted estimates for the next year ending 30 June are as follows:

(i) The maximum capacity of the centre is 50 clients per day for 350 days in the year.

(ii) Clients will be invoiced at a fee per day. The budgeted occupancy level will vary with the client fee level per day and is estimated at different percentages of maximum capacity as follows:

Client fee per day	Occupancy level	Occupancy as percentage of maximum capacity
£180	High	90%
£200	Most likely	75%
£220	Low	60%

(iii) Variable costs are also estimated at one of three levels per client day. The high, most likely and low levels per client day are £95, £85 and £70 respectively.

The range of cost levels reflect only the possible effect of the purchase prices of goods and services.

Required:

(a) Prepare a summary which shows the budgeted contribution earned by Stow Health Centre for the year ended 30 June for each of nine possible outcomes.

(6 marks)

(b) State the client fee strategy for the next year to 30 June which will result from the use of each of the following decision rules: (i) *maximax*; (ii) *maximin*; (iii) *minimax* regret.

Your answer should explain the basis of operation of each rule. Use the information from your answer to (a) as relevant and show any additional working calculations as necessary.

(9 marks)

(c) The probabilities of variable cost levels occurring at the high, most likely and low levels provided in the question are estimated as 0.1, 0.6 and 0.3 respectively.

Using the information available, determine the client fee strategy which will be chosen where maximisation of expected value of contribution is used as the decision basis.

(5 marks)

(d) The calculations in (a) to (c) concern contribution levels which may occur given the existing budget.

Stow Health Centre has also budgeted for fixed costs of £1 200 000 for the next year to 30 June.

Discuss ways in which Stow Health Centre may instigate changes, in ways other than through the client fee rate, which may influence client demand, cost levels and profit.

Your answer should include comment on the existing budget and should incorporate illustrations which relate to each of four additional performance measurement areas appropriate to the changes you discuss.

(15 marks)
(Total 35 marks)
ACCA Paper 9 Information for Control and Decision Making

Capital investment decisions: appraisal methods

Questions to Chapter 13

Intermediate

A machine with a purchase price of £14 000 is estimated to eliminate manual operations costing £4000 per year. The machine will last five years and have no residual value at the end of its life.

You are required to calculate:

(a) the internal rate of return (IRR);

(b) the level of annual saving necessary to achieve a 12% IRR;

(c) the net present value if the cost of capital is 10%.

Intermediate

An investment project has the following expected cash flows over its economic life of three years:

	(£)
Year 0	(142 700)
1	51 000
2	62 000
3	73 000

Required:

(i) Calculate the net present value (NPV) of the project at discount rates of 0%, 10% and 20% respectively.

(ii) Draw a graph of the project NPVs calculated in (i) and use the graph to estimate, and clearly indicate, the project internal rate of return (IRR) to the nearest integer percentage.

(8 marks)
ACCA Foundation Stage Paper 3

Advanced: Calculation of payback, accounting rate of return and NPV

P, a multinational organization, is currently appraising a major capital investment project which will revolutionize its business. This investment involves the installation of an Intranet. *[An Intranet is a private Internet reserved for use by employees and/or customers who have been given the authority and passwords necessary to use that network. It is a private network environment built around Internet technologies and standards.]*

You have recently been appointed as the Management Accountant for this project and have been charged with the responsibility of preparing the financial evaluation of the proposed investment. You have carried out some initial investigations and find that management currently uses a target accounting rate of return of 25% and a target payback period of four years as the criteria for the acceptance or rejection of major capital investments.

You propose to use the net present value method of project appraisal and, having carried out some further investigations, you ascertain the following information for the project:

	£000
Initial outlay	2000
Cash savings:	
Years 1 to 3	400 per annum
Years 4 to 5	500 per annum
Years 6 to 8	450 per annum
Years 9 to 10	400 per annum

At the end of the project's life, no residual value is expected for the project.

The company's cost of capital is 15% per annum. All cash savings are assumed to occur at the end of each year.

Ignore taxation and inflation.

Required:

As Management Accountant for this project,

(a) write a report to the management of P which incorporates the following:
    (i) a full analysis and evaluation of the existing methods of project appraisal and of your proposed method of project appraisal;
    (ii) a recommendation on a purely financial basis as to whether or not the project should be undertaken;
    (iii) a discussion of the difficulties associated with the net present value method when appraising this type of investment;

(15 marks)

(b) describe how you would undertake a post-completion appraisal for this project and discuss the benefits and drawbacks which the management of P might expect when undertaking such an exercise.

(10 marks)
(Total 25 marks)
CIMA Management Accountant – Decision Making

Question 13.4

Advanced: NPV calculation and identification of incremental cash flows

LKL plc is a manufacturer of sports equipment and is proposing to start project VZ, a new product line. This project would be for the four years from the start of year 20X1 to the end of 20X4. There would be no production of the new product after 20X4.

You have recently joined the company's accounting and finance team and have been provided with the following information relating to the project:

Capital expenditure

A feasibility study costing £45 000 was completed and paid for last year. This study recommended that the company buy new plant and machinery costing £1 640 000 to be paid for at the start of the project. The machinery and plant would be depreciated at 20% of cost per annum and sold during year 20X5 for £242 000 receivable at the end of 20X5.

As a result of the proposed project it was also recommended that an old machine be sold for cash at the start of the project for its book value of £16 000. This machine had been scheduled to be sold for cash at the end of 20X2 for its book value of £12 000.

Other data relating to the new product line:

	20X1 (£000)	20X2 (£000)	20X3 (£000)	20X4 (£000)
Sales	1000	1300	1500	1800
Debtors (at the year end)	84	115	140	160
Lost contribution on existing products	30	40	40	36
Purchases	400	500	580	620
Creditors (at the year end)	80	100	110	120
Payments to sub-contractors,	60	90	80	80
including prepayments of	5	10	8	8
Net tax payable associated with this project	96	142	174	275
Fixed overheads and advertising:				
With new line	1330	1100	990	900
Without new line	1200	1000	900	800

Notes

- The year-end debtors and creditors are received and paid in the following year.
- The next tax payable has taken into account the effect of any capital allowances. There is a one year time-lag in the payment of tax.
- The company's cost of capital is a constant 10% per annum.
- It can be assumed that operating cash flows occur at the year end.
- Apart from the data and information supplied there are no other financial implications after 20X4.

Labour costs

From the start of the project, three employees currently working in another department and earning £12 000 each would be transferred to work on the new product line, and an employee currently earning £20 000 would be promoted to work on the new line at a salary of £30 000 per annum. The effect on the transfer of employees from the other department to the project is included in the lost contribution figures given above.

As a direct result of introducing the new product line, four employees in another department currently earning £10 000 each would have to be made redundant at the end of 20X1 and paid redundancy pay of £15 500 each at the end of 20X2.

Agreement had been reached with the trade unions for wages and salaries to be increased by 5% each year from the start of 20X2.

Material costs

Material XNT which is already in stock, and for which the company has no other use, cost the company £6400 last year, and can be used in the manufacture of the new product. If it is not used the company would have to dispose of it at a cost to the company of £2000 in 20X1.

Material XPZ is also in stock and will be used on the new line. It cost the company £11 500 some years ago. The company has no other use for it, but could sell it on the open market for £3000 in 20X1.

Required

(a) Prepare and present a cash flow budget for project VZ, for the period 20X1 and 20X5 and calculate the net present value of the project.

(14 marks)

(b) Write a short report for the board of directors which:
    (i) explains why certain figures which were provided in (a) were excluded from your cash flow budget, and
    (ii) advises them on whether or not the project should be undertaken, and lists other factors which would also need to be considered.

(7 marks)
(Total 21 marks)
ACCA Paper 8 Managerial Finance

Question 13.5

Advanced: Comparison of NPV and IRR and relationship between profits and NPV

Khan Ltd is an importer of novelty products. The directors are considering whether to introduce a new product, expected to have a very short economic life. Two alternative methods of promoting the new product are available, details of which are as follows:

Alternative 1 would involve heavy initial advertising and the employment of a large number of agents. The directors expect that an immediate cash outflow of £100 000 would be required (the cost of advertising) which would produce a net cash inflow after one year of £255 000. Agents' commission, amounting to £157 500, would have to be paid at the end of two years.

Alternative 2 would involve a lower outlay on advertising (£50 000, payable immediately), and no use of agents. It would produce net cash inflows of zero after one year and £42 000 at the end of each of the subsequent two years.

Mr Court, a director of Khan Ltd, comments, 'I generally favour the payback method for choosing between investment alternatives such as these. However, I am worried that the advertising expenditure under the second alternative will reduce our reported profit next year by an amount not compensated by any net revenues from sale of the product in that year. For that reason I do not think we should even consider the second alternative.'

The cost of capital of Khan Ltd is 20% per annum. The directors do not expect capital or any other resource to be in short supply during the next three years.

You are required to:
(a) calculate the net present values and estimate the internal rates of return of the two methods of promoting the new product;

(10 marks)

(b) advise the directors of Khan Ltd which, if either, method of promotion they should adopt, explaining the reasons for your advice and noting any additional information you think would be helpful in making the decision;

(8 marks)

(c) comment on the views expressed by Mr Court.

(7 marks)

Ignore taxation.

(Total 25 marks)
ICAEW Financial Management

Question 13.6

Advanced: NPV evaluation of alternative options

All of the 100 accountants employed by X Ltd are offered the opportunity to attend six training courses per year. Each course lasts for several days and requires the delegates to travel to a specially selected hotel for the training. The current costs incurred for each course are:

Delegate costs:

	£ per delegate per course
Travel	200
Accommodation, food and drink	670
	870

It is expected that the current delegate costs will increase by 5% per annum.

Course costs:

	£ per course
Room hire	1 500
Trainers	6 000
Course material	2 000
Equipment hire	1 500
Course administration	750
	11 750

It is expected that the current course costs will increase by 2.5% per annum.

The Human Resources Director of X Ltd is concerned at the level of costs that these courses incur and has recently read an article about the use of the Internet for the delivery of training courses (e-learning). She decided to hire an external consultant at a cost of £5000 to advise the company on how to implement an e-learning solution. The consultant prepared a report which detailed the costs of implementing and running an e-learning solution:

	Notes	£
Computer hardware	(1)	1 500 000
Software licences	(2)	35 000 per annum
Technical Manager	(3)	30 000 per annum
Camera and sound crew	(4)	4 000 per course
Trainers and course material	(5)	2 000 per course
Broadband connection	(6)	300 per delegate per annum

Notes

(1) The computer hardware will be depreciated on a straight-line basis over five years. The scrap value at the end of the five years is expected to be £50 000.

(2) The company would sign a software licence agreement which fixes the annual software licence fee for five years. This fee is payable in advance.

(3) An employee working in the IT Department currently earning £20 000 per annum will be promoted to Technical Manager for this project. This employee's position will be replaced. The salary of the Technical Manager is expected to increase by 6% per annum.

(4) The company supplying the camera and sound crew for recording the courses for Internet delivery has agreed to hold its current level of pricing for the first two years but then it will increase costs by 6% per annum. All courses will be recorded in the first quarter of the year of delivery.

(5) The trainers will charge a fixed fee of £2000 per course for the delivery and course material in the first year and expect to increase this by 6% per annum thereafter. The preparation of the course material and the recording of the trainers delivering the courses will take place in the first quarter of the year of delivery.

(6) All of the accountants utilizing the training courses will be offered £300 towards broadband costs which will allow them to access the courses from home. They will claim this expense annually in arrears. Broadband costs are expected to decrease by 5% per annum after the first year as it becomes more widely used by Internet users.

X Ltd uses a 14% cost of capital to appraise projects of this nature.

Ignore taxation.

Required:

As the Management Accountant for X Ltd,

(a) prepare a financial evaluation of the options available to the company and advise the directors on the best course of action to take, from a purely financial point of view; (Your answer should state any assumptions you have made.)

(16 marks)

(b) (i) using the annual equivalent technique, calculate the breakeven number of delegates per annum taking each of the six e-learning courses that is required to justify the implementation of the e-learning solution;
(Note that you should assume that the number of delegates taking the e-learning courses will be the same in each of the five years.)

(6 marks)

(ii) comment on the implications of the breakeven number you have calculated in your answer to (b) (i).

(3 marks)
(Total 25 marks)
CIMA Management Accounting – Decision Making

Advanced: Evaluation of alternative options based on NPVs

Question 13.7

CAF plc is a large multinational organization that manufactures a range of highly engineered products/components for the aircraft and vehicle industries. The directors are considering the future of one of the company's factories in the UK which manufactures product A. Product A is coming to the end of its life but another two years' production is planned. This is expected to produce a net cash inflow of £3 million next year and £2.3 million in the product's final year.

Product AA

CAF plc has already decided to replace product A with product AA which will be ready to go into production in two years' time. Product AA is expected to have a life of eight years. It could be made either at the UK factory under consideration or in an Eastern European factory owned by CAF plc. The UK factory is located closer to the markets and therefore if product AA is made in Eastern Europe, the company will incur extra transport costs of £10 per unit. Production costs will be the same in both countries. Product AA will require additional equipment and staff will need training; this will cost £6 million at either location. 200 000 units of product AA will be made each year and each unit will generate a net cash inflow of £25 before extra transport costs. If product AA is made in the UK, the factory will be closed and sold at the end of the product's life.

Product X

Now, however, the directors are considering a further possibility: product X could be produced at the UK factory and product AA at the Eastern European factory. Product X must be introduced in one year's time and will remain in production for three years. If it is introduced, the manufacture of product A will have to cease a year earlier than planned. If this happened, output of product A would be increased by 12.5% to maximum capacity next year, its last year, to build stock prior to the product's withdrawal. The existing staff would be transferred to product X.

The equipment needed to make product X would cost £4 million. 50 000 units of product X would be made in its first year; after that, production would rise to 75 000 units a year. Product X would earn a net cash flow of £70 per unit. After three years' production of product X, the UK factory would be closed and sold. (Product AA would not be transferred back to the factory in the UK at that stage; production would continue at the Eastern European site.)

Sale of factory

It is expected that the UK factory could be sold for £5.5 million at any time between the beginning of year 2 and the end of year 10. If the factory is sold, CAF plc will make redundancy payments of £2 million and the sale of equipment will raise £350 000.

CAF plc's cost of capital is 5% each year.

Required:

(a) Prepare calculations that show which of the three options is financially the best.

(*15 marks*)

(b) The directors of CAF plc are unsure whether their estimates are correct. Calculate and discuss the sensitivity of your choice of option in (a) to:
   (i) changes in transport costs;

(*3 marks*)

   (ii) changes in the selling price of the factory.

(*3 marks*)

(c) Briefly discuss the business issues that should be considered before relocating to another country.

(*4 marks*)
(*Total 25 marks*)
CIMA Management Accounting – Decision Making

Advanced: NPV calculations for alternative options

Question 13.8

Amber plc operates a daily return high speed train service between the UK and mainland Europe, via the channel tunnel. In an attempt to reduce overheads, the company is considering using an outside supplier to take over responsibility for all on-train catering services. Amber invited tenders for a five-year contract, and at the same time the senior management accountant drafted a schedule of costs for in-house provision of an equivalent service. This cost schedule, together with the details of the lowest price tender which was received, are given below. (See Table 1 and additional information.)

TABLE 1 *In-House Provision of Train Catering Services Schedule of Costs, Amber plc*

Variable Costs	Pence Per £ Sales
Direct material	55
Variable overhead	12
Fixed Costs (allocated to products)	
Labour (Year 1)	10
Purchase/storage management	3
Depreciation (catering equipment)	4
Insurance	2
Total cost	86

The train service operates 360 days per year and a single restaurant carriage is adequate to service the catering needs of a train carrying up to 600 passengers. The tendered contract (and the in-house schedule of costs) is for the provision of one catering carriage per train. Past sales data indicates that 45% of passengers will use the catering service, spending an average of £4.50 each per single journey, or £9.00 per return journey. This is expected to remain unchanged over the next five years, unless Amber invests in quality improvements.

Statistical forecasts of the level of demand for the train service, under differing average weather conditions and average exchange rates over the next five years are shown in Table 2.

TABLE 2 *Forecast Passenger Figures (per single journey)*

Exchange rate Euro/£	UK weather conditions		
	Poor	Reasonable	Good
1.52	500	460	420
1.54	550	520	450
1.65	600	580	500

The differing weather conditions are all assumed to be equally likely.

Based upon historical trends, the probability of each different exchange rate occurring is estimated as follows:

Rate Euro/£	Probability
1.52	0.2
1.54	0.5
1.65	0.3

Additional information

1 Labour costs are expected to rise at a rate of 5% per year over the next five years.

2 Variable costs per £ sales are expected to remain unchanged over the next five years.

3 Some catering equipment will need to be replaced at the end of Year 2 at a cost of £500 000. This would increase the depreciation charge on catering equipment to 5 pence per £ sales. The equipment value at the end of Year 5 is estimated to be £280 000.

4 The outside supplier (lowest price tender) has agreed to purchase immediately (for cash) the existing catering equipment owned by Amber plc at a price equal to the current book value i.e. £650 000. The supplier would charge Amber a flat fee of £250 per day for the provision of this catering service, and Amber would receive 5% of gross catering receipts where these exceeded an average of £2200 per day in each 360 day period. The quality of the catering service is expected to be unaffected by the contracting out.

5 In the event of Amber deciding to contract out the catering, the following fixed costs will be saved:

Depreciation	£35 000 per year
Purchasing/storage costs	£18 000 per year
Insurance	£3 000 per year
Labour costs	£74 844 (Year 1)

CAPITAL INVESTMENT DECISIONS: APPRAISAL METHODS

6   The cost of capital for Amber plc is 12%.

Assume that all cash flows occur at the end of each year. Taxation may be ignored in answering this question.

Required:

(a) Calculate the expected number of passengers per single journey for the train service.

(5 marks)

(b) Draft a table of annual cash flows and, using discounted cash flow analysis, determine which of the two alternatives (in-house provision or contracting out) is preferred.

(16 marks)

(c) Calculate and comment upon the financial effect on the decision of a forecast 10% increase in the number of passengers purchasing food and beverages on each train if the in-house catering service were to be improved. Any such improvement would require Amber investing £10 000 per year over five years on staff training.

(7 marks)

(d) Comment on the limitations of using demand forecasts, such as that given in Table 2, for the purposes of the decision in question.

(5 marks)

(e) Identify and critically comment upon three non-financial factors which need to be taken into account when a business is considering this type of decision.

(7 marks)
(Total 40 marks)

Advanced: Evaluation of a proposed investment of computer integrated manufacturing equipment and a discussion of NPV and ARR

Question 13.9

Abert, the production manager of Blom plc, a manufacturer of precision tools, has recently attended a major international exhibition on Computer Integrated Manufacturing (CIM). He has read of the improvements in product quality and profitability achieved by companies which have switched to this new technology. In particular, his Japanese competitors are believed to use CIM equipment extensively. Abert is sufficiently concerned about his company's future to commission a report from Saint-Foix Ltd, a vendor of CIM equipment, as to the appropriateness of utilising CIM for all his manufacturing operations.

The report, which has recently been prepared, suggests that the following costs and benefits will accrue to Blom plc as a result of investing in an appropriate CIM system:

(1) *Costs of implementing CIM*

   (i)   Capital equipment costs will be £40m. The equipment will have an estimated life of 10 years, after which time its disposal value will be £10m.

   (ii) Proper use of the equipment will require the substantial re-training of current employees. As a result of the necessary changes in the production process, and the time spent on retraining, Blom plc will lose production (and sales) in its first two years of implementation. The lost production (and sales) will cost the company £10m per annum.

   (iii) The annual costs of writing software and maintaining the computer equipment will be £4m.

(2) *Benefits of implementing CIM*

    (i) The use of CIM will enhance the quality of Blom plc's products. This will lead to less reworking of products, and a consequent reduction in warranty costs. The annual cost savings are expected to be £12m per annum.

    (ii) The CIM equipment will use less floor space than the existing machinery. As a result one existing factory will no longer be needed. It is estimated that the factory can be let at an annual rental of £2m.

    (iii) Better planning and flow of work will result in an immediate reduction in the existing levels of working capital from £13m to £8m.

The directors of Blom plc currently require all investments to generate a positive net present value at a cost of capital of 15% *and* to show an accounting rate of return in the first year of at least 15%. You may assume that all cash flows arise at the end of the year, except for those relating to the equipment and re-training costs, and the reduction in working capital. It is Blom plc's intention to capitalise re-training costs for management accounting purposes. Requirements:

(a) Determine whether Blom plc should invest in the CIM technology on the basis of its existing investment criteria.

(10 marks)

(b) Discuss possible reasons as to why Blom plc currently requires its long-term investments to meet both the net present value *and* the accounting rate of return criteria.

(8 marks)

(c) Discuss the additional factors Blom plc should consider when deciding whether to switch to CIM technology.

(7 marks)
(Total 25 marks)
ICAEW P2 Financial Management

Capital investment decisions: the impact of capital rationing, taxation, inflation and risk

Questions to Chapter 14

Advanced: Equivalent annual cost to determine optimum replacement cycle

Question 14.1

(a) Explain and illustrate (using simple numerical examples) the Accounting Rate of Return and Payback approaches to investment appraisal, paying particular attention to the limitations of each approach.

(6 marks)

(b) (i) Explain the differences between NPV and IRR as methods of Discounted Cash Flow analysis.

(6 marks)

(ii) A company with a cost of capital of 14% is trying to determine the optimal replacement cycle for the laptop computers used by its sales team. The following information is relevant to the decision:

The cost of each laptop is £2400. Maintenance costs are payable at the end of *each full year* of ownership, but not in the year of replacement e.g. if the laptop is owned for two years, then the maintenance cost is payable at the end of year 1.

Interval between Replacement (years)	Trade-in Value (£)	Maintenance cost (£)
1	1200	Zero
2	800	75 (payable at end of Year 1)
3	300	150 (payable at end of Year 2)

Required:

Ignoring taxation, calculate the equivalent annual cost of the three different replacement cycles, and recommend which should be adopted. What other factors should the company take into account when determining the optimal cycle?

(8 marks)
(Total 20 marks)
ACCA Paper 8 – Managerial Finance

Advanced: Expected NPV and capital rationing

Question 14.2

The Independent Film Company plc is a film distribution company which purchases distribution rights on films from small independent producers, and sells the films on to cinema chains for national and international screening. In recent years the company has found it difficult to source sufficient films to maintain profitability. In response to the problem, the Independent Film Company has decided to invest in commissioning and producing films in its own right. In order to gain the expertise for this venture, the Independent Film Company is considering purchasing an existing filmmaking concern, at a cost of £400 000. The main difficulty that is anticipated for the business is the increasing uncertainty as to the potential success/failure rate of independently produced films. Many cinema chains are adopting a policy of only buying films from large international film companies, as they believe that the market for independent films is very limited and specialist in nature. The Independent Film Company is prepared for the fact that they are likely to have more films that fail than that succeed, but believe that the proposed film production business will nonetheless be profitable.

Using data collected from the existing distribution business and discussions with industry experts, they have produced cost and revenue forecasts for the five years of operation of the proposed investment. The company aims to complete the production of three films per year. The after tax cost of capital for the company is estimated to be 14%.

Year 1 sales for the new business are uncertain, but expected to be in the range of £4–10 million. Probability estimates for different forecast values are as follows:

Sales (£ Million)	Probability
4	0.2
5	0.4
7	0.3
10	0.1

Sales are expected to grow at an annual rate of 5%.

Anticipated costs related to the new business are as follows:

Cost Type	£'000
Purchase of film-making company	400
Annual legal and professional costs	20
Annual lease rental (office equipment)	12
Studio and set hire (per film)	180
Camera/specialist equipment hire (per film)	40
Technical staff wages (per film)	520
Screenplay (per film)	50
Actors' salaries (per film)	700
Costumes and wardrobe hire (per film)	60
Set design and painting (per film)	150
Annual non-production staff wages	60

Additional information

(i) No capital allowances are available.

(ii) Tax is payable one year in arrears, at a rate of 33% and full use can be made of tax refunds as they fall due.

(iii) Staff wages (technical and non-production staff) and actors' salaries, are expected to rise by 10% per annum.

(iv) Studio hire costs will be subject to an increase of 30% in Year 3.

(v) Screenplay costs per film are expected to rise by 15% per annum due to a shortage of skilled writers.

(vi) The new business will occupy office accommodation which has to date been let out for an annual rent of £20 000. Demand for such accommodation is buoyant and the company anticipates no problems in finding future tenants at the same annual rent.

(vii)A market research survey into the potential for the film production business cost £25 000.

Required:

(a) Using DCF analysis, calculate the expected Net Present Value of the proposed investment. (Workings should be rounded to the nearest £'000.)

(15 marks)

(b) Outline the main limitations of using expected values when making investment decisions.

(6 marks)

(c) In addition to the possible purchase of the film-making business, the company has two other investment opportunities, the details of which are given below:

Post-Tax Cash Flows, £'000

	Year 0	Year 1	Year 2	Year 3	Year 4	Year 5	Year 6
Investment X	(200)	200	200	150	100	100	100
Investment Y	(100)	80	80	40	40	40	40

The Independent Film Company has a total of £400 000 available for capital investment in the current year. No project can be invested in more than once.

Required:

(i) Define the term profitability index, and briefly explain how it may be used when a company faces a problem of capital rationing in any single accounting period.

(4 marks)

(ii) Calculate the profitability index for each of the investment projects available to the Independent Film Company, i.e. purchase of the film production company, Investment X and Investment Y, and outline the optimal investment strategy. Assume that all of the projects are indivisible.

(6 marks)

(iii) Explain the limitations of using a profitability index in a situation where there is capital rationing.

(4 marks)

(d) Briefly explain how the tax treatment of capital purchases can affect an investment decision.

(5 marks)
(Total 40 marks)
ACCA Paper 8 – Managerial Finance

Advanced: Inflation adjustments and sensitivity analysis

Question 14.3

(a) Burley plc, a manufacturer of building products, mainly supplies the wholesale trade. It has recently suffered falling demand due to economic recession, and thus has spare capacity. It now perceives an opportunity to produce designer ceramic tiles for the home improvement market. It has already paid £0.5m for development expenditure, market research and a feasibility study.

The initial analysis reveals scope for selling 150 000 boxes per annum over a five-year period at a price of £20 per box. Estimated operating costs, largely based on experience, are as follows:

Cost per box of tiles (£) (at today's prices):

Material cost	8.00
Direct labour	2.00
Variable overhead	1.50
Fixed overhead (allocated)	1.50
Distribution, etc.	2.00

Production can take place in existing facilities although initial re-design and set-up costs would be £2m after allowing for all relevant tax reliefs. Returns from the project would be taxed at 33%.

Burley's shareholders require a nominal return of 14% per annum after tax, which includes allowance for generally-expected inflation of 5.5% per annum. It can be assumed that all operating cash flows occur at year ends.

Required:

Assess the financial desirability of this venture in real terms, finding both the Net Present Value and the Internal Rate of Return to the nearest 1%) offered by the project.

Note: Assume no tax delay.

(*7 marks*)

(b) Briefly explain the purpose of sensitivity analysis in relation to project appraisal, indicating the drawbacks with this procedure.

(*6 marks*)

(c) Determine the values of

(i) price

(ii) volume

at which the project's NPV becomes zero.

Discuss your results, suggesting appropriate management action.

(*7 marks*)
(*Total 20 marks*)
ACCA Paper 8 Managerial Finance

Question 14.4

Advanced: Calculation of expected NPV and impact of writing down allowances

CH Ltd is a swimming club. Potential exists to expand the business by providing a gymnasium as part of the facilities at the club. The Directors believe that this will stimulate additional membership of the club.

The expansion project would require an initial expenditure of £550 000. The project is expected to have a disposal value at the end of 5 years which is equal to 10% of the initial expenditure.

The following schedule reflects a recent market research survey regarding the estimated annual sales revenue from additional memberships over the project's five-year life:

Level of demand	£000	Probability
High	800	0.25
Medium	560	0.50
Low	448	0.25

It is expected that the contribution to sales ratio will be 55%. Additional expenditure on fixed overheads is expected to be £90 000 per annum.

CH Ltd incurs a 30% tax rate on corporate profits. Corporation tax is to be paid in two equal instalments: one in the year that profits are earned and the other in the following year.

CH Ltd's after-tax nominal (money) discount rate is 15.5% per annum. A uniform inflation rate of 5% per annum will apply to all costs and revenues during the life of the project.

All of the values above have been expressed in terms of current prices.

You can assume that all cash flows occur at the end of each year and that the initial investment does not qualify for capital allowances.

Required:

(a) Evaluate the proposed expansion from a financial perspective.

(*13 marks*)

(b) Calculate and then discuss the sensitivity of the project to changes in the expected annual contribution.

(5 marks)

You have now been advised that the capital cost of the expansion will qualify for writing down allowances at the rate of 25% per annum on a reducing balance basis. Also, at the end of the project's life, a balancing charge or allowance will arise equal to the difference between the scrap proceeds and the tax written down value.

Required:

(c) Calculate the financial impact of these allowances.

(7 marks)
(Total 25 marks)
CIMA Management Accounting – Decision Making

Advanced: Expected NPV calculation and taxes on cashflows

Question 14.5

Blackwater plc, a manufacturer of speciality chemicals, has been reported to the anti-pollution authorities on several occasions in recent years, and fined substantial amounts for making excessive toxic discharges into local rivers. Both the environmental lobby and Blackwaters shareholders demand that it clean up its operations.

It is estimated that the total fines it may incur over the next four years can be summarized by the following probability distribution (all figures are expressed in present values):

Level of fine	Probability
£0.5m	0.3
£1.4m	0.5
£2.0m	0.2

Filta & Strayne Ltd (FSL), a firm of environmental consultants, has advised that new equipment costing £1m can be installed to virtually eliminate illegal discharges. Unlike fines, expenditure on pollution control equipment is tax-allowable via a 25% writing-down allowance (reducing balance). The rate of corporate tax is 33%, paid with a one-year delay. The equipment will have no resale value after its expected four-year working life, but can be in full working order immediately prior to Blackwater's next financial year.

A European Union Common Pollution Policy grant of 25% of gross expenditure is available, but with payment delayed by a year. Immediately on receipt of the grant from the EU, Blackwater will pay 20% of the grant to FSL as commission. These transactions have no tax implications for Blackwater.

A disadvantage of the new equipment is that it will raise production costs by £30 per tonne over its operating life. Current production is 10 000 tonnes per annum, but is expected to grow by 5% per annum compound. It can be assumed that other production costs and product price are constant over the next four years. No change in working capital is envisaged.

Blackwater applies a discount rate of 12% after all taxes to investment projects of this nature. All cash inflows and outflows occur at year ends.

Required:

(a) Calculate the expected net present value of the investment assuming a four-year operating period.

Briefly comment on your results.

(12 marks)

(b) Write a memorandum to Blackwater's management as to the desirability of the project, taking into account both financial and non-financial criteria.

(8 marks)
(Total 20 marks)
ACCA Paper 8 Managerial Finance

Question 14.6

Advanced: Expected NPV and decision trees

NP plc is a company that operates a number of different businesses. Each separate business operates its own costing system, which has been selected to suit the particular needs of that business. Data is transferred to Head Office for weekly management control purposes.

NP plc is considering investing in a project named Fantazia, which is a pleasure park consisting of a covered dome and external fun rides. The cost of the dome, which is a covered frame that can be dismantled and erected elsewhere or stored, is £20 million. NP plc is considering two sites for the dome: London or Manchester. The cost of acquiring the land and installing the equipment is expected to be £20 million for the London site and £9 million for the Manchester site.

A market research survey shows that if Fantazia were to be situated in London, there is a 0.5 chance of getting 1.2 million visitors a year for the next four years and a 0.5 chance of getting only 0.8 million visitors a year. Each visitor to the London site is expected to spend £25 on average. This comprises a £10 entrance fee which includes access to fun rides, £10 on souvenir merchandise and £5 on food and drink.

If Fantazia were to be situated in Manchester, there is a 0.4 chance of getting 1.2 million visitors a year for the next four years and a 0.6 chance of getting only 0.8 million visitors. Each visitor to the Manchester site is expected to spend £23 on average. This comprises £9 entrance fee, £10 on merchandise and £4 on food and drink.

The average cost of servicing each visitor (that is, providing rides, merchandise and food and drink) at both sites is estimated to be £10.

After four years, the dome could be kept in operation for a further four years or dismantled. If the dome is kept on the same site, it is estimated that visitor numbers will fall by 0.1 million a year. This means that London would have a 0.5 chance of 1.1 million visitors and a 0.5 chance of 0.7 million visitors in each of years 5 to 8, and Manchester a 0.4 chance of 1.1 million visitors and a 0.6 chance of 0.7 million visitors.

If the dome were to be dismantled after four years, it could be stored at a cost of £0.5 million a year, sold for £4 million or transferred to the other site. The number of visitors and revenue received at this site would be as predicted for years 1 to 4.

The cost of dismantling the dome and equipment would be £3 million and the cost of moving and re-erecting it would be £9 million.

The purchase or sale price of the land at the end of year 4 would be: London £14 million and Manchester £10 million. At the end of year 8, the dome's resale value would be zero and all land values would be as four years previously.

The final cost of dismantling the dome and equipment would be £2 million.

NP plc uses a discount rate of 10% when evaluating all projects.

Required:

(a) Assuming that NP plc intends to terminate the Fantazia project *after four years*:
   (i) draw a decision tree to show the options open to NP plc;

(3 marks)

   (ii) calculate which option would generate the highest net present value. (Use either the decision tree or another method.)

(5 marks)

(b) Assuming that NP plc chose the most advantageous option for years 1 to 4, determined in your answer to (a)(ii) above,

    (i)   draw a decision tree for years 5 to 8, showing the options open to NP plc if Fantazia is not terminated after 4 years;

(3 marks)

    (ii) calculate which of these options generates the highest net present value over years 5 to 8.

(5 marks)

(c) Advise the company which options it should select in order to maximize net present value over the full 8 years of the project. State what that net present value would be.

(5 marks)

(d) NP plc recommends that Fantazia adopts activity based costing (ABC) in order to cost its activities. Discuss whether this would be a suitable system for Fantazia to use in order to assess visitor profitability. If you feel that ABC is not an appropriate system for Fantazia, suggest alternative(s).

(9 marks)
(Total 30 marks)
CIMA Management Accounting – Decision Making

Advanced: NPV calculation, choice of discount rate and sensitivity analysis

Question 14.7

The managing director of Tigwood Ltd believes that a market exists for 'microbooks'. He has proposed that the company should market 100 best-selling books on microfiche which can be read using a special microfiche reader that is connected to a television screen. A microfiche containing an entire book can be purchased from a photographic company at 40% of the average production cost of best-selling paperback books.

It is estimated that the average cost of producing paperback books is £1.50, and the average selling price of paperbacks is £3.95 each. Copyright fees of 20% of the average selling price of the paperback books would be payable to the publishers of the paperbacks plus an initial lump sum which is still being negotiated, but is expected to be £1.5 million. No tax allowances are available on this lump sum payment. An agreement with the publishers would be signed for a period of six years. Additional variable costs of staffing, handling and marketing are 20 pence per microfiche, and fixed costs are negligible.

Tigwood Ltd has spent £100 000 on market research, and expects sales to be 1 500 000 units per year at an initial unit price of £2.

The microfiche reader would be produced and marketed by another company.

Tigwood would finance the venture with a bank loan at an interest rate of 16% per year. The company's money (nominal) cost of equity and real cost of equity are estimated to be 23% per year and 12.6% per year respectively. Tigwood's money weighted average cost of capital and real weighted average cost of capital are 18% per year and 8% per year respectively. The risk free rate of interest is 11% per year and the market return is 17% per year.

Corporate tax is at the rate of 35%, payable in the year the profit occurs. All cash flows may be assumed to be at the year end, unless otherwise stated.

Required

(a) Calculate the expected net present value of the microbooks project.

(5 marks)

(b) Explain the reasons for your choice of discount rate in your answer to part (a). Discuss whether this rate is likely to be the most appropriate rate to use in the analysis of the proposed project.

(5 marks)

(c) (i) Using sensitivity analysis, estimate by what percentage each of the following would have to change before the project was no longer expected to be viable:
   – initial outlay
   – annual contribution
   – the life of the agreement
   – the discount rate.
   (ii) What are the limitations of this sensitivity analysis?

(10 marks)

(d) What further information would be useful to help the company decide whether to undertake the microbook project?

(5 marks)
(Total 25 marks)
ACCA Level 3 Financial Management

The budgeting process

Questions to Chapter 15

Advanced
                                                                                          Question 15.1

Traditional budgeting systems are incremental in nature and tend to focus on cost centres. Activity based budgeting links strategic planning to overall performance measurement aiming at continuous improvement.

(a) Explain the weaknesses of an incremental budgeting system.

(5 marks)

(b) Describe the main features of an activity based budgeting system and comment on the advantages claimed for its use.

(10 marks)
(Total 15 marks)
ACCA Paper 9 Information for Control and Decision Making

Advanced
                                                                                          Question 15.2

Budgeting has been criticized as

- a cumbersome process which occupies considerable management time;
- concentrating unduly on short-term financial control;
- having undesirable effects on the motivation of managers;
- emphasizing formal organization structure.

Requirements:

(a) Explain these criticisms.

(8 marks)

(b) Explain what changes can be made in response to these criticisms to improve the budgeting process.

(12 marks)
(Total 20 marks)
CIMA Stage 4 Management Accounting

Advanced
                                                                                          Question 15.3

For a number of years, the research division of Z plc has produced its annual budget (for new and continuing projects) using incremental budgeting techniques. The company is now under new management and the annual budget for 2004 is to be prepared using zero based budgeting techniques.

Required:

(a) Explain the differences between incremental and zero based budgeting techniques.

(5 marks)

(b) Explain how Z plc could operate a zero based budgeting system for its research projects.

(8 marks)

The operating divisions of Z plc have in the past always used a traditional approach to analysing costs into their fixed and variable components. A single measure of activity was used, which, for simplicity, was the number of units produced. The new management does not accept that such a simplistic approach is appropriate for budgeting in the modern environment and has requested that the managers adopt an activity-based approach to their budgets for 2004.

Required:

(c) (i) Briefly explain activity-based budgeting (ABB).

(3 marks)

(ii) Explain how activity-based budgeting would be implemented by the operating divisions of Z plc.

(9 marks)

(Total 25 marks)

CIMA Management Accounting – Performance Management

Question 15.4

Intermediate: Preparation of functional budgets

Wollongong wishes to calculate an operating budget for the forthcoming period. Information regarding products, costs and sales levels is as follows:

Product	A	B
Materials required		
X (kg)	2	3
Y (litres)	1	4
Labour hours required		
Skilled (hours)	4	2
Semi skilled (hours)	2	5
Sales level (units)	2000	1500
Opening stocks (units)	100	200

Closing stock of materials and finished goods will be sufficient to meet 10% of demand. Opening stocks of material X was 300 kg and for material Y was 1000 litres. Material prices are £10 per kg for material X and £7 per litre for material Y. Labour costs are £12 per hour for the skilled workers and £8 per hour for the semi skilled workers.

Required:

Produce the following budgets:

(a) production (units);

(b) materials usage (kg and litres);

(c) materials purchases (kg, litres and £); and

(d) labour (hours and £).

(10 marks)

ACCA Paper 1.2 – Financial Information for Management

Question 15.5

Intermediate: Preparation of functional budgets and budgeted profit statement

A division of Bud plc is engaged in the manual assembly of finished products F1 and F2 from bought-in components. These products are sold to external customers. The budgeted sales volumes and prices for Month 9 are as follows:

Product	Units	Price
F1	34 000	£50.00
F2	58 000	£30.00

Finished goods stockholding budgeted for the end of Month 9, is 1000 units of F1 and 2000 units of F2, with no stock at the beginning of that month. The purchased components C3 and C4 are used in the finished products in the quantities shown below. The unit price is for just-in-time delivery of the components; the company holds no component stocks.

Product	Component C3	C4
F1 (per unit)	8 units	4 units
F2 (per unit)	4 units	3 units
Price (each)	£1.25	£1.80

The standard direct labour times and labour rates and the budgeted monthly manufacturing overhead costs for the assembly and finishing departments for Month 9 are given below:

Product	Assembly	Finishing
F1 (per unit)	30 minutes	12 minutes
F2 (per unit)	15 minutes	10 minutes
Labour rate (per hour)	£5.00	£6.00
Manufacturing overhead cost for the month	£617 500	£204 000

Every month a predetermined direct labour hour recovery rate is computed in each department for manufacturing overhead and applied to items produced in that month.

The selling overhead of £344 000 per month is applied to products based on a predetermined percentage of the budgeted sales value in each month.

Required:

(a) Prepare summaries of the following budgets for Month 9:
  (i)   component purchase and usage (units and value);
  (ii) direct labour (hours and value);
  (iii) departmental manufacturing overhead recovery rates;
  (iv) selling overhead recovery rate;
  (v)   stock value at the month-end.

(8 marks)

(b) Tabulate the standard unit cost and profit of each of F1 and F2 in Month 9.
(3 marks)

(c) Prepare a budgeted profit and loss account for Month 9 which clearly incorporates the budget values obtained in (a) above.
(3 marks)

(d) Explain clearly the implications of the company's treatment of manufacturing overheads, i.e. computing a monthly overhead rate, compared to a predetermined overhead rate prepared annually.
(6 marks)
(Total 20 marks)
ACCA Paper 8 Managerial Finance

Question 15.6

Intermediate: Preparation of functional budgets, cash budget and master budget

The budgeted balance sheet data of Kwan Tong Umbago Ltd is as follows:

1 March

	Cost (£)	Depreciation to date (£)	Net (£)
Fixed assets			
Land and buildings	500 000	—	500 000
Machinery and equipment	124 000	84 500	39 500
Motor vehicles	42 000	16 400	25 600
	666 000	100 900	565 100
Working capital:			
Current assets			
Stock of raw materials (100 units)		4 320	
Stock of finished goods (110 units)[a]		10 450	
Debtors (January £7680 February £10 400)		18 080	
Cash and bank		6 790	
		39 640	
Less current liabilities			
Creditors (raw materials)		3 900	35 740
			600 840
Represented by:			
Ordinary share capital (fully paid) £1 shares			500 000
Share premium			60 000
Profit and loss account			40 840
			600 840

[a]The stock of finished goods was valued at marginal cost

The estimates for the next four-month period are as follows:

	March	April	May	June
Sales (units)	80	84	96	94
Production (units)	70	75	90	90
Purchases of raw materials (units)	80	80	85	85
Wages and variable overheads at £65 per unit	£4550	£4875	£5850	£5850
Fixed overheads	£1200	£1200	£1200	£1200

The company intends to sell each unit for £219 and has estimated that it will have to pay £45 per unit for raw materials. One unit of raw material is needed for each unit of finished product.

All sales and purchases of raw materials are on credit. Debtors are allowed two months' credit and suppliers of raw materials are paid after one month's credit. The wages, variable overheads and fixed overheads are paid in the month in which they are incurred.

Cash from a loan secured on the land and buildings of £120 000 at an interest rate of 7.5% is due to be received on 1 May. Machinery costing £112 000 will be received in May and paid for in June.

The loan interest is payable half yearly from September onwards. An interim dividend to 31 March of £12 500 will be paid in June.

Depreciation for the four months, including that on the new machinery is:

Machinery and equipment	£15 733
Motor vehicles	£3 500

The company uses the FIFO method of stock valuation. Ignore taxation.

Required:

(a) Calculate and present the raw materials budget and finished goods budget in terms of units, for each month from March to June inclusive.

(5 marks)

(b) Calculate the corresponding sales budgets, the production cost budgets and the budgeted closing debtors, creditors and stocks in terms of value.

(5 marks)

(c) Prepare and present a cash budget for each of the four months.

(6 marks)

(d) Prepare a master budget, i.e. a budgeted trading and profit and loss account, for the four months to 30 June, and budgeted balance sheet as at 30 June.

(10 marks)

(e) Advise the company about possible ways in which it can improve its cash management.

(9 marks)
(Total 35 marks)
ACCA Paper 8 Managerial Finance

Intermediate: Preparation of cash budgets

Question 15.7

The management of Beck plc have been informed that the union representing the direct production workers at one of their factories, where a standard product is produced, intends to call a strike. The accountant has been asked to advise the management of the effect the strike will have on cash flow.

The following data has been made available:

	Week 1	Week 2	Week 3
Budgeted sales	400 units	500 units	400 units
Budgeted production	600 units	400 units	Nil

The strike will commence at the beginning of week 3 and it should be assumed that it will continue for at least four weeks. Sales at 400 units per week will continue to be made during the period of the strike until stocks of finished goods are exhausted. Production will stop at the end of week 2. The current stock level of finished goods is 600 units. Stocks of work in progress are not carried.

The selling price of the product is £60 and the budgeted manufacturing cost is made up as follows:

	(£)
Direct materials	15
Direct wages	7
Variable overheads	8
Fixed overheads	18
Total	£48

Direct wages are regarded as a variable cost. The company operates a full absorption costing system and the fixed overhead absorption rate is based upon a budgeted fixed overhead of £9000 per week. Included in the total fixed overheads is £700 per week for depreciation of equipment. During the period of the strike direct wages and variable overheads would not be incurred and the cash expended on fixed overheads would be reduced by £1500 per week.

The current stock of raw materials are worth £7500; it is intended that these stocks should increase to £11 000 by the end of week 1 and then remain at this level during the period of the strike. *All direct materials are paid for one week after they have been received. Direct wages are paid one week in arrears. It should be assumed that all relevant overheads are paid for immediately the expense is incurred.* All sales are on credit, 70% of the sales value is received in cash from the debtors at the end of the first week after the sales have been made and the balance at the end of the second week.

The current amount outstanding to material suppliers is £8000 and direct wage accruals amount to £3200. Both of these will be paid in week 1. The current balance owing from debtors is £31 200, of which £24 000 will be received during week 1 and the remainder during week 2. The current balance of cash at bank and in hand is £1000.

Required:

(a) (i) Prepare a cash budget for weeks 1 to 6 showing the balance of cash at the end of each week together with a suitable analysis of the receipts and payments during each week.

(13 marks)

(ii) Comment upon any matters arising from the cash budget which you consider should be brought to management's attention.

(4 marks)

(b) Explain why the reported profit figure for a period does not normally represent the amount of cash generated in that period.

(5 marks)
(Total 22 marks)
ACCA Level 1 Costing

Question 15.8

Intermediate: Preparation of production budget and key factor analysis

The management team at MN Limited is considering the budgets it prepared for the year ending 31 December 2003. It has now been revealed that in June 2003 the company will be able to purchase only 10 000 litres of material Q (all other resources will be fully available). In the light of this new information, the management team wants to revise its plans for June to ensure that profits are maximized for that month.

MN Limited can produce three products from the same labour and main raw material Q, though different amounts are required for each product. The standard resource requirements, costs and selling prices, and the customer demand for delivery in June (including those orders already accepted) for each of its finished products are as follows:

	Product V	Product S	Product T
Resources per unit:			
Material Q	10 litres	8 litres	5 litres
Direct labour	8 hours	9 hours	6 hours
	£ per unit	£ per unit	£ per unit
Selling prices and costs:			
Selling price	145.00	134.00	99.00
Material Q	25.00	20.00	12.50
Other materials	10.00	4.00	8.50
Direct labour	40.00	45.00	30.00
Overheads:			
Variable	10.00	11.25	7.50
Fixed*	24.00	30.00	12.00
	109.00	110.25	70.50
Customer demand	1100 units	950 units	1450 units

*based on budgeted costs of £95 000 per month.

MN Limited has already accepted customer orders for delivery in June 2003 as follows:

Product V	34 units
Product S	75 units
Product T	97 units

The management team has decided that these customer orders must be satisfied as the financial and non-financial penalties that would otherwise arise are very significant.

Given the shortage of material Q, the management team has now set the following stock levels for June:

	Opening stock	Closing stock
Material Q**	621 litres	225 litres
Product V	20 units	10 units
Product S	33 units	25 units
Product T	46 units	20 units

**This would mean that 10 396 litres of material Q would be available during the period.

Required:

(a) Prepare a production budget for June 2003 that clearly shows the number of units of each product that should be produced to maximize the profits of MN Limited for June 2003.

(12 marks)

(b) Using your answer to requirement (a) above, calculate the number of units of each product that will be sold in June 2003.

(3 marks)

(c) Using your answer to requirement (b) above, calculate the profit for June 2003 using:
(i) marginal costing;
(ii) absorption costing.

(5 marks)

The Managing Director of MN Limited is concerned about the effect on cashflow caused by the scarcity of material Q during June 2003. She is aware that monthly profit and cashflow are often unequal and has heard that marginal costing profits more closely resemble cashflow than do absorption costing profits.

Required:

(d) (i) Explain briefly why there is a difference between cashflow and profit.

(ii) Briefly discuss the assertion that marginal costing profits are a better indicator of cashflow than absorption costing profits.

(5 marks)
(Total 25 marks)
CIMA Management Accounting – Performance Management

Question 15.9   **Advanced: Comments on budget preparation and zero-based budgeting**

A Public Sector Organization is extending its budgetary control and responsibility accounting system to all departments. One such department concerned with public health and welfare is called 'Homecare'. The department consists of staff who visit elderly 'clients' in their homes to support them with their basic medical and welfare needs.

A monthly cost control report is to be sent to the department manager, a copy of which is also passed to a Director who controls a number of departments. In the system, which is still being refined, the budget was set by the Director and the manager had not been consulted over the budget or the use of the monthly control report.

Shown below is the first month's cost control report for the Homecare department.

Cost Control Report – Homecare Department
Month ending May 2000

	Budget	Actual	(Overspend)/ Underspend
Visits	10 000	12 000	(2 000)
	£	£	£
Department expenses:			
Supervisory salary	2 000	2 125	(125)
Wages (Permanent staff)	2 700	2 400	300
Wages (Casual staff)	1 500	2 500	(1 000)
Office equipment depreciation	500	750	(250)
Repairs to equipment	200	20	180
Travel expenses	1 500	1 800	(300)
Consumables	4 000	6 000	(2 000)
Administration and telephone	1 000	1 200	(200)
Allocated administrative costs	2 000	3 000	(1 000)
	15 400	19 795	(4 395)

In addition to the manager and permanent members of staff, appropriately qualified casual staff are appointed on a week to week basis to cope with fluctuations in demand. Staff use their own transport and travel expenses are reimbursed. There is a central administration overhead charge over all departments. Consumables consist of materials which are used by staff to care for clients. Administration and telephone are costs of keeping in touch with the staff who often operate from their own homes.

As a result of the report, the Director sent a memo to the manager of the Homecare department pointing out that the department must spend within its funding allocation and that any spending more than 5% above budget on any item would not be tolerated. The Director requested an immediate explanation for the serious overspend.

You work as the assistant to the Directorate Management Accountant. On seeing the way the budget system was developing, he made a note of points he would wish to discuss and develop further, but was called away before these could be completed.

Required:

(a) Develop and explain the issues concerning the budgetary control and responsibility accounting system which are likely to be raised by the management accountant. You should refer to the way the budget was prepared, the implications of a 20% increase in the number of visits, the extent of controllability of costs, the implications of the funding allocation, social aspects and any other points you think appropriate. You may include numerical illustrations and comment on specific costs, but you are not required to reproduce the cost control report.

(14 marks)

(b) Briefly explain Zero-Based Budgeting (ZBB), describe how (in a situation such as that above) it might be implemented, and how as a result it could improve the budget setting procedure.

(6 marks)
(Total 20 marks)
ACCA Paper 8 Managerial Finance

Advanced: Preparation of activity-based and flexible budgets

Question 15.10

AHW plc is a food processing company that produces high-quality, part-cooked meals for the retail market. The five different types of meal that the company produces (Products A to E) are made by subjecting ingredients to a series of processing activities. The meals are different, and therefore need differing amounts of processing activities.

Budget and actual information for October 2002 is shown below:

Budgeted data

	Product A	Product B	Product C	Product D	Product E
Number of batches	20	30	15	40	25
Processing activities per batch:					
Processing activity W	4	5	2	3	1
Processing activity X	3	2	5	1	4
Processing activity Y	3	3	2	4	2
Processing activity Z	4	6	8	2	3

Budgeted costs of processing activities:

	£000
Processing activity W	160
Processing activity X	130
Processing activity Y	80
Processing activity Z	200

All costs are expected to be variable in relation to the number of processing activities.

Actual data

Actual output during October 2002 was as follows:

	Product A	Product B	Product C	Product D	Product E
Number of batches	18	33	16	35	28

Actual processing costs incurred during October 2002 were:

	£000
Processing activity W	158
Processing activity X	139
Processing activity Y	73
Processing activity Z	206

Required:

(a) Prepare a budgetary control statement (to the nearest £000) that shows the original budget costs, flexible budget costs, the actual costs, and the total variances of each processing activity for October 2002.

(15 marks)

Your control statement has been issued to the Managers responsible for each processing activity and the Finance Director has asked each of them to explain the reasons for the variances shown in your statement. The Managers are not happy about this as they were not involved in setting the budgets and think that they should not be held responsible for achieving targets that were imposed upon them.

Required:

(b) Explain briefly the reasons why it might be preferable for Managers not to be involved in setting their own budgets.

(5 marks)

(c) (i) Explain the difference between fixed and flexible budgets and how each may be used to control production costs and non-production costs (such as marketing costs) within AHW plc.

(4 marks)

(ii) Give two examples of costs that are more appropriately controlled using a fixed budget, and explain why a flexible budget is less appropriate for the control of these costs.

(3 marks)

Many organizations use linear regression analysis to predict costs at different activity levels. By analysing past data, a formula such as

$$y = ax + b$$

is derived and used to predict future cost levels.

Required:

(d) Explain the meaning of the terms y, a, x and b in the above equation.

(3 marks)
(Total 30 marks)
CIMA Management Accounting – Performance Management

Management control systems

Qestions to Chapter 16

Intermediate

Question 16.1

(a) Identify and explain the essential elements of an effective cost control system.

(13 marks)

(b) Outline possible problems which may be encountered as a result of the introduction of a system of cost control into an organization.

(4 marks)
(Total 17 marks)

Advanced

Question 16.2

You are required, within the context of budgetary control, to:

(a) explain the specific roles of planning, motivation and evaluation;

(7 marks)

(b) describe how these roles may conflict with each other;

(7 marks)

(c) give *three* examples of ways by which the management accountant may resolve the conflict described in (b).

(6 marks)
CIMA P3 Management Accounting

Advanced

Question 16.3

(a) Explain the ways in which the attitudes and behaviour of managers in a company are liable to pose more threat to the success of its budgetary control system than are minor technical inadequacies that may be in the system.

(15 marks)

(b) Explain briefly what the management accountant can do to minimize the disruptive effects of such attitudes and behaviour.

(5 marks)
CIMA P3 Management Accounting

Advanced

Question 16.4

What are the behavioural aspects which should be borne in mind by those who are designing and operating standard costing and budgetary control systems?

(20 marks)
CIMA Cost Accounting 2

Advanced

Question 16.5

One purpose of management accounting is to influence managers' behaviour so that their resulting actions will yield a maximum benefit to the employing organization. In the context of this objective, you are required to discuss:

(a) how budgets can cause behavioural conflict;

(b) how this behavioural conflict may be overcome;

(c) the importance of the feedback of information; and

(d) the purpose of goal congruence.

(20 marks)
CIMA P3 Management Accounting

Question 16.6

Advanced

In his study of 'The Impact of Budgets on People', published in 1952, C. Argyris reported *inter alia* the following comment by a financial controller on the practice of participation in the setting of budgets in his company:

'We bring in the supervisors of budget areas, we tell them that we want their frank opinion, but most of them just sit there and nod their heads. We know they're not coming out with exactly how they feel. I guess budgets scare them.'

You are required to suggest reasons why managers may be reluctant to participate fully in setting budgets, and to suggest also unwanted side effects which may arise from the imposition of budgets by senior management.

(13 marks)
ICAEW Management Accounting

Question 16.7

Advanced

The level of efficiency assumed in the setting of standards has important motivational implications – Discuss.

(8 marks)
ACCA Level 2 Management Accounting

Question 16.8

Advanced

In discussing the standard setting process for use within budgetary control and/or standard costing systems, the following has been written: 'The level of standards appears to play a role in achievement motivation…'

Required:

(a) Briefly distinguish between the motivational and managerial reporting objectives of both budgetary control and standard costing. Describe the extent to which these two objectives place conflicting demands on the standard of performance utilized in such systems.

(6 marks)

(b) Describe three levels of efficiency which may be incorporated in the standards used in budgetary control and/or standard costing systems. Outline the main advantages and disadvantages of each of the three levels described.

(6 marks)

(c) Discuss the advantages and disadvantages of involving employees in the standard setting process.

(8 marks)
(Total 20 marks)
ACCA P2 Management Accounting

Question 16.9

Advanced

The typical budgetary control system in practice does not encourage *goal congruence*, contains *budgetary slack*, ignores the *aspiration levels* of participants and attempts to control operations by *feedback*, when *feedforward* is likely to be more effective; in summary the typical budgetary control system is likely to have dysfunctional effects.

You are required to

(a) explain briefly *each* of the terms in italics;

(*6 marks*)

(b) describe how the major dysfunctional effects of budgeting could be avoided.

(*11 marks*)
(*Total 17 marks*)
CIMA Stage 3 Management Accounting Techniques

Advanced

Question 16.10

Accounting information plays a major part in the planning and control activities of any organization. Often these planning and control activities, in which budgets feature prominently, are undertaken within a structure known as responsibility accounting.

Required:

(a) Briefly explain responsibility accounting and describe three potential difficulties with operating a system of responsibility accounting.

(*6 marks*)

(b) Explain 'feedback' and 'feed-forward' in the context of budgetary control. Present a simple diagram to illustrate each.

(*7 marks*)

(c) Typical purposes of budgets are
   (i)   resource allocation
   (ii) authorization
   (iii) control

Explain each of these giving an example from the setting of a non-profit organization.

(*7 marks*)
(*Total 20 marks*)
ACCA Paper 8 Managerial Finance

Advanced

Question 16.11

One of the major practical difficulties of applying a financial reporting and control system based on flexible budgeting to a service or overhead department is in identifying and measuring an appropriate unit of activity with which to 'flex' the budget.

Required:

(a) Describe and comment on the desirable attributes of such a measure in the context of a valid application of flexible budgeting to a service centre or to a cost centre where standard costing is not applicable.

(*c. 8 marks*)

(b) Explain the difficulties in obtaining such a measure.

(*c. 6 marks*)

(c) List three suitable measures of activity, indicating the circumstances in which each would be suitable and the circumstances in which each of them would be misleading or unsuitable.

(*c. 6 marks*)
(*Total 20 marks*)
ACCA P2 Management Accounting

Question 16.12

Advanced

Several assumptions are commonly made by accountants when preparing or interpreting budgetary information.

You are required to explain why each of the following five assumptions might be made by accountants when designing a system of budgeting, and to set out in each case also any arguments which, in your view, raise legitimate doubts about their validity:

(a) budgeted performance should be reasonably attainable but not too loose,

(5 marks)

(b) participation by managers in the budget-setting process leads to better performance,

(5 marks)

(c) management by exception is the most effective system of routine reporting,

(5 marks)

(d) a manager's budget reports should exclude all matters which are not completely under his control,

(5 marks)

(e) budget statements should include only matters which can be easily and accurately measured in monetary terms.

(5 marks)
(Total 25 marks)
ICAEW Management Accounting

Question 16.13

Intermediate: Preparation of a flexible budget performance report

The Viking Smelting Company established a division, called the reclamation division, two years ago, to extract silver from jewellers' waste materials. The waste materials are processed in a furnace, enabling silver to be recovered. The silver is then further processed into finished products by three other divisions within the company.

A performance report is prepared each month for the reclamation division which is then discussed by the management team. Sharon Houghton, the newly appointed financial controller of the reclamation division, has recently prepared her first report for the four weeks to 31 May. This is shown below:

Performance Report Reclamation Division
4 weeks to 31 May

	Actual	Budget	Variance	Comments
Production (tonnes)	200	250	50 (F)[a]	
	(£)	(£)	(£)	
Wages and social security costs	46 133	45 586	547 (A)	Overspend
Fuel	15 500	18 750	3 250 (F)	
Consumables	2 100	2 500	400 (F)	
Power	1 590	1 750	160 (F)	
Divisional overheads	21 000	20 000	1 000 (A)	Overspend
Plant maintenance	6 900	5 950	950 (A)	Overspend
Central services	7 300	6 850	450 (A)	Overspend
Total	100 523	101 386	863 (F)	

[a](A) = adverse, (F) = favourable

In preparing the budgeted figures, the following assumptions were made for May:

- the reclamation division was to employ four teams of six production employees;
- each employee was to work a basic 42-hour week and be paid £7.50 per hour for the four weeks of May;
- social security and other employment costs were estimated at 40% of basic wages;
- a bonus, shared amongst the production employees, was payable if production exceeded 150 tonnes. This varied depending on the output achieved;

1. if output was between 150 and 199 tonnes, the bonus was £3 per tonne produced;
2. if output was between 200 and 249 tonnes, the bonus was £8 per tonne produced;
3. if output exceeded 249 tonnes the bonus was £13 per tonne produced;

- the cost of fuel was £75 per tonne;
- consumables were £10 per tonne;
- power comprised a fixed charge of £500 per four weeks plus £5 per tonne for every tonne produced;
- overheads directly attributable to the division were £20 000;
- plant maintenance was to be apportioned to divisions on the basis of the capital values of each division;
- the cost of Viking's central services was to be shared equally by all four divisions.

You are the deputy financial controller of the reclamation division. After attending her first monthly meeting with the board of the reclamation division, Sharon Houghton arranges a meeting with you. She is concerned about a number of issues, one of them being that the current report does not clearly identify those expenses and variances which are the direct responsibility of the reclamation division.

Task 1

Sharon Houghton asks you to prepare a flexible budget report for the reclamation division for May in a form consistent with responsibility accounting.

On receiving your revised report. Sharon tells you about the other questions raised at the management meeting when the original report was presented. These are summarized below:

(i) Why are the budget figures based on 2-year-old data taken from the proposal recommending the establishment of the reclamation division?

(ii) Should the budget data be based on what we were proposing to do or what we actually did do?

(iii) Is it true that the less we produce the more favourable our variances will be?

(iv) Why is there so much maintenance in a new division with modern equipment and why should we be charged with the actual costs of the maintenance department even when they overspend?

(v) Could the comments, explaining the variances, be improved?

(vi) Should all the variances be investigated?

(vii) Does showing the cost of central services on the divisional performance report help control these costs and motivate the divisional managers?

Task 2

Prepare a memo for the management of the reclamation division. Your memo should:

(a) answer their queries and justify your comments;

(b) highlight the main objective of your revised performance report developed in Task 1 and give two advantages of it over the original report

AAT Technicians Stage

Question 16.14

Intermediate: Sales forecasting removing seasonal variations, flexible budgets and budget preparation

You work as the assistant to the management accountant for Henry Limited, a medium-sized manufacturing company. One of its products, product P, has been very successful in recent years, showing a steadily increasing trend in sales volumes. Sales volumes for the four quarters of last year were as follows:

	Quarter 1	Quarter 2	Quarter 3	Quarter 4
Actual sales volume (units)	420 000	450 000	475 000	475 000

A new assistant has recently joined the marketing department and she has asked you for help in understanding the terminology which is used in preparing sales forecasts and analysing sales trends. She has said: 'My main problem is that I do not see why my boss is so enthusiastic about the growth in product P's sales volume. It looks to me as though the rate of growth is really slowing down and has actually stopped in quarter 4. I am told that I should be looking at the deseasonalized or seasonally adjusted sales data but I do not understand what is meant by this.'

You have found that product P's sales are subject to the following seasonal variations:

	Quarter 1	Quarter 2	Quarter 3	Quarter 4
Seasonal variation (units)	+25 000	+15 000	0	–40 000

Task 1

(a) Adjust for the seasonal variations to calculate deseasonalized or seasonally adjusted sales volume (i.e. the trend figures) for each quarter of last year.

(b) Assuming that the trend and seasonal variations will continue, forecast the sales volumes for each of the four quarters of next year.

Task 2

Prepare a memorandum to the marketing assistant which explains:

(a) what is meant by seasonal variations and deseasonalized or seasonally adjusted data;

(b) how they can be useful in analysing a time series and preparing forecasts.

Use the figures for product P's sales to illustrate your explanations.

Task 3

Using the additional data below, prepare a further memorandum to the marketing assistant which explains the following:

(a) why fixed budgets are useful for planning but flexible budgets may be more useful to enable management to exercise reflective control over distribution costs,

(b) *two* possible activity indicators which could be used as a basis for flexing the budget for distribution costs,

(c) how a flexible budget cost allowance is calculated and used for control purposes. Use your own examples and figures where appropriate to illustrate your explanations.

Additional data:

The marketing assistant has now approached you for more help in understanding the company's planning and control systems. She has been talking with the distribution manager, who has tried to explain how flexible budgets are used to control distribution costs within Henry Limited. She makes the following comment. 'I thought that budgets were supposed to provide a target to plan our activities and against which to monitor our costs. How can we possibly plan and control our costs if we simply change the budgets when activity levels alter?'

Product Q is another product which is manufactured and sold by Henry Limited. In the process of preparing budgetary plans for next year the following information has been made available to you.

1. Forecast sales units of product Q for the year = 18 135 units.

2. Closing stocks of finished units of product Q at the end of next year will be increased by 15% from their opening level of 1200 units.

3. All units are subject to quality control check. The budget plans are to allow for 1% of all units checked to be rejected and scrapped at the end of the process. All closing stocks will have passed this quality control check.

4. Five direct labour hours are to be worked for each unit of product Q processed, including those which are scrapped after the quality control check. Of the total hours to be paid for, 7.5% are budgeted to be idle time.

5. The standard hourly rate of pay for direct employees is £6 per hour.

6. Material M is used in the manufacture of product Q. One finished unit of producing Q contains 9 kg of M but there is a wastage of 10% of input of material M due to evaporation and spillage during the process.

7. By the end of next year stocks of material M are to be increased by 12% from their opening level of 8000 kg. During the year a loss of 1000 kg is expected due to deterioration of the material in store.

Task 4

Prepare the following budgets for the forthcoming year:

(a) production budget for product Q, in units;

(b) direct labour budget for product Q, in hours and in £;

(c) material usage budget for material M, in kg;

(d) material purchases budget for material M, in kg.

Task 5

The supplier of material M was warned that available supplies will be below the amount indicated in your budget for Task 4 part (d) above. Explain the implications of this shortage and suggest *four* possible actions which could be taken to overcome the problem. For each suggestion, identify any problems which may arise.

AAT Technicians Stage

Intermediate: Preparation of flexible budgets

Question 16.15

Data

Rivermede Ltd makes a single product called the Fasta. Last year, Steven Jones, the managing director of Rivermede Ltd, attended a course on budgetary control. As a result, he agreed to revise the way budgets were prepared in the company. Rather than imposing targets for managers, he encouraged participation by senior managers in the preparation of budgets.

An initial budget was prepared but Mike Fisher, the sales director, felt that the budgeted sales volume was set too high. He explained that setting too high a budgeted sales volume would mean his sales staff would be de-motivated because they would not be able to achieve that sales volume. Steven Jones agreed to use the revised sales volume suggested by Mike Fisher.

Both the initial and revised budgets are reproduced below complete with the actual results for the year ended 31 May.

Rivermede Ltd – budgeted and actual costs for the year ended 31 May

Fast production and sales (units)	Original budget 24 000 (£)	Revised budget 20 000 (£)	Actual results 22 000 (£)	Variances from revised budget 2000 (£)	(F)
Variable costs					
Material	216 000	180 000	206 800	26 800	(A)
Labour	288 000	240 000	255 200	15 200	(A)
Semi-variable costs					
Heat, light and power	31 000	27 000	33 400	6 400	(A)
Fixed costs					
Rent, rates and depreciation	40 000	40 000	38 000	2 000	(F)
	575 000	487 000	533 400	46 400	(A)

Assumptions in the two budgets

1. No change in input prices
2. No change in the quantity of variable inputs per Fasta

As the management accountant at Rivermede Ltd, one of your tasks is to check that invoices have been properly coded. On checking the actual invoices for heat, light and power for the year to 31 May, you find that one invoice for £7520 had been incorrectly coded. The invoice should have been coded to materials.

Task 1

(a) Using the information in the original and revised budgets, identify:

   - the variable cost of material and labour per Fasta;
   - the fixed and unit variable cost within heat, light and power.

(b) Prepare a flexible budget, including variances, for Rivermede Ltd after correcting for the miscoding of the invoice.

Data

On receiving your flexible budget statement, Steven Jones states that the total adverse variance is much less than the £46 400 shown in the original statement. He also draws your attention to the actual sales volume being greater than in the revised budget. He believes these results show that a participative approach to budgeting is better for the company and wants to discuss this belief at the next board meeting. Before doing so, Steven Jones asked for your comments.

Task 2

Write a memo to Steven Jones. Your memo should:

(a) *briefly* explain why the flexible budgeting variances differ from those in the original statement given in the data to task 1;

(b) give *two* reasons why a favourable cost variance may have arisen other than through the introduction of participative budgeting;

(c) give *two* reasons why the actual sales volume compared with the revised budget's sales volume may not be a measure of improved motivation following the introduction of participative budgeting.

AAT Technicians Stage

Intermediate: Demand forecasts and preparation of flexible budgets

Data

Happy Holidays Ltd sells holidays to Xanadu through newspaper advertisements. Tourists are flown each week of the holiday season to Xanadu, where they take a 10-day touring holiday. In 2000, Happy Holidays began to use the least-squares regression formula to help forecast the demand for its holidays.

You are employed by Happy Holidays as an accounting technician in the financial controller's department. A colleague of yours has recently used the least-squares regression formula on a spreadsheet to estimate the demand for holidays per year. The resulting formula was:

$$y = 640 + 40x$$

where y is the annual demand and x is the year. The data started with the number of holidays sold in 1993 and was identified in the formula as year 1. In each subsequent year the value of x increases by 1 so, for example, 1998 was year 6. To obtain the *weekly* demand the result is divided by 25, the number of weeks Happy Holidays operates in Xanadu.

Task 1

(a) Use the least-squares regression formula developed by your colleague to estimate the weekly demand for holidays in Xanadu for 2001.

(b) In preparation for a budget meeting with the financial controller, draft a *brief* note. Your note should identify *three* weaknesses of the least-squares regression formula in forecasting the weekly demand for holidays in Xanadu.

Data

The budget and actual costs for holidays to Xanadu for the 10 days ended 27 November 2000 is reproduced below.

Happy Holidays Ltd Cost Statement
10 days ended 27 November 2000

	Fixed Budget (£)	Actual (£)	Variances (£)
Aircraft seats	18 000	18 600	600 A
Coach hire	5 000	4 700	300 F
Hotel rooms	14 000	14 200	200 A
Meals	4 800	4 600	200 F
Tour guide	1 800	1 700	100 F
Advertising	2 000	1 800	200 F
Total costs	45 600	45 600	0

Key: A = adverse, F = favourable

The financial controller gives you the following additional information:

Cost and volume information

- each holiday lasts 10 days;
- meals and hotel rooms are provided for each of the 10 days;

- the airline charges £450 per return flight per passenger for each holiday but the airline will only sell seats at this reduced price if Happy Holidays purchases seats in blocks of 20;
- the costs of coach hire, the tour guide and advertising are fixed costs;
- the cost of meals was budgeted at £12 per tourist per day;
- the cost of a single room was budgeted at £60 per day;
- the cost of a double room was budgeted at £70 per day;
- 38 tourists travelled on the holiday requiring 17 double rooms and 4 single rooms;

Sales information

- the price of a holiday is £250 more if using a single room.

Task 2

Write a memo to the financial controller. Your memo should:

(a) take account of the cost and volume information to prepare a revised cost statement using flexible budgeting and identifying any variances;

(b) state and justify which of the two cost statements is more useful for management control of costs;

(c) identify *three* factors to be taken into account in deciding whether or not to investigate individual variances.

AAT Technicians Stage

Standard costing and variance analysis 1

Questions to Chapter 17

Intermediate

Despite changes in the environment in which business operates, standard costing and variance analysis may continue to be used in a number of different ways in the operation of a management accounting system. An example of its use would be as a control aid in each accounting period through the investigation of variances.

Required:

Name and explain *five* applications (other than as a control aid each period) of standard costing and/or variance analysis in the operation of a management accounting system.

(15 marks)
ACCA Paper 8 – Managerial Finance

Question 17.1

Intermediate

(a) Outline the uses of standard costing and discuss the reasons why standards have to be reviewed.

(13 marks)

(b) Standard costs are a detailed financial expression of organizational objectives. What non-financial objectives might organizations have? In your answer, identify any stakeholder group that may have a non-financial interest.

(12 marks)
(Total 25 marks)
ACCA Paper 2.4 – Financial Management and Control

Question 17.2

Intermediate: Direct labour and material variances

Newcastle Limited uses variance analysis as a method of cost control. The following information is available for the year ended 30 September 2001:

Budget	Production for the year	12 000 units
	Standard cost per unit:	£
	Direct materials (3 kg at £10/kg)	30
	Direct labour (4 hours at £6/hour)	24
	Overheads (4 hours at £2/hour)	8
		62
Actual	Actual production units for year	11 500 units
	Labour – hours for the year	45 350 hours
	– cost for the year	£300 000
	Materials – kg used in the year	37 250 kg
	– cost for the year	£345 000

Required:

(a) Prepare a reconciliation statement between the original budgeted and actual prime costs.

(7 marks)

Question 17.3

(b) Explain what the labour variances calculated in (a) show and indicate the possible interdependence between these variances.

(3 marks)
(Total 10 marks)
ACCA Paper 1.2 – Financial Information for Management

Question 17.4

Intermediate: Variance analysis and reconciliation of standard with actual cost

SK Limited makes and sells a single product 'Jay' for which the standard cost is as follows:

		£ per unit
Direct materials	4 kilograms at £12.00 per kg	48.00
Direct labour	5 hours at £7.00 per hour	35.00
Variable production overhead	5 hours at £2.00 per hour	10.00
Fixed production overhead	5 hours at £10.00 per hour	50.00
		143.00

The variable production overhead is deemed to vary with the hours worked.

Overhead is absorbed into production on the basis of standard hours of production and the normal volume of production for the period just ended was 20 000 units (100 000 standard hours of production).

For the period under consideration, the actual results were:

Production of 'Jay'	18 000 units (£)
Direct material used – 76 000 kg at a cost of	836 000
Direct labour cost incurred – for 84 000 hours worked	604 800
Variable production overhead incurred	172 000
Fixed production overhead incurred	1 030 000

You are required

(a) to calculate and show, by element of cost, the standard cost for the output for the period;

(2 marks)

(b) to calculate and list the relevant variances in a way which reconciles the standard cost with the actual cost (*Note:* Fixed production overhead sub-variances of capacity and volume efficiency (productivity) are *not* required).

(9 marks)

(c) to comment briefly on the usefulness to management of statements such as that given in your answer to (b) above.

(4 marks)
(Total 15 marks)
CIMA Stage 2 Cost Accounting

Question 17.5

Intermediate: Reconciliation of budgeted and actual contribution

JK plc operates a chain of fast-food restaurants. The company uses a standard marginal costing system to monitor the costs incurred in its outlets. The standard cost of one of its most popular meals is as follows:

		£ per meal
Ingredients	(1.08 units)	1.18
Labour	(1.5 minutes)	0.15
Variable conversion costs	(1.5 minutes)	0.06
The standard selling price of this meal is		1.99

In one of its outlets, which has budgeted sales and production activity level of 50 000 such meals, the number of such meals that were produced and sold during April 2003 was 49 700. The actual cost data was as follows:

		£
Ingredients	(55 000 units)	58 450
Labour	(1 200 hours)	6 800
Variable conversion costs	(1 200 hours)	3 250

The actual revenue from the sale of the meals was 96 480

Required:

(a) Calculate
  (i) the total budgeted contribution for April 2003;
  (ii) the total actual contribution for April 2003.

(3 marks)

(b) Present a statement that reconciles the budgeted and actual contribution for April 2003. Show all variances to the nearest £1 and in as much detail as possible.

(17 marks)

(c) Explain why a marginal costing approach to variance analysis is more appropriate in environments such as that of JK plc, where there are a number of different items being produced and sold.

(5 marks)
(Total 25 marks)
CIMA Management Accounting – Performance Management

Intermediate: Reconciliation of budgeted and actual profit

Question 17.6

ZED plc sells two products, the Alpha and the Beta. These are made from three different raw materials that are bought from local suppliers using a Just-in-Time (JIT) purchasing policy. Products Alpha and Beta are made to customer order using a JIT manufacturing policy. Overhead costs are absorbed using direct labour hours as appropriate.

The following information relates to October 2002:

	Alpha	Beta
Budgeted production (units)	2400	1800

Standard selling price

The standard selling price is determined by adding a 100% mark-up to the standard variable costs of each product.

Standard variable costs per unit	Alpha £	Beta £
Direct material X (£5 per metre)	10.00	12.50
Direct material Y (£8 per litre)	8.00	12.00
Direct material X (£10 per kg)	5.00	10.00
Direct labour (£7 per hour)	14.00	10.50
Variable overhead costs	3.00	2.25

Actual data for October 2002

Direct material X	10 150 metres	costing	£48 890
Direct material Y	5 290 litres	costing	£44 760
Direct material Z	2 790 kg	costing	£29 850
Direct labour	9 140 hours paid	costing	£67 980
Direct labour	8 350 hours worked		
Variable overhead			£14 300
Fixed overhead			£72 000
Actual production	Alpha	3000 units	
	Beta	1500 units	

Sales variances

The following sales variances have been calculated:

	Absorption costing		Marginal costing	
	Alpha £	Beta £	Alpha £	Beta £
Selling price	6 000 (A)	4 500 (F)	6 000 (A)	4 500 (F)
Sales volume	18 000 (F)	11 925 (A)	24 000 (F)	14 175 (A)

Required:

(a) Calculate the budgeted fixed overhead cost for October 2002.

(3 marks)

(b) Calculate the budgeted profit for October 2002.

(2 marks)

(c) Calculate the actual profit for October 2002.

(2 marks)

(d) Prepare a statement, using absorption costing principles, that reconciles the budgeted and actual profits for October 2002, showing the variances in as much detail as possible. Do not calculate material mix and yield variances.

(15 marks)

(e) Explain why it would be inappropriate to calculate material mix and yield variances in requirement (d) above.

(3 marks)
(Total 25 marks)
CIMA Management Accounting – Performance Management

Question 17.7

Intermediate: Calculation of labour variances and actual material inputs working backwards from variances

A company manufactures two components in one of its factories. Material A is one of several materials used in the manufacture of both components.

The standard direct labour hours per unit of production and budgeted production quantities for a 13-week period were:

	Standard direct labour hours	Budgeted production quantities
Component X	0.40 hours	36 000 units
Component Y	0.56 hours	22 000 units

The standard wage rate for all direct workers was £5.00 per hour. Throughout the 13-week period 53 direct workers were employed, working a standard 40-hour week.

The following actual information for the 13-week period is available:

Production:
    Component X, 35 000 units
    Component Y, 25 000 units
Direct wages paid, £138 500
Material A purchases, 47 000 kilos costing £85 110
Material A price variance, £430 F
Material A usage (component X), 33 426 kilos
Material A usage variance (component X), £320.32 A

Required:

(a) Calculate the direct labour variances for the period;

(5 marks)

(b) Calculate the standard purchase price for material A for the period and the standard usage of material A per unit of production of component X.

(8 marks)

(c) Describe the steps, and information, required to establish the material purchase quantity budget for material A for a period.

(7 marks)
(Total 20 marks)
ACCA Cost and Management Accounting 1

Intermediate: Calculation of actual input data working back from variances

Question 17.8

The following data relate to actual output, costs and variances for the four-weekly accounting period number 4 of a company that makes only one product. Opening and closing work in progress figures were the same.

	(£000)
Actual production of product XY	18 000 units
Actual costs incurred:	
Direct materials purchased and used (150 000 kg)	210
Direct wages for 32 000 hours	136
Variable production overhead	38

	(£000)
Variances:	
Direct materials price	15 F
Direct materials usage	9 A
Direct labour rate	8 A
Direct labour efficiency	16 F
Variable production overhead expenditure	6 A
Variable production overhead efficiency	4 F

Variable production overhead varies with labour hours worked.
A standard marginal costing system is operated.

You are required to:

(a) present a standard product cost sheet for one unit of product XY,

(16 marks)

(b) describe briefly *three* types of standard that can be used for a standard costing system, stating which is usually preferred in practice and why.

(9 marks)
(Total 25 marks)
CIMA Cost Accounting Stage 2

Question 17.9

Intermediate: Comparison of absorption and marginal costing variances

You have been provided with the following data for S plc for September:

Accounting method: Variances:	Absorption (£)	Marginal (£)
Selling price	1900 (A)	1900 (A)
Sales volume	4500 (A)	7500 (A)
Fixed overhead expenditure	2500 (F)	2500 (F)
Fixed overhead volume	1800 (A)	n/a

During September production and sales volumes were as follows:

	Sales	Production
Budget	10 000	10 000
Actual	9 500	9 700

Required:

(a) Calculate:
   (i)   the standard contribution per unit;
   (ii) the standard profit per unit;
   (iii) the actual fixed overhead cost total.

(9 marks)

(b) Using the information presented above, explain why different variances are calculated depending upon the choice of marginal or absorption costing.

(8 marks)

(c) Explain the meaning of the fixed overhead volume variance and its usefulness to management.

(5 marks)

(d) Fixed overhead absorption rates are often calculated using a single measure of activity. It is suggested that fixed overhead costs should be attributed to cost units using multiple measures of activity (activity-based costing).

Explain 'activity-based costing' and how it may provide useful information to managers.

(Your answer should refer to both the setting of cost driver rates and subsequent overhead cost control.)

(8 marks)
(Total 30 marks)
CIMA Operational Cost Accounting Stage 2

Question 17.10

Intermediate: Calculation of production ratios

NAB Limited has produced the following figures relating to production for the week ended 21 May:

	Production (in units)	
	Budgeted	Actual
Product A	400	400
Product B	400	300
Product C	100	140

Standard production times were:

	Standard hours per unit
Product A	5.0
Product B	2.5
Product C	1.0

During the week 2800 hours were worked on production.

You are required:

(a) (i) to calculate the production volume ratio and the efficiency ratio for the week ended 21 May;

(4 marks)

    (ii) to explain the significance of the two ratios you have calculated and to state which variances may be related to each of the ratios;

(5 marks)

(b) to explain the three measures of capacity referred to in the following statement:

During the recent recession, increased attention was paid to 'practical capacity' and 'budgeted capacity' because few manufacturing companies could anticipate working again at 'full capacity'.

(6 marks)
(Total 15 marks)
CIMA Stage 2 Cost Accounting

Standard costing and variance analysis 2: further aspects

Questions to Chapter 18

Question 18.1

Advanced

(a) Outline the factors a management accountant should consider when deciding whether or not to investigate variances revealed in standard costing and budgetary control systems.

(b) Indicate briefly what action the management accountant can take to improve the chances of achieving positive results from investigating variances.

(20 marks)
CIMA P3 Management Accounting

Question 18.2

Advanced

Explain:

(a) the problems concerning control of operations that a manufacturing company can be expected to experience in using a standard costing system during periods of rapid inflation;

(b) three methods by which the company could try to overcome the problems to which you have referred in your answer to (a) above, indicating the shortcomings of each method.

(20 marks)
CIMA P3 Management Accounting

Question 18.3

Advanced

(a) Name three bases of valuation of the sales volume variance in a standard cost system and discuss the appropriateness of each valuation basis.

(9 marks)

(b) Expand on arguments supporting the view that the use of sales variances in a standard cost system could be enhanced through the use of a planning and operational approach to the valuation of sales price variances.

(6 marks)
(Total 15 marks)
ACCA Paper 9 – Information for Control and Decision Making

Question 18.4

Advanced

(a) Discuss ways in which standards may be seen as useful aids in management accounting decision-making.

(6 marks)

(b) Suggest ways in which the use of standards may be seen as having a *dysfunctional effect* in relation to decision making about each of materials, labour and overhead cost.

(9 marks)
(Total 15 marks)
ACCA Paper 9 – Information for Control and Decision Making

JC Limited produces and sells one product only, Product J, the standard cost for which is as follows for one unit.

	(£)
Direct material X – 10 kilograms at £20	200
Direct material Y – 5 litres at £6	30
Direct wages – 5 hours at £6	30
Fixed production overhead	50
Total standard cost	310
Standard gross profit	90
Standard selling price	400

The fixed production overhead is based on an expected annual output of 10 800 units produced at an even flow throughout the year; assume each calendar month is equal. Fixed production overhead is absorbed on direct labour hours.

During April, the first month of the financial year, the following were the actual results for an actual production of 800 units.

		(£)
Sales on credit:		320 000
800 units at £400		
Direct materials:		
X 7800 kilogrammes	159 900	
Y 4300 litres	23 650	
Direct wages: 4200 hours	24 150	
Fixed production overhead	47 000	
		254 700
Gross profit		65 300

The material price variance is extracted at the time of receipt and the raw materials stores control is maintained at standard prices. The purchases, bought on credit, during the month of April were:

X 9000 kilograms at £20.50 per kg from K Limited
Y 5000 litres at £5.50 per litre from C plc.

Assume no opening stocks.

Wages owing for March brought forward were £6000.

Wages paid during April (net) £20 150.

Deductions from wages owing to the Inland Revenue for PAYE and NI were £5000 and the wages accrued for April were £5000.

The fixed production overhead of £47 000 was made up of expense creditors of £33 000, none of which was paid in April, and depreciation of £14 000.

The company operates an integrated accounting system.

You are required to

(a) (i) calculate price and usage variances for each material,
   (ii) calculate labour rate and efficiency variances,
   (iii) calculate fixed production overhead expenditure, efficiency and volume variances;

(*9 marks*)

(b) show all the accounting entries in T accounts for the month of April – the work-in-progress account should be maintained at standard cost and each balance on the separate variance accounts is to be transferred to a Profit and Loss Account which you are also required to show;

(18 marks)

(c) explain the reason for the difference between the actual gross profit given in the question and the profit shown in your profit and loss account.

(3 marks)
(Total 30 marks)
CIMA Stage 2 Cost Accounting

Question 18.6   **Advanced: Mix variances and reconciliation of actual and budgeted profit**

The budgeted income statement for one of the products of Derwen plc for the month of May was as follows:

Budgeted income statement – May

	(£)	(£)	(£)
Sales revenue:			
10 000 units at £5			50 000
Production costs:			
Budgeted production			
10 000 units			
Direct materials:			
Material			
A (5000 kg at £0.30)	1 500		
B (5000 kg at £0.70)	3 500		
		5 000	
Direct labour:			
Skilled (4500 hours at £3.00)	13 500		
Semi-skilled (2600 hours at £2.50)	6 500		
		20 000	
Overhead cost:			
Fixed		10 000	
Variable (10 000 units at £0.50)		5 000	
		40 000	
Add Opening stock (1000 units at £4)		4 000	
		44 000	
Deduct Closing stock (1000 units at £4)		4 000	
Cost of goods sold			40 000
Budgeted profit			10 000

During May production and sales were both above budget and the following income statement was prepared:

Income statement – May

	(£)	(£)	(£)
Sales revenue:			
7000 units at £5			35 000
4000 units at £4.75			19 000
			54 000
Production costs:			
Actual production			
12 000 units			

Direct materials:
  Material
    A (8000 kg at £0.20)   1 600
    B (5000 kg at £0.80)   4 000
                                     5 600

Direct labour:
  Skilled (6000 hours at £2.95)   17 700
  Semi-skilled (3150 hours at £2.60)   8 190
                                   25 890

Overhead cost:
  Fixed   9 010
  Variable   7 500
    (12 000 units at £0.625)
                                 48 000
Add Opening stock (1000 units at £4)   4 000
                                 52 000
Deduct Closing stock (2000 units at £4) 8 000
Cost of goods sold   44 000
'Actual' profit   10 000

In the above statement stock is valued at the standard cost of £4 per unit.

There is general satisfaction because the budgeted profit level has been achieved but you have been asked to prepare a standard costing statement analysing the differences between the budget and the actual performance. In your analysis, include calculations of the sales volume and sales price variances and the following cost variances: direct material price, mix, yield and usage variances; direct labour rate, mix, productivity and efficiency variances: and overhead spending and volume variances.

(17 marks)

Provide a commentary on the variances and give your views on their usefulness.

(5 marks)
(Total 22 marks)
ACCA Level 2 Management Accounting

Advanced: Sales mix and quantity variances and planning and operating variances   **Question 18.7**

Milbao plc make and sell three types of electronic game for which the following budget/standard information and actual information is available for a four-week period:

Model	Budget sales (units)	Standard unit data		Actual sales (units)
		Selling price (£)	Variable cost (£)	
Superb	30 000	100	40	36 000
Excellent	50 000	80	25	42 000
Good	20 000	70	22	18 000

Budgeted fixed costs are £2 500 000 for the four-week period. Budgeted fixed costs should be changed to product units at an overall budgeted average cost unit where it is relevant to do so.

Required:

(a) Calculate the sales volume variance for each model and in total for the four-week period where (i) turnover (ii) contribution and (iii) net profit is used as the variance valuation base.

(9 marks)

(b) Discuss the relative merits of each of the valuation bases of the sales volume variance calculated in (a) above.

(6 marks)

(c) Calculate the *total* sales quantity and sales mix variances for Milbao plc for the four-week period, using contribution as the valuation base. (Individual model variances are not required.)

(4 marks)

(d) Comment on why the individual model variances for sales mix and sales quantity may provide misleading information to management. (No calculations are required.)

(4 marks)

(e) The following additional information is available for the four-week period:
1. The actual selling price and variable costs of Milbao plc are 10% and 5% lower respectively, than the original budget/standard.
2. General market prices have fallen by 6% from the original standard. Short-term strategy by Milbao plc accounts for the residual fall in selling price.
3. 3% of the variable cost reduction from the original budget/standard is due to an over-estimation of a wage award, the remainder (i.e. 2%) is due to short-term operational improvements.
    (i) Prepare a summary for a four-week period for model 'Superb' *only*, which reconciles original budget contribution with actual contribution where planning and operational variances are taken into consideration.

(8 marks)

    (ii) Comment on the usefulness to management of planning and operational variance analysis in feedback and feedforward control.

(4 marks)
(Total 35 marks)
ACCA Paper 9 Information for Control and Decision Making

Question 18.8

Advanced: Planning and operating variances

A year ago Kenp Ltd entered the market for the manufacture and sale of a revolutionary insulating material. The budgeted production and sales volumes were 1000 units. The originally estimated sales price and standard costs for this new product were:

	(£)	(£)
Standard sales price (per unit)		100
Standard costs (per unit)		
Raw materials (Aye 10 kg at £5)	50	
Labour (6 hours at £4)	24	74
Standard contribution (per unit)		£26

Actual results were:

First year's results

	(£000)	(£000)
Sales (1000 units)		158
Production costs (1000 units)		
Raw materials (Aye 10 800 kg)	97.2	
Labour (5800 hours)	<u>34.8</u>	<u>132</u>
Actual contribution		<u>£26</u>

'Throughout the year we attempted to operate as efficiently as possible, given the prevailing conditions' stated the managing director. 'Although in total the performance agreed with budget, in every detailed respect, expect volume, there were large differences. These were due, mainly, to the tremendous success of the new insulating material which created increased demand both for the product itself and all the manufacturing resources used in its production. This then resulted in price rises all round.'

'Sales were made at what was felt to be the highest feasible price but, it was later discovered, our competitors sold for £165 per unit and we could have equalled this price. Labour costs rose dramatically with increased demand for the specialist skills required to produce the product and the general market rate was £6.25 per hour – although Kenp always paid below the general market rate whenever possible.'

'Raw material Aye was chosen as it appeared cheaper than the alternative material Bee which could have been used. The costs which were expected at the time the budget was prepared were (per kg): Aye, £5 and Bee, £6. However, the market prices relating to efficient purchases of the materials during the year were:

Aye £8.50 per kg, and
Bee £7.00 per kg.

Therefore it would have been more appropriate to use Bee, but as production plans were based on Aye it was Aye that was used.'

'It is not proposed to request a variance analysis for the first year's results as most of the deviations from budget were caused by the new product's great success and this could not have been fully anticipated and planned for. In any event the final contribution was equal to that originally budgeted so operations must have been fully efficient.'

Required:

(a) Compute the traditional variances for the first year's operations.

(5 marks)

(b) Prepare an analysis of variances for the first year's operations which will be useful in the circumstances of Kenp Ltd. The analysis should indicate the extent to which the variances were due to operational efficiency or planning causes.

(10 marks)

(c) Using, for illustration, a comparison of the raw material variances computed in (a) and (b) above, briefly outline two major advantages and two major disadvantages of the approach applied in part (b) over the traditional approach.

(5 marks)
(Total 20 marks)
ACCA P2 Management Accounting

Question 18.9

Advanced: Planning and operating variances

POV Ltd uses a standard costing system to control and report upon the production of its single product.

An abstract from the original standard cost card of the product is as follows:

	(£)	(£)
Selling price per unit		200
less: 4 kg materials @ £20 per kg	80	
6 hours labour @ £7 per hour	42	122
Contribution per unit		78

For Period 3, 2500 units were budgeted to be produced and sold but the actual production and sales were 2850 units.

The following information was also available:

(i) At the commencement of Period 3 the normal material became unobtainable and it was necessary to use an alternative. Unfortunately, 0.5 kg per unit extra was required and it was thought that the material would be more difficult to work with. The price of the alternative was expected to be £16.50 per kg. In the event, actual usage was 12 450 kg at £18 per kg.

(ii) Weather conditions unexpectedly improved for the period with the result that a £0.50 per hour bad weather bonus, which had been allowed for in the original standard, did not have to be paid. Because of the difficulties expected with the alternative material, management agreed to pay the workers £8 per hour for Period 3 only. During the period 18 800 hours were paid for.

After using conventional variances for some time, POV Ltd is contemplating extending its system to include planning and operational variances.

You are required:

(a) to prepare a statement reconciling budgeted contribution for the period with actual contribution, using conventional material and labour variances;

(4 marks)

(b) to prepare a similar reconciliation statement using planning and operational variances;

(14 marks)

(c) to explain the meaning of the variances shown in statement (b).

(4 marks)
(Total 22 marks)
CIMA Stage 3 Management Accounting Techniques

Question 18.10

Advanced: Activity-based standard costing

X Ltd has recently automated its manufacturing plant and has also adopted a Total Quality Management (TQM) philosophy and a Just in Time (JIT) manufacturing system. The company currently uses a standard absorption costing system for the electronic diaries which it manufactures.

The following information for the last quarter has been extracted from the company records.

	Budget	Actual
Fixed production overheads	$100 000	$102 300
Labour hours	10 000	11 000
Output (electronic diaries)	100 000	105 000

Fixed production overheads are absorbed on the basis of direct labour hours.
The following fixed production overhead variances have been reported:

	$
Expenditure variance	2 300 (A)
Capacity variance	10 000 (F)
Efficiency variance	5 000 (A)
Total	2 700 (F)

If the fixed production overheads had been further analysed and classified under an Activity Based Costing (ABC) system, the above information would then have been presented as follows:

	Budget	Actual
Costs:		
Material handling	$30 000	$30 800
Set up	$70 000	$71 500
Output (electronic diaries)	100 000	105 000
Activity:		
Material handling (orders executed)	5 000	5 500
Set up (production runs)	2 800	2 600

The following variances would have been reported:

		$
Overhead expenditure variance	Material handling	2 200 (F)
	Set ups	6 500 (A)
Overhead efficiency variance	Material handling	1 500 (A)
	Set ups	8 500 (F)
Total		2 700 (F)

Required:

(a) Explain why and how X Ltd may have to adapt its standard costing system now that it has adopted TQM and JIT in its recently automated manufacturing plant.

(9 *marks*)

(b) Explain the meaning of the fixed overhead variances calculated under the standard absorption costing system and discuss their usefulness to the management of X Ltd for decision-making.

(6 *marks*)

(c) For the variances calculated under the ABC classification,
   (i) explain how they have been calculated;
   (ii) discuss their usefulness to the management of X Ltd for decision-making.

(10 *marks*)
(*Total 25 marks*)
CIMA Management Accounting – Decision Making

Advanced: Investigation of variances

Question 18.11

(a) The Secure Locke Company operates a system of standard costing, which it uses amongst other things as the basis for calculating certain management bonuses.

In September the Company's production of 100 000 keys was in accordance with budget. The standard quantity of material used in each key is one unit; the standard price is £0.05 per unit. In September 105 000 units of material were used, at an actual purchase price of £45 per thousand units (which was also the replacement cost).

The materials buyer is given a bonus of 10% of any favourable materials price variance. The production manager is given a bonus of 10% of any favourable materials quantity variance.

You are required:

(i) to calculate the materials cost variances for September;

(4 marks)

(ii) to record all relevant bookkeeping entries in journal form;

(2 marks)

(iii) to evaluate the bonus system from the view-points of the buyer, the production manager, and the company.

(6 marks)

(b) In October there was an adverse materials quantity variance of £500. A decision has to be made as to whether to investigate the key-making process to determine whether it is out of control.

On the basis of past experience the cost of an investigation is estimated at £50. The cost of correcting the process if it is found to be out of control is estimated at £100. The probability that the process is out of control is estimated at .50.

You are required:

(i) to calculate the minimum present value of the expected savings that would have to be made in future months in order to justify making an investigation;

(6 marks)

(ii) to suggest why the monthly cost savings arising from a systematic investigation are unlikely to be as great as the adverse materials variance of £500 which was experienced in the month of October;

(3 marks)

(iii) to calculate, if the expected present value of cost savings were *first* £600 and *second* £250, the respective levels of probability that the process was out of control, at which the management would be indifferent about whether to conduct an investigation.

(4 marks)
ICAEW Management Accounting

Divisional financial performance measures

Questions to Chapter 19

Advanced

Question 19.1

(a) 'Because of the possibility of goal incongruence, an optimal plan can only be achieved if divisional budgets are constructed by a central planning department, but this means that divisional independence is a pseudo-independence.'

Discuss the problems of establishing divisional budgets in the light of this quotation.

(9 marks)

(b) 'Head Office' will require a division to submit regular reports of its performance.

Describe, discuss and compare three measures of divisional operating performance that might feature in such reports.

(8 marks)
ACCA Level 2 Management Accounting

Advanced

Question 19.2

A long-established, highly centralized company has grown to the extent that its chief executive, despite having a good supporting team, is finding difficulty in keeping up with the many decisions of importance in the company.

Consideration is therefore being given to re-organizing the company into profit centres. These would be product divisions, headed by a divisional managing director, who would be responsible for all the divisions' activities relating to its products.

You are required to explain, in outline:

(a) the types of decision areas that should be transferred to the new divisional managing directors if such a reorganization is to achieve its objectives;

(b) the types of decision areas that might reasonably be retained at company head office;

(c) the management accounting problems that might be expected to arise in introducing effective profit centre control.

(20 marks)
CIMA P3 Management Accounting

Advanced

Question 19.3

A recently formed group of companies is proposing to use a single return on capital employed (ROCE) rate as an index of the performance of its operating companies which differ considerably from one another in size and type of activities.

It is, however, particularly concerned that the evaluations it makes from the use of this rate should be valid in terms of measurement of performance.

You are required to:

(a) mention *four* considerations in calculating the ROCE rate to which the group will need to attend, to ensure that its intentions are achieved; for each consideration give an example of the type of problem that can arise;

(8 marks)

(b) mention *three* types of circumstance in which a single ROCE rate might not be an adequate measure of performance and, for each, explain what should be done to supplement the interpretation of the results of the single ROCE rate.

(12 marks)

CIMA P3 Management Accounting

Question 19.4

Advanced

Residual Income and Return on Investment are commonly used measures of performance. However, they are frequently criticized for placing too great an emphasis on the achievement of short-term results, possibly damaging longer-term performance.

You are required to discuss

(a) the issues involved in the long-term:short-term conflict referred to in the above statement;

(11 marks)

(b) suggestions which have been made to reconcile this difference.

(11 marks)
(Total 22 marks)
CIMA Stage 4 Management Accounting – Control and Audit

Question 19.5

Advanced: Impact of various transactions on ROCE and a discussion whether ROCE leads to goal congruence

G Limited, one of the subsidiaries of GAP Group plc., produces the following condensed data in respect of its budgeted performance for the year to 31 December:

	(£000)
Profit	330
Fixed assets:	
Original cost	1500
Accumulated depreciation (as at 31 December)	720
Net current assets (average for the year)	375

In addition, it is considering carrying out the following separate non-routine transactions:

A. It would offer its customers cash discounts that would cost £8000 per annum.

This would reduce the level of its debtors by an average of £30 000 over the year. This sum would be used to increase the dividend to GAP Group plc. payable at the end of the year.

B. It would increase its average stocks by £40 000 throughout the year and reduce by that amount the dividend payable to GAP Group plc. at the end of the year.

This is expected to yield an increased contribution of £15 000 per annum resulting from larger sales.

C. At the start of the year it would sell for £35 000 a fixed asset that originally cost £300 000 and which has been depreciated by 4/5ths of its expected life.

If not sold, this asset would be expected to earn a profit contribution of £45 000 during the year.

D. At the start of the year it would buy for £180 000 plant that would achieve reductions of £52 500 per annum in revenue costs. This plant would have a life of five years, after which it would have no resale value.

The chief accountant of GAP Group plc. has the task of recommending to the Group management committee whether the non-routine transactions should go ahead. The Group's investment criterion is to earn 15% DCF and where no time period is specified, four years is the period assumed.

In measuring the comparative performance of its subsidiaries, GAP Group plc. uses return on capital employed (ROCE) calculated on the following basis:

Profit:	Depreciation of fixed assets is calculated on a straight-line basis. Profit or loss on sale of assets is respectively added to or deducted from operating profits in the year of sale.
Capital employed:	
Fixed assets:	Valued at original cost less accumulated depreciation as at the end of the year.
Net current assets:	At the average value for the year.

You are required

(a) as managing director of G Ltd, to recommend whether *each* of the *four* non-routine transactions (A to D) should independently go ahead;

(8 marks)

(b) as chief accountant of GAP Group plc.,

(i) to state whether you expect there to be goal congruence between G Limited and GAP Group plc. in respect of *each* of the *four* non-routine transactions considered separately;

(8 marks)

(ii) to state whether you would support a proposal to substitute a Group ROCE investment criterion in place of the existing DCF investment criterion.

(4 marks)

Note: You should give supporting calculations and/or explanations in each part of your answer. Ignore taxation.

(Total 20 marks)
CIMA Stage 4 Management Accounting – Decision Making

Advanced: Appropriate performance measures for different goals   **Question 19.6**

The executive directors and the seven divisional managers of Kant Ltd spent a long weekend at a country house debating the company's goals. They concluded that Kant had multiple goals, and that the performance of senior managers should be assessed in terms of all of them.

The goals identified were:

(i) to generate a reasonable financial return for shareholders;

(ii) to maintain a high market share;

(iii) to increase productivity annually;

(iv) to offer an up-to-date product range of high quality and proven reliability;

(v) to be known as responsible employers;

(vi) to acknowledge social responsibilities;

(vii) to grow and survive autonomously.

The finance director was asked to prepare a follow-up paper, setting-out some of the implications of these ideas. He has asked you, as his personal assistant, to prepare comments on certain issues for his consideration.

You are required to set out briefly, with reasons:

(a) suitable measures of performance for each of the stated goals for which you consider this to be possible.

(18 marks)

(b) an outline of your view as to whether any of the stated goals can be considered to be sufficiently general to incorporate all of the others.

(7 marks)
(Total 25 marks)
ICAEW Management Accounting

Question 19.7

Advanced: Comparison of net profit, residual income and ROI performance measures

A large conglomerate with diverse business activities is currently considering whether it should commence Project X and has gathered the following data:

Project X data
1. An initial investment of £54 million will be required on 1 January year 1. The project has a three-year life with a nil residual value. Depreciation is calculated on a straight line basis.
2. The project is expected to generate annual revenue flows of £80m in year 1, £90m in year 2 and £100m in year 3. These values may vary by ± 5%.
3. The incremental costs will be £50m in year 1. £60m in year 2 and £70m in year 3. These may vary by ±10%.
4. The most likely cost of capital is 10%. This may vary from 8% to 13% for the life of the project.

Additional information
Assume that all cash flows other than the initial investment take place at the end of each year.

Use the written down value of the asset at the start of each year to represent the value of the asset for the year. Note: Ignore taxation.

Required:

(a) Prepare two tables showing net profit, residual income and return on investment for each year of the project and also net present value (NPV) for:
 (i) the best outcome;
 (ii) the worst outcome.

(8 marks)

(b) Explain the distinctive features of Residual Income, Return on Investment and Net Present Value in measuring financial performance.

Your answer should include a critique of the strengths and weaknesses of each measure

(8 marks)

(c) What broader issues are likely to be considered when deciding whether the company should proceed with a particular project?

(4 marks)
ACCA P3Performance Measurement

Question 19.8

Advanced: Calculation and comparison of ROI and residual income using straight line and annuity methods of depreciation (This question relates to material covered in Learning Note 19.1)

The CP division of R plc. had budgeted a net profit before tax of £3 million per annum over the period of the foreseeable future, based on a net capital employed of £10 million.

Plant replacement anticipated over this period is expected to be approximately equal to the annual depreciation each year. These figures compare well with the organization's required rate of return of 20% before tax.

CP's management is currently considering a substantial expansion of its manufacturing capacity to cope with the forecast demands of a new customer. The customer is prepared to offer a five-year contract providing CP with annual sales of £2 million.

In order to meet this contract, a total additional capital outlay of £2 million is envisaged, being £1.5 million of new fixed assets plus £0.5 million working capital. A five-year plant life is expected.

Operating costs on the contract are estimated to be £1.35 million per annum, excluding depreciation.

This is considered to be a low-risk venture as the contract would be firm for five years and the manufacturing processes are well understood within CP.

You are required

(a) to calculate the impact of accepting the contract on the CP divisional Return on Capital Employed (ROCE) and Residual Income (RI), indicating whether it would be attractive to CP's management;

(8 marks)

(b) to repeat (a) using annuity depreciation for the newly acquired plant;

(7 marks)

(c) to explain the basis of the calculations in the statements you have produced and discuss the suitability of each method in directing divisional management toward the achievement of corporate goals.

(10 marks)
(Total 25 marks)
CIMA Stage 4 – Control and Audit

Advanced: Computation of divisional performance measures and NPV and impact on bonuses   Question 19.9

Tannadens Division is considering an investment in a quality improvement programme for a specific product group which has an estimated life of four years. It is estimated that the quality improvement programme will increase saleable output capacity and provide an improved level of customer demand due to the enhanced reliability of the product group.

Forecast information about the programme in order that it may be evaluated at each of best, most likely and worst scenario levels is as follows:

(i) There will be an initial investment of £4 000 000 on 1 January, year 1, with a programme life of four years and nil residual value. Depreciation will be calculated on a straight line basis.

(ii) Additional costs of staff training, consultancy fees and the salary of the programme manager are estimated at a most likely level of £100 000 per annum for each year of the proposal. This may vary by ±2.5%. This is the only relevant fixed cost of the proposal.

(iii) The most likely additional output capacity which will be sold is 1000 standard hours in year 1 with further increases in years 2, 3 and 4 of 300, 400 and 300 standard hours respectively. These values may vary by ±5%.

(iv) The most likely contribution per standard hour of extra capacity is £1200. This may vary by ±10%.

(v) The most likely cost of capital is 10%. This may vary from 8% to 12%.

Assume that all cash flows other than the initial investment take place at the end of each year. Ignore taxation.

Required:

(a) Present a table (including details of relevant workings) showing the net profit, residual income and return on investment for each of years 1 to 4 and also the net present value (NPV) for the BEST OUTCOME situation of the programme.

(10 marks)

Using the information provided above, the net profit, residual income (RI), and return on investment (ROI) for each year of the programme have been calculated for the most likely outcome and the worst outcome as follows:

Most likely outcome:	Year 1	Year 2	Year 3	Year 4
Net profit (£)	100 000	460 000	940 000	1 300 000
Residual income (£)	−300 000	160 000	740 000	1 200 000
Return on investment	2.5%	15.3%	47.0%	130.0%

Worst outcome:	Year 1	Year 2	Year 3	Year 4
Net profit (£)	−76 500	231 300	641 700	949 500
Residual income (£)	−556 500	−128 700	401 700	829 500
Return on investment	−1.9%	7.7%	32.1%	95.0%

In addition, the net present value (NPV) of the programme has been calculated as most likely outcome: £1 233 700 and worst outcome: £214 804.

It has been decided that the programme manager will be paid a bonus in addition to the annual salary of £40 000 (assume that this salary applies to the best, most likely and worst scenarios). The bonus will be paid on **ONE** of the following bases:

(A) Calculated and paid each year at 1.5% of any profit in excess of £250 000 for the year.

(B) Calculated and paid each year at 5% of annual salary for each £100 000 of residual income in excess of £250 000.

(C) Calculated and paid at 15% of annual salary in each year in which a positive ROI (%) is reported.

(D) Calculated and paid at the end of year 4 as 2.5% of the NPV of the programme.

Required:

(b) Prepare a table showing the bonus to be paid in each of years 1 to 4 and in total for each of methods (A) to (D) above, where the MOST LIKELY outcome situation applies.

(9 marks)

(c) Discuss which of the bonus methods is likely to be favoured by the programme manager at Tannadens Division. You should refer to your calculations in (b) above as appropriate. You should also consider the total bonus figures for the best outcome and worst outcome situations which are as follows:

	Total bonus	
	Best outcome	Worst outcome
	£	£
Net profit basis	43 890	16 368
Residual income basis	48 150	14 624
ROI basis	24 000	18 000
NPV basis	60 323	5 370

(11 marks)

(d) 'The achievement of the quality improvement programme will be influenced by the programme manager's:
  (i)   level of effort
  (ii) attitude to risk, and
  (iii) personal expectations from the programme'.

  Discuss this statement.

(5 marks)
(Total 35 marks)
ACCA Paper 9 Information for Control and Decision Making

Computation and discussion of economic value added

Question 19.10

The managers of Toutplut Inc were surprised at a recent newspaper article which suggested that the company's performance in the last two years had been poor. The CEO commented that turnover had increased by nearly 17% and pre-tax profit by 25% between the last two financial years, and that the company compared well with others in the same industry.

$ million
Profit and loss account extracts for the year

	2000	2001
Turnover	326	380
Pre-tax accounting profit[1]	67	84
Taxation	23	29
Profit after tax	44	55
Dividends	15	18
Retained earnings	29	37

Balance sheet extracts for the year ending

	2000	2001
Fixed assets	120	156
Net current assets	130	160
	250	316
Financed by:		
Shareholders' funds	195	236
Medium- and long-term bank loans	55	80
	250	316

[1]After deduction of the economic depreciation of the company's fixed assets. This is also the depreciation used for tax purposes.

Other information:
  (i)   Toutplut had non-capitalized leases valued at $10 million in each year 1999–2001.
  (ii)   Balance Sheet capital employed at the end of 1999 was $223 million.
  (iii) The company's pre-tax cost of debt was estimated to be 9% in 2000, and 10% in 2001.
  (iv)   The company's cost of equity was estimated to be 15% in 2000 and 17% in 2001.
  (v)   The target capital structure is 60% equity, 40% debt.
  (vi)   The effective tax rate was 35% in both 2000 and 2001.
  (vii) Economic depreciation was $30 million in 2000 and $35 million in 2001.
  (viii) Other non-cash expenses were $10 million per year in both 2000 and 2001.
  (ix)   Interest expense was $4 million in 2000 and $6 million in 2001.

DIVISIONAL FINANCIAL PERFORMANCE MEASURES

Required:

(a) Estimate the Economic Valued Added (EVA) for Toutplut Inc for both 2000 and 2001. State clearly any assumptions that you make.

Comment upon the performance of the company.

(7 marks)

(b) Explain the relationship between economic value added and net present value.

(2 marks)

(c) Briefly discuss the advantages and disadvantages of EVA.

(6 marks)
(Total 15 marks)
ACCA Paper 3.7 Strategic Financial Management

Transfer pricing in divisionalised companies

Questions to Chapter 20

Advanced

Question 20.1

(a) Transfers between processes in a manufacturing company can be made at (i) cost or (ii) sales value at the point of transfer.

Discuss how each of the above methods might be compatible with the operation of a responsibility accounting system.

(8 marks)

(b) Shadow prices (net opportunity costs or dual prices) may be used in the setting of transfer prices between divisions in a group of companies, where the intermediate products being transferred are in short supply.

Explain why the transfer prices thus calculated are more likely to be favoured by the management of the divisions supplying the intermediate products rather than the management of the divisions receiving the intermediate products.

(9 marks)
(Total 17 marks)
ACCA Level 2 Management Accounting

Advanced

Question 20.2

SK plc is divided into five divisions that provide consultancy services to each other and to outside customers. The divisions are Computing and Information Technology, Human Resources, Legal, Engineering, and Finance.

It has been company policy for all budgets to be prepared centrally with each division being given Sales and Profit targets. However, the divisional managers feel that the targets are unrealistic, as they do not consider the individual circumstances of each division, or the effects on profitability of providing services to other divisions. The current basis of charging for these services is to use the actual marginal cost of the supplying division.

In response to the comments made by the divisional managers, SK plc has now asked the managers to prepare their own budgets for next year and to submit proposals for a new internal charging system.

Required:

(a) (i) State why organizations prepare budgets.

(3 marks)

(ii) Explain the arguments for and against the involvement of managers in the preparation of their budgets.

(7 marks)

(b) Discuss the implications for SK plc, and the consequences for the managers of the supplying and receiving divisions, of each of the following possible cost-based approaches to setting a transfer price:

(i) marginal cost;

(ii) total cost;

(iii) cost plus;

(iv) opportunity cost.

(10 marks)

(c) Discuss whether standard costs or actual costs should be used as the basis for cost-based transfer prices.

(5 marks)

(Total 25 marks)

CIMA Management Accounting – Performance Management

Question 20.3

Advanced: The effect of alternative transfer prices on the divisional performance measure

MCP plc specializes in providing marketing, data collection, data processing and consulting services. The company is divided into divisions that provide services to each other and also to external clients. The performance of the Divisional Managers is measured against profit targets that are set by central management.

During October, the Consulting division undertook a project for AX plc. The agreed fee was £15 500 and the costs excluding data processing were £2600. The data processing, which needed 200 hours of processing time, was carried out by the Data Processing (DP) division. An external agency could have been used to do the data processing, but the DP division had 200 chargeable skilled hours available in October.

The DP division provides data processing services to the other divisions and also to external customers. The budgeted costs of the DP division for the year ending 31 December 2002, which is divided into 12 equal monthly periods, are as follows:

	£
Variable costs:	
Skilled labour (6000 hours worked)	120 000
Semi-skilled labour	96 000
Other processing costs	60 000
Fixed costs	240 000

These costs are recovered on the basis of chargeable skilled labour hours (data processing hours) which are budgeted to be 90% of skilled labour hours worked. The DP division's external pricing policy is to add a 40% mark-up to its total budgeted cost per chargeable hour.

During October 2002, actual labour costs incurred by the DP division were 10% higher than expected, but other costs were 5% lower than expected.

Required:

(a) Calculate the total transfer value that would have been charged by the DP division to the Consulting division for the 200 hours on its AX plc project, using the following bases:

(i) actual variable cost;

(ii) standard variable cost + 40% mark-up;

(iii) market price.

(6 marks)

(b) Prepare statements to show how the alternative values calculated in answer to requirement (a) above would be reflected in the performance measurement of the DP division and the Consulting division.

(12 marks)

(c) Recommend, with supporting calculations, explanations and assumptions, the transfer value that should be used for the 200 hours of processing time in October. Your answer need not be one of those calculated in your answer to requirement (a) above.

(7 marks)
(Total 25 marks)
CIMA Management Accounting – Performance Management

Advanced: ABC implementation and evaluation of a cost-plus transfer pricing system

Question 20.4

M Ltd has two divisions, X and Y. Division X is a chip manufacturer and Division Y assembles mobile phones. Division X currently manufactures many different types of chip, one of which is used in the manufacture of the mobile phones. Division X has no external market for the chips that are used in the mobile phones and currently sets the transfer price on the basis of total cost plus 20% mark-up.

The budgeted profit and loss statement for Division Y for next year shows the following results:

Mobile phone range	P £000	Q £000	R £000
Sales	10 000	9 500	11 750
Less: Total costs	7 200	11 700	9 250
Profit/(loss)	2 800	(2 200)	2 500
Fixed costs	2 000	5 400	5 875

The total costs shown above include the cost of the chips.

Division Y uses a traditional absorption costing system based on labour hours.

M Ltd operates a performance measurement system based on divisional profits. In order to increase profit for the forthcoming year, Division Y has asked permission to buy chips from an external supplier.

The accountant of M Ltd has recently attended a course on activity based costing (ABC) and has recommended that the divisions should implement an ABC system rather than continue to operate the traditional absorption costing system.

Required:

(a) A presenter at the conference stated that 'ABC provides information that is more relevant for decision making than traditional forms of costing'. Discuss this statement, using Division Y when appropriate to explain the issues you raise.

(8 marks)

(b) The management team of M Ltd has decided to implement ABC in all of the divisions. Discuss any difficulties which might be experienced when implementing ABC in the divisions.

(6 marks)

(c) (i) Discuss the current transfer pricing system and explain alternative systems that might be more appropriate for the forthcoming year.

(7 marks)

   (ii) Explain the impact that the introduction of an ABC system could have on the transfer price and on divisional profits.

(4 marks)
(Total 25 marks)
CIMA Management Accounting – Decision Making

Question 20.5

Advanced: Impact of transfer price on bonus payments and recommendation of transfer price to maximize group profits

CTD Ltd has two divisions – FD and TM. FD is an iron foundry division which produces mouldings that have a limited external market and are also transferred to TM division. TM division uses the mouldings to produce a piece of agricultural equipment called the 'TX' which is sold externally. Each TX requires one moulding. Both divisions produce only one type of product.

The performance of each Divisional Manager is evaluated individually on the basis of the residual income (RI) of his or her division. The company's average annual 12% cost of capital is used to calculate the finance charges. If their own target residual income is achieved, each Divisional Manager is awarded a bonus equal to 5% of his or her residual income. All bonuses are paid out of Head Office profits.

The following budgeted information is available for the forthcoming year:

	TM division TX per unit £	FD division Moulding per unit £
External selling price	500	80
Variable production cost	366*	40
Fixed production overheads	60	20
Gross profit	74	20
Variable selling and distribution cost	25	4**
Fixed administration overhead	25	4
Net profit	24	12
Normal capacity (units)	15 000	20 000
Maximum production capacity (units)	15 000	25 000
Sales to external customers (units)	15 000	5 000
Capital employed	£1 500 000	£750 000
Target RI	£105 000	£85 000

*The variable production cost of TX includes the cost of an FD moulding.
**External sales only of the mouldings incur a variable selling and distribution cost of £4 per unit.

FD division currently transfers 15 000 mouldings to TM division at a transfer price equal to the total production cost plus 10%.

Fixed costs are absorbed on the basis of normal capacity.

Required:

(a) Calculate the bonus each Divisional Manager would receive under the current transfer pricing policy and discuss any implications that the current performance evaluation system may have for each division and for the company as a whole.

(7 marks)

(b) Both Divisional Managers want to achieve their respective residual income targets. Based on the budgeted figures, calculate
  (i) the maximum transfer price per unit that the Divisional Manager of TM division would pay.
  (ii) the minimum transfer price per unit that the Divisional Manager of FD division would accept.

(6 marks)

(c) Write a report to the management of CTD Ltd that explains, and recommends, the transfer prices which FD division should set in order to maximize group profits. Your report should also
  • consider the implications of actual external customer demand exceeding 5000 units; and

- explain how alternative transfer pricing systems could overcome any possible conflict that may arise as a result of your recommended transfer prices.

Note: your answer must be related to CTD Ltd. You will not earn marks by just describing various methods for setting transfer prices.

(12 marks)
(Total 25 marks)
CIMA Management Accounting – Decision Making

Advanced: Make or buy decision and intercompany trading

Question 20.6

Companies RP, RR, RS and RT are members of a group. RP wishes to buy an electronic control system for its factory and, in accordance with group policy, must obtain quotations from companies inside and outside of the group.

From outside of the group the following quotations are received:

Company A quoted £33 200.
Company B quoted £35 000 but would buy a special unit from RS for £13 000. To make this unit, however, RS would need to buy parts from RR at a price of £7500.

The inside quotation was from RS whose price was £48 000. This would require RS buying parts from RR at a price of £8000 and units from RT at a price of £30 000. However, RT would need to buy parts from RR at a price of £11 000.

Additional data are as follows:

(1) RR is extremely busy with work outside the group and has quoted current market prices for all its products.

(2) RS costs for the RP contract, including purchases from RR and RT, total £42 000. For the Company B contract it expects a profit of 25% on the cost of its own work.

(3) RT prices provide for a 20% profit margin on total costs.

(4) The variable costs of the group companies in respect of the work under consideration are:

RR: 20% of selling price

RS: 70% of own cost (excluding purchases from other group companies)

RT: 65% of own cost (excluding purchases from other group companies)

You are required, from a group point of view, to:

(a) recommend, with appropriate calculations, whether the contract should be placed with RS or Company A or Company B;

(b) state briefly *two* assumptions you have made in arriving at your recommendations.

(30 marks)
CIMA P3 Management Accounting

Advanced: Return on investment, residual income and transfer pricing

Question 20.7

The NAW Group manufactures healthcare products which it markets both under its own brand and in unbranded packs. The group has adopted a divisional structure. Division O, which is based in a country called Homeland, manufactures three pharmaceutical products for sale in the domestic market. Budgeted information in respect of Division O for the year ending 31 May 2005 is as follows:

Sales information:

Product		'Painfree'	'Digestisalve'	'Awaysafe'
Sales packs (000's)	NAW Brand	5 000	5 000	15 000
	Unbranded	15 000	20 000	—
Selling price per pack (£)	NAW Brand	2.40	4.80	8.00
	Unbranded	1.20	3.60	—

Cost of sales information:

Variable manufacturing costs per pack:	Material and conversion costs	Packaging costs
	£	£
'Painfree'		
NAW Brand	0.85	0.15
Unbranded	0.85	0.05
'Digestisalve'		
NAW Brand	1.85	0.25
Unbranded	1.85	0.15
'Awaysafe'		
NAW Brand	2.80	0.40

Other relevant information is as follows:

(1) Each of the three products is only sold in tablet form in a single pack-size which contains 12 tablets. During the year to 31 May 2005 it is estimated that a maximum of 780 million tablets could be manufactured. All three products are manufactured by the same process therefore management have the flexibility to alter the product mix. Management expect that sales volume will increase by 10% in the year ending 31 May 2006.

(2) Advertising expenditure has been committed to under a fixed term contract with a leading consultancy and is therefore regarded as a fixed cost by management. Advertising expenditure in respect of the turnover of branded products in the year ending 31 May 2005 is apportioned as follows:

Product:	Advertising expenditure as a % of turnover
Painfree	5
Digestisalve	10
Awaysafe	12

(3) The average capital employed in the year to 31 May 2005 is estimated to be £120 million. The company's cost of capital is 10%.

(4) The management of the NAW Group use both Return on Investment (ROI) and Residual Income (RI) to assess divisional performance.

(5) Budgeted fixed overheads (excluding advertising) for Division O during the year ended 31 May 2005 amount to £81 558 000.

(6) There is no planned change in manufacturing capacity between the years ended 31 May 2005 and 31 May 2006.

(7) Ignore taxation for all calculations other than those in part (c).

Required:

(a) (i) Prepare a statement of budgeted profit in respect of Division O for the year ending 31 May 2005.

Your answer should show the annual budgeted contribution of each branded and unbranded product. Calculate BOTH the residual income (RI) and Return of Investment (ROI) for Division O.

(7 marks)

(ii) Name and comment on THREE factors, other than profit maximization, that the management of the NAW Group ought to consider when deciding upon the product mix strategy for the year ending 31 May 2006.

(3 marks)

(iii) Suggest THREE reasons why the management of the NAW Group may have chosen to use Residual Income (RI) in addition to Return on Investment (ROI) in order to assess divisional performance.

(3 marks)

Division L of the NAW Group is based in Farland. The management of Division L purchases products from various sources, including other divisions of the group, for subsequent resale. The manager of Division L has requested two alternative quotations from Division O in respect of the year ended 31 May 2005:

1. Quotation 1 – Purchasing five million packs of 'Awaysafe'.

2. Quotation 2 – Purchasing nine million packs of 'Awaysafe'.

The management of the NAW Group has made a decision that a minimum of 15 million packs of 'Awaysafe' must be reserved for Homeland customers in order to ensure that customer demand can be satisfied and the product's competitive position is further established in the Homeland market.

The management of the NAW Group is willing, if necessary, to reduce the budgeted sales quantities of other products in order to satisfy the requirements of Division L.They wish, however, to minimize the loss of contribution to the group.

The management of Division L is aware of the availability of another product that competes with 'Awaysafe' which could be purchased at a local currency price that is equivalent to £5.50 per pack. The NAW Group's policy is that all divisions are allowed the autonomy to set transfer prices and purchase from whatever sources they choose. The management of Division O intend to use market price less 30% as the basis for each of the quotations.

(b) (i) From the viewpoint of the NAW Group, comment on the appropriateness of the decision by the management of Division O to use an adjusted market price as a basis for the preparation of Quotations 1 and 2, and the implications of the likely decision by the management of Division L.

(3 marks)

(ii) Recommend the prices that should be quoted by Division O for 'Awaysafe', in respect of Quotations 1 and 2, which will ensure that the profitability of the NAW Group as a whole is not adversely affected by the decision of the management of Division L. (3 marks)

(iii) Discuss the proposition that transfer prices should be based on opportunity costs.

(4 marks)

(c) (i) After much internal discussion concerning Quotation 2 by the management of the NAW Group, Division O is not prepared to supply nine million packs of 'Awaysafe' to Division L at a price lower than market price less 30%. All profits earned in Farland are subject to taxation at a rate of 20%. Division O pays tax in Homeland at a rate of 40% on all profits.
Advise the management of the NAW Group whether the management of Division L should be directed to purchase 'Awaysafe' from Division O, or purchase a similar product from a local supplier. Supporting calculations should be provided.

(6 marks)

(ii) Identify and comment on the major issues that can arise with regard to transfer pricing in a multinational organisation.

(5 marks)

(d) Evaluate the extent to which the management of the NAW Group could make use of the product life cycle model in the determination of its product pricing strategy.

(6 marks)
(40 marks)
ACCA Paper 3.3 Performance Management

Question 20.8

Advanced: Determining optimal transfer prices to influence optimal sourcing decisions

Business Solutions is a firm of management consultants which experienced considerable business growth during the last decade. By 2000 the firm's senior managers were beginning to experience difficulties in managing the business. During 2001 the firm was reorganized and a regional divisional structure was introduced with individual profit targets being set for each of the semi-autonomous profit centres. Although North division has its own customer base that is distinct from that of its sister division South, it does occasionally call upon the services of a South consultant to assist with its projects. North has to pay a cross charge to South per consulting day. The amount of the charge is determined by HQ. North is free to choose whether it employs a South consultant or subcontracts the project to an external consultant. The manager of North division believes that the quality of the external consultant and the one from South division are identical and on this basis will always employ the one who is prepared to work for the lower fee.

The following information is also available:

- North division is very busy and it charges its clients £1200 per consulting day
- North division pays its external consultant £500 per consulting day
- The variable cost per internal consulting day is £100

Required:

(a) Determine a possible optimal daily cross charge that should be paid by North for the services of a consultant from South in the scenarios outlined below. The charges that you select must induce both divisional managers to arrive at the same decision independently. Explain how you have determined your cross charges and state any assumptions that you think necessary.

Scenario (i)
- South division has spare consulting capacity.

Scenario (ii)
- South division is fully occupied earning fees of £400 per consulting day.

Scenario (iii)
- South division is fully occupied earning fees of £700 per consulting day.

(10 marks)

(b) Identify the possible factors that may have prompted the senior management to introduce a divisional structure in 2001 and suggest some potential problems that may arise.

(10 marks)
(Total 20 marks)
ACCA Paper 3.3 – Performance Management

TRANSFER PRICING IN DIVISIONALISED COMPANIES

Advanced: Scarce capacity and the use of shadow prices

Black and Brown are two divisions in a group of companies and both require intermediate products Alpha and Beta which are available from divisions A and B respectively. Black and Brown divisions convert the intermediate products into products Blackalls and Brownalls respectively. The market demand for Blackalls and Brownalls considerably exceeds the production possible, because of the limited availability of intermediate products Alpha and Beta.

No external market exists for Alpha and Beta and no other intermediate product market is available to Black and Brown divisions.

Other data are as follows:

Black division
Blackalls: Selling price per unit £45
                        Processing cost per unit £12
                        Intermediate products required per unit:
                        Alpha: 3 units
                        Beta: 2 units

Brown division
Brownalls: Selling price per unit £54
                        Processing cost per unit £14
                        Intermediate products required per unit:
                        Alpha: 2 units
                        Beta: 4 units

A division
Alpha: Variable cost per unit £6
                        Maximum production capacity 1200 units

B division
Beta: Variable cost per unit £4
                        Maximum production capacity 1600 units

The solution to a linear programming model of the situation shows that the imputed scarcity value (shadow price) of Alpha and Beta is £0.50 and £2.75 per unit respectively and indicates that the intermediate products be transferred such that 200 units of Blackalls and 300 units of Brownalls are produced and sold.

Required:

(a) Calculate the contribution earned by the group if the sales pattern indicated by the linear programming model is implemented.

(*3 marks*)

(b) Where the transfer prices are set on the basis of variable cost plus shadow price, show detailed calculations for
   (i) the contribution per unit of intermediate product earned by divisions A and B and
   (ii) the contribution per unit of final product earned by Black and Brown divisions.

(*4 marks*)

(c) Comment on the results derived in (b) and on the possible attitude of management of the various divisions to the proposed transfer pricing and product deployment policy.

(*6 marks*)

(d) In the following year the capacities of divisions A and B have each doubled and the following changes have taken place:

1. *Alpha*: There is still no external market for this product, but A division has a large demand for other products which could use the capacity and earn a contribution of 5% over cost. Variable cost per unit for the other products would be the same as for Alpha and such products would use the capacity at the same rate as Alpha.

2. *Beta*: An intermediate market for this product now exists and Beta can be bought and sold in unlimited amounts at £7.50 per unit. External sales of Beta would incur additional transport costs of £0.50 per unit which are not incurred in inter-divisional transfers.

The market demand for Blackalls and Brownalls will still exceed the production availability of Alpha and Beta.

(i) Calculate the transfer prices at which Alpha and Beta should now be offered to Black and Brown divisions in order that the transfer policy implemented will lead to the maximization of group profit.

(ii) Determine the production and sales pattern for Alpha, Beta, Blackalls and Brownalls which will now maximize group contribution and calculate the group contribution thus achieved. It may be assumed that divisions will make decisions consistent with the financial data available.

(9 marks)
(Total 22 marks)
ACCA Level 2 Management Accounting

Cost management

Questions to Chapter 21

Advanced

Explain your answers to (a) and (b) with figures/calculations where appropriate.

(a) Many manufacturing companies in different countries throughout the world have sought to influence managers' behaviour by the method(s) they employ to charge overheads to products.

Required:

Discuss how overhead systems may be used to:

(i) direct or manipulate decisions made by departmental managers;

(ii) influence product design decisions that affect costs occurring during the product's life cycle.

(15 marks)

(b) Certain types of costing system encourage operational managers to produce in excess of both budget and demand.

Required:

Discuss the statement made above. Your answer should cover the following areas:

● the types of costing system that encourage this behaviour;

● how these costing systems encourage over-production;

● what can be done to overcome the problem of over-production created by a costing system.

(10 marks)
(Total 25 marks)
CIMA Management Accounting – Decision Making

Advanced

A traditional view of the environment in which goods are manufactured and sold is where stocks of materials and components are held. Such stocks are then used to manufacture products to agreed standard specifications, aiming at maximizing the use of production capacity. Finished goods are held in stock to satisfy steady demand for the product range at agreed prices.

Required:

(a) Discuss aspects of the operation of the management accounting function which are likely to apply in the above system.

(5 marks)

(b) Describe an alternative sequence from purchasing to the satisfaction of customer demand, which may be more applicable in the current business environment. Your answer should refer to the current 'techniques or philosophies' which are likely to be in use.

(5 marks)

(c) Name specific ways in which changes suggested in (b) will affect the operation of the management accounting function.

(5 marks)
(Total 15 marks)
ACCA Paper 9 Information for Control and Decision Making

Question 21.3

Advanced

Traditional cost control systems focused on cost containment rather than cost reduction. Today, cost management focuses on process improvement and the identification of how processes can be more effectively and efficiently performed to result in cost reductions.

Required:

Discuss how *each* of the following cost management techniques differs from the traditional cost containment approach and how each seeks to achieve cost reduction:

- Just-in-time;
- Target costing;
- Life cycle costing;
- Activity based management.

(25 marks)
CIMA Management Accounting – Decision Making

Question 21.4

Advanced

Within a diversified group, one division, which operates many similar branches in a service industry, has used internal benchmarking and regards it as very useful.

Group central management is now considering the wider use of benchmarking.

Requirement:

(a) Explain the aims, operation, and limitations of internal benchmarking, and explain how external benchmarking differs in these respects.

(10 marks)

(b) A multinational group wishes to internally benchmark the production of identical components made in several plants in different countries. Investments have been made with some plants in installing new Advanced Manufacturing Technology (AMT) and supporting this with manufacturing management systems such as just-in-time (JIT) and Total Quality Management (TQM). Preliminary comparisons suggest that the standard cost in plants using new technology is no lower than that in plants using older technology.

Requirement:

Explain possible reasons for the similar standard costs in plants with differing technology. Recommend appropriate benchmarking measures, recognizing that total standard costs may not provide the most useful measurement of performance.

(10 marks)
(Total 20 marks)
CIMA Stage 4 Management Accounting – Control Systems

Question 21.5

Advanced

SG plc is a long-established food manufacturer which produces semi-processed foods for fast food outlets. While for a number of years it has recognized the need to produce good quality products for its customers, it does not have a formalized quality management programme.

A director of the company has recently returned from a conference, where one of the speakers introduced the concept of Total Quality Management (TQM) and the need to recognize and classify quality costs.

Required:

(a) Explain what is meant by TQM and use examples to show how it may be introduced into different areas of SG plc's food production business.

(12 marks)

(b) Explain why the adoption of TQM is particularly important within a just-in-time (JIT) production environment.

(5 marks)

(c) Explain four quality cost classifications, using examples relevant to the business of SG plc.

(8 marks)
(Total 25 marks)
CIMA Management Accounting – Performance Management

Advanced

Question 21.6

PG plc manufactures gifts and souvenirs for both the tourist and commercial promotions markets. Many of the items are similar except that they are overprinted with different slogans, logos, and colours for the different customers and markets. For many years, it has been PG plc's policy to produce the basic items in bulk and then overprint them as required, but this policy has now been questioned by the company's new Finance Director.

She has also questioned the current policy of purchasing raw materials in bulk from suppliers whenever the periodic stock review system indicates that the re-order level has been reached.

She has said that it is most important in this modern environment to be as efficient as possible, and that bulk purchasing and production strategies are not necessarily the most efficient strategies to be adopted. She has suggested that the company must carefully consider its approaches to production, and the associated costs.

Required:

(a) Compare and contrast the current strategies of PG plc for raw materials purchasing and production with those that would be associated with a just-in-time (JIT) philosophy.

(15 marks)

(b) Explain what is meant by cost reduction.

(3 marks)

(c) Explain how PG plc might introduce a cost reduction programme without affecting its customers' perceptions of product values.

(7 marks)
(Total 25 marks)
CIMA Management Accounting – Performance Management

Advanced

Question 21.7

Standard costing and target costing have little in common for the following reasons:

- the former is a costing system and the latter is not;
- target costing is proactive and standard costing is not;
- target costs are agreed by all and are rigorously adhered to whereas standard costs are usually set without wide consultation.

Required:

(a) Discuss the comparability of standard costing and target costing by considering the validity of the statements above.

(18 marks)

A pharmaceutical company, which operates a standard costing system, is considering introducing target costing.

Required:

(b) Discuss whether the company should do this and whether the two systems would be compatible.

(7 marks)
(Total 25 marks)
CIMA Management Accounting – Decision Making

Question 21.8

Advanced: Construction of life cycle curves, investment appraisal and sensitivity analysis

(a) Scovet plc uses its production capacity in dedicated product line format to satisfy demand for a rolling range of products. Such products have limited life cycles. A turnover value of £20m is taken as a measure of the annual production capacity of the company. The turnover figures (actual and forecast) are shown below for each of products A, B and C from the beginning of the life cycle of each product up to 2004. These are the only products for which Scovet plc has sales (actual or forecast) for the years 2001 to 2004.

Scovet plc
Sales Turnover (£ million) – actual or forecast

Product	1996	1997	1998	1999	2000	2001	2002	2003	2004
	A	A	A	A	A	F	F	F	F
A	2.0	4.0	6.0	7.0	4.5	3.0	2.0	1.5	nil
B	nil	nil	3.0	6.0	8.0	9.0	3.0	1.0	nil
C	nil	nil	nil	4.0	5.0	6.5	7.5	8.0	7.0

Note A = actual; F = forecast

Other relevant information (forecast) relating to the products for the years 2001 and 2002 is as follows:

1 Contribution to Sales ratios (%): product A (70%); product B (75%); product C (60%).

2 Product specific fixed costs:

	2001 £m	2002 £m
Product A	2.0	1.1
Product B	4.0	1.8
Product C	2.8	3.0

3 Company fixed costs for year; £2.5m.

Required:

(i) Using the graph paper provided, show the life cycle pattern for EACH of products A, B and C expressed in terms of turnover (£m).

(4 marks)

(ii) Comment on the shape of the life cycle curves in the graphs prepared in (i).

(5 marks)

(iii) Prepare a profit/loss analysis for each of years 2001 and 2002 which shows the analysis by product including product turnover, contribution and profit and also company net profit or loss.

(4 marks)

(iv) Comment briefly on the figures in the analysis which you prepared in (iii) above.

(4 marks)

(b) Scovet plc has identified a market for a new product D for which the following estimated information is available:

1   Sales turnover for the years 2002, 2003 and 2004 of £6m, £7m and £6m respectively. No further sales are expected after 2004.

2   Contribution to sales percentage of 60% for each year.

3   Product specific fixed costs in the years 2002, 2003 and 2004 of £2.5m, £2.2m and £1.8m respectively.

4   Capital investment of £4.5m on 1 January 2002 with nil residual value at 31 December 2004. The cost of capital from 1 January 2002 is expected to be 10% per annum.

Assume all cash flows (other than the initial investment) take place on 31 December of each year. Ignore taxation.

Required:

(i)   Determine whether the new product is viable on financial grounds.

(4 marks)

(ii) Calculate the minimum target contribution to sales ratio (%) at which product D will be viable in financial terms where all other factors remain unchanged.

(3 marks)

(iii) Suggest actions which should allow the investigation of variable cost in order that the target contribution to sales ratio (%) calculated in (ii) may be achieved.

(3 marks)

(c) Suggest alternative strategies which may be formulated by Scovet plc in order to improve the overall financial position in the period 2002 to 2004 inclusive where only products A, B, C and D are available for incorporation in the calculations. Comment on the extent of the need for such strategies and include an explanation of any cost/benefit information which would be required.

(8 marks)

(Total 35 marks)

ACCA Paper 9 Information of Control and Decision Making

Advanced: Calculation of costs before and after introduction of a quality management programme

Question 21.9

Calton Ltd make and sell a single product. The existing product unit specifications are as follows:

Direct material X:	8 sq. metres at £4 per sq. metre
Machine time:	0.6 running hours
Machine cost per gross hour:	£40
Selling price:	£100

Calton Ltd require to fulfil orders for 5000 product units per period.
There are no stocks of product units at the beginning or end of the period under review. The stock level of material X remains unchanged throughout the period.

The following additional information affects the costs and revenues:

1. 5% of incoming material from suppliers is scrapped due to poor receipt and storage organization.

2. 4% of material X input to the machine process is wasted due to processing problems.

3. Inspection and storage of material X costs £0.10 pence per sq. metre purchased.

4. Inspection during the production cycle, calibration checks on inspection equipment, vendor rating and other checks cost £25 000 per period.

5. Production quantity is increased to allow for the downgrading of 12.5% of product units at the final inspection stage. Downgraded units are sold as 'second quality' units at a discount of 30% on the standard selling price.

6. Production quantity is increased to allow for returns from customers which are replaced free of charge. Returns are due to specification failure and account for 5% of units initially delivered to customers. Replacement units incur a delivery cost of £8 per unit. 80% of the returns from customers are rectified using 0.2 hours of machine running time per unit and are re-sold as 'third quality' products at a discount of 50% on the standard selling price. The remaining returned units are sold as scrap for £5 per unit.

7. Product liability and other claims by customers is estimated at 3% of sales revenue from standard product sales.

8. Machine idle time is 20% of gross machine hours used (i.e. running hours = 80% of gross hours).

9. Sundry costs of administration, selling and distribution total £60 000 per period.

10. Calton Ltd is aware of the problem of excess costs and currently spends £20 000 per period in efforts to prevent a number of such problems from occurring.

Calton Ltd is planning a quality management programme which will increase its excess cost prevention expenditure from £20 000 to £60 000 per period. It is estimated that this will have the following impact:

1. A reduction in stores losses of material X to 3% of incoming material.

2. A reduction in the downgrading of product units at inspection to 7.5% of units inspected.

3. A reduction in material X losses in process to 2.5% of input to the machine process.

4. A reduction in returns of products from customers to 2.5% of units delivered.

5. A reduction in machine idle time to 12.5% of gross hours used.

6. A reduction in product liability and other claims to 1% of sales revenue from standard product sales.

7. A reduction in inspection, calibration, vendor rating and other checks by 40% of the existing figure.

8. A reduction in sundry administration, selling and distribution costs by 10% of the existing figure.

9. A reduction in machine running time required per product unit to 0.5 hours.

Required:

(a) Prepare summaries showing the calculation of (i) total production units (pre-inspection), (ii) purchases of material X (sq. metres), (iii) gross machine hours. In each case the figures are required for the situation both before and after the implementation of the additional quality management programme, in order that the orders for 5000 product units may be fulfilled.

(10 marks)

(b) Prepare profit and loss accounts for Calton Ltd for the period showing the profit earned both before and after the implementation of the additional quality management programme.

(10 marks)

(c) Comment on the relevance of a quality management programme and explain the meaning of the terms internal failure costs, external failure costs, appraisal costs and prevention costs giving examples for each, taken where possible from the information in the question.

(10 marks)
(Total 30 marks)
ACCA Level 2 Cost and Management Accounting II

Stragegic management accounting

Questions to Chapter 22

Advanced   **Question 22.1**

Required:

(a) Identify and discuss the circumstances that have brought about the proposition that traditional management accounting control systems have lost their 'relevance' to today's manufacturing and organizational environment. *(5 marks)*

(b) Evaluate strategic cost management initiatives which may be used in order to restore the 'relevance' of management accounting control systems in today's manufacturing and organizational environment.

(15 marks)
ACCA Paper 3.3 Performance Management

Advanced   **Question 22.2**

The introduction of improved quality into products has been a strategy applied by many organizations to obtain competitive advantage. Some organizations believe it is necessary to improve levels of product quality if competitive advantage is to be preserved or strengthened.

Requirement:

Discuss how a management accountant can assist an organization to achieve competitive advantage by measuring the increase in added value from improvement in its product quality.

(20 marks)
CIMA Stage 4 Strategic Management Accounting and Marketing

Advanced   **Question 22.3**

Thomas Sheridan, writing in *Management Accounting*, pointed out that Japanese companies have a different approach to cost information with 'the emphasis – based on physical measures', and 'the use of non-financial indices, particularly at shop floor level'. He argues that their approach is much more relevant to modern conditions than traditional cost and management accounting practices.

You are required

(a) to explain what is meant by 'physical measures' and 'non-financial indices';

(3 marks)

(b) to give *three* examples of non-financial indices that might be prepared, with a brief note of what information each index would provide.

(5 marks)

(c) What existing cost and management accounting practices do you consider inappropriate in modern conditions?

(9 marks)
(Total 17 marks)
CIMA Stage 3 Management Accounting Techniques

Question 22.4 Advanced

Discuss the advantages which may be claimed for Kaplan and Norton's balanced scorecard as a basis for performance measurement over traditional management accounting views of performance measurement. Your answer should include specific examples of quantitative measures for each aspect of the balanced scorecard.

(15 marks)

Question 22.5 Advanced

'Product costing and pricing strategies will interact in helping to achieve competitive advantage leading to retention or increase of market share and maintenance or improvement of profit levels.'

(a) Discuss this statement in the context of:
   (i) Cost leadership;
   (ii) Product differentiation.

(7 marks)

(b) Discuss the role of the following in the context of the above statement:
   (i) Penetration pricing;
   (ii) An activity based approach to pricing.

(8 marks)
(Total 15 marks)

Question 22.6 Advanced: Financial and non-financial performance measures

Compuaid Ltd provides advisory services to home computer customers. Three types of advisor are employed offering advice by telephone, written/e-mail replies and home visits respectively.

Appendix 1.1 shows sundry statistics for the past 12 month period for Compuaid Ltd and also for two competitor companies A and B.

Additional information relating to Compuaid Ltd for the past 12 month period is as follows:

(i) Home visit travel and remedial work hours are not charged directly to customers.

(ii) All service workers incur some 'idle time' which is not charged directly to customers.

(iii) A number of customers pay a fixed annual fee of £100 for the advisory service. This entitles them to 24 hour priority access to the service and a maximum of five hours of advice without further charge.

Appendix 1.1 shows the total hours of advice (both budget and actual) taken up by customers. Assume that no customer requires more than the five hours allowable.

(iv) All other time for the advisory service and home visits is billed to customers at £20 per hour.

(v) The budgeted wage rate per hour for advisory service staff is £8. This was also the actual rate paid.

(vi) Sundry operating expenses (other than advisor wages) were budgeted at £950 000. Actual operating expenses incurred were £1 000 000.

Actual information for the period under review for competitor companies A and B is as follows:

(i) Similar policies to those used by Compuaid Ltd are operated with regard to idle time, home visit travel and remedial hours.

(ii) Fixed annual fee advisory service schemes, similar to that of Compuaid Ltd, are operated. The annual fee charged per customer by company A and company B is £75 and £100 respectively.

(iii) Other revenue and cost information is as follows:

	Company A £	Company B £
Total revenue (excluding annual fee income):		
Enquiry advice	756 180	1 266 000
Home visits	87 500	810 000
Total wage costs	720 000	1 099 000
Sundry operating expenses	650 000	1 250 000

Required:

(a) (i) Prepare budgeted and actual profit and loss accounts for the 12 month period under review for Compuaid Ltd and also actual profit and loss accounts for companies A and B.

(8 marks)

(ii) Discuss the financial performance of Compuaid Ltd, incorporating details of relative customer billing rates, company service wage rates and annual agreement advice 'level of uptake' in your answer.

(12 marks)

(b) Comment on the performance of Compuaid Ltd, incorporating relevant percentage and ratio statistics in the context of each of the following:
(i) Competitiveness;
(ii) Quality;
(iii) Resource utilization.

(15 marks)
(Total 35 marks)

Appendix 1.1
Sundry Statistics for the previous 12 month period

	Compuaid Budget	Compuaid Actual	Competitor A Actual	B Actual
Number of service employees:				
Telephone advisor	22	27	25	44
Written/e-mail advisors	15	17	8	10
Home visit staff	12	14	2	21
Service employee hours analysis:				
Home visit travel hours	2 500	4 800	390	4 500
Idle time – home visit staff	2 000	2 600	2 800	6 000
– advisors	4 000	4 800	1 000	7 000
Remedial work for home visits	500	2 000	600	5 200
'Annual agreement' advisor				
call uptake	14 600	15 300	29 700	35 000
Advisor time billed to customers	58 400	72 100	42 010	63 300
Home visits billed to customers	22 000	23 200	3 500	36 000
Total hours	104 000	124 800	80 000	157 000
Number of home visit enquiries				
received	15 000	16 000	2 000	24 000
Number of home visits obtained/				
completed	10 000	8 000	1 400	15 000
Number of home visits requiring				
remedial work	300	1 200	400	3 400
Number of customer complaints –				
home visits	100	160	70	225

Number of customer complaints – advisors	73	131	35	196
Number of annual agreement customers	5 840	7 650	6 600	10 000

ACCA Paper 9 Information for Control and Decision Making

Question 22.7

Advanced: Performance measurement focusing on financial and non-financial measures

Ochilpark plc has identified and defined a market in which it wishes to operate. This will provide a 'millennium' focus for an existing product range. Ochilpark plc has identified a number of key competitors and intends to focus on close co-operation with its customers in providing products to meet their specific design and quality requirements. Efforts will be made to improve the effectiveness of all aspects of the cycle from product design to after sales service to customers. This will require inputs from a number of departments in the achievement of the specific goals of the 'millennium' product range. Efforts will be made to improve productivity in conjunction with increased flexibility of methods.

An analysis of financial and non-financial data relating to the 'millennium' proposal is shown in Schedule 3.1.

Required:

(a) (i) Prepare a table (£m) of the total costs for the 'millennium' proposal for each of years 2000, 2001 and 2002 (as shown in Schedule 3.1), detailing target costs, internal and external failure costs, appraisal costs and prevention costs. The following information should be used in the preparation of the analysis:

	2000	2001	2002
Target costs – variable (as % of sales)	40%	40%	40%
– fixed (total)	£2m	£2m	£2.5m
Internal failure costs (% of total target cost)	20%	10%	5%
External failure costs (% of total target cost)	25%	12%	5%
Appraisal costs	£0.5m	£0.5m	£0.5m
Prevention costs	£2m	£1m	£0.5m

(4 marks)

(ii) Explain the meaning of each of the cost classifications in (i) above and comment on their trend and inter-relationship. You should provide examples of each classification.

(8 marks)

(b) Prepare an analysis (both discursive and quantitative) of the 'millennium' proposal for the period 2000 to 2002. The analysis should use the information provided in the question, together with the data in Schedule 3.1. The analysis should contain the following:

(i) A definition of corporate 'vision or mission' and consideration of how the millennium proposal may be seen as identifying and illustrating a specific sub-set of this 'vision or mission'.

(5 marks)

(ii) Discussion and quantification of the proposal in both marketing and financial terms.

(6 marks)

(iii) Discussion of the external effectiveness of the proposal in the context of ways in which 1. *Quality* and 2. *Delivery* are expected to affect customer satisfaction and hence the marketing of the product.

(4 marks)

(iv) Discussion of the internal efficiency of the proposal in the context of ways in which the management of 1. *Cycle Time* and 2. *Waste* are expected to affect productivity and hence the financial aspects of the proposal.

(4 marks)

(v) Discussion of the links between internal and external aspects of the expected trends in performance.

(4 marks)
(Total 35 marks)
ACCA Paper 9 Information for Control and Decision Making

Schedule 3.1
'Millennium' proposal – estimated statistics

	2000	2001	2002
Total market size (£m)	120	125	130
Ochilpark plc sales (£m)	15	18	20
Ochilpark plc – total costs (£m)	14.1	12.72	12.55
Ochilpark plc sundry statistics:			
Production achieving design quality standards (%)	95%	97%	98%
Returns from customers as unsuitable (% of deliveries)	3.0%	1.5%	0.5%
Cost of after sales service (£m)	1.5	1.25	1.0
Sales meeting planned delivery dates (%)	90%	95%	99%
Average cycle time (customer enquiry to delivery) (weeks)	6	5.5	5
Components scrapped in production (%)	7.5%	5.0%	2.5%
Idle machine capacity (%)	10%	6%	2%

Cost estimation and cost behaviour

Questions to Chapter 23

Question 23.1

Intermediate: Linear regression analysis

A company is seeking to establish whether there is a linear relationship between the level of advertising expenditure and the subsequent sales revenue generated.

Figures for the last eight months are as follows:

Month	Advertising Expenditure	Sales Revenue
	£000	£000
1	2.65	30.0
2	4.25	45.0
3	1.00	17.5
4	5.25	46.0
5	4.75	44.5
6	1.95	25.0
7	3.50	43.0
8	3.00	38.5
Total	26.35	289.5

Further information is available as follows:

Σ(Advertising expenditure $\times$ Sales revenue) = £1055.875
Σ(Advertising expenditure)^2 = £101.2625
Σ(Sales revenue)^2 = £11 283.75

All of the above are given in £ million.

Required:

(a) On a suitable graph plot advertising expenditure against sales revenue or *vice versa* as appropriate. Explain your choice of axes.

(5 marks)

(b) Using regression analysis calculate, using formulae 23.1 and 23.2 in the text, a line of best fit. Plot this on your graph from (a).

(5 marks)
ACCA – Financial Information for Management

Question 23.2

Advanced: Linear regression analysis with price level adjustments

Savitt Ltd manufactures a variety of products at its industrial site in Ruratania. One of the products, the LT, is produced in a specially equipped factory in which no other production takes place. For technical reasons the company keeps no stocks of either LTs or the raw material used in their manufacture. The costs of producing LTs in the special factory during the past four years have been as follows:

	1998 (£)	1999 (£)	2000 (£)	(2001) (estimated) (£)
Raw materials	70 000	100 000	130 000	132 000
Skilled labour	40 000	71 000	96 000	115 000
Unskilled labour	132 000	173 000	235 000	230 000
Power	25 000	33 000	47 000	44 000
Factory overheads	168 000	206 000	246 000	265 000
Total production costs	£435 000	£583 000	£754 000	£786 000
Output (units)	160 000	190 000	220 000	180 000

The costs of raw materials and skilled and unskilled labour have increased steadily during the past four years at an annual compound rate of 20%, and the costs of factory overheads have increased at an annual compound rate of 15% during the same period. Power prices increased by 10% on 1 January 1999 and by 25% on the 1 January of each subsequent year. All costs except power are expected to increase by a further 20% during 2002. Power prices are due to rise by 25% on 1 January 2002.

The directors of Savitt Ltd are now formulating the company's production plan for 2002 and wish to estimate the costs of manufacturing the product LT. The finance director has expressed the view that 'the full relevant cost of producing LTs can be determined only if a fair share of general company overheads is allocated to them'. No such allocation is included in the table of costs above.

You are required to:

(a) use linear regression analysis to estimate the relationship of total production costs to volume for the product LT for 2002 (ignore general company overheads and do *not* undertake a separate regression calculation for each item of cost),

(*12 marks*)

(b) discuss the advantages and limitations of linear regression analysis for the estimation of cost–volume relationships,

(*8 marks*)

(c) comment on the view expressed by the finance director.

(*5 marks*)

Ignore taxation.

ICAEW Elements of Financial Decisions

Advanced: Learning curve

Question 23.3

You have been asked about the application of the learning curve as a management accounting technique.

You are required to:

(a) define the learning curve;

(b) explain the theory of learning curves;

(c) indicate the areas where learning curves may assist in management accounting;

(d) illustrate the use of learning curves for calculating the expected average unit cost of making:
   (i) 4 machines
   (ii) 8 machines

using the data given below.

Data:

Direct labour needed to make the first machine: 1000 hours
Learning curve: 80%
Direct labour cost: £3 per hour
Direct materials cost £1800 per machine
Fixed cost for either size order: £8000

(20 marks)
CIMA P3 Management Accounting

Question 23.4   **Advanced: Estimation of costs and incremental hours using the learning curve**

BL plc has developed a new product, the Webcam IV, to add to its existing range of computer peripherals. Each unit of the Webcam IV will be sold for £60 in a highly competitive market.

The initial estimated unit costs of a Webcam IV are as follows:

	£
Direct materials	28.00
Variable processing cost:	
18 minutes @ £25/hour	7.50
	35.50

There are also annual product specific fixed costs of £240 000. These are to be incurred at a constant rate throughout the year.

No units of the Webcam IV have yet been made.

BL plc plans to make and sell 1000 units each month during the year commencing 1 April 2002.

The following adjustments are to be made to the initial estimated costs when determining the standard cost of the product:

(i)   There is an expected material loss equal to 5% of the material used. This loss has no value and its cost is to be borne by the product.

(ii)   A 90% learning curve effect is expected to apply.

Note: The formula for a 90% learning curve is $y = ax^{-0.1520}$

Required:

(a)   Calculate the standard variable cost of production of the Webcam IV for April 2002.

(3 marks)

(b)   Calculate the standard variable cost of production for September (month 6) given that output in every month will be in accordance with the budgeted output of 1000 units per month and the 90% learning curve effect will continue to apply.

(6 marks)

The actual results for the month of April 2002 were as follows:

Sales	900 units @ £62 each unit
Production	1 000 units
Direct materials used cost	£31 870
Variable processing:	
2425 minutes costing	£1 070
Fixed costs incurred	£24 840

It has now been recognized that an 80% rate of learning should have been used for the original standard cost (instead of the 90% learning curve that was used).

Note: The formula for an 80% learning curve is $y = ax^{-0.320}$

Required:

(c) Prepare a statement for April 2002 using a contribution approach that reconciles the budgeted profit based on the original standard costs (based on the 90% learning curve) with the actual profit. Your statement should clearly identify the revised budgeted profit, the standard profit, and the planning and operating variances in as much detail as possible. Assume that stock is valued at revised standard cost.

(12 marks)

(d) Explain the importance of recognizing the effects of the learning curve when preparing performance reports.

(4 marks)
(Total 25 marks)
CIMA Management Accounting – Performance Management

Advanced: Estimation of costs and incremental hours using the learning curve

Question 23.5

(a) Z plc experiences difficulty in its budgeting process because it finds it necessary to quantify the learning effect as new products are introduced. Substantial product changes occur and result in the need for retraining.

An order for 30 units of a new product has been received by Z plc. So far, 14 have been completed; the first unit required 40 direct labour hours and a total of 240 direct labour hours has been recorded for the 14 units. The production manager expects an 80% learning effect for this type of work.

The company uses standard absorption costing. The direct costs attributed to the centre in which the unit is manufactured and its direct material costs are as follows:

Direct material	£30.00 per unit
Direct labour	£6.00 per hour
Variable overhead	£0.50 per direct labour hour
Fixed overhead	£6000 per four-week operating period

There are ten direct employees working a five-day week, eight hours per day. Personal and other downtime allowances account for 25% of the total available time.

The company usually quotes a four-week delivery period for orders.

You are required to

(i) determine whether the assumption of an 80% learning effect is a reasonable one in this case, by using the standard formula $y = ax^b$

where y = the cumulative average direct labour time per unit (productivity)
a = the average labour time per unit for the first batch
x = the cumulative number of batches produced
b = the index of learning

(5 marks)

(ii) calculate the number of direct labour hours likely to be required for an expected second order of 20 units;

(5 marks)

(iii) use the cost data given to produce an estimated product cost for the initial order, examining the problems which may be created for budgeting by the presence of the learning effect.

(10 marks)

(b) It is argued that in many areas of modern technology, the 'learning curve' effect is of diminishing significance. An 'experience curve' effect would still be present and possibly strengthened in importance. However, the experience curve has little to do with short-term standard setting and product costing.

You are required to discuss the validity of the above statement, in particular the assertion that the experience curve has little relevance to costing.

(6 marks)
(Total 26 marks)
CIMA Stage 4 Management Accounting – Control and Audit

COST ESTIMATION AND COST BEHAVIOUR

Quantitative models for the planning and control of inventories

Questions to Chapter 24

Intermediate **Question 24.1**

Moura uses the economic order quantity formula (EOQ) to establish its optimal reorder quantity for its single raw material. The following data relates to the stock costs:

Purchase price: £15 per item
Carriage costs: *£50 per order*
Ordering costs: *£5 per order*
Storage costs: 10% of purchase price plus £0.20 per unit per annum

Annual demand is 4000 units.

What is the EOQ to the nearest whole unit?

A   153 units
B   170 units
C   485 units
D   509 units.

ACCA Paper 1.2 – Financial information for Management

Advanced: EOQ and JIT management methods **Question 24.2**

TNG Co expects annual demand for product X to be 255 380 units. Product X has a selling price of £19 per unit and is purchased for £11 per unit from a supplier, MKR Co. TNG places an order for 50 000 units of product X at regular intervals throughout the year. Because the demand for product X is to some degree uncertain, TNG maintains a safety (buffer) stock of product X which is sufficient to meet demand for 28 working days. The cost of placing an order is £25 and the storage cost for Product X is 10 pence per unit per year.

TNG normally pays trade suppliers after 60 days but MKR has offered a discount of 1% for cash settlement within 20 days.

TNG Co has a short-term cost of debt of 8% and uses a working year consisting of 365 days.

Required:

(a) Calculate the annual cost of the current ordering policy. Ignore financing costs in this part of the question.

(4 marks)

(b) Calculate the annual saving if the economic order quantity model is used to determine an optimal ordering policy. Ignore financing costs in this part of the question.

(5 marks)

(c) Determine whether the discount offered by the supplier is financially acceptable to TNG Co.

(4 marks)

(d) Critically discuss the limitations of the economic order quantity model as a way of managing stock

(4 marks)

(e) Discuss the advantages and disadvantages of using just-in-time stock management methods.

(8 marks)
ACCA 2.4: Financial Management and Control

Question 24.3
Advanced: Calculation of EOQ, discussion of the limitations of EOQ and a discussion of JIT

The newly-appointed managing director of a division of Bondini plc is concerned about the length of the division's cash operating cycle. Extracts from the latest budget are given below:

Budgeted Profit and Loss Account for the year ending 30 June 2001

	(£000)	(£000)
Sales (43 200 units at £55)		2376
Opening Stock (21 600 units at £30)	648	
Purchases (43 200 units at £30)	1296	
	1944	
Closing Stock (21 600 units at £30)	648	1296
Budgeted Gross Profit		1080

Budgeted Balance Sheet as at 30 June 2001

	(£000)
Current Assets	
Stock	648
Trade debtors	198
Current Liabilities	
Trade creditors	216

The following information has also been gathered for the managing director:

(1) Sales were made evenly during the 12 months to 30 June 2000.

(2) The amount for trade creditors relates only to purchases of stock.

(3) The division is charged interest at the rate of 15% per annum on the average level of net assets held in a year.

(4) The company rents sufficient space in a warehouse to store the necessary stock at an annual cost of £3.25 per unit.

(5) The costs of ordering items of stock are as follows:
Insurance cost per order	£900
Transport cost per order	£750

(6) There will be no change in debtor and creditor payment periods.

In addition, the division maintains a purchasing department at an annual budgeted cost of £72 000.

The managing director has heard about the economic order quantity (EOQ) model and would prefer this basis to be used to calculate the order quantity. He estimates that the buffer stock level should be equal to one month's sales in order to prevent loss of revenue due to stock-outs.

Requirements:

(a) Calculate the EOQ for the division and, assuming that the division uses this as the basis for ordering goods from 1 July 2000, calculate the cash amounts which would be paid to trade creditors in each of the eight months to 28 February 2001.

(12 marks)

QUANTITATIVE MODELS FOR THE PLANNING AND CONTROL OF INVENTORIES

(b) Determine the length of the cash operating cycle at 30 June 2000 and calculate the improvement that will have taken place by 30 June 2001.

(4 marks)

(c) Discuss the practical limitations of using the EOQ approach to determining order quantities.

(5 marks)

(d) Describe the advantages and disadvantages of the just-in-time approach (i.e. when minimal stocks are maintained and suppliers deliver as required).

(4 marks)

(Total 25 marks)

ICAEW P2 Financial Management

Advanced: Calculation of EOQ and safety stocks assuming uncertainty

Question 24.4

The retailing division of Josefa plc sells Hofers and its budget for the coming year is given below:

	(£)	(£)
Sales (4200 units at £85 each)		357 000
Cost of goods sold:		
Opening stock (200 units at £65 per unit)	13 000	
Purchases (4200 units at £750 per unit)	294 000	
	307 000	
Closing stock (200 units at £70 per unit)	14 000	293 000
Gross profit		64 000
Purchasing department cost		
Variable (7 orders at £300 per order)	2 100	
Fixed	8 400	
Transportation costs for goods	5 250	
received (7 orders at £750 per order)		
Stock insurance costs based on	2 000	
average stockholding		
(500 units at £4 per unit)		
Fixed warehouse costs	43 000	
		60 750
Budgeted net profit		3 250

The supplier of Hofers is responsible for their transportation and charges Josefa plc accordingly. Recently the supplier has offered to reduce the cost of transportation from £750 per order to £650 per order if Josefa plc will increase the order size from the present 600 units to a minimum of 1000 units.

The management of Josefa plc is concerned about the retailing division's stock ordering policy. At present, a buffer stock of 200 units is maintained and sales occur evenly throughout the year. Josefa plc has contracted to buy 4200 Hofers and, irrespective of the order quantity, will pay for them in equal monthly instalments throughout the year. Transportation costs are to be paid at the beginning of the year. The cost of capital of Josefa plc is 20% p.a.

Requirements:

(a) Determine the quantity of Hofers which Josefa plc should order, assuming the buffer stock level of 200 units is maintained, and calculate the improvement in net profit that will result.

(11 marks)

(b) Calculate what the buffer stock level should be, assuming that:
  (i) Josefa plc changes its ordering frequency to one order (of 700 units) every two months;
  (ii) stockout costs are £18 per unit;
  (iii) the distribution of sales within each two-month period is not even but the following two-monthly sales pattern can occur:

2-monthly sales	Probability
500 units	0.15
600 units	0.20
700 units	0.30
800 units	0.20
900 units	0.15

(7 marks)

(c) Discuss the problems which might be experienced in attempting to maintain a stock control system based upon economic order quantities and buffer stocks.

(7 marks)
(Total 25 marks)

Ignore taxation.

ICAEW P2 Financial Management

Question 24.5

Advanced: Safety stocks and uncertain demand and quantity discounts

Runswick Ltd is a company that purchases toys from abroad for resale to retail stores. The company is concerned about its stock (inventory) management operations. It is considering adopting a stock management system based upon the economic order quantity (EOQ) model.

The company's estimates of its stock management costs are shown below:

Percentage of purchase price of toys per year	
Storage costs	3
Insurance	1
Handling	1
Obsolescence	3
Opportunity costs of funds invested in stock	10

'Fixed' costs associated with placing each order for stock are £311.54

The purchase price of the toys to Runswick Ltd is £4.50 per unit. There is a two week delay between the time that new stock is ordered from suppliers and the time that it arrives.

The toys are sold by Runswick at a unit price of £6.30. The variable cost to Runswick of selling the toys is £0.30 per unit. Demand from Runswick's customers for the toys averages 10 000 units per week, but recently this has varied from 6000 to 14 000 units per week. On the basis of recent evidence the probability of unit sales in any two week period has been estimated as follows:

Sales (units)	Probability
12 000	0.05
16 000	0.20
20 000	0.50
24 000	0.20
28 000	0.05

If adequate stock is not available when demanded by Runswick's customers in any two week period approximately 25% of orders that cannot be satisfied in that period will be lost, and approximately 75% of customers will be willing to wait until new stock arrives.

Required:

(a) Ignoring taxation, calculate the optimum order level of stock over a one year planning period using the economic order quantity model.

(3 marks)

(b) Estimate the level of safety stock that should be carried by Runswick Ltd.

(6 marks)

(c) If Runswick Ltd were to be offered a quantity discount by its suppliers of 1% for orders of 30 000 units or more, evaluate whether it would be beneficial for the company to take advantage of the quantity discount. Assume for this calculation that no safety stock is carried.

(4 marks)

(d) Estimate the expected total annual costs of stock management if the economic order quantity had been (i) 50% higher (ii) 50% lower than its actual level. Comment upon the sensitivity of total annual costs to changes in the economic order quantity. Assume for this calculation that no safety stock is carried.

(4 marks)

(e) Discuss briefly how the effect of seasonal sales variations might be incorporated within the model.

(3 marks)

(f) Assess the practical value of this model in the management of stock.

(5 marks)
(Total 25 marks)
ACCA Level 3 Financial Management

The application of linear programming to management accounting

Questions to Chapter 25

Question 25.1

Advanced: Throughput accounting, determining optimal product mix and interpretation of linear programme output

QP plc is a food processing company that produces pre-prepared meals for sale to consumers through a number of different supermarkets. The company specializes in three particular pre-prepared meals and has invested significantly in modern manufacturing processes to ensure a high-quality product. The company is very aware of the importance of training and retaining high quality staff in all ares of the company and, in order to ensure their production employees' commitment to the company, the employees are guaranteed a weekly salary that is equivalent to their normal working hours paid at their normal hourly rate of £7 per hour.

The meals are produced in batches of 100 units. Costs and sellling prices per batch are as follows:

Meal	TR	PN	BE
	£/batch	£/batch	£/batch
Selling price	340	450	270
Ingredient K (£5/kg)	150	120	90
Ingredient L (£10/kg)	70	90	40
Ingredient M (£15/kg) 30	30	75	45
Labour (£7/hour)	21	28	42
Factory costs absorbed	20	80	40

OP plc has adopted throughput accounting for its short-term decisions.

Required

(a) State of principles of throughput accounting and the effects of using it for short-term decision making.

(6 marks)

(b) QP plc is preparing its production plans for the next three months and has estimated the maximum demand from its customers to be as follows:

TR   500 batches
PN   400 batches
BE   350 batches

These demand maximums are amended figures because a customer has just delayed its request for a large order and QP has unusually got some spare capacity over the next three months. However, these demand maximums do include a contract for the delivery of 50 batches of each to an important customer. If this minimum contract is not satisfied then QP plc will have to pay a substantial financial penalty for non-delivery.

The Production Director is concerned at hearing news that two of the ingredients used are expected to be in short supply for the next three months. QP plc does not hold inventory of these ingredients and although there are no supply problems for ingredient K, the supplies of ingredients L and M are expected to be limited to:

Ingredient L   7000 kilos
Ingredient M   3000 kilos

The Production Director has researched the problem and found that ingredient V can be used as a direct substitute for ingredient M. It also costs the same as ingredient M. There is an unlimited supply of ingredient V.

Required:

Prepare calculations to determine the production mix that will maximize the profit of QP plc during the next three months.

(10 marks)

(c) The World Health Organization has now announced that ingredient V contains dangerously high levels of a chemical that can cause life-threatening illnesses. As a consequence it can no longer be used in the production of food.

As a result, the production director has determined the optimal solution to the company's production mix problem using linear programming. This is set out below:

Objective function value	110 714
TR value	500
PN value	357
BE value	71
TR slack value	0
PN slack value	43
BE slack value	279
L value	3
M value	28

Required:

Explain the meaning of each of the values contained in the above solution.

(9 marks)

CIMA P2 Management Accounting: Decision Management

Advanced: Optimal output and calculation of shadow prices using graphical approach

Question 25.2

MF plc manufactures and sells two types of product to a number of customers. The company is currently preparing its budget for the year ending 31 December 2003 which it divides into 12 equal periods.

The cost and resource details for each of the company's product types are as follows:

	Product type M £	Product type F £
Selling price per unit	200	210
Variable costs per unit		
Direct material P (£2.50 per litre)	20	25
Direct material Q (£4.00 per litre)	40	20
Direct labour (£7.00 per hour)	28	35
Overhead (£4.00 per hour)	16	20
Fixed production cost per unit	40	50
	Units	*Units*
Maximum sales demand in period 1	1000	3000

The fixed production cost per unit is based upon an absorption rate of £10 per direct labour hour and a total annual production activity of 180 000 direct labour hours. One-twelfth of the annual fixed production cost will be incurred in period 1.

In addition to the above costs, non-production overhead costs are expected to be £57 750 in period 1.

During period 1, the availability of material P is expected to be limited to 31 250 litres. Other materials and sufficient direct labour are expected to be available to meet demand.

It is MF plc's policy not to hold stocks of finished goods.

Required:

(a) Calculate the number of units of product types M and F that should be produced and sold in period 1 in order to maximize profit.

(4 marks)

(b) Using your answer to (a) above, prepare a columnar budgeted profit statement for period 1 in a marginal cost format.

(4 marks)

After presenting your statement to the budget management meeting, the production manager has advised you that in period 1 the other resources will also be limited. The maximum resources available will be:

Material P	31 250 litres
Material Q	20 000 litres
Direct labour	17 500 hours

It has been agreed that these factors should be incorporated into a revised plan and that the objective should be to make as much profit as possible from the available resources.

Required:

(c) Use graphical linear programming to determine the revised production plan for period 1. State clearly the number of units of product types M and F that are to be produced.

(10 marks)

(d) Using your answer to part (c) above, calculate the profit that will be earned from the revised plan.

(3 marks)

(e) Calculate and explain the meaning of the shadow price for material Q.

(5 marks)

(f) Discuss the other factors that should be considered by MF plc in relation to the revised production plan.

(4 marks)
(Total 30 marks)
CIMA Management Accounting – Performance Management

Question 25.3

Advanced: Optimal output, shadow prices and decision making using the graphical approach

The instruments department of Max Ltd makes two products: the XL and the YM. Standard revenues and costs per unit for these products are shown below:

	XL		YM	
	(£)	(£)	(£)	(£)
Selling price		200		180
Variable costs:				
Material A (£10 per kg)	(40)		(40)	
Direct labour (£8 per hour)	(32)		(16)	
Plating (£12 per hour)	(12)		(24)	
Other variable costs	(76)		(70)	
		(160)		(150)

Fixed overheads (allocated at £7 per direct labour hour)	(28)	(14)
Standard profit per unit	12	16

Plating is a separate automated operation and the costs of £12 per hour are for plating materials and electricity.

In any week the maximum availability of inputs is limited to the following:

Material A	120 kg
Direct labour	100 hours
Plating time	50 hours

A management meeting recently considered ways of increasing the profit of the instrument department. It was decided that each of the following possible changes to the existing situation should be examined *independently* of each other.

(1) The selling price of product YM could be increased.

(2) Plating time could be sold as a separate service at £16 per hour.

(3) A new product, ZN, could be sold at £240 per unit. Each unit would require the following:

Material A	5 kg
Direct labour	5 hours
Plating time	1 hour
Other variable costs	£90

(4) Overtime could be introduced and would be paid at a premium of 50% above normal rates.

Requirements:

(a) Formulate a linear programme to determine the production policy which maximizes the profits of Max Ltd in the present situation (i.e. ignoring the alternative assumptions in 1 to 4 above), solve, and specify the optimal product mix and weekly profit.

(6 marks)

(b) Determine the maximum selling price of YM at which the product mix calculated for requirement (a) would still remain optimal.

(3 marks)

(c) Show how the linear programme might be modified to accommodate the sale of plating time at £16 per hour (i.e. formulate but do not solve).

(3 marks)

(d) Using shadow prices (dual values), calculate whether product ZN would be a profitable addition to the product range.

(4 marks)

(e) Ignoring the possibility of extending the product range, determine whether overtime working would be worthwhile, and if so state how many overtime hours should be worked.

(3 marks)

(f) Discuss the limitations of the linear programming approach to the problems of Max Ltd.

(6 marks)
(Total 25 marks)
ICAEW P2 Management Accounting

Question 25.4

Advanced: Formulation of an initial tableau and interpretation of final matrix using the Simplex method

Hint: Reverse the signs and ignore the entries of 0 and 1. You are not required to solve the model.

A chemical manufacturer is developing three fertilizer compounds for the agricultural industry. The product codes for the three products are X1, X2 and X3 and the relevant information is summarized below:

Chemical constituents: percentage make-up per tonne

	Nitrate	Phosphate	Potash	Filler
X1	10	10	20	60
X2	10	20	10	60
X3	20	10	10	60

Input prices per tonne

Nitrate	£150
Phosphate	£ 60
Potash	£120
Filler	£ 10

Maximum available input in tonnes per month

Nitrate	1200
Phosphate	2000
Potash	2200
Filler	No limit

The fertilizers will be sold in bulk and managers have proposed the following prices per tonne.

X1	£83
X2	£81
X3	£81

The manufacturing costs of each type of fertilizer, excluding materials, are £11 per tonne.

You are required to:

(a) formulate the above data into a linear programming model so that the company may maximize contribution;

(4 marks)

(b) construct the initial Simplex tableau and state what is meant by 'slack variables' (Define X4, X5, X6 as the slack variables for X1, X2, and X3 respectively);

(2 marks)

(c) indicate, with explanations, which will be the 'entering variable' and 'leaving variable' in the first iteration;

(2 marks)

(d) interpret the final matrix of the simplex solution given below:

Basic Variable	X_1	X_2	X_3	X_4	X_5	X_6	Solution
X1	1	0	3	20	−10	0	4 000
X2	0	1	−1	−10	10	0	8 000
X6	0	0	−0.4	−3	1	1	600
Z	0	0	22	170	40	0	284 000

(8 marks)

THE APPLICATION OF LINEAR PROGRAMMING TO MANAGEMENT ACCOUNTING

(e) use the final matrix above to investigate:
   (i)   the effect of an increase in nitrate of 100 tonnes per month;
   (ii) the effect of a minimum contract from an influential customer for 200
         tonnes of X3 per month to be supplied.

(4 marks)
(Total 20 marks)
CIMA Stage 3 Management Accounting Techniques

Part II
Solutions

An introduction to cost terms and concepts

Solutions to Chapter 2 questions

In Chapters 1 and 2 it was pointed out that a management accounting system should generate information to meet the following requirements: **Question 2.1**

1. to allocate costs between cost of goods sold and inventories for internal and external profit measurement and inventory valuation;
2. to provide relevant information to help managers to make better decisions;
3. to provide information for planning, control and performance measurement.

The question relates to how costs can be classified for meeting the planning, control and decision-making requirements.

Planning relates to the annual budgeting and long-term processes described in Chapter 15. Within these processes costs can be classified by:

- *Behaviour* – By classifying costs into fixed, variable, semi-fixed and semi-variable categories the outcomes from different activity levels can be examined.
- *Function* – Functions are the different responsibility centres within the organization. The budget is built up by the functional levels so that everyone in the organization has a clear understanding of the role that their responsibility centre has in achieving the annual budget.
- *Expense type* – Classifying by expense types provides useful information on the nature, content and trend of different expense categories that is useful for planning how much should be authorized on spending within the different categories.
- *Controllability* – Classifying expenses by responsibility centres determines the individuals who are accountable for achieving the budget and who should thus be involved in setting the budget for the specific responsibility centres.

The management function of control consists of the measurement, reporting and the subsequent correction of performance in an attempt to ensure that a firm's objectives and plans are achieved. Within the control process costs can be classified by:

- *Behaviour* – Costs must be classified by behaviour for comparing actual and budgeted performance using flexible budgets. You should refer to Chapter 16 for a description of flexible budgeting.
- *Function* – For control, cost and revenues should be traced to the heads of the responsibility centres who are responsible for incurring them. For a description of this process you should refer to 'Responsibility Accounting' in Chapter 2.
- *Expense type* – This will ensure that like items are compared with one another when budget and actual performance are compared and trends in revenues and different expense categories are monitored.
- *Controllability* – Costs and revenues must be assigned to the responsibility heads who are made accountable for them so that effective control can be exercised.
- *Relevance* – Attention should only be focused on those expense categories where there are significant deviations from the budget. Insignificant deviations are not relevant for cost control. See 'Management by Exception' in Chapter 1 for a more detailed explanation of this point.

Decision-making involves choosing between alternative courses of actions. The following classifications are important for decision-making:

- *By behaviour* – Classification of costs by fixed, variable, semi-fixed and semi-variable is necessary for predicting future costs for alternative courses of action. In particular, classification is necessary for cost–volume–profit analysis and identifying break-even levels. You should refer to Chapter 8 for a more detailed discussion of these topics.
- *By expense type* – This is necessary to identify how different cost categories will change as a result of pursuing alternative courses of action.
- *By relevance* – For decision-making it is necessary to distinguish between relevant and irrelevant costs and revenues for alternative courses of action. For a more detailed explanation you should refer to 'Relevant and Irrelevant Costs and Revenues' in Chapter 2.

It is apparent from the above discussion that costs should be classified in different ways for different purposes. This is explained in more detail in the section entitled 'Maintaining a cost database' in Chapter 2.

Question 2.2 (a) A large proportion of non-manufacturing costs are of a discretionary nature. In respect of such costs, management has some significant range of discretion as to the amount it will budget for the particular activity in question. Examples of discretionary costs (sometimes called *managed* or *programmed costs*) include advertising, research and development, and training costs. There is no optimum relationship between inputs (as measured by the costs) and outputs (as measured by revenues or some other objective function) for these costs. Furthermore, they are not predetermined by some previous commitment. In effect, management can determine what quantity of service it wishes to purchase. For example, it can choose to spend small or large amounts on research and development or advertising. The great difficulty in controlling such costs is that there is no established method for determining the appropriate amount to be spent in particular periods.

For a description of fixed and variable costs see Chapter 2. Examples of fixed costs include depreciation of the factory building, supervisors' salaries and leasing charges. Examples of variable costs include direct materials, power and sales commissions.

(b) The £500 000 is a sunk cost and cannot be avoided. It is therefore not a relevant cost for decision-making purposes. The project should be continued because the incremented/relevant benefits exceed the incremental/relevant costs:

	(£000)
Incremental benefits	350
Incremental costs	200
Net incremental benefit	150

(c) An opportunity cost is a cost that measures the opportunity lost or sacrificed when the choice of one course of action requires that an alternative course of action be given up. The following are examples of opportunity costs:

(i) If scarce resources such as machine hours are required for a special contract then the opportunity cost represents the lost profit that would have been earned from the alternative use of the machine hours.

(ii) If an employee is paid £5 per hour and is charged out at £11 per hour for committed work then, if that employee is redirected to other work, the lost contribution of £6 per hour represents the opportunity cost of the employee's time.

The CIMA terminology defines a notional cost as: 'A hypothetical cost taken into account in a particular situation to represent a benefit enjoyed by an entity in respect of which no actual cost is incurred.' The following are examples of notional costs:

(i) interest on capital to represent the notional cost of using an asset rather than investing the capital elsewhere;

(ii) including rent as a cost for premises owned by the company so as to represent the lost rent income resulting from using the premises for business purposes.

(a) See Chapter 2 for a description of opportunity costs. Out of pocket cost can be viewed as being equivalent to incremental or relevant costs as described in Chapter 2.

Question 2.3

(b) Depreciation is not a relevant cost since it will be the same for both alternatives. It is assumed that tyres and miscellaneous represent the additional costs incurred in travelling to work. The relevant costs are:

Using the car to travel to work:

	(£)
Petrol	128
Tyres and miscellaneous	52
	180
Contribution from passenger	120
Relevant cost	60

Using the train:

Relevant cost	£188

(c)

	(£000)	(£000)	(%)
Sales		2560.0	100
Direct materials	819.2		32
Direct wages	460.8		18
Variable production overhead	153.6		6
Variable administration/selling	76.8		3
Total variable cost		1510.4	59
Contribution		1049.6	41
Fixed production overhead[a]	768		30
Fixed administration/selling[b]	224		8.75
		992	
Profit		57.6	2.25

Notes

[a] $100/80 \times £2\,560\,000 \times 0.24$

[b] $100/80 \times £2\,560\,000 \times 0.07$

Cost assignment

Solutions to Chapter 3 questions

Question 3.1

(a) Calculation of department overhead rates

	Department P (£)	Department Q (£)	Department R (£)
Repairs and maintenance	42 000	10 000	10 000
Depreciation	17 000^a	14 000	9 000
Consumable supplies	4 500^b	2 700	1 800
Wage related costs	48 250	26 250	12 500
Indirect labour	45 000	27 000	18 000
Canteen/rest/smoke room	15 000^c	9 000	6 000
Business rates and insurance	13 000^d	10 400	2 600
	184 750	99 350	55 900
Direct labour hours	50 000	30 000	20 000
Overhead absorption rate	£3.70	£3.31	£3.00

Notes:
The calculations for Department P are:
^{a}Depreciation = £170 000/£400 000 × £40 000.
^{b}Consumable supplies = 50 000/100 000 × £9000.
^{c}Canteen = 25/50 × £30 000.
^{d}Business rates insurance = 5000/10 000 × £26 000.

(b) Job 976: Sample quotation

		(£)	(£)
Direct materials			800.00
Direct labour	P (30 × £7.72^a)	231.60	
	Q (10 × £7.00^b)	70.00	
	R (5 × £5.00^c)	25.00	326.60
Overhead absorbed	P (30 × £3.70)	111.00	
	Q (10 × £3.31)	33.10	
	R (5 × £3.00)	15.00	159.10
Production cost			1285.70
Selling, distribution and administration costs (20% × £1285.70)			257.14
Total cost			1542.84
Profit margin (20% of selling price)			385.71
Selling price (£1542.84 × 100/800)			1928.55

Notes:
^{a}£386 000/50 000.
^{b}£210 000/30 000.
^{c}£100 000/20 000.

(c)

	(£)
Direct materials	800.00
Direct labour	326.60
Prime cost	1126.60
Overhead applied (125%)	1408.25
Total cost	2534.85

The auditor's system results in a higher cost for this quotation. However, other jobs will be overcosted with the previous system. The auditor's system will result in the reporting of more accurate job costs with some job costs being higher, and others being lower, than the present system. For a more detailed answer see the section on plant-wide (blanket) overhead rates in Chapter 3.

(a)   *Calculation of overhead absorption rates*   **Question 3.2**

	Machining (£000)	Assembly (£000)	Finishing (£000)	Stores (£000)	Maintenance (£000)
Allocated costs	600.00	250.00	150.00	100.00	80.00
Stores apportionment (10%)	40.00 (40%)	30.00 (30%)	20.00 (20%)	(100.00)	10.00
Maintenance apportionment	49.50 (55%)	18.00 (20%)	18.00 (20%)	4.50 (5%)	(90.00)
Stores apportionment[a]	2.00 (4/9)	1.50 (3/9)	1.00 (2/9)	(4.50)	
Total	691.50	299.50	189.00	—	—
Machine hours	50 000				
Labour hours		30 000	20 000		
Overhead absorption rates[b]	13.83	9.98	9.45		

Notes

[a] Costs have become too small at this stage to justify apportioning 10% of the costs to the maintenance department. Therefore stores costs are apportioned in the ratio 40: 30: 20.

[b] Machine hours are the predominant activity in the machine department whereas labour hours are the predominant activity in the assembly and finishing departments. Therefore machine hours are used as the allocation base in the machining department and direct labour hours are used for the assembly and finishing departments.

(b)   *Quotation for Job XX 34*

	(£)	(£)
Direct material		2400.00
Direct labour		1500.00
Overhead cost:		
Machining (45 machine hours at £13.83)	622.35	
Assembly (15 labour hours at £9.98)	149.70	
Finishing (12 labour hours at £9.45	113.40	885.45
Total cost		4785.45
Selling price (Profit margin = 20% of selling price		
∴ selling price = £4785.45/0.8)		5981.81

(c)   *Overhead control account*

	(£)		(£)
Overhead incurred	300 000	WIP control (30 700 hrs at £9.98)	306 386
Balance – over-recovery transferred to costing profit and loss account	6 386		
	306 386		306 386

(d) For the answer to this question see 'An illustration of the two-stage process for an ABC system' in Chapter 3. In particular, the answer should stress that cost centres will consist of activity cost centres rather than departmental centres. Separate cost driver rates would also be established for the service departments and the costs would be allocated to cost objects via cost driver rates rather than being reallocated to production departments and assigned within the production department rates. The answer should also stress that instead of using just two volume-based cost drivers (e.g. direct labour and machine hours) a variety of cost drivers would be used, including non-volume-based drivers such as number of set-ups and number of material issues. The answer could also stress that within the machining department a separate set-up activity centre might be established with costs being assigned using the number of set-ups as the cost driver. The current system includes the set-up costs within the machine hour overhead rate.

Question 3.3

(a)

	Department A	Department B
Allocated costs	£217 860	£374 450
Apportioned costs	45 150	58 820
Total departmental overheads	263 010	433 270
Overhead absorption rate	£19.16 (£263 010/13 730)	£26.89 (£433 270/16 110)

(b)

	Department A (£)	Department B (£)	Department C (£)
Allocated costs	219 917	387 181	103 254
Apportionment of 70% of Department C costs [a]	32 267	40 011	(72 278)
Apportionment of 30% of Department C costs [b]	11 555	19 421	(30 976)
Total departmental overheads	263 739	446 613	
Overheads charged to production	261 956 [c]	455 866 [d]	
Under/(over-recovery)	1 783	(9 253)	

Notes:
[a] Allocated on the basis of actual machine hours
[b] Allocated on the basis of actual direct labour hours
[c] £19.16 × 13 672 actual machine hours
[d] £26.89 × 16 953 actual direct labour hours

(c)
See Appendix 3.1 (Chapter 3) for the answer to this question.

Question 3.4

(a) *Year 1*
  (1) Budgeted machine hours   132 500
  (2) Budgeted fixed overheads   £2 411 500 (132 500 × £18.20)
  (3) Actual machine hours   134 200 (£2 442 440/£18.20)
  (4) Fixed overheads absorbed   £2 442 440
  (5) Actual fixed overheads incurred £2 317 461

  Over-absorption of fixed overheads   £124 979 (5 − 4)

The section on 'Under- and over-recovery of fixed overheads' in Chapter 3 indicates that an under- or over-recovery will arise whenever actual activity or expenditure differs from budgeted activity or expenditure. Actual activity was 1700 hours in excess of budget and this will result in an over-recovery of fixed overheads of

£30 940. Actual overheads incurred were £94 039 (£2 317 461 – £2 411 500) less than budget and this is the second factor explaining the over-absorption of fixed overheads.

Summary	(£)
Over-recovery due to actual expenditure being less than budgeted expenditure	94 039
Over-recovery due to actual activity exceeding budgeted activity	30 940
Total over-recovery of overhead for year 1	124 979

Year 2

(1) Budgeted machine hours (134 200 × 1.05)	140 910
(2) Budgeted fixed overheads	£2 620 926
(3) Fixed overhead rate (£2 620 926/140 900 hours)	£18.60
(4) Actual fixed overheads incurred	£2 695 721
(5) Fixed overheads absorbed (139 260 × £18.60)	£2 590 236
(6) Under-recovery of overhead for year 2 (4 – 5)	£105 485

Analysis of under-recovery of overhead	(£)
Under-recovery due to actual activity being less than budgeted activity (139 260 – 140 910) × £18.60	30 690
Under-recovery due to actual expenditure being greater than budgeted expenditure (£2 695 721 – £2 620 926	74 795
Total under-recovery for the year	105 485

Change in the overhead rate

Change in the rate (£18.60 – £18.20)/£18.20	=	+ 2.198%
This can be analysed as follows:		
Increase in budgeted expenditure (£2 620 926 – £2 411 500)/£2 411 500	=	+ 8.684%
Increase in budgeted activity (140 910 hours – 132 500 hrs)/132 500	=	+ 6.347%

The increase of 2.198% in the absorption rate is due to an expenditure increase of 8.684% in budgeted expenditure partly offset by an increase in budgeted activity of 6.347% over the 2 years.

Proof
(1.08684/1.06347) – 1 = 0.02198 (2.198%)

(b) See 'Plant-wide (blanket) overhead rates' and 'Budgeted overhead rates' in Chapter 3 for the answers to these questions.

(a) (i) and (ii) An activity increase of 150 hours (1650 – 1500) results in an increase in total overheads of £675. It is assumed that the increase in total overheads is due entirely to the increase in variable overheads arising from an increase in activity. Therefore the variable overhead rate is £4.50 (£675/150 hours) per machine hour. The cost structure is as follows:

Question 3.5

1. Activity level (hours)	1 500	1 650	2 000
2. Variable overheads at £4.50 per hour	£6 750	£7 425	£9 000
3. Total overheads	£25 650	£26 325	£27 900
4. Fixed overheads (3 – 2)	£18 900	£18 900	£18 900

(iii) The fixed overhead rate is £10.50 (£15 − £4.50 variable rate)

normal activity = fixed overheads (£18 900)/fixed overhead rate (£10.50)
= 1800 machine hours

(iv) Under-absorption = 100 machine hours (1800 − 1700) at £10.50 = £1050

(b) (i) A machine hour rate is recommended for the machine department because most of the overheads (e.g. depreciation and maintenance) are likely to be related to machine hours. For non-machine labour-intensive departments, such as the finishing department, overheads are likely to be related to direct labour hours rather than machine hours. Overheads are therefore charged to jobs performed in the finishing department using the direct labour hour method of recovery.

Calculation of overhead rates

	Machining department	Finishing department
Production overhead	£35 280	£12 480
Machine hours	11 200	
Direct labour hours		7800
Machine hour overhead rate	£3.15	
Direct labour hour overhead rate		£1.60

(ii)

	Machining department (£)	Finishing department (£)
Direct materials		
(189 × 1.1 × £2.35/0.9)	542.85	—
Direct labour[a]		
25 hours × £4	100.00	
28 hours × £4		112.00
Production overhead		
46 machine hours at £3.15	144.90	
28 direct labour hours at £1.60		44.80
	787.75	156.80

Total cost of job = £944.55 (£787.75 + £156.80)

Note
[a]Overtime premiums are charged to overheads, and are therefore not included in the above job cost.

Question 3.6

(a)
$$\text{Overhead rate} = \frac{\text{Budgeted overhead}}{\text{Budgeted direct wages}} \times 100$$

$$= \frac{£225\,000}{£150\,000} \times 100$$

$$= \underline{\underline{150\%}}$$

(b)

	(£)
Direct materials	190
Direct wages	170
Production overhead (150% × £170)	255
Production cost	615
Gross profit (¹/₃ × £615)	205
	820

(c) (i) Each department incurs different overhead costs. For example, the overhead costs of department A are considerably higher than those of the other departments. A blanket overhead rate is only appropriate where jobs spend the same proportion of time in each department. See the section on blanket overhead rates in Chapter 3 for an explanation of why departmental overhead rates are preferable.

(ii) *Department A machine-hour overhead rate:*

$$\frac{£120\,000}{40\,000 \text{ machine hours}} = £3 \text{ per machine hour}$$

A machine-hour rate is preferable because machine hours appear to be the dominant activity. Also, most of the overheads incurred are likely to be related to machine hours rather than direct labour hours. Possibly one worker operates four machines since the ratio is 40 000 machine hours to 10 000 direct labour hours. If some jobs do not involve machinery but others do, then two separate cost centres should be established (one related to machinery and the other related to jobs which involve direct labour hours only).

Department B direct labour hour overhead rate:

$$\frac{£30\,000}{50\,000 \text{ direct labour hours}} = £0.60 \text{ per labour hour}$$

Because direct labour hours are five times greater than machine hours a direct labour hour overhead rate is recommended. A comparison of direct labour hours and direct wages for budget, actual and job 657 for department B suggests that wage rate are not equal throughout the department. Therefore the direct wages percentage method is inappropriate.

Department C direct labour hour overhead rate:

$$\frac{£75\,000}{25\,000 \text{ direct labour hours}} = £3 \text{ per direct labour hour}$$

This method is chosen because it is related to time and machine hours are ruled out. A comparison of budgeted direct wages and labour hours for budget, actual and job 657 for department C suggests that wage rates are equal at £1 per hour throughout the department. Therefore direct labour hours or direct wages percentage methods will produce the same results.

(d) Department A (40 machine hours × £3)   120
　　　　　　 B (40 labour hours × £0.60)   24
　　　　　　 C (10 labour hours × £3)   <u>30</u>
　　　　　　　　　　　　　　　　　　　　 174

(e) (i) *Current rate (actual wages × 150%):*

	Absorbed	Actual	Over/(under)-absorbed
	(£000s)	(£000s)	(£000s)
Department A	45	130	(85)
B	120	28	92
C	<u>45</u>	<u>80</u>	<u>(35)</u>
	<u>210</u>	<u>238</u>	<u>(28)</u>

(ii) *Proposed rates:*

	Absorbed (£000s)	Actual (£000s)	Over/(under)-absorbed (£000s)
Department A	135	130	5
B	27	28	(1)
C	90	80	10
	252	238	14

Question 3.7

(a) It is easier to allocate service department B first because it provides services to both of the other service departments.

	Centre 1 (£)	Centre 2 (£)	Service A (£)	Service B (£)	Service C (£)
	2000	3500	300	500	700
Service B	250 (50%)	100 (20%)	100 (20%)	(500)	50 (10%)
	2250	3600	400		750
Service A	180 (45%)	180 (45%)	(400)	40 (10%)	
	2430	3780		40	750
Service C	450 (60%)	300 (40%)			(750)
	2880	4080		40	
Service B	20 (50%)	8 (20%)	8 (20%)	(40)	4 (10%)
	2900	4088	8		4
Service A	4 (45%)	4 (45%)	(8)		
Service C (Balance shared equally)	2	2			(4)
Total	2906	4094			

(b) It would appear that the department is machine intensive so it is preferable to use machine hours. The overhead absorption rate per machine hour is £0.969 (£2906/3000 machine hours).

Question 3.8

(a) (i) *Direct apportionment*

	Heat (£000)	Maintenance (£000)	Steam (£000)	Processing (£000)	Assembly (£000)	Total (£000)
Allocation	90	300	240			630
Heat (4 : 5)	(90)			40	50	—
Maintenance (1 : 2)		(300)		100	200	—
Steam (2 : 1)			(240)	160	80	—
				300	330	630

With the direct method of allocation, inter-service department apportionments are ignored; service department costs are reapportioned to *production* departments only.

(ii) *Step-down method*

This method is the specified order of closing described in Appendix 3.1. There the service department that provided the largest proportion of services for other services was closed first. In this answer the service department providing the largest value of cost inputs to other service departments (namely the maintenance department) is closed first, and the department providing the second largest value of cost input to other service departments (namely steam) is closed next. Return charges are not made.

	Heat (£000)	Maintenance (£000)	Steam (£000)	Processing (£000)	Assembly (£000)	Total (£000)
Allocation	90	300	240			630
Maintenance[a]	30	(300)	45	75	150	
Steam[a]	60		(285)	150	75	
Heat[a]	(180)			80	100	
				305	325	630

Note
[a]Proportions allocated to each department:
  Maintenance = 3/30, 4.5/30, 7.5/30, 15/30
  Steam = 192/912, 480/912, 240/912
  Heat = 4/9, 5/9.

(iii) *Reciprocal method*
Either the algebraic method or the repeated distribution method can be used to take account of reciprocal service arrangements. Both are illustrated in this answer.

Algebraic method
Let
h = total cost of heating
m = total cost of maintenance
s = total cost of steam
Then
$h = 90 + (3/30)m + (192/960)s$
$m = 300 + (5/100)h + (48/960)s$
$s = 240 + (5/100)h + (4.5/30)m$

Expressing these equations in decimal form, we get:

$$h = 90 + 0.10m + 0.2s \qquad (1)$$
$$m = 300 + 0.05h + 0.05s \qquad (2)$$
$$s = 240 + 0.05h + 0.15m \qquad (3)$$

Substituting for s,

$$h = 90 + 0.10m + 0.2(240 + 0.05h + 0.15m)$$
$$m = 300 + 0.05h + 0.05(240 + 0.05h + 0.15m)$$

Expanding these equations gives:

$$h = 90 + 0.10m + 48 + 0.01h + 0.03m$$
$$m = 300 + 0.05h + 12 + 0.0025h + 0.0075m$$

Rearranging,

$$0.99h = 138 + 0.13m \qquad (4)$$
$$0.9925m = 312 + 0.0525h \qquad (5)$$

Substituting in equation (4) for m,

$$0.99h = 138 + 0.13 \frac{(312 + 0.0525h)}{0.9925}$$

$$0.99h = 138 + 40.866 + 0.0069h$$

$$h = \frac{138 + 40.866}{0.99 - 0.0069} = 181.941$$

Substituting for h in equation (5),

$$0.9925m = 312 + 0.0525(181.941)$$

$$m = \frac{312 + 0.0525}{(181.941)} = 324.165$$

Substituting into equation (3),

$$s = 240 + 0.05\,(181.941) + 0.15\,(324.165) = 297.722$$

We now apportion the values of h, m and s to the production departments according to the basis of allocation specified:

	Processing (£000)	Assembly (£000)
Heat (181.941)	72.776 (40/100)	90.970 (50/100)
Maintenance (324.165)	81.041 (7.5/30)	162.082 (15/30)
Steam (297.722)	148.861 (480/960)	74.431 (240/960)
	302.678	327.483

Repeated distribution method

	Heat (£000)	Maintenance (£000)	Steam (£000)	Processing (£000)	Assembly (£000)
Allocation per question	90.00	300.00	240.00		
Heat reallocation	(90.00)	4.50(5%)	4.50(5%)	36.00(40%)	45.00(50%)
Maintenance reallocation	30.45(10%)	(304.50)		45.67(15%)	76.13(25%)	152.25(50%)
Steam reallocation	58.03(20%)	14.51(5%)	(290.17)	145.09(50%)	72.54(25%)
Heat reallocation	(88.48)	4.42(5%)	4.42(5%)	35.40(40%)	44.24(50%)
Maintenance reallocation	1.89(10%)	(18.93)	2.84(15%)	4.73(25%)	9.47(50%)
Steam reallocation	1.45(20%)	0.36(5%)	(7.26)	3.63(50%)	1.82(25%)
Heat reallocation	(3.34)	0.16(5%)	0.17(5%)	1.34(40%)	1.67(50%)
Maintenance reallocation[a]		(0.52)		0.17	0.35
Steam[a]			(0.17)	0.11	0.06
				302.6	327.4

Note

[a]At this stage the costs are so small that no further reallocations between service departments are justified. The costs of the maintenance department are reapportioned in the ratio 7.5:15, while those of the steam department are reapportioned in the ratio 480:240.

(b) The main problems encountered are as follows:
  (i) The costs allocated to the service departments are the result of arbitrary apportionments. The costs are then reallocated from the service to production departments using further arbitrary allocations. Consequently, the associated costs attached to products will be arbitrary and dependent upon the selected apportionment methods.

(ii) If a substantial part of the service department costs are fixed and costs are allocated to production departments on the basis of usage, there is a danger that the resulting unit product costs will fail to distinguish between the fixed and variable cost categories. This could result in misleading information being used for short-term decisions.

(iii) If the responsibility accounting system allocates the actual costs of the service departments to the production departments, the production departments will be accountable for the inefficiencies arising in the service departments. Consequently, the production managers will be demotivated and the service department managers will not be motivated to be efficient because they will always be able to recover their costs.

Possible solutions include the following:

(i) Avoid the use of arbitrary apportionments and identify appropriate cost drivers for the main activities undertaken by the service/support departments using an activity-based costing (ABC) system. See Chapters 3 and 10 for an explanation of an ABC system.

(ii) Separate fixed and variable costs when reallocating service department costs to production departments.

(iii) Charge service department costs to production departments on the basis of actual usage at standard cost. If the production managers have no control over the usage of the service, the service department costs should be regarded as uncontrollable (see 'Guidelines for applying the controllability principle in Chapter 16 for a discussion of this point). The service department managers will be motivated to control costs if they are accountable for the difference between actual and standard usage multiplied by the standard cost.

(c) The answer should include a discussion of the following points:

(i) In today's production environment an increasing proportion of total costs are fixed, and short-term variable costs do not provide a useful measure of the cost of producing a product. Managers require an estimate of long-run product costs. The allocation of fixed costs to products provides a rough guide of a product's long-run cost. The answer should draw attention to the criticisms that Kaplan and Cooper (see Chapter 10) have made of traditional cost allocation methods and explain that an ABC system is an approach that has been recommended to overcome the problems of arbitrary overhead allocations.

(ii) It is a tradition in some industries (e.g. Government contracts) for selling prices to be based on full product costs plus a percentage profit margin.

(iii) Total manufacturing costs are required for stock valuation for external reporting. However, it is questionable whether costs computed for stock valuation ought to be used for decision-making.

(iv) It is sometimes claimed that fixed costs should be allocated to managers in order to draw their attention to those costs that the company incurs to support their activities. This is because the manager may be able to indirectly influence these costs, and should therefore be made aware of the sums which are involved. If this approach is adopted, controllable and non-controllable costs ought to be distinguished in the performance reports.

Question 3.9   (a) *Cost of Job 123*

	(£)	(£)
Direct materials:		
Y (W1) (400 kg × £0.505)	202.00	
Z (W2) (265 kg × £1.45)	384.25	586.25
Direct labour:		
Department A (W3) (76 hrs × £4.50)	342.00	
Department B (W4) (110 hrs × £4)	440.00	782.00
Overhead (W5):		
Department A (76 hrs × £2.70)	205.20	
Department B (110 hrs × £2.25)	247.50	452.70
		1820.95

Workings and comments

(W1)

$$\frac{(£529.75) + (600 \times £0.50) + (500 \times £0.50) + (400 \times £0.52)}{1050 + 600 + 500 + 400} = £0.505 \text{ weighted average price}$$

400 kg issued to job 123 is a direct cost

(W2)
$$\frac{£9946.50 + (16\,000 \times £1.46)}{6970 + 16\,000} = £1.45 \text{ weighted average price.}$$

Direct issues to the job are 270 kg (300 − 30), but 5 kg were damaged and destroyed. It is unlikely that the materials are a direct consequence of the job, and therefore it is incorrect to regard the 5 kg as a direct cost to the job. If such losses are expected to occur from time to time, the cost of the lost materials should be charged to departmental overheads and included in the departmental overhead rate calculation. If such losses are abnormal (as indicated in the question), they should not be charged as product costs. Instead, they should be charged to an abnormal losses account (see Chapter 5) and written off to profit and loss account as a period cost.

(W3) 76 hours have been directly identified to the job at the hourly rate of £4.50. Six hours were overtime, resulting in excess payments. As these hours are likely to be due to the general high level of production, the overtime premium is included in the overhead rate and shared out amongst all jobs. An additional 3 hours rectification were spent on the job, but such work is a *normal* part of the work *generally* undertaken by the department. The cost of rectification is therefore charged to overheads and included in the overhead absorption rate.

(W4) 110 hours are charged to the job. Of these, 30 hours were overtime, but this was a direct result of a customer's requirement on another job. Therefore the overtime premium is not charged to the job.

(W5) All direct items can be ignored when calculating overhead rates, but direct materials include scrapped materials and direct labour includes rectification work. However, scrapped materials are to be regarded as abnormal costs, but 20 hours rectification should be charged to overheads. Department A overtime premium is part of the overhead cost, but the overtime premium for Department B is charged directly to another customer.

Calculation of overhead rates	Department A (£)	Department B (£)
Rectification (20 × £4.50)	90	—
Indirect labour	2420	2960
Overtime premium	450	—
Lubricants	520	680
Maintenance	720	510
Other	1200	2150
	5400	6300
Direct labour hours	$2000 \left(\dfrac{£9000^a}{£4.50} \right)$	$2800 \left(\dfrac{£11\,200}{£4} \right)$
Direct labour hour overhead rate	£2.70	£2.25

Note
[a] £9000 − £90 rectification cost.

(b) Information on the cost of individual jobs can be used as follows:
   (i) for stock valuation of partly completed and completed jobs;
   (ii) to determine the selling price of a product where no established market price exists;
   (iii) as an assessment of the profitability of a job when the selling price is market determined.
   Note that the job cost calculation derived here may be inappropriate for decision-making purposes. The major objective is to use the cost for stock valuation purposes.

Accounting entries for a job costing system

Solutions to Chapter 4 questions

Question 4.1

The company's cost accounts are not integrated with the financial accounts. For a description of a non-integrated accounting system see 'Interlocking accounts' in Chapter 4. The following accounting entries are necessary:

Cost ledger control account

	(£)			(£)
Sales a/c	410 000	1.5.00	Balance b/f	302 000
Capital under	50 150		Stores ledger	42 700
construction a/c			a/c – Purchases	
Balance c/f	237 500		Wages control a/c	124 000
			Production overhead a/c	152 350
			WIP a/c – Royalty	2 150
			Selling overhead a/c	22 000
			Profit	52 450
	697 650			697 650

Stores ledger control account

		(£)		(£)
1.5.00	Balance b/f	85 400	WIP a/c	63 400
	Cost ledger control	42 700	Production overhead a/c	1 450
	a/c – Purchases		Capital a/c	7 650
			31.5.X0 Balance c/f	55 600
		£128 100		£128 100

Wages control account

	(£)		(£)
Cost ledger control a/c	124 000	Capital a/c	12 500
		Production	35 750
		WIP a/c	7 550
	£124 000		£124 000

Production overhead control account

	(£)			(£)
Stores ledger a/c	1 450	Capital a/c	30 000	
Wages control a/c	35 750	WIP a/c – Absorption		152 000
Cost ledger control a/c	152 350	(balancing figure)		
		Costing P/L a/c (under		7 550
		absorption)		
	£189 550			£189 550

Work in progress control account

		(£)		(£)
1.5.00	Balance b/f	167 350	Finished goods control a/c	281 300
	Stores ledger a/c –		(balancing figure)	
	Issues	63 400		
	Wages control a/c	75 750	31.5.X0 Balance c/f[a]	179 350
Production overhead		152 000		
absorbed				
Cost ledger control				
a/c – Royalty		2 150		
		£460 650		£460 650

Finished goods control account

	(£)		(£)
1.5.00 Balance b/f	49 250	Cost sales a/c[b]	328 000
WIP a/c	281 300	31.5.X0 Balance c/f	2 550
	£330 550		£330 550

Capital under construction account

	(£)		(£)
Stores ledger a/c	7 650	Cost ledger control a/c	50 150
Wages control a/c	12 500		
Production overhead absorbed	30 000		
	£50 150		£50 150

Sales account

	(£)		(£)
Costing P/L a/c	£410 000	Cost ledger control a/c	£410 000

Cost of sales account

	(£)		(£)
Finished goods a/c[b]	£328 000	Cost P/L a/c	£328 000

Selling overhead account

	(£)		(£)
Cost ledger control a/c	£22 000	Costing P/L a/c	£22 000

Costing profit and loss account

	(£)		(£)
Selling overhead a/c	22 000	Sales a/c	410 000
Production overhead (under absorbed)	7 550		
Cost of sales a/c	328 000		
Profit – Cost ledger control a/c	52 450		
	£410 000		£410 000

Notes

[a]Closing balance of work in progress = £167 350 (opening balance)
                £12 000 (increase per question)
                £179 350

[b]Transfer from finished goods stock to cost of sales account: £410 000 sales × (100/125) = £328 000

Question 4.2

(a)

Raw materials stores account

	(£)		(£)
Balance b/d	49 500	Work in progress	104 800
Purchases	108 800	Loss due to flood to P&L a/c	2 400
		Balance c/d	51 100
	£158 300		£158 300
Balance b/d	51 100		

Work in progress control account

	(£)		(£)
Balance b/d	60 100	Finished goods	222 500
Raw materials	104 800	Balance c/d	56 970
Direct wages	40 200		
Production overhead	74 370		
	£279 470		£279 470
Balance b/d	56 970		

Finished goods control account

	(£)		(£)
Balance b/d	115 400	Cost of sales	212 100
Work in progress	222 500	Balance c/d	125 800
	£337 900		£337 900
Balance b/d	125 800		

Production overhead

	(£)		(£)
General ledger control	60 900	Work in progress	
Notional rent (3 × £4000)	12 000	(185% × £40 200)	74 370
Overhead over absorbed	1 470		
	£74 370		£74 370

General ledger control account

	(£)		(£)
Sales	440 000	Balance b/d	
Balance c/d	233 870	(49 500 + 60 100 +	
		115 400)	225 000
		Purchases	108 800
		Direct wages	40 200
		Production overhead	60 900
		Notional rent	12 000
		P & L a/c	226 970
		(profit for period: see (b))	
	673 870		673 870

(b) *Calculation of profit in cost accounts*

	(£)	(£)
Sales		440 000
Cost of sales	212 100	
Loss of stores	2 400	
	214 500	
Less overhead over absorbed	1 470	213 030
Profit		226 970

Reconciliation statement[a]

	(£)	(£)	(£)
Profit as per cost accounts			226 970
Differences in stock values:			
Raw materials opening stock	1500		
Raw materials closing stock	900		
WIP closing stock	1030	3 430	
WIP opening stock	3900		
Finished goods opening stock	4600		
Finished goods closing stock	3900	(12 400)	(8 970)
Add items not included in financial accounts:			
Notional rent			12 000
Profit as per financial accounts			230 000

Note

[a]Stock valuations in the financial accounts may differ from the valuation in the cost accounts. For example, raw materials may be valued on a LIFO basis in the cost accounts, whereas FIFO or weighted average may be used in the financial accounts. WIP and finished stock may be valued on a marginal (variable costing) basis in the cost accounts, but the valuation may be based on an absorption costing basis in the financial accounts. To reconcile the profits, you should start with the profit from the cost accounts and consider what the impact would be on the profit calculation if the financial accounting stock valuations were used. If the opening stock valuation in the financial accounts exceeds the valuation in the cost accounts then adopting the financial accounting stock valuation will reduce the profits. If the closing stock valuation in the financial accounts exceeds the valuation in the cost accounts then adopting the financial accounting stock valuation will increase profits. Note that the notional rent is not included in the financial accounts and should therefore be deducted from the costing profit in the reconciliation statement.

(c) The over recovery of overhead could be apportioned between cost of goods sold for the current period and closing stocks. The justification for this is based on the assumption that the under/over recovery is due to incorrect estimates of activity and overhead expenditure, which leads to incorrect allocations being made to the cost of sales and closing stock accounts. The proposed adjustment is an attempt to rectify this incorrect allocation.

The alternative treatment is for the full amount of the under/over recovery to be written off to the cost accounting profit and loss account in the current period as a period cost. This is the treatment recommended by SSAP 9.

(a)

Question 4.3

Stores ledger control account

	(£)		(£)
Opening Balance	60 140	Finished Goods Control A/c (1)	95 200
Cost Ledger Control A/c	93 106	Closing Balance	58 046
	153 246		153 246

Production wages control account

	(£)		(£)
Cost Ledger Control A/c (2)	121 603	Finished Goods Control A/c	87 480
		Production Overhead	
		Control A/c (2)	34 123
		(indirect wages)	
	121 603		121 603

Production overhead control account

	(£)		(£)
Cost Ledger Control A/c	116 202	Finished Goods Control A/c (3)	61 236
Production Wages		Profit & Loss A/c – Fixed	
Control A/c (2)	34 123	Overhead (3)	90 195
Profit & Loss A/c – over			
absorbed variable			
production overhead (3)	1 106		
	151 431		151 431

Finished goods control account

	(£)		(£)
Opening Balance	147 890	Variable Production Cost of	
Stores Ledger Control A/c	95 200	Sales A/c (balance)	241 619
Production Wages Control A/c	87 480	Closing Balance	150 187
Production Overhead			
Control A/c	61 236		
	391 806		391 806

Workings

(1)

	(Kg)	(£)
Opening stock	540	7 663
Purchases	1 100	15 840
	1 640	23 503

Issue price £23 503/1 640 = £14.33 per kg

Cost of material issues: Material Y = £14.33 × 1 164kg = £16 680

Other materials = £78 520

£95 200

(2) *Analysis of wages*

	Direct labour (£)	Indirect labour (£)
Direct workers productive time (11 664 × £7.50)	87 480	
Direct workers unproductive time at £7.50 (12 215 hours – 11 664)		4 132.50
Overtime premium (1 075 hours × £2.50)		2 687.50
Indirect workers basic time (4 655 hours × £5.70)		26 533.50
Indirect workers overtime premium (405 hours × £1.90)		769.50
	87 480	34 123.00

Total wages for the period £121 603 (£87 480 + £34 123)

(3) *Analysis of overheads*

Production overheads	= £150 325 (£116 202 + £34 123)
Fixed overheads	= 90 195 (60% × £150 325)
Variable overheads	= 60 130 (40% × £150 325)
Variable overheads absorbed	= 61 236 (70% of the direct labour cost of £87 480)
Over-absorbed overheads	= 1 106 (£61 236 – £60 130)

Note that with a marginal costing system fixed overheads are charged directly to the profit and loss account and not included in the product costs. Therefore they are not included in the finished stocks.

(b) See working (2) in part (a) for the answer to this question.

(c)

	(£)	(£)
Sales		479 462
Less: Variable production cost of sales	241 619	
Variable selling and administration overheads	38 575	
Over-absorbed variable production overheads	(1 106)	279 088
Contribution		200 374
Less: Fixed production overheads	90 195	
Fixed selling and administration overheads	74 360	164 655
Net profit		35 819

Question 4.4

(a)

Stores ledger card

Date	Kilos	Total value (£)	Average price per kilo (£)	
Opening balance	21 600	28 944	1.34	
1 Issue	(7 270)	(9 742)	1.34	
7 Purchase	17 400	23 490		
	31 730	42 692	1.3455	(£42 692/31 730)
8 Issue	(8 120)	(10 925)	1.3455	
15 Issue	(8 080)	(10 872)	1.3455	
20 Purchase	19 800	26 730		
	35 330	47 625	1.348	(£47 625/35 330)

22 Issue	(9 115)	(12 287)	1.348
Closing balance	26 215	35 338	1.348

Summary of transactions

	(£)
Opening balance	28 944
Purchases	50 220
Issues	(43 826)
Closing balance	35 338

Raw material stock control account

	(£)		(£)
Opening balance	28 944	WIP	43 826
Purchases	50 220	Closing balance	35 338
	79 164		79 164

Production costs for the period:	(£)
Raw materials	43 826
Labour and overhead	35 407
	79 233
Cost per unit (£79 233/17 150 units)	£4.62

Units sold = opening stock (16 960) + production (17 150)
        − closing stock (17 080) = 17 030 units

Finished goods stock control account

	(£)		(£)
Opening balance	77 168	Cost of sales	
Raw materials	43 826	(difference/balancing figure)	77 491
Labour and overhead	35 407	Closing balance	
		(17 080 × £4.62)	78 910
	156 401		156 401

(b) The financial ledger control account is sometimes described as a cost control account or a general ledger adjustment account. For an explanation of the purpose of this account see 'Interlocking accounting' in Chapter 4.

(c) Budgeted production (units):

Sales	206 000	
Add closing stock	18 128	(206 000 × 1.10 × 20/250)
Less opening stock	(17 080)	
	207 048	units

For month 12 the raw material usage is 1.90 kilos per unit of output:

(7270 + 8120 + 8080 + 9115 = 32 585 kg used)/17 150 units produced
∴ Budgeted material usage = 207 048 units × 1.9 kg per unit
                    = 393 391 kg

Budgeted material purchases

Budgeted usage	393 391 kg
Add closing stock	22 230 (11 700 × 1.9)
Less opening stock	(26 215)
	389 406 kg

Question 4.5   (a)

Raw material stock control account

	(£)		(£)
Opening balance	72 460	Finished goods (1)	608 400
Creditors	631 220	Closing balance	95 280
	703 680		703 680

Production overhead control account

	(£)		(£)
Bank/Creditors	549 630	Finished goods (3)	734 000
Wages (2)	192 970	P & L – under absorption (3)	8 600
	742 600		742 600

Finished goods stock control account

	(£)		(£)
Opening balance	183 560	Production cost of sales (6)	1 887 200
Raw materials	608 400	Closing balance	225 960
Wages (5)	587 200		
Production overhead	734 000		
	2 113 160		2 113 160

Workings

(1) Raw materials issues:
    Product A: 41 000 units at £7.20 per unit =£295 200
    Product B: 27 000 units at £11.60 per unit =£313 200

    £608 400

(2) Indirect labour charged to production overhead:
    3 250 overtime premium hours at £2 per hour = £6 500 + £186 470 = £192 970

(3) Production overhead absorbed charged to finished goods:
    Product A: 41 000 × 1 hour × £10   =£410 000
    Product B: 27 000 × 1.2 hours × £10 =£324 000

    £734 000

    Production overhead under-absorbed = £549 630 + £192 970 – £734 000
    = £8 600

(4) Direct labour charge to finished goods stock:
    Product A: 41 000 × 1 hour × £8   =£328 000
    Product B: 27 000 × 1.2 hours × £8   =£259 200

    £587 200

(5) Production cost of sales:
    Cost of product A = £7.20 materials + £8 direct labour + £10 overhead =
        £25.20
    Cost of product B = £11.60 materials + £9.60 direct labour (1.2 hours × £8)
            + £12 overhead (1.2 hours × £10) = £33.20
    Cost of sales: Product A = 38 000 units × £25.20 per unit = £957 600
                Product B = 28 000 units × £33.20 per unit = £929 600

    £1 887 200

ACCOUNTING ENTRIES FOR A JOB COSTING SYSTEM

(6) Valuation of closing stocks of finished goods:
    Product A: 6200 units at £25.20 =   £156 240
    Product B: 2100 units at £33.20 =   £69 720
                                              £225 960

The above figure can also be derived from the balance of the account.

(b)

	Product A (£000)	Product B (£000)	Total (£000)
Sales	1330	1092	2422
Production cost of sales	(957.6)	(929.6)	(1887.2)
Gross profit (before adjustment)	372.4	162.4	534.8
Under absorbed production overheads			(8.6)
Gross profit (after adjustment)			526.2
Non-production overheads			(394.7)
Net profit			131.5

(c) With a marginal costing system fixed production overheads are charged directly against profits whereas with an absorption costing system they are included in the product costs and therefore included in the stock valuations. This means that with absorption costing cost of sales and profits will be affected by the changes in stocks. An increase in stocks will result in some of the fixed overheads incurred during the period being deferred to future periods whereas with a decrease in stocks the opposite situation will apply. Thus, absorption costing profits will be higher than marginal costing profits when stocks increase and lower when stocks decrease. For a more detailed explanation of the difference in profits you should refer to 'Variable costing and absorption costing: a comparison of their impact on profit' in Chapter 7.

In this question there is a stock increase of 3000 units for product A resulting in absorption costing profits exceeding marginal costing profits by £20 400 (3000 units at £6.80 per unit fixed overhead). Conversely, for product B there is a 1000 units stock reduction resulting in marginal costing profits exceeding the absorption costing profits by £8160 (1000 units at £8.16 per unit fixed overhead). The overall impact is that absorption costing profits exceed marginal costing profits by £12 240.

(a) A wages control account is a summary account which records total wages payable including employers' national insurance contributions. The account is cleared by a credit and corresponding debits in respect of total wages costs charged to WIP and the overhead control account. The detail which supports the control account is maintained in subsidiary payroll records.   **Question 4.6**

(b) (i)

	Dr (£)	Cr (£)
Wages control	122 300	
Bank		122 300
Wages control	58 160	
Employees' National Insurance		14 120
Employees' pension fund contributions		7 200
Income tax		27 800
Court order retentions		1 840
Trade union subscriptions		1 200
Private health plans		6 000
	180 460	180 460

Production overhead control Dr	18 770	
Employer's National Insurance		18 770
	18 770	18 770

(ii)

Work-in-progress control:		
Wages	77 460	
Overtime wages – direct	16 800	
Production overhead control:		
Overtime premium	9 000	
Shift premium	13 000	
Indirect wages	38 400	
Overtime wage – indirect	10 200	
Warehouse construction account	2 300	
Statutory sick pay	9 000	
Idle time	4 300	
Wages control		180 460
	180 460	180 460

Question 4.7

(a) *Calculation of gross wages:*

	Direct workers		Indirect workers		Total
		(£)		(£)	(£)
Attendance time	2640 × 5.00 =	13 200	940 × 4.00 =	3760	
Overtime premium	180 × 2 =	360	75 × 1.60 =	120	
Group bonuses		2 840		710	
Gross wages		16 400		4590	20 990

(b) *Analysis of gross wages:*

	Direct charge (to WIP)		Indirect charge to production overhead		Total
		(£)		(£)	(£)
Attendance time:					
Direct workers	2515 × 5.00 =	12 575	125 × 5.00 =	625	
Indirect workers			940 × 4.00 =	3760	
Overtime premium:					
Direct workers	72 × 2.00 =	144	108 × 2.00 =	216	
Indirect workers	30 × 1.60 =	48	45 × 1.60 =	72	
Group bonuses					
Direct workers				2840	
Indirect workers				710	
		12 767		8223	20 990

Wages control account

	(£)		(£)
Cost ledger control	20 990	Work in progress	12 767
(Gross wages)		Production overhead	8 223
	20 990		20 990

Production overhead control account:

	(£)
Wages control	8223
Cost ledger control	1865
(Employers' employment costs)	

Process costing

Solutions to Chapter 5 questions

(a) (i)

Process A account

	(kg)	(£)		(kg)	(£)	(£)
Direct material	2000	10 000	Normal loss	400	0.50	200
Direct labour		7 200	Process B	1400	18.575	26 005
Process costs		8 400	Abnormal loss	200	18.575	3 715
Overhead		4 320				
	2000	29 920		2000		29 920

Unit cost = (£29 920 − £200)/1600 = £18.575

(ii)

Process B account

	(kg)	(£)		(kg)	(£)	(£)
Process A	1400	26 005	Finished goods	2620	21.75	56 989
Direct material	1400	16 800	Normal loss	280	1.825	511
Direct labour		4 200	(10% × 2800)			
Overhead		2 520				
Process costs		5 800				
		55 325				
Abnormal gain	100	2 175				
	2900	57 000		2900		57 500

Unit cost = (£55 325 − £511)/(2800 − 280) = £21.75

(iii)

Normal loss/gain account

	(kg)	(£)		(kg)	(£)
Process A	400	200	Bank (A)	400	200
Process B	280	511	Abnormal gain (B)	100	182.5
			Bank (B)	180	328.5
	680	711		680	711

(iv)

Abnormal loss/gain

	(£)		(£)
Process A	3715	Process B	2175
Normal loss/gain (B)	182.5	Bank	100
		Profit & Loss	1622.5
	3897.5		3897.5

(v)

Finished goods

	(£)		(£)
Process B	56 989		

(vi)

Profit and loss account (extract)

	(£)		(£)
Abnormal loss/gain	1622.5		

Question 5.2   (a)   Units completed = 8250 − Closing WIP (1600) = 6650

Calculation of number of equivalent units produced

	Completed units	Closing WIP	Total equivalent units
Previous process	6650	1600	8250
Materials	6650	1600	8250
Labour and overhead	6650	960 (60%)	7610

(b)

	(£)	Total equivalent units	Cost per unit (£)
Previous process cost	453 750	8250	55
Materials	24 750	8250	3
Labour and overheads	350 060	7610	46
			104

(c)

Process account

	Units	(£)		Units	(£)
Input from previous			Finished goods^a	6650	691 600
process	8250	453 750	Closing WIP^b	1600	136 960
Materials		24 750			
Labour and overheads		350 060			
	8250	828 560		8250	828 560

Note
^a Cost of completed production = 6650 units × £104 = £691 600
^b   (£)
Closing WIP: Previous process cost (1600 × £55) =   88 000
                        Materials (1600 × £3)   =   4 800
                        Labour and overhead (960 × £46) = 44 160
                                                                           136 960

(d) See the introduction to Chapter 6 and 'Accounting for by-products' in Chapter 6 for the answer to this question.

Question 5.3   (a)

	Units
Input:	
Opening WIP	12 000
Transferred from process 1	95 000
	107 000
Output:	
Closing WIP	10 000
Normal loss	200
Completed units (balance)	96 800
	107 000

Statement of completed production and calculation of cost per unit (Process 2)

	Opening WIP (£)	Current cost (£)	Total cost (£)	Completed units	Closing WIP	Total equiv. units	Cost per unit (£)	WIP (£)
Previous process cost	13 440	107 790	121 230	96 800	10 000	106 800	1.135	11 350
Materials added	4 970	44 000	48 970	96 800	9 000	105 800	0.463	4 167
Conversion costs	3 120	51 480	54 600	96 800	7 000	103 800	0.526	3 682
	21 530	203 270	224 800				2.124	19 199

Completed units (96 800 × £2.124) 205 601

224 800

Note that the above answer is based on the short-cut approach described in Appendix 5.1

(b)

Process 2 Account

	Units	(£)		Units	(£)
Opening WIP	12 000	21 530	Finished goods	96 800	205 601
Transferred from process 1	95 000	107 790	Normal loss	200	—
Materials		44 000	Closing WIP	10 000	19 199
Conversion cost		51 840			
	107 000	224 800		107 000	224 800

(c) If losses are not expected to occur the loss would be abnormal. Because abnormal losses are not an inherent part of the production process and arise from inefficiencies they are not included in the process costs. Instead, they are charged with their full share of production costs and removed (credited) from the process account and reported separately as an abnormal loss. The abnormal loss is treated as a period cost and written off in the profit and loss account.

(d) Workings would be different because FIFO assumes that the opening WIP is the first group of units to be completed during the current period. The opening WIP is charged separately to completed production, and the cost per unit is based only on current period costs and production for the current period. This requires that opening WIP equivalent units are deducted from completed units to derive current period equivalent units. The cost per unit is derived from dividing current period costs by current period total equivalent units.

Question 5.4

(a)

Cost element	Current period costs (£)	Completed units less opening WIP equiv. units	Closing WIP equiv. units	Current total equiv. units	Cost per unit (£)
Materials	2255	2800	1300	4100	0.55
Conversion costs[a]	3078	3300	975	4275	0.72
	5333				
	(£)	(£)			

Completed production:		
Opening WIP (£540 + £355)	895	
Materials (2800 × £0.55)	1540	
Conversion cost (3300 × £0.72)	2376	
		4811
Closing work in progress:		
Materials (1300 × £0.55)	715	
Conversion cost (975 × £0.72)	702	
		1417
		6228

Note
^aBonus = Current total equivalent units (4275) – Expected output (4000)
  = 275 units × £0.80 = £220
 Labour cost = 6 men × 37 hours × £5 = £1110 + Bonus (£220) = £1330
 Conversion cost = £1748 overhead + £1330 labour = £3078

Process account

	(£)		(£)
Opening WIP	895	Completed output	4811
Materials	2255	Closing WIP	1417
Labour and overhead	3078		
	6228		6228

(b) (i) In most organizations the purchasing function is centralized and all goods are purchased by the purchasing department. To purchase goods, user departments complete a purchase requisition. This is a document requesting the purchasing department to purchase the goods listed on the document.

(ii) See 'Materials recording procedure' in Chapter 4 for the answer to this question.

Question 5.5

(a) *Calculation of input for process 1*

	(litres)	(£)
Opening stock	4 000	10 800
Receipts	20 000	61 000
Less closing stock	(8 000)	(24 200)
Process input	16 000	47 600

Output		(litres)
Completed units		8 000
Closing WIP		5 600
Normal loss (15% of input)		2 400
		16 000

Because input is equal to output, there are no abnormal gains or losses.

Calculation of cost per unit (Process 1)

The calculation (based on the short-cut method) is as follows:

Element of cost	(£)	Completed units	Closing WIP	Total equiv. units	Cost per unit (£)	WIP (£)
Materials	47 600	8000	5600	13 600	3.50	19 600
Conversion cost	21 350	8000	4200	12 200	1.75	7 350
					£5.25	£26 950

Completed units 8000 × £5.25 = £42 000

Process 1 account – May 2000

	(litres)	(£)		(litres)	(£)
Materials	16 000	47 600	Transfers to process 2	8 000	42 000
Labour		4 880	Normal loss	2 400	—
Direct expenses		4 270	Closing stock C/f	5 600	26 950
Overheads absorbed		12 200			
	16 000	68 950		16 000	68 950

With process 2, there is no closing WIP. Therefore it is unnecessary to express output in equivalent units. The cost per unit is calculated as follows:

$$\frac{\text{cost of production less scrap value of normal loss}}{\text{expected output}} = \frac{£54\ 000^{a}}{(90\% \times 8000)} = £7.50$$

Note
^aCost of production = transferred in cost from process 1 (42 000) + labour (£6000) + overhead (£6000).

Process 2 account – May 2000

	Litres	(£)		Litres	(£)
Transferred from Process 1	8000	42 000	Finished goods store[b]	7500	56 250
Labour		6 000	Normal loss	800	
Overheads absorbed		6 000	Closing stock	—	—
Abnormal gain[a]	300	2 250			
	8300	56 250		8300	56 250

Finished goods account

	Litres	(£)			
Ex Process 2	7500	56 250			

Abnormal gain account

	(£)		Litres	(£)
Profit and loss account	2250	Process 2 account	300	2250

Notes
[a]Input = 8000 litres. Normal output = 90% × 8000 litres = 7200 litres. Actual output = 7500 litres.
Abnormal gain = 300 litres × £7.50 per litre = £2250.
[b]7500 litres at £7.50 per litre.

(b) If the materials can be replaced then the loss to the company will consist of the replacement cost of materials. If the materials cannot be replaced then the loss will consist of the lost sales revenue less the costs not incurred as a result of not processing and selling 100 litres.

Question 5.6

a)
Expected output from an input of 39 300 sheets:	3 144 000 cans	(39 300 × 80)
Less 1% rejects	31 440 cans	
Expected output after rejects	3 112 560 cans	

The normal loss arising from the rejects (31 440 cans) is sold at £0.26 per kg. It is therefore necessary to express the rejects in terms of kilos of metal. Each sheet weighs 2 kilos but wastage in the form of offcuts is 2% of input. Therefore the total weight of 80 cans is 1.96 kg (0.98 × 2 kg) and the weight of each can is 0.0245 kilos (1.96 kg/80 cans). The weight of the normal loss arising from the rejects is 770.28 kg (31 440 × 0.0245 kg). The normal loss resulting from the offcuts is 1572 kg (39 300 × 2 kg × 0.02). Hence the total weight of the normal loss is 2342.28 kilos (1572 kg + 770.28 kg), with an expected sales value of £609 (2342.28 kg × £0.26).

Process account

	(£)		(£)
Direct materials		Finished goods	
(39 300 × £2.50)	98 250	(3 100 760 cans × £0.042[a])	130 232
		Normal loss	609
Direct labour and		Abnormal loss	
overheads	33 087	(11 800 kg[b] at £0.042[a])	496
	131 337		131 337

Abnormal loss account

	(£)		(£)
Process account	496	Sale proceeds[c]	75
		Profit and loss account	421
	496		496

Notes
[a]Cost per unit = $\dfrac{£98\ 250 + £33\ 087 - £609}{\text{expected output (3 112 560 cans)}}$ = £0.042 per can

^{b}Expected output (3 112 560) − actual output (3 100 760 cans) = 11 800 cans
^{c}Abnormal loss = 11 800 cans (3 112 560 − 3 100 760)
This will yield 289.1 kilos (11 800 × 0.0245 kilos) of metal with a sales value of
£75 (289.1 × £0.26).

(b) (i) See 'Opening and closing work in progress' in Chapter 5 for the answer to this
question.

(ii) See 'Weighted average method' and 'First in, first out method' in Chapter 5 for
the answer to this question.

Question 5.7

(a) Opening WIP (100) + input – closing WIP (200) = Normal loss (0.10 × input)
+ output (1250)
Input – Normal loss (0.10 × input) = 1250 –100 + 200
0.90 input = 1350
Input = 1500 (1350/0.9)

(b) The short cut approach is adopted resulting in the normal loss not being
included in the calculation of equivalent units (see Appendix 5.1).

	Completed units less opening WIP equivalent units	Closing WIP equiv. units	Current total equiv. units
Materials	1 150 (1 250 – 100)	200	1 350
Conversion cost	1 220 (1 250 – 30)	80 (200 × 40%)	1 300

(c) Cost per unit = Input cost/current total equivalent units
Conversion cost = 1 300 × £1.50 = £1950
With materials the normal loss will be deducted from the input cost to derive the cost per
unit so that:
Materials = 1350 × £2.60 = £3510 + (10% × 1500 × £2) = £3810.

Question 5.8

(a)

Production statement

Input:	Units
Opening WIP	20 000
Transfer from previous process	180 000
	200 000

Output:	
Closing WIP	18 000
Abnormal loss	60
Completed units (balance)	181 940
	200 000

Statement of equivalent production and calculation of cost of completed production and WIP

	Current costs (£)	Completed units less opening WIP equivalent units	Abnormal loss	Closing WIP equivalent units	Current total equivalent units	Cost per unit (£)
Previous process cost	394 200	161 940	60	18 000	180 000	2.19
Materials	110 520	167 940	60	16 200	184 200	0.60
Conversion cost	76 506	173 940	60	12 600	186 600	0.41
	581 226					3.20

	(£)	(£)
Cost of completed production:		
Opening WIP (given)	55 160	
Previous process cost (161 940 × £2.19)	354 649	
Materials (167 940 × £0.60)	100 764	
Conversion costs (173 940 × £0.41)	71 315	581 888
Cost of closing WIP:		
Previous process cost (18 000 × £2.19)	39 420	
Materials (16 200 × £0.60)	9 720	
Conversion costs (12 600 × £0.41)	5 166	54 306
Value of abnormal loss (60 × £3.20)		192
		636 386

Process 3 account

	(£)		(£)
Opening WIP	55 160	Transfer to finished goods	
Transfer from process 2	394 200	stock	581 888
Materials	110 520	Abnormal loss	192
Conversion costs	76 506	Closing WIP	54 306
	636 386		636 386

(b) Normal losses are unavoidable losses that are expected to occur under efficient operating conditions. They are an expected production cost and should be absorbed by the completed production whereas abnormal losses are not included in the process costs but are removed from the appropriate process account and reported separately as an abnormal loss. See 'Losses in process and partially completed units' in the appendix to Chapter 5 for a more detailed explanation of the treatment of normal losses.

(c) If the weighted average method is used, both the units and value of WIP are merged with current period costs and production to calculate the average cost per unit. The weighted average cost per unit is then applied to all completed units, any abnormal losses and closing WIP equivalent units. In contrast, with the FIFO method the opening WIP is assumed to be the first group of units completed during the current period. The opening WIP is charged separately to completed production, and the cost per unit is based only on current costs and production for the period. The closing WIP is assumed to come from the new units that have been started during the period.

The physical input and output to the process are as follows:

Question 5.9

Input:	Rolls	Output:	Rolls
Opening WIP	1000	Spoiled	550
Started from new	5650	Closing WIP	800
Reworked	500	Completed (balance)	5800
	7150		7150

The 5800 rolls will include the reworked output of 500 rolls, which is assumed to be completed during the period. Therefore the un-reworked output is 5300 rolls. It is assumed that the normal loss is 10% of the un-reworked output of 5300 units. Hence the abnormal loss is 20 rolls (550 − 530 rolls). Because the question specifically states that the loss can be identified only at the end of the process, losses are not allocated to closing WIP. Therefore the short-cut method is not applied.

(a) *Schedule of completed production and cost per roll*

	Current cost (£)	Un-reworked completed rolls less opening WIP equivalent rolls	Reworked equivalent rolls[a]	Normal loss	Abnormal loss	Closing WIP equivalent rolls	Total equivalent rolls	Cost per roll (£)
Materials	72 085	4300	300	530	20	640	5790	12.4499
Labour	11 718	4700	250	530	20	320	5820	2.0134
Overheads[b]	41 013	4700	250	530	20	320	5820	7.0469
	124 816							21.5102

Notes

[a] Reworked equivalent rolls refers to production for the current period only. Previous period costs are not included in the cost per unit calculation when the FIFO method is used.

[b] Note that overheads are charged to production at the rate of £3.50 per £1 of labour.

(b) *Allocation of costs*

Completed units:

	(£)
Un-reworked completed rolls	
[(4300 × £12.4499) + (4700 × £2.0134) + (4700 × £7.0469)]	96 118
Reworked rolls	
[(300 × £12.4499) + (250 × £2.0134) + (250 × £7.0469)]	6 000
Cost of normal spoilage (530 × £21.5102)	11 400
Opening WIP (£12 000 + £4620 + £16 170[a])]	32 790
	146 308

Value of closing WIP	
[(640 × £12.4499) + (320 × £2.0134) + (320 × £7.0469)]	10 868
Cost of abnormal spoilage (20 × £21.5102)	430
	157 606

Note

[a] Overhead costs at the rate of £3.50 per £1 of labour should be added to the value of the opening WIP.

(c) The advantages of converting to a standard costing system are as follows:

  (i) Calculations of *actual* costs per unit for each period will not be required. Completed production and stocks can be valued at standard costs per unit for each element of cost.

  (ii) Targets can be established and a detailed analysis of the variances can be presented. This process should enable costs to be more effectively controlled.

(d) Actual costs computed in (a) and (b) imply that cost-plus pricing is used. Possible disadvantages of this approach include:

  (i) Prices based solely on costs ignore demand and the prices that competitors charge.

  (ii) Overheads will include fixed overheads, which are arbitrarily apportioned and may distort the pricing decision.

  (iii) Replacement costs are preferable to historic costs for pricing decisions. Standard costs represent future target costs and are therefore more suitable for decision-making than historic costs based on a FIFO system.

For additional comments see 'Limitations of cost-plus pricing' in Chapter 11.

(e) The implications are:
   (i) Replacement costs should be used for management accounting, but they will have to be adjusted for external reporting.
   (ii) Practical difficulties in using replacement costs. For example, it is necessary to constantly monitor the current market price for all stock items.
   (iii) The benefits from the use of replacement costs will depend upon the rate of inflation. The higher the rate of inflation, the greater the benefits.

Joint and by-product costing

Solutions to Chapter 6 questions

Question 6.1

(a) Normal loss (toxic waste) = 50 kg per 1000 kg of input (i.e. 5%)
Actual input = 10 000 kg
Abnormal loss = Actual toxic waste (600) less normal loss (500) = 100 kg

By-product R net revenues of £1750 are credited to the joint (main) process account and normal and abnormal losses are valued at the average cost per unit of output:

$$\frac{\text{Net cost of production } (£35\ 750 - £1750)}{\text{Expected output of the joint products } (8500\ \text{kg})} = £4$$

The cost of the output of the joint products is £33 600 (8400 kg × £4) and this is to be allocated to the individual products on the basis of final sales value (i.e. 4800 kg × £5 = £24 000 for P and 3600 kg × £7 = £25 200 for Q):
P = £24 000/£49 200 × £33 600 = £16 390
Q = £25 200/£49 200 × £33 600 = £17 210

The main process account is as follows:

Main process account

	(kg)	(£)		(kg)	(£)
Materials	10 000	15 000	P Finished goods	4 800	16 390
Direct labour	—	10 000	Q Process 2	3 600	17 210
Variable overhead	—	4 000	By-product R	1 000	1 750
Fixed overhead	—	6 000	Normal toxic waste	500	—
Toxic waste disposal a/c	—	750	Abnormal toxic waste	100	400
	10 000	35 750		10 000	35 750

(b)

Toxic waste disposal (Creditors' account)

	(£)		(£)
Bank	900	Main process account	750
		Abnormal toxic waste	150
	900		900

Abnormal toxic waste account

	(£)		(£)
Main process account	400	Profit and Loss Account	550
Toxic waste disposal account	150		
(100 × £1.50)			
	550		550

Process 2 account

	kg	(£)		kg	(£)
Main process Q	3600	17 210	Finished goods Q[b]	3 300	26 465
Fixed cost		6 000	Closing work-in-progress[b]	300	1 920
Variable cost		5 175[a]			
	3600	28 385		3600	28 385

Notes:
^{a} $3300 + (50\% \times 300) \times £1.50 = £5175$
^{b}

	(£)	Completed units	WIP equiv. units	Total equiv. units	Cost per unit
Previous process cost	17 210	3300	300	3600	£4.78
Conversion cost	11 175	3300	150	3450	£3.24
					£8.02

	(£)
Completed units (3 300 units × £8.02)	26 465
WIP (300 × £4.78) + (150 × £3.24)	1 920
	28 385

(c) See the section on methods of apportioning joint costs to joint products in Chapter 6 for the answer to this question.

(d)

	(£)
Incremental sales revenue per kg from further processing (£7 − £4.30)	2.70
Incremental (variable) cost per kg of further processing	1.50
Incremental contribution per kg from further processing	1.20

	(£)
At an output of 3600 kg the incremental contribution is	4320
Avoidable fixed costs	3600
Net benefit	720

$$\text{Break-even point} = \frac{\text{Avoidable fixed costs (£3600)}}{\text{Incremental unit contribution (£1.20)}} = 3000 \text{ kg}$$

Further processing should be undertaken if output is expected to exceed 3000 kg per week.

(a) See Figure Q6.2

Question 6.2

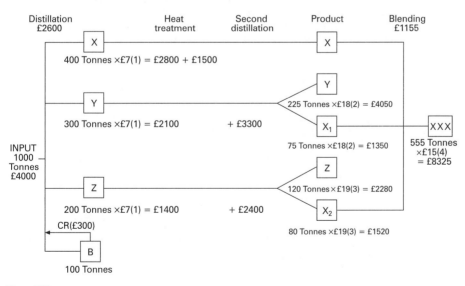

Figure Q6.2

Workings
(W1) $(4000 + 2600 - 300)/900 = £7$
(W2) $(2100 + 3300)/300 = £18$
(W3) $(1400 + 2400)/200 = £19$
(W4) $(2800 + 1500 + 1155 + 1350 + 1520)/555 = £15$

(b)

Product	Output (tonnes)	Total cost (£)	Cost per tonne (£)
XXX	555	8325	15
Y	225	4050	18
Z	120	2280	19

(c) An alternative treatment is to credit the income direct to the profit and loss account rather than crediting the proceeds to the process from which the byproduct was derived.

Question 6.3

(a) You can see from the question that the input is 240 000 kg and the output is 190 000 kg. It is assumed that the difference of 50 000 kg is a normal loss in output which occurs at the start of processing. Therefore the loss should be charged to the completed production and WIP. By making no entry for normal losses in the cost per unit calculation the normal loss is automatically apportioned between completed units and WIP.

	Opening WIP (£)	Current cost (£)	Total cost (£)	Completed units	Closing WIP	Total equivalent units	Cost per unit (£)	WIP value (£)
Materials	20 000	75 000	95 000	160 000	30 000	190 000	0.50	15 000
Processing costs	12 000	96 000	108 000	160 000	20 000	180 000	0.60	12 000
			203 000				1.10	27 000
				Completed units (160 000 units × £1.10)				176 000
								203 000

(b) This question requires a comparison of incremental revenues and incremental costs. Note that the costs of process 1 are irrelevant to the decision since they will remain the same whichever of the two alternatives are selected. You should also note that further processing 120 000 kg of the compound results in 240 000 kg of Starcomp.

Incremental sales revenue:

	(£)	(£)
Starcomp (120 000 × 2 kg × £2)	480 000	
Compound (120 000 × £1.60)	192 000	288 000
Incremental costs:		
Materials	120 000	
Processing costs	120 000	240 000
Incremental profits		48 000

It is therefore worthwhile further processing the compound.

(c) The sales revenue should cover the additional costs of further processing the 40 000 kg compound and the lost sales revenue from the 40 000 kg compound if it is sold without further processing.
Additional processing costs:

$$
\begin{array}{lr}
 & (£) \\
\text{Materials } (£160\,000 - £120\,000) & 40\,000 \\
\text{Processing costs } (£140\,000 - £120\,000) & 20\,000 \\
\text{Lost compound sales revenue } (40\,000 \times £1.60) & 64\,000 \\
\hline
 & 124\,000 \\
\end{array}
$$

$$
\text{Minimum selling price per kg of Starcomp} = \frac{£124\,000}{40\,000 \text{ kg} \times 2}
$$

$$
= £1.55
$$

(a) See Chapters 5 and 6 for an explanation of the meaning of each of these terms.

(b) No specific apportionment method is asked for in this problem. It is recommended that the joint costs should be apportioned (see Chapter 6) according to the sales value at split-off point:

Product	Sales value (£)	Proportion to total (%)	Joint costs apportioned (£)
A	60 000	20	40 000
B	40 000	13.33	26 660
C	200 000	66.67	133 340
	300 000	100.00	200 000

(c) Assuming all of the output given in the problem can be sold, the initial process is profitable – the sales revenue is £300 000 and the joint costs are £200 000. To determine whether further processing is profitable the additional revenues should be compared with the additional relevant costs:

	A (£)	B (£)	C (£)
Additional relevant revenues	10 (20–10)	4 (8–4)	6 (16–10)
Additional relevant costs	14	2	6
Excess of relevant revenue over costs	(4)	2	–

Product B should be processed further, product A should not be processed further, and if product C is processed further, then profits will remain unchanged.

(a) *Profit and loss account*

	W (£)	X (£)	Z (£)	Total (£)
Opening stock	—	—	8 640	8 640
Production cost	189 060	228 790	108 750	526 600
Less closing stock	(14 385)	(15 070)	(15 010)	(44 465)
Cost of sales	174 675	213 720	102 380	490 775
Selling and administration costs	24 098	27 768	10 011	61 877
Total costs	198 773	241 488	112 391	552 652
Sales	240 975	277 680	100 110	618 765
Profit/(loss)	42 202	36 192	(12 281)	66 113

Workings
Joint process cost per kilo of output = £0.685 per kg (£509 640/744 000 kg)
Production cost for products W, X and Y:

$$
\begin{array}{ll}
\text{Product W} & (276\,000 \text{ kg} \times £0.685) = £189\,060 \\
\text{X} & (334\,000 \text{ kg} \times £0.685) = £228\,790 \\
\text{Y} & (134\,000 \text{ kg} \times £0.685) = £91\,790 \\
\end{array}
$$

Closing stocks for products W and X:

$$\text{Product W} \quad (21\,000 \text{ kg} \times £0.685) = £14\,385$$
$$\text{X} \quad (22\,000 \text{ kg} \times £0.685) = £15\,070$$

Cost per kilo of product Z:

	(£)
Product Y (128 000 kg × £0.685) =	87 680
Further processing costs	17 920
Less by-product sales (8000 × £0.12) =	(960)
	104 640
Cost per kilo (£104 640/96 000 kg)	£1.09

Closing stock of product Z (10 000 kg × £1.09)	= £10 900
Add closing stock of input Y (6000 × £0.685)	= £4 110
Closing stock relating to product Z	£15 010

Production cost relating to final product Z:

	(£)
Product Y (134 000 kg × £0.685) =	91 790
Further processing costs	17 920
Less by-product costs	(960)
	108 750

(b) The joint costs are common and unavoidable to both alternatives, and are therefore not relevant for the decision under consideration. Further processing from an input of 128 000 kg of Y has resulted in an output of 96 000 kg of Z. Thus it requires 1.33 kg of Y to produce 1 kg of Z (128/96).

	(£)
Revenue per kilo for product Z	1.065 (£100 110/94 000 kg)
Sale proceeds at split-off point	
(1.33 × £0.62)	0.823
Incremental revenue per kg from further	
processing	0.242
Incremental costs of further processing	0.177 [(£17 920 − £960)/96 000]
Incremental profit from further processing	0.065

It is assumed that selling and administration costs are fixed and will be unaffected by which alternative is selected. The company should therefore process Y further into product Z and not accept the offer from the other company to purchase the entire output of product Y.

(c) See 'Methods of allocating joint costs to joint products' in Chapter 6 for the answer to this question.

Question 6.6

(a) In a manufacturing organization product costs are required for stock valuation, the various types of decisions illustrated in Chapter 9 and pricing decisions (see 'Role of cost information in pricing decisions' in Chapter 11).

(b) The total net cost of the output for process 1 is calculated as follows:

	(£)
Materials (36 000 kg at £1.50)	54 000
Labour	28 000
Overheads (120%)	33 600
	115 600
Less: Sale of waste (14 400 kg at £0.30)	4 320
	111 280

Output for each category of fish is as follows:

Superior	3 600 kg
Special	7 200
Standard	10 800 (50% × (36 000 – 14 400))
	21 600

The allocation of costs based on weight and the resulting profits are as follows:

	Superior (£)	Special (£)	Standard (£)	Total (£)
Costs	18 547 [a]	37 093 [a]	55 640 [a]	111 280
Sales	27 000	48 960	43 200	119 160
Profit/(Loss)	8 453	11 867	(12 440)	7 880

Note
[a] Allocated pro-rata to output (e.g. Superior = £111 280 × 3600/21 600)

The allocation of costs based on market value and the resulting profits are as follows:

	Superior (£)	Special (£)	Standard (£)	Total (£)
Costs	25 215 [b]	45 722 [b]	40 343 [b]	111 280
Sales	27 000	48 960	43 200	119 160
Profit/(Loss)	1 785	3 238	2 857	7 880

Note
[b] Allocated in proportion to sales revenues (e.g. Superior = £111 280 × £27 000/ 119 160)

(c) Since all of the costs are joint and unavoidable in relation to all products, dropping a product with a reported loss will not result in any reduction in costs but sales revenues from the product will be forgone. Therefore, an individual loss-making product should not be dropped provided that the process as a whole is profitable. In the circumstances given in the question, the emphasis should be on whether the joint process as a whole is making a profit. In the question none of the products incur further processing costs that can be specifically attributed to them. Where this situation occurs, a joint product should be produced as long as the sales revenues from the product exceed the costs that are specifically attributable to the product (assuming that the joint process as a whole makes a profit).

(d) Further process is worthwhile as long as the incremental revenues exceed the incremental costs. The calculations are as follows:

	£ per kilo		
	Superior	Special	Standard
Incremental costs:			
Materials	0.10	0.10	0.10
Labour	0.60	0.60	0.60
Variable overhead	0.27	0.27	0.27
	0.97	0.97	0.97
Incremental revenue	1.20	0.70	1.20
Incremental contribution	0.23	(0.27)	0.23

The incremental revenues exceed the incremental costs for superior and standard. Special should not be further processed because the incremental revenues are insufficient to cover the incremental costs. Superior will generate a total contribution of £828 (3600 kg × £0.23) and the total contribution from standard is £2484 (10 800 kg × £0.23). Therefore, the total contribution from further processing is £3312. Further processing is profitable as long as the incremental contribution exceeds the fixed costs that are attributable to process 2 and that are avoidable. The fixed costs are not given but they would appear to exceed £3312. Assuming that the overhead rate has been derived from the output in (a) the total labour costs (included in the calculation in (d) are £12 960 (21 600 kg × £0.60). Fixed costs would appear to be £17 496 (0.75 × 180% × £12 960). The process would not appear to be worthwhile if all of the fixed costs can be avoided by not undertaking process 2.

Question 6.7

(a) Figure Q6.7 indicates that the relative sales value of each product is as follows:

	Boddie (£000)	Soull (£000)	Total (£000)
Total sales	8400	36 000	44 400
Plus NRV of Threekeys		2 170 (W1)	2 170
	8400	38 170	46 570

Workings
(W1)   (280 000 litres × £8) − £70 000 delivery costs

Allocation of joint costs:

$$\text{Boddie} = £840\ 000 \left(\frac{8400}{46\ 570} \times £4\ 657\ 000 \right)$$

$$\text{Soull} = \frac{£3\ 817\ 000}{4\ 657\ 000} \left(\frac{38\ 170}{46\ 570} \times £4\ 657\ 000 \right)$$

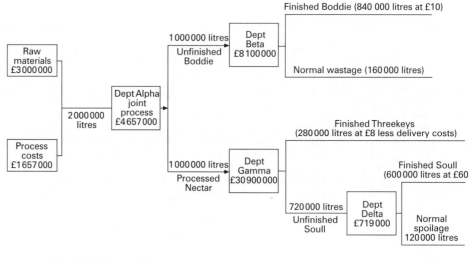

Figure Q6.7 *Diagram of joint cost system.*

(b) *Profit and loss statement*

	Boddie (£000)	Soull (£000)	Threekeys (£000)	Total (£000)
Sales	8400	36 000	2240	46 640
Less specifically attributable costs:				
Department Beta	8100			
Department Gamma		30 900		
Department Delta		719		
Delivery costs			70	
Contribution to joint costs	300	4 381	2170	6 851
Less apportioned joint costs	840	3 817	–	4 657
Profit/(loss)	(540)	564	2170	2 194

(c) The incremental revenues are in excess of the incremental costs for all three products. In other words, each product provides a contribution towards the joint costs. Consequently, all three products should be produced.

(a) *Preliminary workings*

Question 6.8

The joint production process results in the production of garden fertilizer and synthetic fuel consisting of 80% fertilizer and 20% synthetic fuel. The question indicates that 1 600 000 kg of fertilizer are produced. Therefore total output is 2 000 000 kg, and synthetic fuel accounts for 20% (400 000 kg) of this output. The question also states that a wholesaler bought 160 000 kg of the synthetic fuel, and the remaining fuel (400 000 kg − 160 000 kg = 240 000 kg) was used to heat the company greenhouses. The greenhouses produce 5 kg of fruit and vegetables per kg of fuel. Therefore 1 200 000 kg of fruit and vegetables were produced during the period.

Summary profit statements

	Garden fertilizer (£000)	Synthetic fuel (£000)	Fruit and vegetables (£000)
Sales revenue/internal transfers[a]	4800	560	600
Less costs:			
Internal transfers[a]			(336)
Joint costs[b]	(2880)	(720)	
Variable packing costs		(192)	
Direct fixed costs		(40)	
Variable costs			(420)
Fixed labour costs			(100)
Apportioned fixed costs	(720)	(18)	(90)
Net profit/(Loss)	1200	(410)	(346)

Notes

[a]Garden fertilizer: 1 600 000 kg at £3 per kg
Synthetic fuel: 160 000 kg external sales at £1.40 per kg
240 000 kg internal transfers at £1.40 per kg
Fruit and vegetables: 1 200 000 kg at £0.50 per kg

[b]The question states that the fertilizer has a contribution/sales ratio of 40% after the apportionment of joint costs. Therefore joint costs of £2 880 000 (60% × £4 800 000 sales) will be apportioned to fertilizers. Joint costs are apportioned on a weight basis, and synthetic fuel represents 20% of the total weight. Thus £2 880 000 joint costs apportioned to fertilizers represents 80% of the joint costs. The remaining 20% represents the joint costs apportioned to synthetic fuel. Joint costs of £720 000 [20% × (100/80) × £2 880 000] will therefore be apportioned to synthetic fuel.

(b) Apportioned joint and fixed costs are not relevant costs since they will still continue if the activity ceases. The relevant revenues and costs are as follows:

	(£)	
Relevant revenues	224 000	(160 000 kg at £1.40)
Less packing costs	(192 000)	
avoidable fixed costs	(40 000)	
Net benefit to company	(8 000)	

The percentage reduction in avoidable fixed costs before the relevant revenues would be sufficient to cover these costs is 20% (£8000/£40 000).

(c) The notional cost for internal transfers and the apportioned fixed costs would still continue if the fruit and vegetables activity were eliminated. These costs are therefore not relevant in determining the net benefit arising from fruit and vegetables. The calculation of the net benefit is as follows:

	(£)
Relevant revenues	600 000
Less variable costs	(420 000)
avoidable fixed labour costs	(100 000)
Net benefit	80 000

(d) Proposed output of synthetic fuel is 400 000 kg, but there is a contracted requirement to supply a minimum of 100 000 kg to the wholesaler. Consequently, the maximum output of fruit and vegetables is 1 500 000 kg (300 000 kg of synthetic fuel × 5 kg). In determining the optimum price/output level the fixed costs will remain unchanged whatever price/output combination is selected. Internal transfers are a notional cost and do not represent any change in company cash outflows arising from the price/output decision. The price/output decision should be based on a comparison of the relevant revenues less incremental costs (variable costs) for each potential output level. In addition, using synthetic fuel for fruit and vegetable production results in a loss of contribution of £0.20 per kg (£1.40 − £1.20 packing) of synthetic fuel used. This opportunity cost is a relevant cost which should be included in the analysis. The net contributions for the relevant output levels are as follows:

Sales (000kg)	Contribution per kg[a] (£)	Total contribution (£)	Contribution forgone on fuel sales (£)	Net contribution (£)
1200	0.15	180 000	0[b]	180 000
1300	0.145	188 500	4 000[c]	184 500
1400	0.135	189 000	8 000[d]	181 000
1500	0.125	187 500	12 000[e]	175 500

The optimum output level is to sell 1 300 000 kg of fruit and vegetables. This will require 260 000 kg of synthetic fuel. Sales of synthetic fuel to the wholesaler will be restricted to 140 000 kg.

Notes
[a]Average selling price less variable cost of fruit and vegetable production (£420 000/1 200 000 kg = £0.35 per kg).
[b]240 000 kg of synthetic fuel used, resulting in 160 000 kg being sold to the wholesaler. Therefore existing sales to the wholesaler of 160 000 kg will be maintained.
[c]260 000 kg of synthetic fuel used, resulting in 140 000 kg being sold to the wholesaler. Therefore sales will decline by 20 000 kg and the lost contribution will

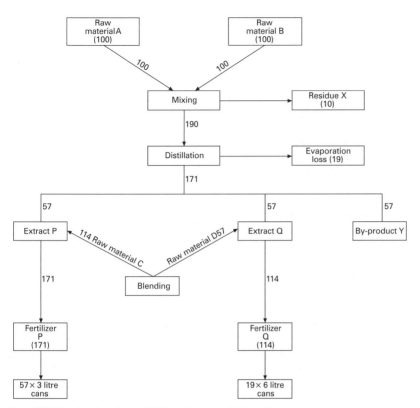

Figure Q6.9 *Flowchart for an input of 100 litres of raw materials A and B*

be £4000 (20 000 kg × £0.20 per kg).
[d]280 000 kg of synthetic fuel used, resulting in 120 000 kg being sold to the wholesaler. Therefore lost contribution is £8000 (40 000 kg × £0.20).
[e]300 000 kg used, resulting in 100 000 kg being sold to the wholesaler. Therefore the lost contribution is £12 000 (60 000 kg × £0.20).

(a) Figure Q6.9 shows a flowchart for an input of 100 litres of raw material A and 100 litres of raw material B. The variable costs for an input of 100 litres of raw materials for each product are shown below: **Question 6.9**

	(£)	(£)	Fertilizer P (£)	Fertilizer Q (£)
Raw materials:				
100 litres of A at £25 per 100 litres	25.00			
100 litres of B at £12 per 100 litres	12.00	37.00		
Mixing:				
200 litres at £3.75 per 100 litres	7.50			
Residue × (10 litres at £0.03)	(0.30)	7.20		
Distilling:				
190 litres at £5 per 100 litres	9.50			
By-product Y (57 litres × £0.04)	(2.28)	7.22		
Total joint costs		51.42	25.71[a]	25.71[a]
Raw material C (114 litres at £20 per 100 litres)			22.80	

Raw material D (57 litres at £55 per 100 litres)		31.35
Blending:		
P (171 litres at £7 per 100 litres)	11.97	
Q (114 litres at £7 per 100 litres)		7.98
Cans:		
P (57 cans at £0.32 per can)	18.24	
Q (19 cans at £0.50 per can)		9.50
Labels:		
P (57 cans at £3.33 per 1000 cans)	0.19	
Variable cost from 100 litres input of each raw material	78.91	74.54

Output is restricted to 570 000 litres of Q. An input of 100 litres of raw materials A and B yields an output of 114 litres of Q. Therefore an input of 500 000 litres [570 000/(114/110)] of each raw material will yield an output of 570 000 litres of Q. An input to the joint process of 500 000 litres of each raw material will yield an output of 855 000 litres (171 × 5000) of P. The total manufacturing cost based on an input of 500 000 litres of each raw material is shown below:

	Fertilizer P (£)	Fertilizer Q (£)
Total variable cost: 5000 × £78.91	394 550	
5000 × £74.54		372 700
Mixing and distilling fixed costs	13 000[a]	13 000[a]
Blending fixed costs	19 950[b]	13 300[b]
(i) *Total manufacturing cost*	427 500	399 000

Notes
[a]Joint costs are apportioned to the main products on the basis of the output from each process. The mixing and distilling processes yield identical outputs for each product. Therefore 50% of the costs are apportioned to each product.
[b]Apportioned on the basis of an output of 171 litres of P and 114 litres of Q.

(ii) *Manufacturing cost per litre*

$$\text{Fertilizer P} = £0.50 \ (£427\ 500/855\ 000 \text{ litres})$$
$$\text{Fertilizer Q} = £0.70 \ (£399\ 000/570\ 000 \text{ litres})$$

(iii) *List price per litre*
  Costs and profit as a percentage of list price are:

	(%)
List price	100
Net selling price	75
Profit (20% × 75%)	15
Total cost (75% − 15%)	60
Selling and distribution (13.33% × 75%)	10
Manufacturing cost (60% − 10%)	50

List price per litre is, therefore, twice the manufacturing cost per litre:

$$P = £1.00$$
$$Q = £1.40$$

(iv) *Profit for the year*

$$P = £128\ 250\ (15\%\ of\ £1) \times 855\ 000\ litres$$
$$Q = £119\ 700\ (15\%\ of\ £1.40) \times 570\ 000\ litres$$

(b) Manufacturing joint product Q will also result in an additional output of P. The break-even point will depend on whether or not P is sold at split-off point as scrap or further processed and sold at the normal market price. The following analysis assumes that P is further processed and sold at the normal market price:

	(£)
Variable cost of producing 50 000 litres of Q	
[(50 000 × £372 700)/570 000]	32 693
Variable selling costs of Q	2 000
	34 693
Contribution from sale of 75 000 litres of P:	16 500
75 000 litres × £0.22[a]	
Net cost	18 193

The selling price should at least cover the net cost per litre of £0.364 (£18 193/50 000 litres). Therefore the break-even selling price is £0.364 per litre.

Note
[a]Output of P is 1.5 times the output of Q (see the Flowchart). Therefore output of P is 75 000 litres (50 000 × 1.5)
Variable manufacturing cost per litre of P = £0.46
$$(394\ 500/855\ 000\ litres)$$
Variable selling cost per litre of P = £0.07
$$[0.7 \times (13.33\%\ of\ £0.75)]$$
Selling price per litre = £0.75
Contribution per litre = £0.22

(c) There is no specific answer to this question. The recommendation should be based on price/demand relationships and the state of competition. The normal mark-up is 25% on cost (20% of selling price equals 25% mark-up on cost).

$$Selling\ price\ based\ on\ normal\ mark\text{-}up = [1.25\ (£18\ 193)]/50\ 000\ litres$$
$$= £0.455$$

The above price assumes that the additional output of P can be sold at the normal market price. If P cannot be sold then the following costs will be incurred:

	(£)
Variable costs of Q	34 693
Pre-separation variable costs previously apportioned to P:	
5000 at £25.71 per 100 = £128 550 (for 570 000 output)	
Pre-separation variable costs for an output of 50 000 litres	
[(£128 550/570 000) × 50 000]	11 276
	45 969

Minimum selling price = £0.919 (£45 969/50 000)
Note that pre-separation variable costs previously allocated to P will still be incurred if P is not produced. The recommended price will depend on the circumstances, competition, demand and the company's pricing policy.

Income effects of alternative cost accumulation systems

Solutions to Chapter 7 questions

Question 7.1

(a) Manufacturing cost per unit of output = variable cost (£6.40) + fixed cost
(£92 000/20 000 = £4.60) = £11
Absorption costing profit statement

	(£000)
Sales (22 000 units at £14 per unit)	308.0
Manufacturing cost of sales (22 000 units × £11)	242.0
Manufacturing profit before adjustment	66.0
Overhead over-absorbed [a]	4.6
Manufacturing profit	70.6

Note:
[a] The normal activity that was used to establish the fixed overhead absorption rate was 20 000 units but actual production in period 2 was 21 000 units. Therefore a period cost adjustment is required because there is an over-absorption of fixed overheads of £4 600 [(22 000 units – 21 000 units) × £4.60].

(b)

	(£000)
Sales	308.0
Variable cost of sales (22 000 units × £6.40)	140.8
Contribution to fixed costs	167.2
Less fixed overheads	92.0
Profit	75.2

(c) (i) Compared with period 1 profits are £34 800 higher in period 2 (£70 600 – £35 800). The reasons for the change are as follows:

	(£000)
Additional sales (7000 units at a profit of £3 per unit)	21 000
Difference in fixed overhead absorption (3000 units extra production at £4.60 per unit) [a]	13 800
Additional profit	34 800

Note:
[a] Because fixed overheads are absorbed on the basis of normal activity (20 000 units) there would have been an under-recovery of £9200 (2000 units × £4.60) in period 1 when production was 18 000 units. In period 2 production exceeds normal activity by 1000 units resulting in an over-recovery of £4600. The difference between the under- and over-recovery of £13 800 (£9200 + £4600) represents a period cost adjustment that is reflected in an increase in profits of £13 800. In other words, the under-recovery of £9200 was not required in period 2 and in addition there was an over-recovery of £4600.

(c) (ii) Additional profits reported by the marginal costing system are £4600 (£75 200 – £70 600). Because sales exceed production by 1000 units in period 2 there is a stock reduction of 1000 units. With an absorption costing system the stock reduction will result in a release of £4600 (1000 units at £4.60) fixed overheads as an expense during the current period. With a marginal costing system changes in stock levels do not have an impact on the fixed overhead that is treated as an expense for the period. Thus, absorption costing profits will be £4600 lower than marginal costing profits.

(a)

Question 7.2

January	(£)	Marginal costing (£)	(£)	Absorption costing (£)
Sales revenue (7000 units)		315 000		315 000
Less: Cost of sales (7000 units)				
Direct materials	77 000		77 000	
Direct labour	56 000		56 000	
Variable production overhead	28 000		28 000	
Variable selling overhead	35 000	196 000		
Fixed overhead (7000 × £3)			21 000	182 000
Contribution		119 000		
Gross profit				133 000
Over absorption of fixed production overhead (1)				1 500
				134 500
Fixed production costs (2)	24 000			
Fixed selling costs (2)	16 000		16 000	
Variable selling costs			35 000	
Fixed admin costs (2)	24 000	64 000	24 000	75 000
Net profit		55 000		59 500

February	(£)	Marginal costing (£)	(£)	Absorption costing (£)
Sales revenue (8750 units)		393 750		393 750
Less: Cost of sales (8750 units)				
Direct materials	96 250		96 250	
Direct labour	70 000		70 000	
Variable production overhead	35 000		35 000	
Variable selling overhead	43 750	245 000		
Fixed overhead (8750 × £3)			26 250	227 500
Contribution		148 750		
Gross profit				166 250
Under absorption of fixed production overhead				750
				165 500
Fixed production costs (2)	24 000			
Fixed selling costs (2)	16 000		16 000	
Variable selling costs			43 750	
Fixed admin costs (2)	24 000	64 000	24 000	83 750
Net profit		84 750		81 750

Workings:

(1) Fixed production overhead has been unitized on the basis of a normal monthly activity of 8000 units (96 000 units per annum). Therefore monthly production fixed overhead incurred is £24 000 (8000 × £3). In January actual production exceeds normal activity by 500 units so there is an over-absorption of £1500 resulting in a period cost adjustment that has a positive impact on profits. In February production is 250 units below normal activity giving an under-absorption of production overheads of £750.

(2) With marginal costing fixed production overheads are treated as period costs and not assigned to products. Therefore the charge for fixed production overheads is £24 000 per month (see note 1). Both marginal and absorption costing systems treat non-manufacturing overheads as period costs. All of the non-manufacturing overheads have been unitized using a monthly activity level of 8000 units. Therefore the non-manufacturing fixed overheads incurred are as follows:

Selling   = £16 000 (8000 × £2)
Administration = £24 000 (8000 × £3)

(b) In January additional profits of £4500 are reported by the absorption costing system. Because production exceeds sales by 1500 units in January there is a stock increase of 1500 units. With an absorption costing system the stock increase will result in £4500 (1500 units × £3) being incorporated in closing stocks and deferred as an expense to future periods. With a marginal costing system changes in stock levels do not have an impact on the fixed overhead that is treated as an expense for the period. Thus, absorption costing profits will be £4500 higher than marginal costing profits. In February sales exceed production by 1000 units resulting in a stock reduction of 1000 units. With an absorption costing system the stock reduction will result in a release of £3000 (1000 units at £3) fixed overheads as an expense during the current period. Thus, absorption costing profits are £3000 lower than marginal costing profits.

(c) (i) Contribution per unit = Selling price (£45) – unit variable cost (£28) = £17
Break-even point (units) = Annual fixed costs (£64 000)/unit contribution (£17) = 3765 units
Break-even point (£ sales) = 3765 units × £45 selling price = £169 424
The above calculations are on a monthly basis. The sales value of the annual break-even point is £2 033 100 (£169 425 × 12).

(ii) Required contribution for an annual profit of £122 800

= Fixed costs (£64 000 × 12) + £122 800
= £899 800

Required activity level = Required contribution (£899 800)

$$\frac{\text{Required contribution (£899 800)}}{\text{Unit contribution (£17)}}$$

= 52 400 units

(d) See 'Cost–volume–profit analysis assumptions' in Chapter 8 for the answer to this question.

Question 7.3

(a) *Preliminary calculations*

	January–June (£)	July–December (£)
Production overheads	90 000	30 000
(Over)/underabsorbed	(12 000)	12 000
	78 000	42 000

Change in overheads	£36 000	
Change in production volume (units)	12 000	

Production variable overhead rate per unit		£3
Fixed production overheads (£78 000 – (18 000 × £3)) £24 000		
Distribution costs	£45 000	£40 000
Decrease in costs		£5 000
Decrease in sales volume (units)		5 000
Distribution cost per unit sold		£1
Fixed distribution cost (£45 000 – (15 000 × £1))		£30 000

Unit costs are as follows:

	(£)	(£)
Selling price		36
Direct materials	6	
Direct labour	9	
Variable production overhead	3	
Variable distribution cost	1	19
Contribution		17

Note that the unit direct costs are derived by dividing the total cost by units produced

Marginal costing profit statement

	January–June		July–December	
	(£000)	(£000)	(£000)	(£000)
Sales		540		360
Variable costs at £19 per unit sold		285		190
Contribution		255		170
Fixed costs:				
Production overhead	24		24	
Selling costs	50		50	
Distribution cost	30		30	
Administration	80	184	80	184
Profit		71		(14)

(b) Marginal costing stock valuation per unit = £18 per unit production variable cost

Absorption costing stock valuation per unit = £20 per unit total production cost

	January–June	July–December
	(£000)	(£000)
Absorption costing profit	77	(22)
Fixed overheads in stock increase of 3000 units	6	
Fixed overheads in stock decrease of 4000 units		(8)
Marginal costing profit	71	14

(c) Absorption gross profit per unit sold = Annual gross profit (£400 000)/Annual production (15 000 units)

= £16

	(£000)
Profit from January–June	77
Reduction in sales volume (5000 × £16)	(80)
Difference in overhead recovery (£12 000 over recovery and £12 000 under recovery)	(24)
Reduction in distribution cost	5
	(22)

(d) Fixed cost £184 000 × 2= £368 000
Contribution per unit   £17
Break-even point   21 647 units (Fixed costs/contribution per unit)

(e) See 'Some arguments in support of variable costing' in Chapter 7 for the answer
to this question.

Question 7.4

(a)
$$\text{Fixed overhead rate per unit} = \frac{\text{Budgeted fixed overheads (£300 000)}}{\text{Budgeted production (40 000 units)}} = £7.50$$

Absorption Costing (FIFO) Profit Statement:

		(£000)
Sales (42 000 × £72)		3024
Less cost of sales:		
Opening stock (2000 × £30)	60	
Add production (46 000 × £52.50[a])	2415	
	2475	
Less closing stock (6000 × £52.50)	315	2160
		864
Add over-absorption of overheads[b]		27
Profit		891

Notes:
[a] Variable cost per unit = £2070/46 000 = £45
Total cost per unit = £45 + £7.50 Fixed overhead = £52.50
[b] Overhead absorbed (46 000 × £7.50) = £345 000
Actual overhead incurred   = £318 000
Over-recovery   £27 000

Marginal Costing (FIFO) Profit Statement:

	(£000)	(£000)
Sales		3024
Less cost of sales:		
Opening stock (2000 × £25)	50	
Add production (46 000 × £45)	2070	
	2120	
Less closing stock (6000 × £45)	270	1850
Contribution		1174
Less fixed overheads incurred		318
Profit		856

Reconciliation:
Absorption profit exceeds marginal costing profit by £35 000 (£891 000 − £856 000). The difference is due to the fixed overheads carried forward in the stock valuations:

	(£)
Fixed overheads in closing stocks (6000 × £7.50)	45 000
Less fixed overheads in opening stocks (2000 × £5)	10 000
Fixed overheads included in stock movement	35 000

Absorption costing gives a higher profit because more of the fixed overheads are carried forward into the next accounting period than were brought forward from the last accounting period.

(b) *Absorption Costing (AVECO) Profit Statement:*

	(£000)	(£000)
Sales		3024
Opening stock plus production		
(48 000 × £51.56[a])	2475	
Less closing stock (6000 × £51.56)	309	2166
		858
Add over-absorption of overheads		27
Profit		885

Marginal Costing (AVECO) Profit Statement:

	(£000)	(£000)
Sales		3024
Less cost of sales		
Opening stock plus production		
(48 000 × £44.17[b])	2120	
Less closing stock (6000 × £44.17)	265	1855
Contribution		1169
Less fixed overheads		318
Profit		851

Notes:
[a] With the AVECO method the opening stock is merged with the production of the current period to ascertain the average unit cost:
Opening stock (2000 × £30) + Production cost (£2 415 000) = £2 475 000
Average cost per unit = £2 475 000/48 000 units
[b] Average cost = (Production cost (£2 070 000) + Opening stock (50 000))/48 000 units.

Reconciliation:

	(£000)
Difference in profits (£885 − £851)	34
Fixed overheads in closing stocks (309 − 265)	44
Less fixed overheads in opening stock (2000 × £5)	10
Fixed overheads included in stock movement	34

The variations in profits between (a) and (b) are £6000 for absorption costing and £5000 for marginal costing. With the FIFO method all of the lower cost brought forward from the previous period is charged as an expense against the current period. The closing stock is derived only from current period costs. With the AVECO method the opening stock is merged with the units produced in the current period and is thus allocated between cost of sales and closing stocks. Therefore some of the lower cost brought forward from the previous period is incorporated in the closing stock at the end of the period.

Question 7.5

(a) It is assumed that opening stock valuation in 2001 was determined on the basis of the old overhead rate of £2.10 per hour. The closing stock valuation for 2001 and the opening and closing valuations for 2002 are calculated on the basis of the new overhead rate of £3.60 per hour. In order to compare the 2001 and 2002 profits, it is necessary to restate the 2001 opening stock on the same basis as that which was used for 2002 stock valuations.

We are informed that the 2002 closing stock will be at the same physical level as the 2000 opening stock valuation. It should also be noted that the 2001 opening stock was twice as much as the 2000 equivalent. The 2000 valuation on the revised basis would have been £130 000, resulting in a 2001 revised valuation of £260 000. Consequently, the 2001 profits will be £60 000 (£260 000 − £200 000) lower when calculated on the revised basis.

From the 2001 estimate you can see that stocks increase and then decline in 2002. It appears that the company has over-produced in 2001 thus resulting in large opening stocks at the start of 2002. The effect of this is that more of the sales demand is met from opening stocks in 2002. Therefore production declines in 2002, thus resulting in an under recovery of £300 000 fixed overheads, which is charged as a period cost. On the other hand, the under recovery for 2001 is expected to be £150 000.

The reconciliation of 2001 and 2002 profits is as follows:

	(£)
2001 profits	128 750
Difference in opening stock valuation for 2001	(60 000)
Additional under recovery in 2002	(150 000)
Budgeted loss for 2002	(81 250)

(b) To prepare the profit and loss accounts on a marginal cost basis, it is necessary to analyse the production costs into the fixed and variable elements. The calculations are:

	2000 (£)	2001 (£)	2002 (£)
Total fixed overheads incurred	600 000	600 000	600 000
Less under recovery	300 000	150 000	300 000
Fixed overheads charged to production	300 000	450 000	300 000
Total production cost	1 000 000	975 000	650 000
Proportion fixed	3/10	6/13 (450/975)	6/13
Proportion variable (balance)	7/10	7/13	7/13

Profit and loss accounts (marginal cost basis)

	Actual 2000 (£)	(£)	Estimated 2001 (£)	(£)	Budget 2002 (£)	(£)
Sales		1 350 000		1 316 250		1 316 250
Opening finished goods stock at marginal cost	70 000[a]		140 000[a]		192 500[b]	
Variable factory cost	700 000[a]		525 000[b]		350 000[b]	
	770 000		665 000		542 500	
Closing finished goods stock at marginal cost	140 000[a]	630 000	192 500[b]	472 500	70 000[b]	472 500
		720 000		843 750		843 750
Fixed factory cost	600 000		600 000		600 000	
Administrative and financial costs	220 000		220 000		220 000	
		820 000		820 000		820 000
Profit/(loss)		(£100 000)		£23 750		£23 750

Notes
[a] 7/10 × absorption cost figures given in the question.
[b] 7/13 × absorption cost figures given in the question.

(c) The under absorption of overhead may be due to the fact that the firm is operating at a low level of activity. This may be due to a low demand for the firm's products. The increase in the overhead rate will cause the product costs to increase. When cost-plus pricing is used the selling price will also be increased. An increase in selling price may result in a further decline in demand. Cost-plus pricing ignores price/demand relationships. For a more detailed discussion of the answer required to this question see section on 'Limitations of cost-plus pricing' in Chapter 11.

(d) For an answer to this question see section on 'Reasons for using cost-based pricing formulae' in Chapter 11 and 'Some arguments in favour of absorption costing' in Chapter 7. Note that SSAP 9 requires that absorption costing (full costing) be used for external reporting.

(a) Sales for the second six-monthly period have increased for department A, but profit has declined, whereas sales for department B have declined and profit has increased. This situation arises because stocks are valued on an absorption cost basis. With an absorption costing system, fixed overheads are included in the stock valuations, and this can result in the amount of fixed overhead charged as an expense being different from the amount of fixed overhead incurred during a period. The effect of including fixed overheads in the stock valuation is shown below: **Question 7.6**

	1 July–31 December		1 January–30 June	
	Department A	Department B	Department A	Department B
	(£000)	(£000)	(£000)	(£000)
Fixed overheads brought forward in opening stock of finished goods[a]	36	112	72	96
Fixed overheads carried forward in closing stock of goods[b]	72	96	12	160
Profit increased by	36			64
Profit reduced by		16	60	
Net profit as per absorption costing profit and loss account	94	50	53	83
Profit prior to stock adjustment	58	66	113	19

Notes

[a]Stocks are valued at factory cost with an absorption costing system. The opening stock valuation for department A for the first six months is £60 000 based on a product cost of £20 per unit. Therefore opening stock comprises 3000 units. Fixed manufacturing overheads are charged to the product made in department A at £12 per unit. Consequently, the stock valuation includes £36 000 for fixed overheads. The same approach is used to calculate the fixed overheads included in the opening stock valuation for the second period and department B.

[b]Closing stock for department B (first period) = 6000 units (£120 000/£20). Fixed overheads included in closing stock valuation = £72 000 (6000 units × £12).

The same approach is used to calculate fixed overheads included in the remaining stock valuations.

Comments

During the first six months for department A, stocks are increasing so that the stock adjustment results in a reduction of the fixed overhead charge for the period of £36 000. Fixed manufacturing overheads of £132 000 have been incurred during the period. Therefore the total fixed manufacturing overhead charge for the period is £96 000. In the first period for department B stocks are declining and the stock adjustment will result in an additional £16 000 fixed manufacturing overheads being included in the stock valuation. Consequently, the fixed manufacturing overhead charge for the period is £320 000 (£304 000 + £16 000). When stocks are increasing, the stock adjustment will have a favourable impact on profits (department A, period 1), and when stocks are declining, the stock adjustment will have an adverse impact on profits (department B, period 1).

In the second period stocks decline in department A and the stock adjustment will have an adverse impact on profits, whereas in department B stocks increase and this has a favourable impact on profit. When the two periods are compared, the stock adjustment has an adverse impact on the profits of department A and a favourable impact on the profits of department B. With an absorption costing system, profit is a function of sales and stock movements, and these stock movements can have an adverse impact on profits even when sales are increasing.

(b) *Departmental profit and loss accounts (marginal costing basis)*

	1 July–31 December		1 January–30 June	
	Department A	Department B	Department A	Department B
	(£000)	(£000)	(£000)	(£000)
Sales revenue	300	750	375	675
Variable manufacturing costs:				
Direct material	52	114	30	132
Direct labour	26	76	15	88
Variable overheads	26	76	15	88
Variable factory cost of production	104	266	60	308
Add opening stock of finished goods	24	98	48	84
	128	364	108	392
Less closing stock of finished goods	48	84	8	140
Variable factory cost of goods sold	80	280	100	252
Total contribution	£220	£470	£275	£423
Less:				
Fixed factory overheads	132	304	132	304
Fixed administrative and				
selling costs	30	100	30	100
Net profit	58	66	113	19

INCOME EFFECTS OF ALTERNATIVE COST ACCUMULATION SYSTEMS

Cost–volume–profit analysis

Solutions to Chapter 8 questions

(a) See Figure Q8.1.

Question 8.1

(b) See Chapter 8 for the answer to this question.
(c) The major limitations are:
  (i) Costs and revenue may only be linear within a certain output range.
  (ii) In practice, it is difficult to separate fixed and variable costs, and the calculations will represent an approximation.
  (iii) It is assumed that profits are calculated on a variable costing basis.
  (iv) Analysis assumes a single product is sold or a constant sales mix is maintained.
(d) The advantages are:
  (i) The information can be absorbed at a glance without the need for detailed figures.
  (ii) Essential features are emphasized.
  (iii) The graphical presentation can be easily understood by non-accountants.

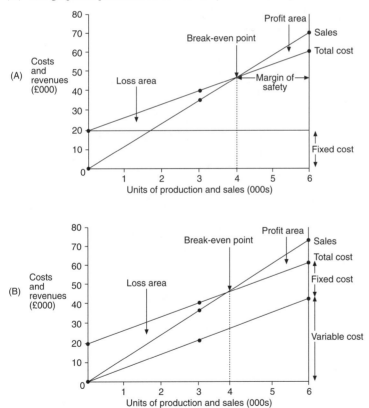

Figure Q8.1 *(A) Break-even chart. (B) Contribution graph*

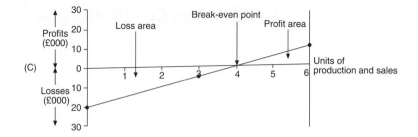

Figure Q8.1 *(C) Profit-volume graph*

Question 8.2

(a) Break-even point = $\dfrac{\text{fixed costs } (£1\,212\,000)}{\text{average contribution per £ of sales } (£0.505)} = £2\,400\,000$

Average contribution per £ of sales = $[0.7 \times (£1 - £0.45)] + [0.3 \times (£1 - £0.6)]$

(b) The graph (Figure Q8.2) is based on the following calculations:

Zero activity: loss = £1 212 000 (fixed costs)
£4 m existing sales: (£4m × £0.505) − £1 212 000 = £808 000 profit
£4 m revised sales: (£4m × £0.475) − £1 212 000 = £688 000 profit
Existing break-even point: £2 400 000
Revised break-even point: £2 551 579 (£1 212 000/£0.475)
Revised contribution per £ of sales: (0.5 × £0.55) + (0.5 × £0.40) = £0.475

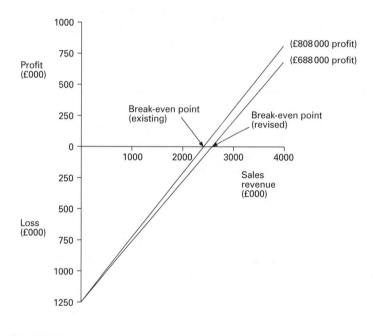

Figure Q8.2 *Profit-volume chart*

(c) $$\frac{\text{Required contribution}}{\text{Contribution per £ of sales}} = \frac{£455\ 000 + £700\ 000}{£0.55} = £2\ 100\ 000$$

(a) See Figures Q8.3(A) and Q8.3(B) for the break-even charts.

(b) Both charts indicate that each product has three break-even points. With the Standard quality, profits are earned on sales from 80 000 to 99 999 units and above 140 000 units; whereas with the De Luxe quality, profits are earned on sales from 71 429 − 99 999 units and above 114 286 units. The charts therefore provide guidance regarding the level of sales at which to aim.

(c) *Expected unit sales*

Standard: $(172\ 000 \times 0.1) + (160\ 000 \times 0.7) + (148\ 000 \times 0.2) = 158\ 800$

De Luxe: $(195\ 500 \times 0.3) + (156\ 500 \times 0.5) + (109\ 500 \times 0.2) = 158\ 800$

Expected profits

	Standard (£)	De Luxe (£)
Total contribution	397 000 (158 800 × £2.50)	555 800 (158 800 × £3.50)
Fixed costs	350 000	400 000
Profit	47 000	155 800

Margin of safety

Standard: expected sales volume (158 800) − break-even point (140 000)
= 18 800 units

De Luxe: expected sales volume (158 800) − break-even point (114 286)
= 44 514 units

(d) The profit probability distributions for the products are:

	Standard			De Luxe	
Demand	probability	Profits (£)	Demand	Probability	Profits/(loss) (£)
172 000	0.1	80 000	195 500	0.3	284 250
160 000	0.7	50 000	156 500	0.5	147 750
148 000	0.2	20 000	109 500	0.2	(16 750)

The De Luxe model has the higher expected profit, but is also more risky than the Standard product. There is a 0.2 probability that the De Luxe model will make a loss, whereas there is a zero probability that the Standard product will make a loss. The decision as to which product to produce will depend upon management's attitude towards risk and the future profitability from its other products. If the company is currently making a loss it may be inappropriate to choose the product that could make a loss. On the other hand, the rewards from the De Luxe model are much higher, and, if the company can survive if the worst outcome occurs, there is a strong argument for producing the De Luxe product.

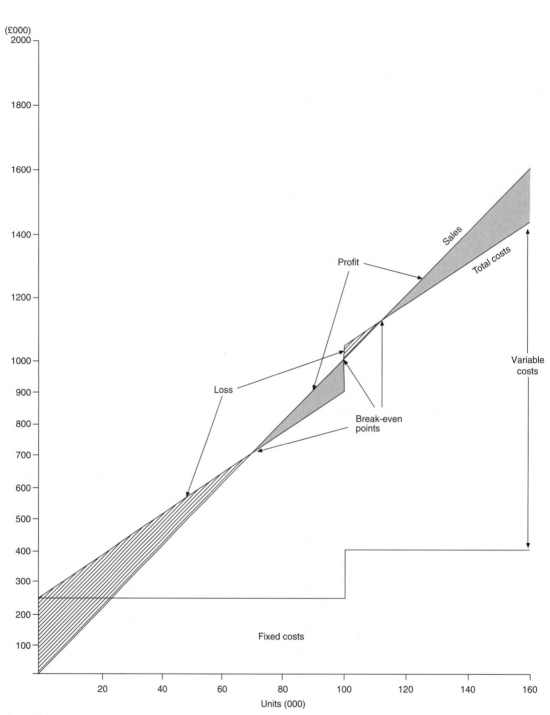

Figure Q8.3 *(A) Break-even chart – Deluxe quality*

COST–VOLUME–PROFIT ANALYSIS

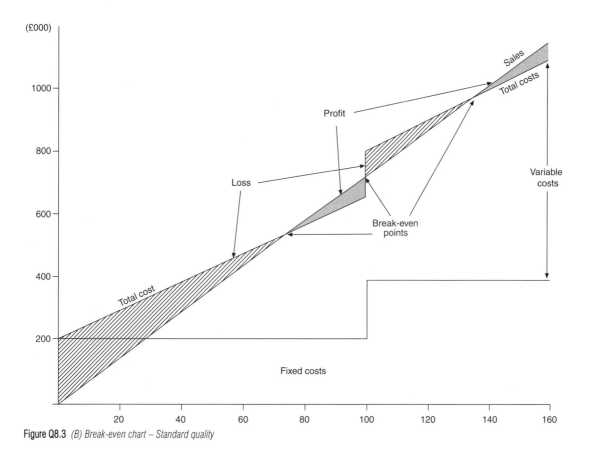

Figure Q8.3 *(B) Break-even chart – Standard quality*

(a) (i)

Question 8.4

Products	1	2	3	Total
1. Unit contribution	£1.31	£0.63	£1.87	
2. Specific fixed costs per unit	£0.49	£0.35	£0.62	
3. General fixed costs per unit	£0.46	£0.46	£0.46	
4. Sales volume (000s units)	98.2	42.1	111.8	252.1
5. Total contribution (1 × 4)	£128.642	£26.523	£209.066	£364.231
6. Total specific fixed costs (2 × 4)	£48.118	£14.735	£69.316	£132.169
7. Total general fixed costs (3 × 4)	£45.172	£19.366	£51.428	£115.966
8. Unit selling price	£2.92	£1.35	£2.83	
9. Total sales revenue (8 × 4)	£286.744	£56.835	£316.394	£659.973

Average contribution per unit = Total contribution (£364.231)/sales volume
(252.1)
= £1.4448

Average selling price per unit = Total sales revenue (£659.973)/sales
volume (252.1)
= £2.6179

Break-even point (units) = $\dfrac{\text{Total fixed costs}}{\text{Average contribution per unit}}$

= (£132.169 + £115.966)/£1.4448
= 171.743 units

Break-even point (sales value) = 171.743 units × average selling price
(£2.6179)
= £449.606

Alternatively, the break-even point (sales value) can be calculated using the following formula:

$$\text{Break-even point} = \frac{\text{Fixed costs } (£132.169 + £115.966)}{\text{Total contribution } (£364.231)} \times \text{Total sales } (£659.973)$$

$$= £449.606$$

It is assumed that the question requires the calculation of the break-even point to cover both general and specific fixed costs. An alternative answer would have been to present details of the break-even point to cover only specific fixed costs.

(ii) The planned sales mix for Product 2 that was used to calculate the break-even point in (i) is 42.1/252.1. Therefore the number of units of Product 2 at the break-even point is:

42.1/252.1 × 171 743 units = 28 681

(b) At the forecast sales volume the profit/contributions are as follows:

	(£000s)
Contributions to all fixed costs	26.523
Less specific fixed costs	14.735
Contribution to general fixed costs	11.788
Less share of general fixed costs	19.366
Net loss	7.578

Product 2 provides a contribution of £11 788 towards general fixed costs and, unless savings in general fixed costs in excess of £11 788 can be made if Product 2 is abandoned, it is still viable to produce Product 2. If the company ceases production of Product 2 it will lose a contribution of £11 788 and total profits will decline by £11 788. The company should investigate whether a greater contribution than £11 788 can be generated from the resources. If this is not possible the company should continue production of Product 2.

Question 8.5

Task 1	(£)	(£)
Sales		2 106 000
Less variable cost of sales:		
Cost of beds	1 620 000	
Commission	210 600	
Transport	216 000	2 046 600
Contribution		59 400

Average contribution per bed sold = £59 400/5400   = £11
Fixed costs (£8450 + £10 000 + £40 000 + £40 000)   = £98 450

$$\text{Break-even point (units)} = \frac{\text{Fixed costs } (£98\,450)}{\text{Contribution per unit } (£11)} = 8950 \text{ beds}$$

Average selling price per unit (£2 106 000/5400 beds)   = £390
Break-even point (sales revenue) = 8950 beds at £390   = £3 490 500

Task 2
The letter should include the items listed in (a) to (e) below:

(a) Required contribution: (£)

	(£)
Salary	36 550
Interest lost	15 000
Fixed costs shown in Task 1	98 450
	150 000
Less manager's salary saved	40 000
Total contribution	110 000

The minimum profit required to compensate for loss of salary and interest is £11 550 (£110 000 − £98 450 fixed costs).

(b) Required volume = Required contribution (£110 000)/Contribution per unit (£11) = 10 000 beds

(c) Average life of a bed = (9 years × 0.10) + (10 years × 0.60) + (11 years × 0.3) = 10.2 years

Total bed population = 44 880 households × 2.1 beds per market = 94 248

$$\text{Estimated annual demand} = \frac{94\ 248 \text{ beds}}{\text{Average replacement period (10.2 years)}}$$
$$= 9\ 240 \text{ beds}$$

(d) The proposal will not achieve the desired profit. Estimated annual sales are 9240 beds but 10 000 beds must be sold to achieve the desired profit. The shortfall of 760 beds will result in profit being £8360 (760 × £11) less than the desired profit.

(e) The estimate of maximum annual sales volume may prove to be inaccurate because of the following reasons:
  (i) The population of Mytown may differ from the sample population. For example the population of Mytown might contain a greater proportion of elderly people or younger people with families. Either of these situations may result in the buying habits of the population of Mytown being different from the sample proportion.
  (ii) The data is historic and does not take into account future changes such as an increase in wealth of the population, change in composition or a change in buying habits arising from different types of beds being marketed.

Task 3
This question requires a knowledge of the material covered in Chapter 9. Therefore you should delay attempting this question until you have understood the content of Chapter 9.

	A	B	C	Total
	(£)	(£)	(£)	
Selling price	240	448	672	
Unit purchase cost	130	310	550	
Carriage inwards	20	20	20	
Contribution	90	118	102	
Square metres per bed	3	4	5	
Contribution per square metre	£30	£29.50	£20.40	
Ranking	1	2	3	
Maximum demand	35	45	20	
Storage required (square metres)	105	180	100	385

Monthly sales schedule and statement of profitability:

	(£)	(£)
Contribution from sales of A (35 × £90)		3150
Contribution from sales of B (45 × £118)		5310
Contribution from sales of C (3^a × £102)		306
		8766
Less specific avoidable fixed costs:		
Staff costs	3780	
Departmental fixed overheads	2000	5780
Contribution to general fixed overheads		2986
Less general fixed overheads		2520
Departmental profit		466

Note:
[a] The balance of storage space available for Model C is 300 square metres less the amount allocated to A and B (285 metres) = 15 metres. This will result in the sales of 3 beds (15 metres/5 metres per bed).

Question 8.6

(a) *Analysis of semi-variable costs*[a]

$$\text{Method A: variable element} = \frac{\text{increase in costs}}{\text{increase in activity}} = \frac{£10\,000}{100\,000 \text{ copies}}$$

$$= £0.10 \text{ per copy}$$

fixed element = total semi-variable cost (£55 000) − variable cost (£35 000) at an activity level of 350 000 copies

Therefore   fixed element = £20 000

$$\text{Method B: variable element} = \frac{\text{increase in costs}}{\text{increase in activity}} = \frac{£5000}{100\,000 \text{ copies}}$$

$$= £0.05 \text{ per copy}$$

fixed element = total semi-variable cost (£47 500) − variable costs (£17 500) at an activity level of 350 000 copies

Therefore   fixed element = £30 000

Note
[a]The analysis is based on a comparison of total costs and activity levels at 350 000 and 450 000 copies per year.

Contribution per copy of new magazine

	Method A (£)	Method B (£)
Selling price	1.00	1.00
Variable cost (given)	(0.55)	(0.50)
Variable element of semi-variable cost	(0.10)	(0.05)
Lost contribution from existing magazine	(0.05)	(0.05)
Contribution	0.30	0.40

Calculation of net increase in company profits

	Method A			Method B		
Copies sold	500 000	400 000	600 000	500 000	400 000	600 000
Contribution per copy	£0.30	£0.30	£0.30	£0.40	£0.40	£0.40
Total contribution	£150 000	£120 000	£180 000	£200 000	£160 000	£240 000
Fixed costs[a]	£100 000	£100 000	£100 000	£150 000	£150 000	£150 000
Net increase in profit	£50 000	£20 000	£80 000	£50 000	£10 000	£90 000

Note
[a]Method A = specific fixed costs (£80 000) + semi-variable element (£20 000)
= £100 000
Method B = specific fixed costs (£120 000) + semi-variable element (£30 000)
= £150 000

(b)
$$\text{Break-even point} = \frac{\text{fixed costs}}{\text{contribution per unit}}$$

Method A = £100 000/0.30 = 333 333 copies
Method B = £150 000/0.40 = 375 000 copies

The margin of safety is the difference between the anticipated sales and the break-even point sales:

Method A = 500 000 − 333 333 = 166 667 copies
Method B = 500 000 − 375 000 = 125 000 copies

(c) Method B has a higher break-even point and a higher contribution per copy sold. This implies that profits from Method B are more vulnerable to a decline in sales volume. However, higher profits are obtained with Method B when sales are high (see 600 000 copies in (B)).

The break-even point from the sale of the existing magazine is 160 000 copies (£80 000/£0.50) and the current level of monthly sales is 220 000 copies. Therefore sales can drop by 60 000 copies before break-even point is reached. For every 10 copies sold of the new publication, sales of the existing publication will be reduced by one copy. Consequently, if more than 600 000 copies of the new publication are sold, the existing magazine will make a loss. If sales of the new magazine are expected to consistently exceed 600 000 copies then the viability of the existing magazine must be questioned.

Question 8.7

(a) (i) The opportunity costs of producing cassettes are the salary forgone of £1000 per month and the rental forgone of £400 per month.
(ii) The consultant's fees and development costs represent sunk costs.
(b) The following information can be obtained from the report.

	£10 selling price	£9 selling price
Sales quantity	7500–10 000 units	12 000–18 000 units
Fixed costs[a]	£13 525	£17 525
Profit at maximum sales[b]	£3 975	£4 975
Profit/(loss) at minimum sales[c]	(£400)	(£2 525)
Break-even point[d]	7 729 units	14 020 units
Margin of safety:		
Below maximum	2 271 units	3 980 units
Above minimum	229 units	2 020 units

Notes
[a] Fixed production cost + £1400 opportunity cost
[b] (10 000 units × £1.75 contribution) − £13 525 fixed costs = £3975 profit
(18 000 units × £1.25 contribution) − £17 525 fixed costs = £4975 profit
[c] (7 500 units × £1.75 contribution) − £13 525 fixed costs = £400 loss
(12 000 units × £1.25 contribution) − £17 525 fixed costs = £2525 loss
[d]Fixed costs/contribution per unit

Conclusions
(i) The £10 selling price is less risky than the £9 selling price. With the £10 selling price, the maximum loss is lower and the break-even point is only 3% above minimum sales (compared with 17% for a £9 selling price).

(ii) The £9 selling price will yield the higher profits if maximum sales quantity is achieved.
(iii) In order to earn £3975 profits at a £9 selling price, we must sell 17 200 units (required contribution of 17 525 fixed costs plus £3975 divided by a contribution per unit of £1.25).

Additional information required
  (i) Details of capital employed for each selling price.
 (ii) Details of additional finance required to finance the working capital and the relevant interest cost so as to determine the cost of financing the working capital.
(iii) Estimated probability of units sold at different selling prices.
 (iv) How long will the project remain viable?
  (v) Details of range of possible costs. Are the cost figures given in the question certain?

Question 8.8

(a) *Impact of stitching elimination*
Loss of contribution from 10% sales reduction

(£300 000 × 10% × £4.50)	£135 000
Production cost reduction (270 000 × £0.60)	£162 000
Net gain from the stitching elimination	£27 000

Note
Contribution per unit − Fixed cost per unit (£1.50) = Net profit per unit (£3). Therefore contribution per unit = £4.50.

Use of plastic eyes
The reduction in sales volume arising from the stitching elimination also applies to the evaluation of the proposals for the change in type of eye and change in filling.
  Glass eyes required for production = £540 000 (270 000 × 2)

Input required to allow for 5% input losses (540 000/0.95 × £0.20) =	£113 684
Plastic eyes required to allow for 10% input losses	
(540 000/0.90 × £0.15) =	£90 000
Net saving from plastic eyes	£23 684

Use of scrap fabric for filling

Cost of synthetic filling (270 000/2000 × £80)	£10 800
Additional production cost of scrap fabric (270 000 × £0.05)	£13 500
Net increase in cost from use of scrap fabric	£2 700

The overall net increase in annual net profit arising from the implementation of the three proposals is £47 984 − (£27 000 + £23 684 − £2700)

(b) Additional contribution from all three changes

(£162 000 + £23 684 − £2700)/270 000 =	£0.678
Existing contribution	£4.50
Revised contribution per unit	£5.178

Number of toys required to give the same contribution prior to the changes:
  (£4.50 × 300 000)/£5.178 = 260 718 toys
Therefore the reduction in sales required to leave net profit unchanged
  = (300 000 − 260 718)/300 000
  = 13.1%

(c) The report should indicate that answers to the following questions should be obtained before a final decision is taken:
  (i) How accurate is the estimate of demand? Demand is predicted to fall by 10% but the answer to (b) indicates that if demand falls by more than 13%, profit will be lower if the changes are implemented.
  (ii) Have all alternative courses of action been considered? For example, would a price reduction, or advertising and a sales promotion, stimulate demand and profits?
  (iii) Will the change to using scrap fabric result in a loss of revenues from the sale of scrap?
  (iv) Will the elimination of stitching result in redundancy payments and possible industrial action?
  (v) Consideration should be given to eliminating stitching and using plastic eyes but not using scrap fabric for filling.

(a) Actual patient days   = 22 000 (£4.4 million/£200)

Bed occupancy   = 75% (22 000/29 200)

Profit/(Loss)	(£)	(£)
Total revenue		4 400 000
Variable costs		1 100 000
Contribution to direct and general fixed costs		3 300 000
Staffing costs: Supervisors	4 × £22 000	
Nurses	13 × £16 000	
Assistants	24 × £12 000	584 000
Fixed charges		1 650 000
Profit		1 066 000

Break-even point   = Fixed costs (£584 000 + £1 650 000)/ Contribution per patient day (£150) [a]
                        = 14 893 patient days.

The above calculation is based on the actual outcomes for the period. Because of the stepped nature of the fixed costs other break-even points can be calculated based on actual patient days for the period being less than 20 500 or over 23 000.

Note
[a] £3 300 000/22 000 patient days

(b) It is assumed that estimated bed occupancy will be at the 2001 level plus an extra 20 beds for 100 days giving an occupancy of 24 000 patient days [22 000 + (100 × 20)]. This will result in an estimated bed occupancy of 66% (24 000/ (100 × 365)) = 66%.

Revised Profit/(Loss)

	(£)	(£)
Total revenue (24 000 × £200)		4 800 000
Variable costs (24 000 × £50)		1 200 000
Contribution to direct and general fixed costs		3 600 000
Staffing costs: Supervisors	4 × £24 200	
Nurses	15 × £17 600	
Assistants	28 × £13 200	730 400
Fixed charges (£1 650 000 × 100/80)		2 062 500
Profit		807 100

(c) Attempting to cover the 100 days demand by increasing capacity by 20 beds for 365 days has resulted in a decline in the occupancy percentage from 75% to 66%. To meet the increased demand of 2000 patient days (100 days × 20 beds) extra capacity of 7300 potential patient days were provided (365 days × 20 beds). This has had a detrimental impact on the occupancy percentage. The extra contribution from the increased demand was £300 000 but this was offset by a higher allocation of fixed charges of £412 500 arising from the increase in bed capacity. The additional personnel costs arising from increases in stepped fixed costs and increased salaries further contributed to the reduction in profit.

Assuming that fixed costs (administration, security and property costs) will remain unchanged the extra demand has generated an additional contribution to these common and unavoidable fixed costs and should therefore increase the profit for the hospital as a whole. However, the way in which the fixed costs are allocated reduces the profit for the paediatric unit. A possible solution to overcome this problem is to make the units accountable for the contribution to unavoidable fixed costs (assumed to be contribution less staffing costs). Adopting this approach would result in a contribution to general fixed costs of £2 716 000 being reported in 2001 and £2 869 000 in 2002. An alternative approach would be to allocate fixed costs on the basis of patient days rather than bed capacity. The danger with both approaches is that there is no incentive to encourage managers to restrict bed capacity.

(d) For organizations that have profit making objectives a reasonable financial return must be generated to satisfy the providers of the funds. However, for an organization to survive it must satisfy the objectives of other stakeholders (e.g. employees, customers and social objectives). Conflicts between financial and social objectives occur when a greater financial return can be achieved at the expense of poorer social provision or increased social provision can be obtained but this has a detrimental impact on meeting financial objectives. In a private healthcare organization higher profits might be obtained by charging higher fees and treating fewer patients compared with treating many patients at a lower fee. Thus financial objectives are being pursued at the expense of lower social provision. Determining the optimal balance between financial and social objectives represents a major problem for a private hospital. To ensure that an adequate level of social provision is provided, such as treating patients requiring expensive treatment, requires that the provision is provided within the public sector.

Question 8.10

(a)

	Estimated variable cost per unit Normal materials (£)	Cheaper-grade materials (£)
Direct material	36.00	31.25
Direct labour	10.50	10.50
Variable overheads	10.50	10.50
	57.00	52.25
Wastage (5/95 × £52.25)		2.75
	57.00	55.00

Contribution from using normal grade of materials

Selling price (£)	80	84	88	90	92	96	100
Variable cost (£)	57	57	57	57	57	57	57
Unit contribution (£)	23	27	31	33	35	39	43
Demand (000)	25	23	21	20	19	17	15
Contribution to general fixed costs (£000)	575	621	651	660	665	663	645

Contribution from using cheaper grade of materials

Selling price (£)	80	84	88	90	92	96	100
Variable cost	55	55	55	55	55	55	55
Unit contribution	25	29	33	35	37	41	45
Demand (000)	25	23	21	20	19	17	15
Contribution to specific fixed costs (£000)	625	667	693	700	703	697	675
Specific fixed costs (£000)	30	30	30	30	30	30	30
Contribution to general fixed costs (£000)	595	637	663	670	673	667	645

The selling price that maximizes profit is £92 and the optimum output is 19 000 units. For all levels of demand (other than 15 000 units), profits are higher for the cheaper-grade material. At 15 000 units, profits are identical for both grades of materials.

If the reject rate for the cheaper grade of materials increased from 5% to 6% then at the optimum output level higher profits would be earned from using the normal grade of materials. Fixed inspection costs can increase by 10%, and profits will still be higher with the cheaper-grade materials for all output levels other than 15 000 units. As long as demand is in excess of 15 000 units (£30 000 inspection costs/£2 variable cost saving), it is preferable to use the cheaper-grade materials. Profits are not very sensitive to selling prices within the range £90–£96.

(b) Total revenues and total costs are required to construct a cost–volume–profit graph (Figure Q8.10).

Demand (000)	25	23	21	20	19	17	15
Total revenue (£000)	2000	1932	1848	1800	1748	1632	1500
Total variable cost (£000) (normal grade)	1425	1311	1197	1140	1083	969	855
Total variable cost plus £30 000 inspection cost (cheaper grade)	1405	1295	1185	1130	1075	965	855

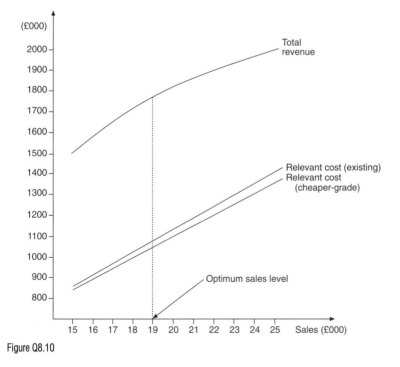

Figure Q8.10

The above costs and revenues are plotted on the CVP diagram, and optimum output is determined at the point where the difference between the total cost and revenue line is the greatest. This occurs at an output level of 19 000 units. The selling price with a demand of 19 000 units is £92.

Question 8.11   (a)

	Manual production		Computer-aided	
	Thingone	Thingtwo	Thingone	Thingtwo
	(£)	(£)	(£)	(£)
Selling price	20	50	20.00	50.00
Variable production costs	(15)	(31)	(12.75)	(26.35)
Bad debts[a]	—	(2)	—	(2.00)
Finance cost[b]		(3)	—	(3.00)
Contribution	5	14	7.25	18.65
Fixed costs per month	£31 500		£43 500	

Notes
[a] 4% of selling price
[b] $2\% \times £50 \times 3$ months

(i) *Thingone only is sold*
Manual process break-even point = 6300 units (£31 500/£5)
                         = £126 000 sales revenue
Computer-aided break-even point = 6000 units (£43 500/£7.25)
                         = £120 000 sales revenue

Point of indifference:
Let x = point of indifference
Then indifference point is where:

$$5x - 31\ 500 = 7.25x - 43\ 500$$
$$= 5333.33 \text{ units}$$
$$= £106\ 667 \text{ sales revenue}$$

(ii) *Sales of Thingone and Thingtwo in the ratio 4 : 1*
Manual process:

$$\text{average contribution per unit} = \frac{(4 \times £5) + (1 \times £14)}{5} = £6.80$$

break-even point   = 4632.35 units (£31 500/£6.80)
                         = £120 441 sales revenue (4632.35 × £26 (W1))

Computer-aided process:
$$\text{average contribution per unit} = \frac{(4 \times £7.25) + (1 \times £18.65)}{5} = £9.53$$

break-even point   = 4564.53 units (£43 500/£9.53)
                         = £118 678 sales revenue (4564.53 × £26 (W1))

Indifference point:
Let x = point of indifference
Then indifference point is where:

$$6.80x - 31\ 500 = 9.53x - 43\ 500$$
$$= 4395.60 \text{ units}$$
$$= £114\ 286 \text{ sales revenue} (4395.60 \times £26 \text{ (W1)})$$

Workings
(W1) Break-even point (sales revenue) = break-even point in units × average selling price per unit sold

$$\text{Therefore, average sales revenue per unit} = \frac{(4 \times £20) + (1 \times £50)}{5} = £26$$

(b) If Thingone alone is sold, budgeted sales are 4000 units, and break-even sales are 6000 units (computer-aided process) and 6300 units (manual process). Hence there is little point producing Thingone on its own. Even if the two products are substitutes, total budgeted sales are 6000 units, and Thingone is still not worth selling on its own. Only if sales are limited to £180 000 (budgeted sales revenue) is Thingone worth selling on its own. However, the assumption that the products are perfect substitutes and £180 000 sales can be generated is likely to be over-optimistic. In other words, the single-product policy is very risky.

Assuming that Thingone and Thingtwo are sold in the ratio of 4:1, the break-even point is 4565 units using the computer-aided process. This consists of a sales mix of 3652 units of Thingone and 913 units of Thingtwo, representing individual margins of safety of 348 units and 1087 units when compared with the original budget. Launching both products is clearly the most profitable alternative.

It should be noted that the budgeted sales mix is in the ratio of 2:1, and this gives an average contribution per unit of £8 (manual process) and £11.05 (computer-aided process). The break-even point based on this sales mix is 3937 units for both the manual and computer-aided process, consisting of 2625 units of Thingone and 1312 units of Thingtwo. This represents a margin of safety of 1375 units of Thingone (34%) and 688 units of Thingtwo (34%). It is obviously better to sell Thingtwo in preference to Thingone. It is recommended that both products be sold and the computer-aided process be adopted.

(c) For the answer to this question see 'Pricing policies' in Chapter 11. In particular, the answer should stress the need to obtain demand estimates for different selling prices and cost estimates for various demand levels. The optimal *short-run* price is where profits are maximized. However, the final price selected should aim to maximize *long-run* profits and the answer should include a discussion of relevant pricing policies such as price skimming and pricing penetration policies. Competitors' reactions to different selling prices should also be considered.

Before demand estimates are made, market research should be undertaken to find customers' reaction to the new product. In addition, research should be undertaken to see whether a similar product is being developed or sold by other firms. This information might be obtained from trade magazines, market research or the company's sales staff. If a similar product is currently being sold, a decision must be made whether to compete on price or quality. The degree of interdependence of new and existing products must also be considered, and any lost sales from existing products should be included in the analysis. It may be necessary to differentiate the new product from existing products.

Measuring relevant costs and revenues for decision-making

Solutions to Chapter 9 questions

Question 9.1

(a)

	Relevant costs of the project
Material A	(1 750)
Material B	8 000
Direct labour	7 000
Net cost of machinery	4 750
Relevant cost	18 000
Contract price	30 000
Contribution	12 000

Notes:

(1) There is a saving in material costs of £1750 if material A is not used.

(2) The actual cost of material B represents the incremental cost.

(3) The hiring of the labour on the other contract represents the additional cash flows of undertaking this contract.

(4) The net cost of purchasing the machinery represents the additional cash flows associated with the contract.

(5) Supervision and overheads will still continue even if the contract is not accepted and are therefore irrelevant.

(b) The report should indicate that the costs given in the question do not represent incremental cash flows arising from undertaking the contract. As the company is operating at an activity level in excess of break-even point any sales revenue in excess of £18 000 incremental costs will provide an additional contribution which will result in an increase in profits. Assuming that the company has spare capacity, and that a competitor is prepared to accept the order at £30 000, then a tender price slightly below £30 000 would be appropriate.

(c) Before accepting the contract the following non-monetary factors should be considered.
(i) Is there sufficient spare capacity to undertake the project?
(ii) Is the overseas customer credit worthy?
(iii) Has the workforce the necessary skills to undertake the project?
(iv) Is the contract likely to result in repeat business with the customer?

(d) If the company were operating below the break-even point, acceptance of the order would provide a further contribution towards fixed costs and reduce the existing loss. In the short term it is better to accept the order and reduce the total loss but if, in the long run, there are not enough orders to generate sufficient contributions to cover total fixed costs, then the company will not survive.

(a)   (£)   **Question 9.2**
   Purchase price of component from supplier   50
   Additional cost of manufacturing (variable cost only)   34
   Saving if component manufactured   16

The component should be manufactured provided the following assumptions are correct:
(i) Direct labour represents the *additional* labour cost of producing the component.
(ii) The company will not incur any additional fixed overheads if the component is manufactured.
(iii) There are no scarce resources. Therefore the manufacture of the component will not restrict the production of other more profitable products.

(b) (i) Additional fixed costs of £56 000 will be incurred, but there will be a saving in purchasing costs of £16 per unit produced. The break-even point is 3500 units (fixed costs of £56 000/£16 per unit saving). If the quantity of components manufactured per year is less than 3500 units then it will be cheaper to purchase from the outside supplier.
(ii) The contribution per unit sold from the existing product is £40 and each unit produced uses 8 scarce labour hours. The contribution per labour hour is £5. Therefore if the component is manufactured, 4 scarce labour hours will be used, resulting in a lost contribution of £20. Hence the relevant cost of manufacturing the components is £54, consisting of £34 incremental cost plus a lost contribution of £20. The component should be purchased from the supplier.

(c) The book value of the equipment is a sunk cost and is not relevant to the decision whether the company should purchase or continue to manufacture the components. If we cease production now, the written-down value will be written off in a lump sum, whereas if we continue production, the written-down value will be written off over a period of years. Future cash outflows on the equipment will not be affected by the decision to purchase or continue to manufacture the components. For an illustration of the irrelevance of the written down value of assets for decision-making purposes see 'Replacement of equipment' in Chapter 13.

(a) *Calculation of minimum selling price:*   **Question 9.3**

	(£)
Direct materials: Steel[a]	55.00
Brass Fittings[b]	20.00
Direct Labour: Skilled[c]	300.00
Semi-skilled[d]	—
Overhead[e]	7.50
Estimating time[f]	—
Administration[g]	—
Relevant cost of the order	382.50

Notes:
[a] Using the materials for the order will result in them having to be replaced. Therefore future cash outflows will increase by £55.
[b] Future cash outflows of £20 will be incurred.
[c] The required labour hours can be obtained by reducing production of another product involving a lost contribution before deducting the labour cost of £21 (£13 + £8) per hour (note that the labour cost will be incurred for all alternatives and

therefore is not an incremental cash flow). Alternatively, the company can pay additional wages involving overtime of £300 (25 hours × £12). Therefore the latter course of action is the most economical and the incremental cash flows from undertaking the order will be £300.

[d] No incremental cost is involved since the alternative is paid idle time.

[e] The only incremental cost is power consisting of 10 hours at £0.75 per hour.

[f] Estimating time is a sunk cost.

[g] Administration does not involve any incremental cash flows.

(b) Factors to be considered include:

   (i) time period for repeat orders, the number of repeat orders and the likely demand;

  (ii) the cash flows generated from the alternative use of the capacity;

 (iii) competition to obtain future orders from Exe plc;

 (iv) estimated price quotations from competitors.

(c) *Limiting factor presentation:*

	Product X	Product Y
Product contribution	£10	£20
Kg of material used per product	1	4
Contribution per kg	£10	£5

Thus scarce materials should be allocated to Product X since it yields a contribution of £5 per kg in excess of the contribution derived from Product Y.

Opportunity cost approach:

	Product X	Product Y
Product contribution at acquisition cost	£10	£20
Lost contribution from alternative use:		
1 kg allocated to Y at £5 per kg	(£5)	
4 kg allocated to X at £10 per kg		£40
Cash flow impact per product	+£5	−£20
Cash flow impact per kg	+£5 (£5/1 kg)	−£5 (£20/4 kg)

The above analysis shows that X yields a contribution of £5 per kg when taking alternative uses of the materials into consideration. Producing Product Y results in the contribution being reduced by £5 per kg taking into account the alternative use of the materials. This is consistent with the limiting factor approach which indicates that the company is £5 per kg better off using the materials for X or £5 per kg worse off from using the materials for Y.

Question 9.4   (a) (i)

	Product I (£000)	Product II (£000)	Product III (£000)	Total (£000)
Sales	2475	3948	1520	7943
Contribution	1170	1692	532	3394
Attributable fixed costs	(275)	(337)	(296)	(908)
General fixed costs[a]	(520)	(829)	(319)	(1668)
	(795)	(1166)	(615)	(2576)
Profit	375	526	(83)	818
	= £1.6/unit	= £1.40/unit	= (£0.04/unit)	

Note

[a]General fixed costs are allocated to products at 21% of total sales revenue (£1668/£7943)

MEASURING RELEVANT COSTS AND REVENUES FOR DECISION-MAKING

(ii) If Product III is discontinued it is assumed that variable costs and attributable (i.e. specific) fixed costs are avoidable. It is assumed that general fixed costs are common and unavoidable to all products and will remain unchanged if Product III is discontinued. However, it is possible that some general fixed costs may be avoidable in the longer term. The revised profits if Product III is discontinued will be:

	(£000s)
Contribution of Products I and II (£1170 + £1692)	2862
Attributable fixed costs (£275 + £337)	(612)
General fixed costs	(1668)
Profit	582

Profits will decline by £236 000 (£818 − £582) if Product III is discontinued because A Ltd will no longer obtain a contribution of £236 000 (£532 − £296) towards general fixed costs.

(iii) Extra sales of 15 385 units (£80 000 additional fixed costs/£5.20 unit contribution) will be required to cover the additional advertising expenditure. It is assumed that existing fixed costs will remain unchanged.

(iv) The revised unit contribution will be £3.45 (£9.45 − £6).

$$\text{Required sales} = \frac{£1\,692\,000 \text{ (existing total contribution)}}{£3.45 \text{ revised unit contribution}}$$

= 490 435 units (an increase of 30.4% over the budgeted sales of 376 000 units)

(b) The following factors will influence cost behaviour in response to changes in activity:
  (i) The magnitude of the change in activity (more costs are likely to be affected when there is a large change in activity).
  (ii) Type of expense (some expenses are directly variable with volume such as direct materials, whereas others are fixed or semi-fixed).
  (iii) Management policy (some expenses are varied at the discretion of management, e.g. advertising).
  (iv) The time period (in the long term, all costs can be changed in response to changes in activity whereas in the short term, some costs, e.g. salaries of supervisors, will remain unchanged).

Task 1

Question 9.5

(a) and (b)

Selling price	£60	£70	£80	£90
Sales volume (units)	25 000	20 000	16 000	11 000
	(£ per unit)	(£ per unit)	(£ per unit)	(£ per unit)
Direct material	14.00	14.00	14.00	16.10 (£14 × 115/100)
Direct labour	13.00	13.00	11.70 (90%)	11.70
Variable production overhead	4.00	4.00	4.00	4.00
Sales commission (10% of selling price)	6.00	7.00	8.00	9.00
Total variable cost per unit	37.00	38.00	37.70	40.80
Contribution per unit	23.00	32.00	42.30	49.20
	£000	£000	£000	£000
Total contribution	575	640	676.8	541.2

Fixed costs:

production overhead
(25 000 × £8)	200	200	190	190

selling and distribution

| (25 000 × £3) | 75 | 70 | 70 | 70 |

administration

(25 000 × £2)	50	50	50	50
Total fixed costs	325	320	310	310
Total annual profit	250	320	366.8	231.2

Task 2

(a) A selling price of £80 maximizes company profits at £366 800 per annum.

(b) Factors to be considered include:

  (i) The effect on morale arising from a large reduction in direct labour and the resulting redundancies.

  (ii) If competitors do not increase their prices customers may migrate to competitors in the long term and long-term annual profits may be considerably less than the profits predicted in the above schedule. The migration of customers may also enable competitors to reap the benefits of economies of scale thus resulting in their having lower unit costs than Rane Ltd.

Task 3

(a) The products should first be ranked according to their contribution per component used.

	Product A £ per unit	Product B £ per unit	Product C £ per unit	Product D £ per unit
Selling price	14	12	16	17
Variable costs	11	11	12	12
Contribution	3	1	4	5
Number of components used per unit	2 (£4/£2)	1 (£2/£2)	3 (£6/£2)	4 (£8/£2)
Contribution per component	£1.50	£1.00	£1.33	£1.25
Ranking	1	4	2	3

The scarce components should be allocated as follows:

Product	Units	Components used	Balance unused
A	4000	8 000	14 400
C	3600	10 800	3 600
D	900	3 600	—
		22 400	

(b) Profit to be earned next period:

Product	Units	Contribution per unit (£)	Total (£)
A	4000	3	12 000
C	3600	4	14 400
D	900		4 500
Total contribution			30 900
Fixed costs			8 000
Profit			22 900

(a)

	Product X	Product Y	Total	**Question 9.6**
(1) Estimated demand (000 units)	315	135		
(2) Machine hours required (per 000 units)	160	280		
(3) Machine hours required to meet demand (1 × 2)	50 400	37 800	88 200	

The machine hours required to meet demand are in excess of the machine hours that are available. Therefore machine hours are the limiting factor and the company should allocate capacity according to contribution per machine hour.

	Product X (£)	Product Y (£)
Selling price	11.20	15.70
Variable cost	6.30	8.70
Contribution	4.90	7.00
Machine hours required per unit[a]	0.16	0.28
Contribution per machine hour	£30.625	£25

Note:
[a] Product X = 160/1000   Product Y = 280/1000

The company should concentrate on maximizing output of Product X. Meeting the maximum demand of Product X will require 50 400 machine hours and this will leave 34 600 hours (85 000 hrs − 50 400 hrs) to be allocated to Product Y. Therefore 123 571 units (34 600 hrs/0.28 hrs) of Y and 315 000 units of X should be produced.

(b)

	Product X (£)	Product Y (£)	Total (£)
Contribution per unit	4.90	7.00	
Sales volume	315 000	123.571	
Contribution (£000s)	1543.5	864.997	2 408.497
Less fixed costs[a]			2 124.997
Profit			283.500

Note:
[a] Fixed costs: Product X = 315 000 units × £4 per unit = £1 260 000
Product Y = 123 571 units × £7 per unit = £864 997
                                                                 2 124 997

(c) There are now two limiting factors and linear programming techniques must be used.

Let   X = Number of units of X produced (in 000s of units)
       Y = Number of units of Y produced (in 000s of units)

160X + 280Y = 85 000 Machine hours   (1)
120X + 140Y = 55 000 Labour hours   (2)

Multiply equation (2) by 2 and equation (1) by 1

160X + 280Y = 85 000   (1)
240X + 280Y = 110 000   (2)

Subtract equation (2) from equation (1)

− 80X = −25 000
   X = 312.5 (i.e. 312 500 units)

Substitute for X in equation (1)

$$160 (312.5) + 280Y = 85\,000$$
$$50\,000 + 280Y = 85\,000$$
$$280Y = 35\,000$$
$$Y = 125 \text{ (i.e. } 125\,000)$$

Therefore the optimal output to fully utilize both labour and machine capacity is 312 500 units of Product X and 125 000 units of Product Y.

Question 9.7

(a) The statement includes the following errors:

1　It focuses only on next year's figures but this is not a typical year. Some of the costs are one-off costs and will not be repeated each year. The decision is also likely to be influenced by the level of demand and this varies over the years. Therefore, the analysis should be over a longer time period.

2　The additional cost of purchasing SCB's ignores relevant costs. It should be based on the purchase price less incremental cost and not the full cost of £112 per unit.

3　Half of the purchasing officer's salary is unlikely to be saved since there is no evidence to suggest that he/she will be placed on a fractional contract.

4　The cost of placing orders are not an incremental cost since they are already reflected in the salary, which is likely to remain unchanged.

5　The new liaison officer's salary and redundancy costs are omitted.

6　The cost of transportation of materials is unlikely to be an incremental cost. The cost will be included within the cost of direct materials.

(b) (i)　There are a number of different approaches that can be adopted to answer this question. Where you are faced with more than two alternatives, you will probably find it easier to list the costs and revenues associated with each of the alternatives. For the irrelevant costs you can either ensure that the same amount is included in all alternatives, thus ensuring that they become irrelevant, or omit them from the analysis.

Evaluation of the three alternatives

	2002/03	2003/04	2004/05	Total
Produce internally (Alternative 1)				
Sales volume (units)	58 000	60 500	60 500	
	(£000's)	(£000's)	(£000's)	(£000's)
Sales at normal contribution of £312				
(£400 – £88) per unit	18 096	18 876	18 876	
Less: Overtime at £75 per unit in excess				
of 55 000 units	(225)	(412.5)	(412.5)	
Avoidable fixed costs – SCB's	(250)	(380)	(380)	
Fixed costs – sensors [a]	(2 600)	(2 900)	(2 900)	
Contribution to profits	15 021	15 183.5	15 183.5	45 388
Purchase SCB's externally (Alternative 2)				
Sales volume (units)	58 000	62 000	65 000	
	(£000's)	(£000's)	(£000's)	(£000's)
Sales at a contribution of £284				
(£400 – £116) per unit	16 472	17 608	18 460	
Less: Extra stockholding costs	(10)	(10)	(10)	
Redundancy costs (72 × £4 000)	(288)			
Liaison officer	(30)	(30)	(30)	
Fixed costs – sensors [a]	(2 600)	(2 900)	(3 100)	
Contribution to profits	13 544	14 668	15 320	43 532

　MEASURING RELEVANT COSTS AND REVENUES FOR DECISION-MAKING

Purchase SCB's externally and rental of extra space (Alternative 3)

Sales volume (units)	58 000	60 500	60 500	
	(£000's)	(£000's)	(£000's)	(£000's)
Sales at a contribution of £284				
(£400 – £116) per unit	16 472	17 182	17 182	
Additional rental income (240 × 120 × £45)		1 296	1 296	
Less: Extra stockholding costs	(10)	(10)	(10)	
Redundancy costs (72 × £4 000)	(288)			
Liaison officer	(30)	(30)	(30)	
Fixed costs – sensors [a]	(2 600)	(2 900)	(2 900)	
Contribution to profits	13 544	15 538	15 538	44 620

Note

[a] Note that the same amount is entered for 2002/03 and 2003/04 for the fixed costs relating to sensors, thus making them irrelevant. In 2004/05 the figures reflect incremental fixed costs of £200 000 associated with the higher output level for the second alternative in 2004/05.

Based on the time horizon specified in the question it is preferable to continue producing SCB's and work overtime.

(b) (ii) It is assumed that, in the long term, annual output for the first and third alternatives would still be restricted to 60 500 units but with the second alternative output can be increased to 70 000 units. Over the three year time horizon shown in (b) (i) the first alternative generates £1 856 000 (£45 388 – £43 532) greater contribution than the second alternative and £768 000 (£45 388 – £44 620) more than the third alternative. Assuming that demand remains at 65 000 units the second alternative will generate an extra contribution of £136 500 each year compared with the first alternative (difference between year 3 figures for the two alternatives) thus taking approximately another 13 years (£1 856 000/£136 500) to make up the shortfall in contribution. However, if demand increases to 68 000 units (based on the same 3000 units increase in 2004/05) an additional contribution of £852 000 (3000 units × £284) will be obtained for the second alternative from 2005/06 onwards thus exceeding alternative 1 by £988 500 (£852 000 + £136 500) per annum. Therefore, after two years alternative 2 would be preferred to the first alternative.

A similar analysis could be undertaken based on a comparison of alternatives 1 and 3 to show that in 2004/05 alternative 3 generates £354 500 (£15 538 – £15 183.5) greater contribution. Thus after approximately two years the shortfall in profits would be achieved and beyond a five-year time horizon alternative 3 would be preferred to alternative 1.

The choice of alternatives therefore depends on future demand levels. If demand can be maintained at 68 000 units, alternative 2 is the most attractive option. If demand is expected to remain at 65 000 units the third alternative is preferable. It should be noted that qualitative factors, such as the impact of redundancies on the morale of the workforce, should be incorporated into the final decision.

Question 9.8

(a) The relevant cost of producing the new product is the variable cost plus the lost contribution from selling the processing time to another manufacturer. It is assumed that it is more profitable to spend three days per week producing the established main products. The calculations of the variable overhead rates are:

	Department 4	Department 5
Normal hours (0.9 × 40 hrs × 50 weeks)	1800	1800
Fixed overhead rate per hour (£)	20 (36 000/1800)	28 (50 400/1800)
Total overhead rate per hour (£)	40	40
Variable overhead rate per hour (£)	20	12

The variable costs per hour are:

Department 4: £60 (£40 power cost + £20 variable overhead)
Department 5: £72 (£60 power cost + £12 variable overhead)

Note that labour costs are fixed.

If the new product is not developed, Department 4 should sell unused processing time at £70 per hour, but it is not profitable for Department 5 to sell processing time because hourly variable cost is in excess of the selling price. Therefore the relevant costs per processing hour are:

Department 4: £70 (£60 variable cost + £10 lost contribution)
Department 5: £72

We can now calculate the relevant cost of producing the new product:

	(£)
Direct material	10.00
Department 4 variable operating cost (0.75 hrs × £70)	52.50
Department 5 variable operating cost (0.33 hrs × £72)	24.00
	86.50

The total *additional* contributions for various selling prices and demand levels are:

	(£)	(£)	(£)
Selling price	100	110	120
Unit contribution	13.50	23.50	33.50
Demand	1067[a]	1000	500
Total contribution	14 404	23 500	16 750

Note
[a]Maximum output in Department 4 is 1067 units [(16 weeks × 50 hrs)/0.75 hrs] and 2400 units in Department 5. Output is therefore restricted to 1067 units. Optimum output of the new product is 1000 units at a selling price of £110. An output of 1000 units will require 15 hours per week (20 units per week × 0.75 hrs) in Department 4 and 6.67 hours in Department 5. Department 4 should therefore sell 1 hour per week at £70 per hour, but it is not profitable for Department 5 to sell its spare capacity of 9.33 hours per week.

The weekly *additional* gain from this programme is £470 (20 units × £23.50 contribution). The overall weekly gain is calculated without including the lost contribution of £10 per hour for Department 4. Variable cost is £79 (£86.50 relevant cost less opportunity cost of 0.75 hrs at £10) and contribution is £31 per unit. The total week gain is £630 (20 units at £31 per week plus £10 from the sale of one hour). Without the new product, weekly contribution will be £160 (16 hrs × £10). Therefore there is an additional gain of £470 from introducing the new product.

(b) The shadow prices indicate that if an hour is lost from the existing optimum plan, contribution will decline by £76 for Department 4 and £27 for Department 5. The relevant hourly cost for a scarce resource is:

Variable cost per hour plus lost contribution per hour

Therefore the relevant cost of producing the new product is:

	(£)
Direct material	10
Department 4: 0.75 hrs × (£60 + £76)	102
Department 5: 0.33 hrs × (£72 + £27)	33
	145

The new product will not increase total contribution if the selling price is less than £145.

(c) The shadow price of a scarce resource represents the increase in total contribution that will be obtained if a scarce resource can be increased by 1 unit. Alternatively, the shadow price can be expressed as the loss in total contribution that will occur if the availability of a scarce resource is reduced by 1 unit. The opportunity cost of using a resource is the lost benefit that occurs from using it in the most profitable manner. Shadow prices represent the contribution that would be lost if one unit of a resource were removed from the optimal production programme. In other words, it represents the lost benefit from using it in the most profitable manner. Therefore shadow prices are equivalent to opportunity costs.

(a) *Alternative uses of spare electric motor*

Question 9.9

Use with exhaust gas extraction equipment

Production/sales enhancement resulting in the reduction of the loss in production enhancement from 30% to 10% of 30 000 units thus increasing sales volume by

2000 units at a contribution of £5 (£8–£3)	£10 000
Less fitting and dismantling costs	(2 500)
Add sales value after one year	2 000
Net cash flow	9 500

Use in cooling process	
Hiring cost avoided	£3000
Less modification cost	(1000)
Less disposal cost	(250)
Net cash flow	1750

Hold in store and sell in one year	
Net cash flow (sale proceeds in one year)	£3500

The company should use the motor in conjunction with the exhaust gases for the space heating proposal during the coming year.

(b) The answer in part (a) indicates that if conversion is implemented now, the spare electric motor should be used in the coming year to enhance production and then sold after one year for £2000. The consequences of adopting this alternative are incorporated into the financial evaluation of converting now or in one year's time. Note that the production enhancement will therefore be 9000 units (10 000 units less 10%) for one year only and 10 000 units after the running in period.

Evaluation of decision to convert now or in one year's time

	Convert now (£)	Convert in one year's time (£)	Net benefit/ (cost) of delay for one year (£)
Cash inflows:			
Production/sales enhancement (at £8)	72 000	80 000	8 000
Sales of space heating equipment (ducted air)	20 000	18 000	(2 000)
Gas extraction machine sale	40 000	30 000	(10 000)
Electric motor sale	2 000	3 500	1 500
	134 000	131 500	
Cash outflows:			
Production/sales enhancement – (VC at £3)	27 000	30 000	(3 000)
Exhaust gas extraction machine			
Incremental fixed costs		16 000	(16 000)
dismantling cost	5 000	5 500	(500)
Space heating (ducted air)			
running costs		10 000	(10 000)
dismantling cost	3 000	3 500	(500)
Alternative exhaust gas extraction machinery			
running cost	12 000		12 000
leasing cost	4 000		4 000
Electric motor conversion cost	2 500		2 500
	53 500	65 000	
Net cash flow	80 500	66 500	
Net cost of delay for one year (£14 000)			(£14 000)

(a) In order to evaluate the three alternatives, it is necessary to estimate the annual income receivable from customers if the company undertakes to service the appliances itself. The calculation of income receivable from customers is:

	(£)
Labour: maintenance contract (100/10 × £30 000)	300 000
Labour: ad hoc work (100/15 × £12 000)	80 000
Materials: maintenance contract (137.5[a]/10 × £18 000)	247 500
Materials: ad hoc work (137.5[a]/10 × £6000)	82 500
	710 000

Note
[a]The material price calculation per £100 cost is:

	(£)
Company cost	100
Contractors' price (£100 + 10%)	110
Customers' price (£110 + 25%)	137.5

In other words, it is assumed that for every £137.50 charged to customers the subcontractor obtains £27.50 profit and the remaining £10 represents income received by the company from the sub-contractor.

Option 1

	(£)	(£)
Sales from small items (40% × £710 000)		284 000
Costs: Incremental fixed costs	148 000	
Materials [40% × 100/137.5 × (247 500 + 82 500)]	96 000	244 000
Income from own operations		40 000
Income from subcontractors of large items (60% × £66 000)	_____	39 600
Total net income	_____	79 600

Option 2

	(£)	(£)
Sales from large items (60% × £710 000)		426 000
Costs: Incremental fixed costs	285 000	
Materials [60% × 100/137.5 × (247 500 + 82 500)]	144 000	429 000
Deficit from own operations		(3 000)
Income from subcontracting small items (40% × £66 000)		26 400
Total net income		23 400

Option 3

	(£)	(£)
Sales from large and small items		710 000
Costs: Incremental fixed costs	385 000	
Materials [100/137.5 × (247 500 + 82 500)]	240 000	625 000
Income from own operations		85 000

It is assumed that all of the fixed costs relating to own operations represent incremental costs.

Option 3 is recommended since it yields the highest profit and is £19 000 in excess of existing operations. Insufficient information is given to incorporate in the answer the effect of repair work undertaken in the first 6 months of operation for which the subcontractor receives 3.5% of the selling price. It is assumed that this payment is common and unavoidable for all alternatives.

(b) Favourable non-financial features:
   (i) The company will have better control over repairs and maintenance of its products and can ensure that a good customer service is provided.
   (ii) The company's mechanics will specialize only in maintaining the company's own appliances, whereas the subcontractors may service many different manufacturers' appliances. Consequently, the company mechanics may become more experienced in maintaining the appliances.

Adverse non-financial features:
   (i) The new system requires the customers to bring the small appliances to the repair centre. Customers may find this inconvenient compared with the present system.
   (ii) The subcontractors may compete and seek to offer present customers a better service.

(a) Total hours = 36 750 (120 000 × 0.25) + (45 000 × 0.15)

Question 9.11

Fixed overhead rate per hour = £40 (£1 470 000/36 750 hours)

	Product A (£)	Product B (£)
Direct materials	2	40
Variable production overhead	28	4
Fixed production overhead	10 (0.25 × £40)	6 (0.15 × 40)
Total cost	40	50
Selling price	60	70
Profit	20	20

Assuming that the company focuses on profits per unit it will be indifferent between the 2 products.

Total net profit = £3 300 000 (120 000 × £20) + (45 000 × £20)

(b)

	Product A	Product B
Contribution per unit	£30 (60–30)	£26 (70–44)
Bottleneck hours	0.02	0.015
Contribution per bottleneck hour	£1500	£1733

Based on the contribution per bottleneck hour the maximum demand of product B should be produced.

The maximum demand of product B requires 810 hours (54 000 × 0.015) leaving 2 265 hours (3075 – 810) to be allocated to product A. This will result in the production of 113 250 units (2265 hours/0.02) of A. The maximum profit is calculated as follows:

	£
Contribution from product A (113 250 × £30)	3 397 500
Contribution from product B (54 000 × £26)	1 404 000
	4 801 500
Less Fixed overhead cost	1 470 000
Net profit	3 331 500

(c) (i) Return per bottleneck hour = (Selling price – material cost)/(Time on bottleneck resource)

Product A = £2900 [(£60 – £2)/0.02 hours]
Product B = £2000 [(£70 – £40)/0.015 hours]

Product A should be sold up to its maximum capacity of utilizing 2880 bottleneck hours (144 000 units × 0.02 hours). This will leave 195 hours for product B thus enabling 13 000 units (195/0.015) to be produced. The maximum profit is calculated as follows:

	£
Throughput return from product A (144 000 × £58)	8 352 000
Contribution from product B (13 000 × £30)	390 000
	8 742 000
Less: variable overheads[a]	3 540 000
fixed overhead cost	1 470 000
Net profit	3 732 000

Note
[a]It is assumed that the variable overheads (e.g. direct labour) are fixed in the short-term. They are derived from part (a) – [(120 000 × £28) + (45 000 × £4)]

(c) (ii) Total overhead cost (£3 540 000 + £1 470 000) = £5 010 000
Overhead cost per bottleneck hour = £1629.27
(£5 010 000/3075 hours)

Throughput return per bottleneck hour = £2000 (see c (i))
Throughput accounting ratio = 1.2275 (£2000/£1 629.27)

(c) (iii) With throughput accounting a product should be sold if the throughput return per bottleneck hour is greater than the production cost (excluding direct materials) per throughput hour. In other words, the throughput accounting ratio should exceed 1.00. Increasing a product's throughput ratio can increase profits. The throughput ratio can be increased by:

1. Increasing the selling price or reducing material costs (note that product B has a very high material cost).
2. Reducing the time required on the bottleneck resource.
3. Creating more capacity of the bottleneck resource and if possible increase the capacity so that the bottleneck can be removed (subject to any additional financial outlays being justified).

Note that product B should be sold because its throughput ratio exceeds 1 but product A has the higher ranking because it has a higher throughput ratio.

(c) (iv) If material costs increase by 20% for product B the revised return per bottleneck hour will be £1467 [(£70 – £48)/0.015] giving a throughput ratio of 0.9 (£1467/£1629.27). Although this is less than 1, production of B can be justified in the short-term, given the special circumstances that apply. Product A is being produced up to its maximum demand and the balance of capacity applied to product B has no incremental cost and is thus fixed in the short-term. Therefore product B will contribute a cash flow of £22 (£70 – £48) per unit.

Activity-based costing

Solutions to Chapter 10 questions

Question 10.1

(a) Three cost poolss and cost drivers have been identified for the proposed ABC system. The cost pools are mileage travel cost incurred in visiting clients, accommodation costs and other costs. Miles travelled, number of overnight stays and chargeable hours have been identified as the respective cost drivers. Details relating to the number of cost drivers are as follows:

	D	E	F	Total
Miles travelled[a]	3000	5600	3000	11600
Nights accommodation[b]		40	15	55
Chargeable hours[c]	1000	3500	1500	6000

Notes

[a] Return miles travelled × number of visits × number of clients (e.g. 100 miles × 3 visits × 10 clients for D)

[b] Number of visits per client × number of clients (only applies to visits in excess of 50 miles)

[c] Chargeable hours per client × number of clients

The cost driver rates are:

Mileage costs = £1.293 per mile (£15 000/11 600 miles)
Accommodation costs = £200 per night (£11 000/55 nights)
Other costs = £70.833 per chargeable hour (£425 000/6000 hours)

Note that the other costs consist of marketing consultants (4 × £60 000) + administration (£120 000) + office premises (£50 000) + advertising (£5000) + telephones etc. (£10 000). The costs allocated to each client profile are as follows:

	D	E	F
Mileage costs (£)	3879 (3000 × £1293)	7241 (5600 × 1.293)	3880 (3000 × £1.293)
Accommodation costs(£)		8000 (40 × £200)	3000 (15 × £200)
Other costs (£)	70833 (1000 × 70.833)	247 915 (3500 × £70.833)	106 252 (1500 × £70.833)
Total costs	74 712	263 156	113 132

	D	E	F
(b) Total costs assigned with the current system (£)[a]	75 000	262 500	112 500
Total costs assigned with the ABC system (£)	74 712	263 156	113 132

Note:
[a] Chargeable hours × £75 per hour

The difference in costs assigned to the client profiles with the ABC system compared with the existing system is very small. This is because ABC system assigns only £26 000 of the total cost of £451 000 (approximately 6%) using different cost drivers. Therefore the proposed system can only be justified if the costs of obtaining the information required are only minimal. There would have to be a considerable change in the cost structure and client profile to provide a justification for implementing an ABC system.

(c) See 'Activity hierarchies' in Chapter 10 for an explanation of the four cost categories. For a firm of consultants the consultants' salaries could be classified as unit-level activities. This is because the costs are likely to be determined by the number of chargeable hours. If the chargeable hours were to change significantly the number of consultants employed would be likely to change. Accommodation costs can be viewed as batch-related costs since the accommodation costs are the same irrespective of the unit-level activities (i.e. chargeable hours). In other words, the accommodation cost is the same for a client with a small number of chargeable hours as for a client with a large number of chargeable hours. Where administrative staff are responsible for administering the workload and providing support for a specific client, or a category of clients, then such costs represent the equivalent of product-sustaining costs but where customers are the cost object they are described as customer-sustaining costs. Finally, faculity sustaining costs consist of infrastructure costs such as maintenance and upkeep of the consultancy premises.

(a) (i) *Conventional Absorption Costing Profit Statement:*

Question 10.2

		XYI	YZT	ABW
(1)	Sales volume (000 units)	50	40	30
		£	£	£
(2)	Selling price per unit	45	95	73
(3)	Prime cost per unit	32	84	65
(4)	Contribution per unit	13	11	8
(5)	Total contribution in £000s (1 × 4)	650	440	240
(6)	Machine department overheads[a]	120	240	144
(7)	Assembly department overheads[b]	288.75	99	49.5
	Profit (£000s)	241.25	101	46.5

Total profit = £388 750

Notes:
[a] XYI = 50 000 × 2 hrs × £1.20, YZT = 40 000 × 5 hrs × £1.20
[b] XYI = 50 000 × 7 hrs × £0.825, YZT = 40 000 × 3 hrs × £0.825

(ii) *Cost pools:*

	Machining services	Assembly services	Set-ups	Order processing	Purchasing
£000	357	318	26	156	84
Cost drivers	420 000 machine hours	530 000 direct labour hours	520 set-ups	32 000 customer orders	11 200 suppliers' orders
Cost driver rates	£0.85 per machine hour	£0.60 direct labour hour	£50 per set-up	£4.875 per customer order	£7.50 per suppliers' order

ABC Profit Statement:

	XYI (£000)	YZT (£000)	ABW (£000)
Total contribution	650	440	240
Less overheads:			
Machine department at £0.85 per hour	85	170	102
Assembly at £0.60 per hour	210	72	36
Set-up costs at £50 per set-up	6	10	10
Order processing at £4.875 per order	39	39	78
Purchasing at £7.50 per order	22.5	30	31.5
Profit (Loss)	287.5	119	(17.5)

Total profit = £389 000

(b) See the sections on 'Comparison of traditional and ABC costing systems' and 'Volume-based and non-volume-based cost drivers' in Chapter 10 for the answer to this question.

Question 10.3   (a) (i) The package material requirements are as follows:

John Ltd	30 000 units (30 000 × 1)
George Ltd	90 000 units (45 000 × 2)
Paul Ltd	75 000 units (25 000 × 3)
	195 000 units

Cost per unit of packaging = £1 950 000/195 000 = £10

Product costs per cubic metre

	John Ltd (£)	George Ltd (£)	Paul Ltd (£)
Packaging material	10 (1 × £10)	20 (2 × £10)	30 (3 × £10)
Labour and overhead[a]	9.40	9.40	9.40
	19.40	29.40	39.40

Note
[a]Labour and overhead average cost per metre = £940 000/100 000 metres
= £9.40.

(ii) The costs are assigned to the following activities:

	Receipt and inspection (£)	Storage (£)	Packing (£)
Labour: Basic	52 500 (15%)	35 000 (10%)	262 500 (75%)
Overtime	15 000 (50%)	4 500 (15%)	10 500 (35%)
Occupancy	100 000 (20%)	300 000 (60%)	100 000 (20%)
Administration and management	24 000 (40%)	6 000 (10%)	30 000 (50%)
	191 500	345 500	403 000

The resource usage for each of the cost drivers is:

	Receipt and inspection hours	Storage (m²)	Packing hours
John Ltd.	2 500 (30 000 × 5 mins.)	9 000 (30 000 × 0.3)	18 000 (30 000 × 36 min)
George Ltd.	6 750 (45 000 × 9 mins.)	13 500 (45 000 × 0.3)	33 750 (45 000 × 45 min)
Paul Ltd.	6 250 (25 000 × 15 mins.)	5 000 (25 000 × 0.2)	25 000 (25 000 × 1 hr)
	15 500	27 500	76 750

The cost driver rates are:

£12.355 per receipt and inspection hour (£191 500/15 500 hours)
£12.564 per m² of material stored (£345 500/27 500 m²)
£5.251 per packing hour (£403 000/76 750 hrs)

Product cost per cubic metre

	John Ltd (£)	George Ltd (£)	Paul Ltd (£)
Packing material	10.00	20.00	30.00
Receipt and inspection[a]	1.03	1.85	3.09

Storage cost[b]	3.77	3.77	2.51
Packing cost[c]	3.15	3.94	5.25
	17.95	29.56	40.85

Notes
[a] £12.355 × 5/60 hrs = £1.03;
   £12.355 × 9/60 hrs = £1.85;   £12.355 × 15/60 hrs = £3.09.
[b] £12.564 × 0.3 m = £3.77;   £12.564 × 0.2 m = £2.51.
[c] £5.25 × 36/60 hrs = £3.15;   £5.25 × 45/60 hrs = £3.94, £5.25 × 1 hr.

(b) The company has established cost pools for three major activities (receipt and inspection, storage and packing). The cost driver that causes the receipt and inspection costs to be incurred is the fragility of the different goods (measured by receipt and inspection time). The storage cost is influenced by the average size (measured in square metres) of the incoming product and packing costs are caused by the complexity of packaging and this is measured by the time required to pack the products.

ABC results in the computation of more accurate costs by seeking to measure resources consumed by products. ABC systems assume that activities cause costs and that products create the demand for activities. Costs are assigned to products based on individual products' consumption or demand for each activity. ABC systems simply recognize that businesses must understand the factors that cause each major activity, the cost of activities and how activities relate to products.

ABC has attracted a considerable amount of interest because it provides not only a basis for calculating more accurate product costs but also a mechanism for managing and controlling overhead costs. By collecting and reporting on the significant activities in which a business engages, it is possible to understand and manage costs more effectively. The aim is to manage the forces that cause activities (i.e. the cost drivers), and by reducing cost driver volume, costs can be managed and controlled in the long run.

(a) For the answer to this question see Chapter 10.

Question 10.4

(b) *Machine-related costs*
Machine hours for the period:

$$A = 500 \times \tfrac{1}{4} \quad = \quad 125$$
$$B = 5000 \times \tfrac{1}{4} \quad = \quad 1\,250$$
$$C = 600 \times 1 \quad = \quad 600$$
$$D = 7000 \times 1\tfrac{1}{2} = 10\,500$$
$$\overline{12\,475}$$

Machine hour rate = £3 per hour (£37 424/12 475 hrs)

Set-up related costs
Cost per set-up = £256.18 (£4355/17)
Set-up cost per unit of output:

$$\text{Product A } (1 \times £256.18)/500 \quad = £0.51$$
$$B \ (6 \times £256.18)/5000 \quad = £0.31$$
$$C \ (2 \times £256.18)/600 \quad = £0.85$$
$$D \ (8 \times £256.18)/7000 \quad = £0.29$$

Material ordering related costs
Cost per order = £1920/10 orders = £192 per order

Material ordering cost per unit of output:

$$\begin{array}{ll}
\text{Product A } (1 \times £192)/500 & = £0.38 \\
\text{B } (4 \times £192)/5000 & = £0.15 \\
\text{C } (1 \times £192)/600 & = £0.32 \\
\text{D } (4 \times £192)/7000 & = £0.11
\end{array}$$

Material handling related costs
Cost per material handing = £7580/27 = £280.74
Material handling cost per unit of output:

$$\begin{array}{ll}
\text{Product A } (2 \times £280.74)/500 & = £1.12 \\
\text{B } (10 \times £280.74)/5000 & = £0.56 \\
\text{C } (3 \times £280.74)/600 & = £1.40 \\
\text{D } (12 \times £280.74)/7000 & = £0.48
\end{array}$$

Spare parts
Cost per part = £8600/12 = £716.67
Administration of spare parts cost per unit of output:

$$\begin{array}{ll}
\text{Product A } (2 \times £716.67)/500 & = £2.87 \\
\text{B } (5 \times £716.67)/5000 & = £0.72 \\
\text{C } (1 \times £716.67)/600 & = £1.19 \\
\text{D } (4 \times £716.67)/7000 & = £0.41
\end{array}$$

Overhead cost per unit of output

Product	A (£)	B (£)	C (£)	D (£)
ABC overhead cost:				
Machine overheads	0.75	0.75	3.00	4.50
Set-ups	0.51	0.31	0.85	0.29
Material ordering	0.38	0.15	0.32	0.11
Material handling	1.12	0.56	1.40	0.48
Spare parts	2.87	0.72	1.19	0.41
	5.63	2.49	6.76	5.79
Present system	1.20	1.20	4.80	7.20
Difference	+4.43	+1.29	+1.96	−1.41

The present system is based on the assumption that all overhead expenditure is volume-related, measured in terms of machine hours. However, the overheads for the five support activities listed in the question are unlikely to be related to machine hours. Instead, they are related to the factors that influence the spending on support activities (i.e. the cost drivers). The ABC system traces costs to products based on the quantity (cost drivers) of activities consumed. Product D is the high volume product, and thus the present volume-based system traces a large share of overheads to this product. In contrast, the ABC system recognizes that product D consumes overheads according to activity consumption and traces a lower amount of overhead to this product. The overall effect is that, with the present system, product D is overcosted and the remaining products are undercosted. For a more detailed explanation of the difference in resource consumption between products for an ABC and traditional cost system see 'A comparison of traditional and ABC systems' and 'Volume-based and non-volume-based cost drivers' in Chapter 10 for the answer to this question.

Question 10.5

(a) For short-term decision-making, contribution to fixed costs is often advocated. Contribution is defined as sales less variable costs. It therefore attempts to include only those costs and revenues that will change as a result of a decision. Fixed costs are assumed to be unavoidable and remain unchanged and irrelevant for decision-making. Ignoring fixed costs can only be justified in certain circumstances. For example, the contribution approach can be applied to one-time only special orders where the company has a temporary excess supply of spare capacity. In this situation a short-term approach can be adopted by focusing only on the sales revenues and variable costs. The contribution approach is also advocated for pricing off-peak business and ranking products where limiting factors apply (see 'Product-mix decisions when capacity constraints apply' in Chapter 9). In the latter situation a company may be faced with short-term capacity constraint and profit is maximized by ranking products by their contributions per limiting factor.

The contribution approach can only be applied when decisions have no long-term implications. However, most decisions do have long-term implications and in these circumstances fixed costs cannot be ignored. With the contribution approach there is a danger that only those direct costs that are uniquely attributable to individual products will be regarded as relevant for decision-making. Those fixed costs relating to the joint resources that fluctuate according to the demand for them will also be relevant for decision-making. An ideal answer should emphasize, why in the longer-term, fixed costs are likely to change and be relevant for decision-making. For a more detailed discussion of this issue you should refer to 'The need for a cost accumulation system in generating relevant cost information for decision-making' in Chapter 10. Points 1 (many indirect costs are relevant for decision-making) and 3 (product decisions are not independent) are of particular importance.

(b) See section 'Designing ABC systems' in Chapter 10 for the answer to this question.

(c) See sections on 'A comparison of traditional and ABC systems' and 'Volume-based and non-volume-based cost drivers' in Chapter 10 for the answer to this question.

(d) See 'Activity hierarchies' in Chapter 10 for the answer to this question.

Part one

Question 10.6

(a) Single factory direct labour hour overhead rate = £310 000/2000 hours = £155 per direct labour hour

Component	r (£)	s (£)	t (£)
Direct labour costs at £12 per hour	300	5 760	600
Direct materials	1200	2 900	1 800
Overheads (direct labour hours × £155 per hour)	3875	74 400	7 750
Total costs	5375	83 060	10 150
Cost per unit	£9.60	£6.49	£4.23

(b) In Chapter 10 it was pointed out that ABC systems involve the following stages:
   (i)   identifying the major activities that take place in an organization;
   (ii) creating a cost pool/cost centre for each activity;
   (iii) determining the cost driver for each activity;
   (iv) assigning the cost of activities to cost objects (e.g. products, components, customers, etc.) according to their demand for activities.

The consultants have already identified the most significant activities. They are receiving component consignments from suppliers, setting up equipment for production runs, quality inspections and dispatching orders to customers. The following shows the assignment of the costs to these activities:

	Receiving supplies (£000)	Set-ups (£000)	Quality inspections (£000)	Dispatching (£000)	Total (£000)
Equipment operation expenses[a]	18.75	87.50		18.75	125.00
Maintenance[a]	3.75	17.50		3.75	25.00
Technicians' wages initially allocated to maintenance (30% of £85 = £25.50) and then reallocated to activities on the same basis as maintenance[a]	3.83	17.85		3.82	25.50
Technicians wages allocation (excluding portion allocated to maintenance)[b]		34.00	25.50		59.50
Stores wages[c]	35.00				35.00
Dispatch wages[d]				40.00	40.00
Total	61.33	156.85	25.50	66.32	310.00

Notes
[a]Allocated on the basis 15%, 70% and 15% as specified in the question
[b]Allocated on the basis 30%, 40% and 30% (of £85) as specified in the question
[c]Directly attributable to the receiving component supplies activity
[d]Directly attributable to the dispatching activity

The next stage is to identify cost drivers for each activity and establish cost driver rates by dividing the activity costs by a measure of cost driver usage for the period. The calculations are as follows:

Receiving supplies (£61 330/980)   = £62.58 per component consignment received
Performing set-ups (£156 850/1020) = £153.77 per set-up
Quality inspections (£25 500/640)   = £39.84 per quality inspection
Dispatching goods (£66 320/420)   = £157.93 per goods order dispatched

Finally, the costs are assigned to components based on their cost driver usage. The assignments are as follows:

	r (£)	s (£)	t (£)
Direct labour	300.00	5 760.00	600.00
Direct materials	1 200.00	2 900.00	1 800.00
Receiving supplies	2 628.36	1 501.92	1 752 24
Performing set-ups	2 460.32	2 767.86	1 845.24
Quality inspection	398.40	318.72	717.12
Dispatching goods	3 474.46	13 424.05	7 264.78
Total costs	10 461.54	26 672.55	13 979.38
Number of units produced	560	12 800	2 400
Cost per unit	£18.68	£2.08	£5.82

For component r the overhead costs have been assigned as follows:
Receiving supplies (42 receipts at £62.58)
Performing set-ups (16 production runs at £153.77)
Quality inspection (10 at £39.84)
Dispatching goods (22 at £157.93)

(c)

Cost assigned to component z

Quarterly charge (for 1000 units)		(£)
Design cost	£40 000 ÷ 8	5 000
Direct labour	80 × £12	960
Direct materials		2 000
Overheads:		
Receiving supplies	£62.58 × 20	1 252
Set-ups	£153.77 × 15	2 307
Quality inspection	£39.84 × 30	1 195
Dispatching goods	£157.93 × 4	632
Total		13 346
25% mark up		3 337
Charge per quarter		16 683

According to the information provided in the question the short-term incremental cost attributable to the order is as follows:

	(£)
Design costs (£40 000/7.02 annuity factor[a])	5 698
Direct labour (80 hours at £12)	960
Direct materials	2 000
Labour related variable overheads[b]	3 720
Inspection related variable overheads[b]	4 359
	16 737

Notes

[a]Represents the present value of £8000 received in 8 quarterly instalments by dividing £40 000 by the annuity factor for 8 periods at 3% (present values are explained in Chapter 13).

[b]The question states that 40% of the overheads are variable in the short-term and 50% of these costs vary with direct labour hours and the remaining 50% vary with the number of quality inspections. Therefore the variable overhead rates are:
Labour related = (310 000 × 0.6 × 0.5)/2000 = £46.50 per direct labour hour
Inspection related = (310 000 × 0.6 × 0.5)/640 = £145.31 per quality inspection
Charge to component Z
  Labour related = 80 hours at £46.50 = £3720
  Inspection related = 30 inspections at £145.31 = £4359

The method suggested by the sales manager results in a reported product cost that is lower than the short-term incremental costs of the order. This suggests that the proposed costing system does not accurately assign costs to cost objects or that the variable cost analysis implied in the question is incorrect. The discrepancy between the above reported costs should be investigated and the design of the costing system reviewed.

(Part two)

Question 10.6

(a) For the ideas concerning cost behaviour that underpin ABC see 'A comparison of traditional and ABC systems' and activity hierarchies in Chapter 10. You should refer to 'The emergence of ABC systems' in Chapter 10 for an explanation of why ABC may be better attuned to the modern manufacturing environment. For an explanation of why the company might not obtain a more meaningful impression of product costs through the use of ABC see 'Cost versus benefits considerations' and 'Pitfalls in using ABC information' in Chapter 10 and Learning Note 10.2 on the open access website.

(b) The answer should point out that the current system uses a blanket overhead rate and can be improved by retaining the traditional system and establishing separate departmental or cost centre overhead rates. For a discussion of these issues you should refer to 'Cost-benefit issues and cost system design', 'Blanket overhead rates' in Chapter 3.

(c) See 'Pitfalls in using ABC information' in Learning Note 10.2 on the open access website for the answer to this question.

Question 10.6   *(Part three)*

(a) See 'Just-in-time systems', 'Cost of quality' and 'Cost management and the value chain' in Chapter 21 for the answer to this question.

(b) Manufacturing in large batches leads to a build up of WIP, increases inventory holding costs and consumes large amounts of space because large batch production normally requires a functional production layout. For a more detailed discussion of the costs associated with large batch sizes you should refer to 'Just-in-time systems' in Chapter 21. However, manufacturing in small batch sizes can also result in additional costs. Examples include the increase in set-up costs (arising from more set-ups associated with producing in small batches) and quality inspection costs where a sample from each batch must be inspected to ensure that the batch meets quality requirements. The statement in the question is referring to the costs associated with different batch sizes.

Traditional volume-based costing systems, such as the one operated by KL's, fail to distinguish between the different costs associated with producing products or components in different batch sizes. To capture the costs associated with producing in different batch sizes requires that non-volume-based cost drivers are used. The use of non-volume-based cost drivers is a distinguishing feature of ABC systems. For a more detailed explanation of how traditional costing systems provide misleading cost information because of their failure to identify and assign batch-related costs you should refer to 'Volume based and non-volume based cost drivers' and 'Batch-level activities' in Chapter 10.

(c) This is a very open ended question and there is no specific answer. Academic research can be viewed as providing a constantly updated stock of concepts and techniques that are available to practitioners and that should be considered alongside existing techniques used in practice. In particular the choice of a particular technique should be based on cost–benefit criteria. If academic research is ignored, or misunderstood, accounting systems would be implemented without an awareness of alternative systems that are available. Consequently, there would be a tendency to perpetuate existing practices rather than selecting a preferable alternative. Also an understanding of research enables practitioners to be aware of the conceptual weaknesses of the techniques that are used in practice and thus seek to avoid the pitfalls when interpreting the information generated by these techniques. Academic research often represents a theoretical ideal and not necessarily a set of techniques that must be implemented. The cost versus benefits criteria must always be considered in determining the extent to which a cost system approximates the theoretical Ideal.

Pricing decisions and profitability analysis

Solutions to Chapter 11 questions

(a) *Computation of full costs and budgeted cost-plus selling price* **Question 11.1**

	EXE (£m)	WYE (£m)	Stores (£m)	Maintenance (£m)	Admin (£m)
Material	1.800	0.700	0.100		
Other variable	0.800	0.500	0.100	0.200	0.200
Gen factory	1.440	1.080	0.540	0.180	0.360
					0.560
Admin reallocation	0.224	0.168	0.112	0.056	(0.560)
				0.536	
Maintenance reallocation	0.268	0.134	0.134	(0.536)	
			0.986		
Stores	0.592	0.394	(0.986)		
	5.124	2.976			
Volume	150 000	70 000			
	(£)	(£)			
Full cost	34.16	42.51			
Mark up (25%)	8.54	10.63			
Price	42.70	53.14			

(b) (i) The incremental costs for the order consist of the variable costs. The calculation of the unit variable cost is as follows:

	EXE (£m)	WYE (£m)	Stores (£m)	Maintenance (£m)	Admin (£m)
Material	1.800	0.700	0.100	0.100	
Other variable	0.800	0.500	0.100	0.200	0.200
Admin	0.080	0.060	0.040	0.020	(0.200)
				0.320	
Maintenance	0.160	0.080	0.080	(0.320)	
			0.320		
Stores	0.192	0.128	(0.320)		
	3.032	1.468			
Volume	150 000	70 000			
	(£)	(£)			
Variable cost	20.21	20.97			

The proposed selling price exceeds the incremental cost and provides a contribution towards fixed costs and profits of £14.03 (£35 – £20.97) per unit thus giving a total contribution of £42 090. Given that the company has spare capacity no lost business will be involved and it appears that the order is a one-off short-term special order. Therefore the order is acceptable provided it does not have an impact on the selling price in the existing market or utilize capacity that has alternative uses. Given that the markets are segregated, the former would appear to be an unlikely event. However, if the order were to generate further regular business the longer-term cost considerations described in Chapter 11 should be taken into account in determining an acceptable long-run price.

(b) (ii) The proposed selling price is £46.76 (full cost of £42.51 plus 10%). This will generate a contribution of £25.79 (£46.76 – £20.97) per unit. Un-utilized capacity is 30 000 units but the order is for 50 000 units. Therefore the order can only be met by reducing existing business by 20 000 units. The financial evaluation is as follows:

Increase in contribution from existing business	
(50 000 units at a contribution of £25.79)	£1 289 500
Lost contribution from existing business	
(20 000 units at a contribution of (£53.14 – £20.97))	643 400
Net increase in contribution	646 100

Before accepting the order the longer term implications should be considered. The inability to meet the full demand from existing customers may result in a significant reduction in customer goodwill and the lost contribution from future sales to these customers may exceed the short-term gain of £646 100. Also the above analysis has not considered the alternative use of the un-utilized capacity of 30 000 units. If the cost savings from reducing the capacity exceed £646 100 for the period under consideration the order will not be worthwhile. The order will also result in the company operating at full capacity and it is possible that the cost structure may change if the company is operating outside its normal production range.

If the company does not rely on customer repeat orders and customer goodwill it is unlikely to be affected and the order would appear to be profitable. It is important, however, that long-term considerations are taken into account when evaluating the order. In particular, consideration should be given to the negotiation of a longer-term contract on both price and volume.

(c) See 'Alternative denominator level measures' in Chapter 7 and 'Selecting the cost driver denominator level' in Learning Note 10.1 on the open access website for the answer to this question.

Question 11.2

(a) For the answer to this question you should refer to Chapter 11. In particular the answer should discuss the role of cost information in the following situations:
1   a price setting firm facing short-run pricing decisions;
2   a price setting firm facing long-run decisions;
3   a price taker firm facing short-run product-mix decisions;
4   a price taker firm facing long-run decisions.

(b) *Calculation of variable overhead absorption rates*

	Moulding (£000)	Finishing (£000)	General Factory (£000)
Allocated overheads	1600	500	1050
Reallocation of General Factory			
based on machine hours	600	450	(1050)
	2200	950	
Machine hours	800	600	
Variable overhead rate per hour	£2.75	£1.583	

Calculation of fixed overhead absorption rates

	Moulding (£000)	Finishing (£000)	General Factory (£000)
Allocated overheads	2500	850	1750
Reallocation of General Factory based on machine hours	1050	700	(1750)
	3550	1550	
Machine hours	800	600	
Variable overhead rate per hour	£4.4375	£2.583	

Calculation of full manufacturing cost

		(£)
Direct material		9.00
Direct labour	10.00 (2 × £5)	
	16.50 (3 × £5.50)	26.50
Variable overheads	11.00 (4 × £2.75)	
	4.75 (3 × £1.583)	15.75
Variable manufacturing cost		51.25
Fixed overheads	17.75 (4 × £4.4375)	
	7.75 (3 × £2.583)	25.50
Full manufacturing cost		76.75

Prices based on full manufacturing cost
25% mark up = £95.94
30% mark up = £99.78
35% mark up = £103.61

Minimum prices based on short-term variable cost and incremental cost are as follows:

Variable cost = £51.25
Incremental cost = £59.60 (£51.25 plus specific fixed costs of £8.35)

The specific fixed cost per unit is calculated by dividing the fixed costs of £167 000 by the estimated sales volume (10% × 200 000).

(c) The cost information is more likely to provide a general guide to the pricing decision but the final pricing decision will be influenced by the prices of competitors' products (£90 – £100). The full cost prices indicate prices within a range of £96 – £104. The variable/incremental price indicates a minimum short-run price that may be appropriate if the company wishes to pursue a price skimming policy. Given that the product is an improvement on competitors, a price in the region of £100 would seem to be appropriate but the final decision should be based on marketing considerations drawing off the knowledge of the marketing staff. The role of the cost information has been to indicate that a price within this range should provide a reasonable margin and contribution to general fixed costs.

Question 11.3

(a) Presumably the question is intended to indicate that if competitors increase their prices by 6% and the company maintains its current price then this is equivalent to a price reduction by the company of 6%. An estimated price reduction of 6% and a price elasticity of demand of 1.5 would be expected to increase demand by 9%.

To predict costs for the next period it is necessary to analyse the costs into their fixed and variable elements. The high–low method can be used by comparing the changes in costs between the periods with the changes in activity. However, the current period costs must be deflated by the inflation factor so that they are expressed in the current prices for the previous period.

Current period's costs adjusted to previous period's prices = £1036 (£1077.4/1.04). Applying the high–low method:

	Units (000)	Costs (£000)
Current period	106	1036
Previous period	100	1000
	6	36

Variable cost per unit = Increase in costs (£36 000)/Increase in activity (6000 units)
= £6 per unit
Fixed costs   = £1 000 000 − (100 000 units × £6) = £400 000

Costs have increased by 4% from the previous to the current period and by a further 6% from the current to the next period:

Variable cost per unit next period = £6 (1.04) (1.06) = £6.6144
Fixed costs next period = £400 000 (1.04) (1.06)   = £440 960

Budgeted profit at a selling price of £13

	(£)
Sales (106 000 × 1.09[a] × £13)	1 502 020
Variable costs (106 000 × 1.09[a] × £6.6144)	764 228
Contribution	737 792
Less fixed costs	440 960
Profit	296 832

Note
[a]It is assumed that sales volume and production increase by 9% as a result of the price increase by competitors.

(b) *Budgeted profit assuming that the selling price is increased by 6%*

	(£)
Sales (106 000 × £13 (1.06))	1 460 680
Variable costs (106 000 × £6.6144)	(701 126)
Contribution	759 554
Fixed costs	440 960
	318 594

If the selling price is increased to match that of the competitors it is assumed that demand will remain unchanged.

(c) The report should indicate that on the basis of the information specified in parts (a) and (b) the price should be increased by 6%.

(d) It is assumed that:
  (i) Total market volume will remain unchanged and that the sales of the company will not decline as a result of both the firm and its competitors increasing prices by 6%;
  (ii) The estimate of the elasticity of demand is correct;
  (iii) All costs are affected by the same rate of inflation;
  (iv) All other factors remain constant so that sales will not be influenced by changes in advertising, customer preferences and general economic conditions.

(a) The following represents the quantity of sales that would be required to break even for a range of selling prices within each of the three selling price categories:

	Selling price (£)	Variable costs[a] (£)	Unit contribution (£)	Break-even point[b] (units)	Break-even % share of market
Category 1					
Low selling price	600	850	0	Not applicable	—
Medium selling price	825	917.50	0	Not applicable	—
High selling price	1050	985	65	8462	38
Category 2					
Low selling price	1450	1105	345	1594	27
Medium selling price	1675	1172.5	502.5	1095	18
High selling price	1900	1240	660	833	14
Category 3					
Low selling price	2500	1420	1080	509	68
Medium selling price	2750	1495	1255	438	58
High selling price	3000	1570	1430	385	51

Notes
[a] (30% × selling price) + £670 variable cost.
[b] (£550 000 fixed costs)/unit contribution.

The average market share per manufacturer in category 1 is 5500 units. AB Ltd would have to sell 8462 units (that is, capture a 38% share of the market) at the maximum price within the range in order to break even. It is likely that there will be a significant demand in the category 1 market for a lower-quality and lower-priced product. It may therefore be unwise to enter the category 1 market.

The average market share per manufacturer in the category 2 market is 1200 units. Given that AB will be able to enter the market with a product of advanced technology and distinctive design, it is likely that it will be able to sell the break-even sales volume of 1594 units (that is, obtain a market share of 27%) at the lowest selling price within the range. At the medium and high selling prices the break-even sales volume is below the average sales volume per manufacturer.

For the category 3 market the average market share per manufacturer is 375 units. This is in excess of the break-even point for the three prices considered in the above analysis. The company would also have to obtain a market share in excess of 50% in order to break even. The technology in this market is also advanced, and consequently competition will be more intensive.

It is therefore suggested that the company market the product within a selling price range of £1450–£1900.

(b) The question does not provide any details of demand information within each price range, and it is therefore questionable whether or not it is possible to recommend a price from the data given. AB's product incorporates some of the most advanced techniques available, together with a very distinctive design, and it is therefore likely that a large market share will be obtained at selling prices at the lower end of the price range. Assuming that a 50% market share could be obtained at a £1500 selling price, 40% at £1700, 30% at £1800 and 20% at £1900, the profits would be as follows:

Selling price	£1500	£1700	£1800	£1900
3000 units (50%)	£590 000			
2400 units (40%)		£698 000		
1800 units (30%)			£512 000	
1200 units (20%)				£242 000

Note that the above figures have been calculated as follows:

demand × (70% of selling price − £670 variable cost) − £550 000 fixed costs

Assuming that the above estimates of demand were correct, a selling price of £1700 would be recommended.

Question 11.5

(a) The answer should include a discussion of the following points:
- the benefits and limitations of cost-plus pricing;
- price skimming and price penetration policies;
- pricing based on demand estimates approximating economic theory.

A detailed description of each of the above approaches is provided in Chapter 11. You will find an explanation of the approach involving demand estimates in the sections relating to economic theory and pricing non-customized products in Chapter 11 and Learning Note 11.1 on the open access website.

(b) (i) To increase demand by one unit, price must be reduced by £0.01 (£10/1000) so that:

Selling price = £750 − £0.10x
Marginal revenue = £750 − £0.02x
Marginal cost = £320
At the optimum output level where MR = MC:
£320 = £750 − £0.02x
x = 21 500
Selling price = £750 − 21 500 (0.01) = £535
Therefore the maximum annual profit is:

Total contribution (21 500 × unit contribution (£535 − £320)	= £4 622 500
Less fixed costs (15 000 × £80)	= 1 200 000
	= 3 422 500

(b) (ii) Current contribution = £4 622 500

Contribution from exporting to L = [(930 × 0.60) − £300] × 25 000 = £6 450 000

Based on the above information R Ltd. should sell all of the output to L. However, if the exchange rate falls below €1 = £0.521 R Ltd. will be worse off. This rate is calculated as follows:

Required unit contribution = £4 622 500/25 000 = £184.90

Required selling price in UK currency = £484.90 (£300 variable cost + £184.90)

The exchange rate can fall to €1 = £0.521 (£484.90/[€]930) before R Ltd. will be worse off.

Also note that if the exchange rate falls to €1 = £0.25 the following negative contribution will be generated:

((€930 × 0.25) − £300) × 25 000 = − £1 687 500

The above items can now be plotted on the graph (see Figure 11.5).

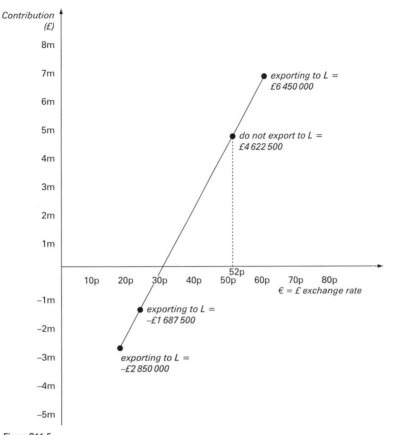

Figure Q11.5

(c)

Purchase Year	Outlay	Capital allowances	Tax savings on capital allowances[a]	Net cash flow	Discount factor	Present value
	(£)	(£)	(£)	(£)	(£)	(£)
0	(1 000 000)			(1 000 000)	1.000	(1 000 000)
1		(250 000)	37 500	37 500	0.893	33 488
2		(187 500)	65 625	65 625	0.893	52 303
3		(140 625)	49 219	49 219	0.712	35 044
4		(421 875)	84 375	84 375	0.636	53 663
5			63 281	63 281	0.567	35 880
		(1 000 000)				(789 622)

Lease Year	Payments	Tax cash flow	Net cash flow	Discount factor	Present value
	(£)	(£)	(£)	(£)	(£)
0	(300 000)	45 000	(255 000)	1.000	(255 000)
1	(300 000)	90 000	(210 000)	0.893	(187 530)
2	(300 000)	90 000	(210 000)	0.797	(167 370)
3	(300 000)	90 000	(210 000)	0.712	(149 520)
4		45 000	45 000	0.636	28 620
					(730 800)

therefore, leasing is the least cost option with savings of £58 822.

Question 11.6

(a) (i) If the selling price is £200, demand will be zero. To increase demand by one unit, selling price must be reduced by £1/1000 units or £0.001. Hence the maximum selling price attainable for an output of x units is:

$$P = £200 - 0.001x$$

At an output level of 100 000 units,

$$P = £200 - £0.001 \times 10\ 000$$
$$= £100 \text{ per unit}$$

Total contribution at an output level of 100 000 units

100 000 × (£100 − £50)	5 000 000
Less fixed costs (100 000 × £25)	2 500 000
Profit	2 500 000

(ii) Profit is maximized where MC = MR

MC = £50 per unit variable cost (given)

$$MR = \frac{dTR}{dx}$$

$$TR = x\ (200 - 0.001x)$$
$$= 200x - 0.001x^2$$

$$\frac{dTR}{dx} = 200 - 0.002x$$

Therefore optimum output is where $50 = 200 - 0.002x$ (i.e. where MC = MR). And so

$$150 = 0.002x$$

That is,

$$x = 75\ 000 \text{ units}$$

At an output level of 75 000 units, the selling price is £200 − (£0.001 × 75 000) = £125. Therefore profit at 75 000 units:

	(£)
Contribution (75 000 × £75)	5 625 000
Less fixed costs	2 500 000
	3 125 000

(b) (i) Revised fixed costs = £3 000 000.
The optimal output level will not be affected by a change in fixed costs. Therefore the selling price should not be changed. Profit will decline by £500 000.

(ii) Revised marginal cost = £60.
The new optimum is where $60 = 200 - 0.002x$
$$0.002x = 140$$
Therefore $x = 70\ 000$ units
At this output level, $P = £200 - £0.001 \times 70\ 000$
$$= £130$$

(c) Profit before advertising expenditure:

	(£)
Total contribution [70 000 × (£130 − £60)]	4 900 000
Less fixed costs	3 000 000
Profit	1 900 000

After the introduction of the advertising expenditure:

$$P = 210 - 0.001x$$
$$\text{TR} = x(210 - 0.001x)$$
$$= 210x - 0.001x^2$$

Therefore MR $= 210 - 0.002x$

The revised optimum output is where $60 = 210 - 0.002x$
$$0.002x = 150$$
$$x = 75\ 000$$

The optimum price at this output level is where $P = £210 - £0.001 \times 75\ 000$
$$= £135$$

	(£)
Total contribution [75 000 × (£135 − £60)]	5 625 000
Revised fixed costs	4 000 000
Profit	1 625 000

Therefore profits will decline by £275 000 if the advertising campaign is undertaken.

(d) The original budgeted output of 100 000 units was higher than the optimum output level. The solution to (a) (ii) indicates that the optimum output level is achieved by reducing production to 75 000 units and increasing the selling price to £125. Beyond an output level of 75 000 units, marginal cost per unit is in excess of marginal revenue. This is because selling price is reduced in order to expand output. Consequently, marginal revenue declines and is less than marginal cost. This means that profits decline when output is in excess of 75 000 units. This analysis is based on the following assumptions:
  (i) The demand schedule can be predicted accurately.
  (ii) Marginal cost per unit is constant at all output levels.
  (iii) Fixed costs are constant throughout the entire output range.
The analysis also showed that the change in fixed costs had no effect on the MR and MC function, so that the optimum output level and price did not change. When MC increases, the effect is to decrease output level and increase price.

   The effect of the advertising campaign is to shift the demand curve to the right, thus causing sales demand to be higher at each selling price or the selling price to be higher at each demand level. However, the increased advertising costs are in excess of the additional revenue, thus resulting in a reduction in profits.

Question 11.7

Several factors should be considered in the determination of pricing policy. The most important is price elasticity of demand, but if price is to be set in order to maximize profits then knowledge of cost structures and cost behaviour will also be of great importance. Knowledge of price–demand relationships and costs at different output levels is necessary to determine the optimum price. This is the price that results in marginal revenue being equal to marginal cost. The emphasis should be placed on providing information on the effect of changes in output on total cost rather than providing average unit cost information.

   When cost information is presented using absorption costing, the resulting selling price calculation will be a function of the overhead apportionments and recovery methods used and the assumed volume of production. At best, the calculated selling price will only be appropriate for one level of production, and a different selling price would be produced for different output levels. Single cost figures calculated using absorption costing also fail to supply information on the effect of changes in output on total cost. For other disadvantages that appear when absorption costing is used in the determination of pricing policy see 'Limitations of cost-plus pricing' in Chapter 11.

The advantage claimed from the use of absorption costing in price determination is that all manufacturing costs are included in the cost per unit calculation, so that no major manufacturing cost is overlooked. With variable costing, there is a danger that output will be priced to earn a low contribution that is insufficient to cover total fixed costs. Also, the use of production facilities entails an opportunity cost from the alternative use of capacity forgone. The fixed cost per unit of capacity used can be regarded as an attempt to approximate the opportunity cost from the use of productive capacity. In spite of these claimed advantages, the presentation of relevant costs for pricing decisions (see Chapter 11) is likely to be preferable to information based on absorption cost.

Question 11.8

(a) See Chapters 9–11 for the answer to this question. In particular, the answer should indicate:
  (i) Information presented to the product manager should be *future* costs, not past costs.
  (ii) *Incremental* cost and revenue information should be presented, and the excess of incremental revenues over incremental costs compared for different selling price and sales quantity levels. Costs that are common to all alternatives are not relevant for decision-making purposes.
  (iii) Decisions involve a choice between alternatives, and this implies that a choice leads to forgoing *opportunities*. Therefore relevant cost information for a pricing decision should include future cash costs and imputed (opportunity) cost.
  (iv) *Sunk costs* are past costs and not relevant to the pricing decision.
  (v) Pricing decisions should be based on estimates of demand schedules and a comparison of marginal revenues and costs.
(b) See 'Reasons for using cost-based pricing formulae' in Chapter 11 for the answer to this question. Note that overhead allocation is an attempt to provide an estimate of the long-run costs of producing a product.
(c) There is no specific answer to this question. The author's views on this question are expressed in Chapters 10 and 11.

Decision-making under conditions of risk and uncertainty

Solutions to Chapter 12 questions

The decision tree is shown in Figure 12.1. The company is faced with choosing between three alternatives at the decision point (represented by the box labelled 1 in the diagram). The circles represent the possible outcomes that can occur and the probabilities of these outcomes are shown on the lines emanating from the circles. Note that for the first alternative (undertaking the survey) the probabilities for the two branches in the top right hand corner of the diagram are derived from the joint probabilities of two events occurring (i.e. the multiplication of the probability of one event occurring by the probability of the other event occurring). Therefore the probabilities are 0.76 (0.95 × 0.8), 0.004 (0.8 × 0.05) and 0.2 (1 × 0.2).

The highest expected value is £840 000 for the third alternative (build the small premises without any survey) and, based on the expected value decision rule, this alternative should be chosen.

FIGURE 12.1 *Decision tree*

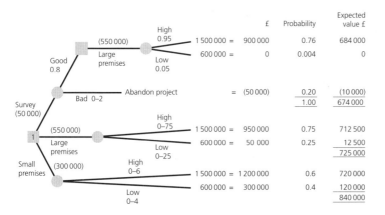

(a) *Profit and Loss Statement for Period Ending 31 May 2000*

	(£)
Revenue (14 400 000 journeys):	
0–3 miles (7 200 000 × £0.20)	1 440 000
4–5 miles (4 320 000 × £0.30)	1 296 000
Over 5 miles (2 880 000 × £0.50)	1 440 000
Juvenile fares (4 800 000 × £0.15)	720 000
Senior citizen fares (4 800 000 × £0.10)	480 000
	5 376 000
Advertising revenue	250 000
	5 626 000

Less: Variable costs (20 routes × 4 buses × 150 miles ×

                330 days × £0.75)   (2 970 000)

        Fixed costs   (1 750 000)

Net profit   906 000

(b) Assuming the same passenger mix as 2000 the weighted average fare per passenger for year ending 31 May 2001 is (£5 376 000 × 1.05)/24 000 000 = £0.2352.

The break-even point is where:

Total revenue from fares + Advertising revenue = Total cost

Let x = number of passenger journeys

Break-even point: $0.2352x + £250\ 000 = (2\ 970\ 000 + £1\ 750\ 000)\ 1.1$

$$0.2352x = £4\ 942\ 000$$
$$x = 21\ 011\ 905$$

Maximum capacity utilization   = 40 000 000 passenger journeys (24 000 000/0.6)

Break-even capacity utilization = 21 011 905/40 000 000 = 52.5%

(c) (i)

Expected value and probability estimates for 2001

Capacity Utilization		Revenue		Inflation		Costs	Combined	Net profit	Expected value
		Fares	Adverts				probability		
%	(Probability)	(£000)	(£000)	(%)	(Probability)	(£000)		(£000)	(£000)
70	0.1	6585.6[a]	250	8	0.3	5097.6[b]	0.03	1738.0	52.14
		6585.6	250	10	0.6	5192.0[b]	0.06	1643.6	98.62
		6585.6	250	12	0.1	5286.4[b]	0.01	1549.2	15.49
60	0.5	5644.8[a]	250	8	0.3	5097.6	0.15	797.2	119.58
		5644.8	250	10	0.6	5192.0	0.30	702.8	210.84
		5644.8	250	12	0.1	5286.4	0.05	608.4	30.42
50	0.4	4704.0[a]	250	8	0.3	5097.6	0.12	−143.6	−17.23
		4704.0	250	10	0.6	5192.0	0.24	−238.0	−57.12
		4704.0	250	12	0.1	5286.4	0.04	−332.4	−13.30
							1.00		439.44

Notes

[a]Fare revenues at 60% capacity for 2000 were £5 376 000. Assuming 5% inflation fare revenues for 2001 at 60% capacity will be £5 644 800 (£5 376 000 × 1.05). At 70% and 50% capacity utilization fare revenues will be as follows:

$$70\% = 70/60 × £5\ 644\ 800 = £6\ 585\ 600$$
$$50\% = 50/60 × £5\ 644\ 800 = £4\ 704\ 000$$

[b]Variable costs vary with bus miles which are assumed to remain unchanged. Predicted costs at the different inflation levels are as follows:

$$8\% = (£2\ 970\ 000 + £1\ 750\ 000)1.08 = £5\ 097\ 600$$
$$10\% = (£2\ 970\ 000 + £1\ 750\ 000)1.10 = £5\ 192\ 000$$
$$12\% = (£2\ 970\ 000 + £1\ 750\ 000)1.12 = £5\ 286\ 400$$

(c) (ii) The answer to this question requires the preparation of a cumulative probability distribution that measures the cumulative probability of profits/ (losses) being greater than specified levels.

Cumulative probability distribution

Losses greater than £300 000   = 0.04 probability
Probability of a loss occurring   = 0.40
Profits greater than £600 000   = 0.60
Profits greater than £700 000   = 0.55
Profits greater than £800 000   = 0.10
Profits greater than £1 500 000 = 0.10

(d) The following factors have not been incorporated into the analysis:
   (i) Change in the passenger mix.
   (ii) Changes in the number of routes and the number of days operation per year.
   (iii) Changes in fare structure such as off-peak travel or further concessions for juveniles and senior citizens.
   (iv) Changes in cost levels due to factors other than inflation (e.g. more efficient operating methods).

Question 12.3

(a) For each selling price there are three possible outcomes for sales demand, unit variable cost and fixed costs. Consequently, there are 27 possible outcomes. In order to present probability distributions for the two possible selling prices, it would be necessary to compute profits for 54 outcomes. Clearly, there would be insufficient time to perform these calculations within the examination time that can be allocated to this question. It is therefore assumed that the examiner requires the calculations to be based on an expected value approach.
The expected value calculations are as follows:

(i) *Variable cost*	(£)	(ii) *Fixed costs*	(£)
(£10 + 10%) × 10/20 =	5.50	£82 000 × 0.3 =	24 600
£10 × 6/20 =	3.00	£85 000 × 0.5 =	42 500
(£10 − 5%) × 4/20 =	1.90	£90 000 × 0.2 =	18 000
	10.40		85 100

(iii) *£17 selling price*	(units)	(iv) *£18 selling price*	(units)
21 000 units × 0.2 =	4 200	19 000 units × 0.2 =	3 800
19 000 units × 0.5 =	9 500	17 500 units × 0.5 =	8 750
16 500 units × 0.3 =	4 950	15 500 units × 0.3 =	4 650
	18 650		17 200

Expected contribution

£17 selling price = (£17 − £10.40) × 18 650 = £123 090
£18 selling price = (£18 − £10.40) × 17 200 = £130 720

The existing selling price is £16, and if demand continues at 20 000 units per annum then the total contribution will be £112 000 [(£16 − £10.40) × 20 000 units].
Using the expected value approach, a selling price of £18 is recommended.
(b) Expected profit = £130 720 − £85 100 fixed costs = £45 620
Break-even point = fixed costs (£85 100)/contribution per unit (£7.60)
          = 11 197 units
Margin of safety = expected demand (17 200 units) − 11 197 units = 6003 units
% margin of safety = 6003/17 200 = 34.9% of sales
Note that the most pessimistic estimate is above the break-even point.
(c) An expected value approach has been used. The answer should draw attention to the limitations of basing the decision solely on expected values. In particular,

it should be stressed that risk is ignored and the range of possible outcomes is not considered. The decision ought to be based on a comparison of the probability distributions for the proposed selling prices. For a more detailed answer see 'Probability distributions and expected value' and 'Measuring the amount of uncertainty' in Chapter 12.

(d) Computer assistance would enable a more complex analysis to be undertaken. In particular, different scenarios could be considered, based on different combinations of assumptions regarding variable cost, fixed cost, selling prices and demand.

Question 12.4

(a)

Alternative types of machine hire	Possible outcomes (level of orders)	Probability of outcomes	Payoff (£000)
High	High	0.25	2200 [(0.3 × £15 000) − £2300]
	Medium	0.45	250 [(0.3 × £8500) − £2300]
	Low	0.30	−1100 [(0.3 × £4000) − £2300]
Medium	High	0.25	1700 (0.3 × £15 000) − £1500 − £1300
	Medium	0.45	1050 [(0.3 × £8500) − £1500]
	Low	0.30	−300 [(0.3 × £4000) − £1500]
Low	High	0.25	1350 (0.3 × £15 000) − £1000 − £2150
	Medium	0.45	700 (0.3 × £8500) − £1000 − £850
	Low	0.30	200 [(0.3 × £4000) − £1000]

(b) Expected values:

$$\text{High hire level} = (0.25 \times £2200) + (0.45 \times £250) - (0.3 \times £1100)$$
$$= £332\ 500$$
$$\text{Medium hire level} = (0.25 \times £1700) + (0.45 \times £1050) - (0.3 \times £300)$$
$$= £807\ 500$$
$$\text{Low hire level} = (0.25 \times £1350) + (0.45 \times £700) + (0.3 \times £200)$$
$$= £712\ 500$$

Using the expected value decision rule, the medium hire contract should be entered into.

(c) Managers may be risk-averse, risk-neutral or risk-seeking. A risk-averse manager might adopt a maximin approach and focus on the worst possible outcome for each alternative and then select the alternative with the largest payoff. This approach would lead to the selection of the low initial hire level. A risk-seeking manager might adopt a maximax approach and focus on the best possible outcomes. This approach would lead to choosing the high initial hire contract, since this has the largest payoff when only the most optimistic outcomes are considered.

(d) With perfect information, the company would select the advance plant and machinery hire alternative that would maximize the payoff. The probabilities of the consultants predicting high, medium and low demand are respectively 0.25, 0.45 and 0.30. The expected value calculation with the consultant's information would be:

DECISION-MAKING UNDER CONDITIONS OF RISK AND UNCERTAINTY

	Advance hire level	Payoff (£000)	Probability	Expected value (£000)
High market	high	2200	0.25	550
Medium market	medium	1050	0.45	472.5
Low market	low	200	0.30	60
				1082.5

	(£)
Expected value with consultant's information	1 082 500
Expected value without consultant's information	807 500
Maximum amount payable to consultant	275 000

(a)

Selling price (£)	70	80	90
Maximum demand (£)	75 000	60 000	40 000
Maximum revenue (£)	5 250 000	4 800 000	3 600 000
Total variable cost (£)	3 750 000	3 000 000	2 000 000
Fixed costs (£)	800 000	800 000	800 000
R & D cost (£)	250 000	250 000	250 000
	4 800 000	4 050 000	3 050 000
Estimated profit (£)	450 000	750 000	550 000

Question 12.5

The above analysis is based on the maximum sales demand. On this basis, the analysis indicates that profits are maximized at an output level of 60 000 units when the selling price is £80. It is preferable to use the 'most likely' demand level and to incorporate uncertainty around the 'most likely' demand into the analysis.

(b) For a selling price of £90 there are three different demand levels, and for each demand level there are three different outcomes for actual unit variable cost. Therefore there are nine possible outcomes. The contribution and probability of each outcome is presented in the following schedule:

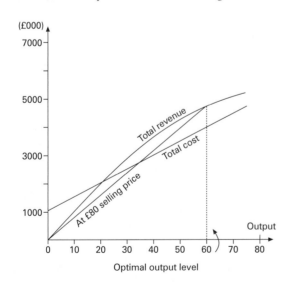

Figure Q12.5

(1)	(2)	(3)	(4)	(5)	(6)	(7)	(8)
Demand (000)	Probability	Unit variable cost (£)	Probability	Unit contribution (£)	Total contribution (£000)	Joint probability (2 × 4)	Weighted outcome (6 × 7) (£000)
20	0.2	60	0.2	30	600	0.04	24.00
20	0.2	55	0.7	35	700	0.14	98.00
20	0.2	50	0.1	40	800	0.02	16.00
35	0.7	60	0.2	30	1050	0.14	147.00
35	0.7	55	0.7	35	1225	0.49	600.25
35	0.7	50	0.1	40	1400	0.07	98.00
40	0.1	60	0.2	30	1200	0.02	24.00
40	0.1	55	0.7	35	1400	0.07	98.00
40	0.1	50	0.1	40	1600	0.01	16.00
						1.00	1121.25

	(£)
Expected total contribution	1 121 250
Fixed costs	1 050 000
Expected profit	71 250

(c) To compare the three selling prices, it is necessary to summarize the information in part (b) for a £90 selling price in the same way as part (c) of the question. Note that fixed costs are deducted from the total contribution column in the schedule presented in (b) to produce the following statement:

		Prices under review	
	£70	£80	£90
Probability of a loss			
Greater than or equal to £500 000	0.02	0	0
£300 000	0.07	0.05	0.18
£100 000	0.61	0.08	0.20
0	0.61	0.10	0.34
Probability of a profit			
Greater than or equal to 0	0.39	0.91	0.80
£100 000	0.33	0.52	0.66
£300 000	0.03	0.04	0.15
£500 000	0	0.01	0.01
Expected profit	Loss (£55 750)	£68 500	£71 250

The following items should be included in the memorandum:
  (i) The £90 selling price has the largest expected profit, but there is also a 0.34 probability of not making a profit.
 (ii) Selling price of £80 may be preferable, because there is only a 0.10 probability of not making a profit. A selling price of £80 is least risky, and the expected value is only slightly lower than the £90 selling price.
(iii) Subjective probability distributions provide details of the uncertainty surrounding the estimates and enable the decision-maker to select the course of action that is related to his personal risk/profit trade-off (see Chapter 12 for an explanation of this).
(iv) Subjective probabilities are subject to all the disadvantages of any subjective estimate (e.g. bias).
 (v) Calculations are based on discrete probabilities. For example, this implies that there is a 0.7 probability that demand will be exactly 35 000. A more realistic interpretation is that 35 000 represents the mid-point of demand

falling within a certain range.

(d) If the increase in fixed costs represents an additional cost resulting from an increase in volume then this incremental cost is relevant to the pricing decision. If the fixed costs represent an apportionment then it is not relevant. Nevertheless, we noted in Chapter 11 that selling prices should be sufficient to cover the common and unavoidable long-run fixed costs.

The research and development expenditure is a sunk cost, and is not a relevant cost as far as the pricing decision is concerned. However, the pricing policy of the company may be to recover the research and development expenditure in the selling price. The amount recovered per unit sold should be a policy decision. Note that the decision to write off research and development in one year instead of three will affect the reported profits.

(a) The calculations of the product variable costs per unit are:

Question 12.6

	Newone (£)	Newtwo (£)
Labour and materials	82	44
Variable overheads	6 (6 hrs × £1)	2 (2 hrs × £1)
Unit variable cost	88	46

Low-price alternative: The contributions per unit are £32 for Newone (£120 − £88) and £14 (£60 − £46) for Newtwo. The probability distributions are as follows:

	Newone			Newtwo	
Demand	Probability	Contribution (£)	Demand	Probability	Contribution (£)
1000	0.2	32 000	3000	0.2	42 000
2000	0.5	32 000[a]	3000	0.5	42 000
3000	0.3	32 000[a]	3000	0.3	42 000

Note

[a]Machine capacity restricts outputs to 1000 units of Newone and 3000 units of Newtwo.

Note that estimates indicate with 100% certainty that Newone will yield a contribution of £32 000 and Newtwo will yield a contribution of £42 000.

Higher price alternative: The contributions per unit are £42 for Newone (£130 − £88) and £24 (£70 − £46) for Newtwo. The probability distributions are as follows:

	Newone			Newtwo	
Demand	Probability	Contribution (£)	Demand	Probability	Contribution (£)
500	0.2	21 000	1500	0.2	36 000
1000	0.5	42 000	2500	0.5	60 000
1500	0.3	42 000[a]	3500	0.3	72 000[a]
	Expected value	37 800		Expected value	58 800

Note

[a]Output is restricted to 1000 units of Newone and 3000 units of Newtwo.

Recommendations

The above probability distributions indicate that Newtwo is preferable to Newone, irrespective of which price is set. At the higher selling price Newtwo yields a higher expected value. There is only a 0.2 probability that a lower contribution will be earned if the higher price is selected in preference to the lower price. The advantage of the lower price is that the outcome is certain, but, given the high probability (0.8) of earning higher profits with the higher-price alternative, a selling price of £70 is recommended. With the higher-price alternative, there is a 0.70 probability that machine hours will not be utilized. Any unused capacity should be used to sell Newone at £130 selling price.

(b) Decision problems require estimates of changes in costs and revenues for choosing alternative courses of action. It is therefore necessary to distinguish between fixed and variable costs. Regression analysis can be used to estimate a cost equation, and tests of reliability can be applied to ascertain how reliable the cost equation is in predicting costs. For a description of regression analysis and tests of reliability you should refer to Chapter 23. A common test of reliability is the coefficient of determination, which can be calculated by squaring the correlation coefficient. The coefficient of determination for the cost equation used in the question is 0.64 (0.8^2). Consequently, 36% of the variation in cost is not explained by the cost equation used in the question. It is possible that activity bases other than machine hours might provide a better explanation of the relationship between costs and activities. Alternatively, changes in costs might be a function of more than one variable. In such circumstances, cost equations based on multiple regression techniques should provide more reliable cost estimates.

Question 12.7

The following is a decision tree relating to the question:

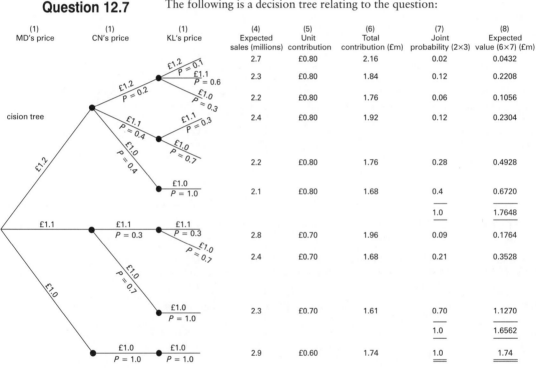

Figure Q12.7

The variable cost per litre is as follows:

	(£)
Direct materials	0.12
Direct wages	0.24
Indirect wages etc. ($16\frac{2}{3}\% \times £0.24$)	0.04
	0.40

and the range of contributions are:

> £0.80 for a selling price of £1.20
> £0.70 for a selling price of £1.10
> £0.60 for a selling price of £1.00

The decision tree indicating the possible outcomes presented in Figure Q12.7 shows that the expected value of the contribution is maximized at a selling price of £1.20. Fixed costs are common and unavoidable to all alternatives, and are therefore not included in the analysis. However, management might prefer the certain contribution of £1.74 million at a selling price of £1.00. From columns 6 and 7 of the decision tree it can be seen that there is a 0.60 probability that contribution will be in excess of £1.74 million when a selling price of £1.20 is implemented. The final decision depends on management's attitude towards risk.

Question 12.8

(a) Budgeted net Profit/Loss outcomes for year ending 30 June

Client Days	Fee per Client day (£)	Variable cost per client day (£)	Contribution per client day (£)	Total contrib. per year (£)
15 750	180	95	85	1 338 750
15 750	180	85	95	1 496 250
15 750	180	70	110	1 732 500
13 125	200	95	105	1 378 125
13 125	200	85	115	1 509 375
13 125	200	70	130	1 706 250
10 500	220	95	125	1 312 500
10 500	220	85	135	1 417 500
10 500	220	70	150	1 575 000

(b) The *maximax* rule looks for the largest contribution from all outcomes. In this case the decision maker will choose a client fee of £180 per day where there is a possibility of a contribution of £1 732 500.

The *maximin* rule looks for the strategy which will maximize the minimum possible contribution. In this case the decision maker will choose client fee of £200 per day where the lowest contribution is £1 378 125. This is better than the worst possible outcome from client fees per day of £180 or £220 which will provide contribution of £1 338 750 and £1 312 500 respectively.

The *minimax regret* rule requires the choice of the strategy which will minimize the maximum regret from making the wrong decision. Regret represents the opportunity lost from making the wrong decision.

The calculations in part (a) are used to list the opportunity losses in the following regret matrix:

State of nature

	Low variable cost of £70	Most likely variable cost of £85	High variable cost of £95
Choose a fee of £180	0	£13 125	£39 375
Choose a fee of £200	£26 250	0	0
Choose a fee of £220	£157 500	£91 875	£65 625

At a variable cost of £70 the maximum contribution is £1 732 500 derived from a fee of £180. Therefore there will be no opportunity loss. At a fee of £200 the opportunity loss is £26 250 (£1 732 500 − £1 706 250) and at the £220 fee the opportunity loss is £157 500 (£1 732 500 − £1 575 000). The same approach is used to calculate the opportunity losses at variable costs of £85 and £95.

The maximum regrets for each fee are as follows:

	(£)
£180	39 375
£200	26 250
£220	157 500

The minimum regret is £26 250 and adopting a minimum regret strategy will result in choosing the £200 fee per day alternative.

(c) The expected value of variable cost

$$= £95 \times 0.1 + £85 \times 0.6 + £70 \times 0.3 = £81.50$$

For each client fee strategy the expected value of budget contribution for the year is calculated as follows:

* fee of £180 : 15 750 (180 – 81.50) = £1 551 375
* fee of £200 : 13 125 (200 – 81.50) = £1 555 312.50
* fee of £220 : 10 500 (220 – 81.50) = £1 454 250

A client fee of £200 per day is required to give the maximum expected value contribution of £1 555 312.50. Note that there is virtually no difference between this and the contribution where a fee of £180 per day is used.

(d) Profit can be increased by making cost savings provided that such actions do not result in a fall in demand and a reduction in revenues. Alternatively, investments may be made that will increase the level of service and thus demand. Profits will increase if the extra revenues exceed the increase in costs. The balanced scorecard approach to performance measurement and the determinants of performance measurement relating to service organizations described in Learning Note 22.1 on the open access website can be used to identify appropriate performance areas for the health centre. The performance areas identified in Exhibit LN 22.1 in Learning note 22.1 include quality of service, flexibility, resource utilization and innovation. Each of these areas is discussed below.

(i) Quality of service may be improved by upgrading facilities such as a cafeteria, free daily newspapers and better waiting room facilities. This may increase demand and generate additional revenues which exceed the cost increases.

(ii) Flexibility of service may be improved by providing additional sports/exercise facilities that are not currently available. In addition, additional exercise and dietary consultants who can provide services that are not currently available.

(iii) Resource utilization may be improved by better scheduling relating to the use of the exercise equipment and staff time and extending the opening hours. The aim should be to provide at least the same level of service with fewer resources.

(iv) Innovation may take the form of *new* services such as an extension of the range of health advice that can be provided and introducing on-line booking systems which can be directly accessed by the clients.

Capital investment decisions: appraisal methods

Solutions to Chapter 13 questions

(a) The IRR is where:

annual cash inflows × discount factor = investment cost
i.e.   £4000 × discount factor = £14 000
Therefore   discount factor = $\frac{£14\ 000}{£4\ 000}$

= 3.5

We now work along the five-row table of the cumulative discount tables to find the discount rate with a discount factor closed to 3.5. This is 13%. Therefore the IRR is 13%.

(b) The annual saving necessary to achieve a 12% internal rate of return is where:

annual savings × 12% discount factor = investment cost
i.e. annual savings × 3.605   = £14 000
Therefore annual savings   = $\frac{£14\ 000}{3.605}$

= £3 883

(c) NPV is calculated as follows:

£4000 received annually from years 1–5: (£)
£4000 × 3.791 discount factor   15 164
  Less investment cost   14 000
NPV   1 164

(i) Net present values:

Year	0% NPV (£)	10% Discount Factor	10% NPV (£)	20% Discount Factor	20% NPV (£)
0	(142 700)	1 000	(142 700)	1.000	(142 700)
1	51 000	0.909	46 359	0.833	42 483
2	62 000	0.826	51 212	0.694	43 028
3	73 000	0.751	54 823	0.579	42 267
NPV	43 300		9 694		(14 922)

(ii) **Project NPV Profile**

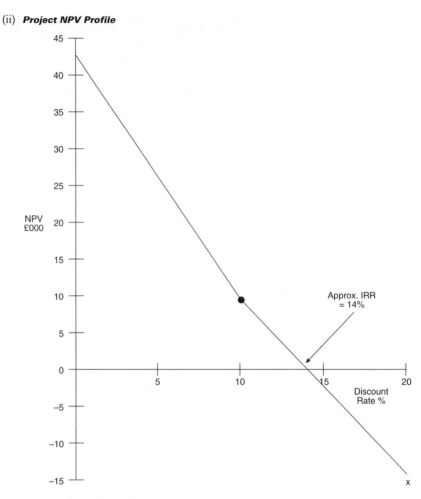

Figure Q13.2

Question 13.3

(a) The answer should include the following points:

1 Computations of the payback period and accounting rate of return (see below for the calculations), a description of the methods and their benefits and limitations (see text for a discussion of the payback and accounting rate of return methods).

2 A computation of the net present value (see below) and an explanation as to why this method is preferred to the other methods (see text for an explanation).

3 A recommendation that since the project has a positive net present value it should be accepted.

4 A discussion of the difficulties associated with NPV. These include the greater potential for a lack of understanding by non-accountants, difficulties in estimating cash flows over the whole life of the asset and the difficulty in deriving the discount rate.

Computation of the payback period

The cumulative cash flows for years 4 and 5 are £1 700 000 and £2 200 000. Therefore, the payback period occurs between years 4 and 5. Assuming that cash flows accrue evenly throughout the year, a cash flow of £300 000 is required in year 5 to reach the payback period. This represents 7 months (£300 000/£500

000 × 12 months). Therefore, the payback period is 4 years and 7 months. This is above the target payback period of 4 years, so the project would be rejected using this method.

Computation of accounting rate of return

Total cash flows = (£400 × 3) + (£500 × 2) + (£450 × 3) + (£400 × 2)	= £4 350 000
Less depreciation/initial outlay	= £2 000 000
Total profits over the period	= £2 350 000
Average annual profit	= £235 000
Average investment (Initial cost/2)	= £1 000 000
Accounting rate of return	= 23.5%

This is below the target return so the project would be rejected.

Computation of NPV

Year	Cash flows (£000's)	Discount factor (15%)[a]	Present value (£000's)
1 – 3	400	2.283	913.20
4 – 5	500	1.069	534.50
6 – 8	450	1.135	510.75
9 – 10	400	0.531	212.40
			2170.85
Less initial outlay			2000.00
NPV			170.85

Note
[a] The discount factors are derived by summing the factors for years 1–3, 4–5, 6–8 and 9–10 in the discount tables.

The project has a positive NPV and should be accepted.

(b) 1 For the answer to this question see 'Controlling the capital expenditure during the installation stage' and 'Post-completion audits' in Chapter 14.

(a)

Estimated incremental net cash flows and NPV from project VZ

Question 13.4

Inflows:	20X1 (£000)	20X2 (£000)	20X3 (£000)	20X4 (£000)	20X5 (£000)
Sales[a]	916	1269	1475	1780	160
Savings in salaries of employees made redundant[b]		42	44.1	46.3	
Residual value of new machine					242
Material XNT, savings on cost of disposal	2				
	918	1311	1519.1	1826.3	402

Outflows:					
Purchases[c]	320	480	570	610	120
Loss of sale proceeds from old machine		12			
Employee promoted[d]	10	10.5	11.03	11.58	
Redundancy pay		62			
Material XPZ, lost residual value	3				

Sub-contractors	60	90	80	80
Lost contribution from existing product	30	40	40	36
Overheads and advertising^e	130	100	90	100
Taxation		96	142	174	275
	553	890.5	933.03	1011.58	395

Total

Incremental net cash flow	365	420.5	586.01	814.72	7	
Discount factors at 10%	0.9091	0.8264	0.7513	0.683	0.6209	
Present value (£000)	331.8	347.5	440.3	556.4	4.3	1680.3
Less net investment outlay (1640–16)						1624.0
NPV (£000s)						56.3

Notes
^{a}The cash inflows from sales are calculated as follows:

	20X1 (£000)	20X2 (£000)	20X3 (£000)	20X4 (£000)	20X5 (£000)
Opening debtors	—	84	115	140	160
Add sales	1000	1300	1500	1800	—
	1000	1384	1615	1940	160
Less closing debtors	84	115	140	160	—
Cash from sales	916	1269	1475	1780	160

^{b}Four employees at £10 000 per year inflated at 5% per annum
^{c}The cash outflows for purchases is calculated as follows:

Opening creditors	—	80	100	110	120
Add purchases	400	500	580	620	—
	400	580	680	730	120
Less closing creditors	80	100	110	120	—
Cash paid for purchases	320	480	570	610	120

^{d}£10 000 incremental costs inflated at 5% per annum
^{e}Difference in costs between new and old product line
(b) (i) The report should explain that the figures incorporate only the incremental cash flows arising from undertaking the project. In addition the following information should be included in the report:
  (i) The feasibility study is a sunk cost.
  (ii) Depreciation is a non-cash item and the net investment cost is incorporated as a deduction from the total present value of the net cash flows. Including depreciation will result in double counting.
  (iii) The £12 000 paid to the three employees is not a relevant cash flow because it will be paid whether or not the project goes ahead.
  (iv) The original purchase price for both types of materials is a sunk cost and is not relevant to the decision.
  (v) The relevant figures for a NPV calculations are cash flows and therefore no adjustment is required for prepayments.
(b) (ii) The report should indicate that on the basis of the financial appraisal the project should be undertaken because it has a positive NPV. However, it should

be pointed out that the cash flows have been discounted at the company's average cost of capital of 10%. If the risk of the project is higher than the average for the firm as a whole then a higher cost of capital should be used. Other factors that should be incorporated in the report include the effect on staff morale of the redundancies, the reliability of the estimates, the likely response from the competitors and the alternative use of the capacity.

(a) *Alternative 1*
NPV:

Year	Cash flow (£000)	Discount factor	PV (£000)
0	−100	1.00	−100
1	+255	0.83	+211.65
2	−157.5	0.69	−108.675
		NPV =	2.975

IRR: The cash flow sign changes after year 1, which implies that the project will have two IRRs. Using the interpolation method, the NPV will be zero at a cost of capital of 5% and 50%. Therefore the IRRs are 5% and 50%.

Alternative 2
NPV:

Year	Cash flow (£000)	Discount factor	PV (£000)
0	−50	1.00	−50
1	0	0.83	0
2	+42	0.69	+28.98
3	+42	0.58	+24.36
		NPV =	+3.34

IRR: At a 25% discount rate the project has an NPV of −1.616. Using the interpolation formula:

$$\text{IRR} = 20 + \frac{3340}{3340 - (-1616)} \times (25 - 20)$$

$$= 23.4\%$$

Summary

	NPV	IRR
Alternative 1	£2975	5% or 50%
Alternative 2	£3340	23.4%

(b) The projects are mutually exclusive and capital rationing does not apply. In these circumstances the NPV decision rule should be applied and alternative 2 should be selected. Because of the reasons described in Chapter 13, the IRR method should not be used for evaluating mutually exclusive projects. Also, note that alternative 1 has two IRRs. Therefore, the IRR method cannot be used to rank the alternatives.

Before a final decision is made, the risk attached to each alternative should be examined. For example, novelty products are generally high-risk investments with short lives. Therefore alternative 1 with a shorter life might be less risky. Other considerations include the possibility of whether the promotion of this novelty product will adversely affect the sales of the other products sold by the company. Also, will the large expenditure on advertising for alternative 1 have a beneficial effect on the sales of the company's other products?

(c) The answer should include a discussion of the payback method, particularly the limitations discussed in Chapter 13. It should be stressed that payback can be a useful method of investment appraisal when liquidity is a problem and the speed of a project's return is particularly important. It is also claimed that payback allows for uncertainty in that it leads to the acceptance of projects with fast paybacks. This approach can be appropriate for companies whose products are subject to uncertain short lives. Therefore there might be an argument for using payback in Khan Ltd.

The second comment by Mr Court concerns the relationship between reported profits and the NPV calculations. Projects ranked by the NPV method can give different rankings to projects that are ranked by their impact on the reported profits of the company. The NPV method results in the maximization of the present value of future cash flows and is the correct decision rule. If investors give priority to reported profits in valuing shares (even if reported profits do not give an indication of the true economic performance of the company) then Mr Court's comments on the importance of a project's impact on reported profits might lead to the acceptance of alternative 1. However, if investors are aware of the deficiencies of published reported profits and are aware of the company's future plans and cash flows then share values will be based on PV of future cash flows. This is consistent with the NPV rule.

Question 13.6

(a) *Attending 6 training courses per year*

Year	Travel and accommodation etc. (£000's)[a]	Course costs (£000's)[a]	Total cash flows (£000's)	Discount factor	Present value (£000's)
1	522.00	70.50	592.50	0.877	519.62
2	548.10	72.26	620.36	0.769	477.06
3	575.51	74.07	649.58	0.675	438.47
4	604.29	75.92	680.21	0.592	402.68
5	634.50	77.82	712.32	0.519	369.69
					2207.52

Note:
[a] Travel etc. = £870 × 100 delegates × 6 courses = £522 000
Courses = £11 750 × 6 courses = £70 500
Travel etc. Year 2 = £522 (1.05), Year 3 = £522 $(1.05)^2$ and so on.
Course costs Year 2 = £70.5 (1.025), Year 3 = £70.5 $(1.025)^2$ and so on.

Proposed e-learning solution

Year	0 (£000's)	1 (£000's)	2 (£000's)	3 (£000's)	4 (£000's)	5 (£000's)
Hardware[a]	1500					(50)
Software	35	35	35	35	35	
Technical manager and trainers (30 + 12)[b]		42	44.52	47.19	50.02	53.02
Camera and sound		24	24	25.44	26.97	28.59
Broadband connection		30	28.50	27.08	25.73	24.44
		131	132.02	134.71	137.72	56.05
Discount factor	1.000	0.877	0.769	0.675	0.592	0.519
Present value	1 535	114.89	101.52	90.93	81.53	29.09

Total present value = £1 953 257
The e-learning solution should be recommended since this has the lowest present value.

Notes:
[a] Depreciation is not a relevant cost and should not be included in the analysis.
[b] The technical manager will have to be replaced resulting in an incremental cash flow of £20 000 per annum.

(b) (i) Note that equivalent annual costs/cash flows are explained in Chapter 14. To answer this question it is necessary to separate those costs that are variable with the number of delegates and those that are fixed and thus do not change with the number of candidates. It is assumed that 6 courses will be provided per year. For the course attendance alternative, the course costs are fixed and travel, etc. is variable with the number of delegates. Separate present values must be calculated for course costs and travel, etc. If you discount the second and third columns for the course attendance alternative you will find that the present values are £1 954 800 (variable cost) and £252 720 (fixed cost). Dividing both of these items by an annuity factor for 5 years at 14% (3.433) gives annual equivalent costs of £569 415 (variable costs) and £73 615 (fixed cost).

For the e-learning costs alternative, the broadband connection is variable with the number of delegates and the remaining costs are fixed. The respective present values are £94 421 (variable) and £1 858 836 (fixed) giving equivalent annual costs of £27 504 (variable) and £541 461 (fixed). Therefore, the additional annual equivalent fixed costs for the e-learning alternative are £467 846. The savings in annual equivalent variable costs from this alternative are £541 911 (£569 415 – £27 504) per 100 delegates or £5419 per delegate. Therefore the minimum number of delegates required to achieve the fixed cost savings is 86.33 (£467 846/£5419).

(b) (ii) The required number of delegates to break even is 87%. This is a very high required take-up rate and so the company must ensure that virtually all of the delegates will favour this method of delivery.

Question 13.7

(a) Three alternatives can be identified from the question:
  1 Produce product A and replace it with AA at the UK factory.
  2 Produce product A, then sell the UK factory in year 2 and make AA in Eastern Europe for 8 years.
  3 Produce product A for a limited period, replace with product X and sell the UK factory in year 4 and make Product AA in Eastern Europe for 8 years.

Alternative 1

Years		Cash flows (£m)	Discount factor	NPV (£m)
1	Normal sales of product A	3.0	0.952	2.856
2	Normal sales of product A	2.3	0.907	2.086
2	Equipment and training costs for product AA	–6.0	0.907	– 5.442
3–10	Net cash inflows from AA	5.0	5.863 (7.722 – 1.859)	29.315
10	Sale of factory [a]	3.85	0.614	2.364
				31.179

Note:
[a] £5.5m + £0.35m – redundancy costs (2m) = 3.85m

Alternative 2

Years		Cash flows (£m)	Discount factor	NPV (£m)
1	Normal sales of product A	3.0	0.952	2.856
2	Normal sales of product A	2.3	0.907	2.086
2	Sale of factory	3.85	0.907	3.492
2	Equipment and training costs for product AA	−6.0	0.907	−5.442
3–10	Net cash flows from AA with additional transport costs	3.0	5.863 (7.722 − 1.859)	17.589
				20.581

Alternative 3

Years		Cash flows (£m)	Discount factor	NPV (£m)
1	Purchase of equipment for X	−4.0	0.952	−3.808
1	Normal sales of product A	3.0	0.952	2.856
2	Sales of stock of A (0.125 × £3m)	0.375	0.907	0.340
2	Inflows from product X (50 000 × £70)	3.5	0.907	3.175
3	Inflows from product X (75 000 × £70)	5.25	0.864	4.536
4	Inflows from product X (75 000 × £70)	5.25	0.823	4.321
4	Sale of factory	3.85	0.823	3.169
2	Equipment and training costs for product AA	−6.0	0.907	− 5.442
3–10	Sales of AA with additional transport costs	3.0	5.863 (7.722 − 1.859)	17.589
				26.736

The first alternative yields the highest NPV.

(b) (i) Both alternatives 2 and 3 involve the same transport cost but alternative 3 yields a significantly higher NPV. Therefore it is appropriate to test the sensitivity of transport costs by comparing alternative 3 against alternative 1, which does not involve transport costs. The NPV of alternative 1 exceeds the NPV of alternative 3 by £4.443m (£31.179m − £26.736). The present value of the transport costs is £11.726m (200 000 × £10 × a discount factor of 5.863 for years 3–10). Therefore, the present value of transport costs would have to fall below £7.283m (£11.726m − £4.443m) for alternative 3 to be preferred to alternative 1. This represents annual cash flows of £1 242 000 (£7.283m/5.863 discount factor). Estimated annual cash flows for transport costs are £2m so cash flows would have to decline by £758 000 which represents a 37.9% decline.

(b) (ii) Based on the discussion in (b) (i), it is again appropriate to compare alternatives 1 and 3 where the NPV for alternative 1 exceeds that of alternative 3 by £4 443 000.

Let SV = net difference in sales value for NPV to be the same for both alternatives so that:

SV × year 4 discount factor (0.823) − SV × year 10 discount factor (0.614)
= £4 443 000
0.209SV = £4 443 000
SV = £21 258 373

Given that the existing sales value is £5.5m, the sales value can increase to £26.758m (£21.258m + £5.5m), representing an increase of approximately 400%.

(c) The answer should include a discussion of the following points:
1   the availability of skilled labour;
2   closeness to the market in terms of being able to respond quickly to demand;
3   taxation implications;
4   management problems arising from differences in national cultures;
5   the difficulties that may be encountered in operating a business that is located a considerable distance from central headquarters.

(a) The expected number of passengers is derived from the demand at each exchange **Question 13.8** rate:

Expected demand at 1.52 €/£ = 0.33 (500 + 460 + 420) = 460
Expected demand at 1.54 €/£ = 0.33 (550 + 520 + 450) = 506.67
Expected demand at 1.65 €/£ = 0.33 (600 + 580 + 500) = 560
Expected demand = 0.2(460) + 0.5(506.67) + 0.3(560) = 513.335 per train (or 1026.7 per day).

(b) *Cash flows: in-house option*

Year	1	2	3	4	5
Sales[a]	748 440	748 440	748 440	748 440	748 440
Variable costs[b]	(501 455)	(501 455)	(501 455)	(501 455)	(501 455)
Contribution	246 985	246 985	246 985	246 985	246 985
Labour costs[c]	(74 844)	(78 586)	(82 516)	(86 641)	(90 973)
Purchase and insurance[d]	(37 422)	(37 422)	(37 422)	(37 422)	(37 422)
Asset sale/purchase		(500 000)			280 000
Net cash flow	134 719	(369 023)	127 047	122 922	398 590
Discount factor at 12%	0.893	0.797	0.712	0.636	0.567
Present value	120 304	(294 111)	90 457	78 178	226 000

Net present value = £220 828

Cash flows: contract out option

Year	0	1	2	3	4	5
Contract fee[f]		(90 000)	(90 000)	(90 000)	(90 000)	(90 000)
Asset purchase/sale	650 000					
Purchase and insurance[e]		(16 422)	(16 422)	(16 422)	(16 422)	(16 422)
Net cash flow	650 000	(106 422)	(106 422)	(106 422)	(106 422)	(106 422)
Discount factor	1.0	0.893	0.797	0.712	0.636	0.567
Present value	650 000	(95 035)	(84 818)	(75 772)	(67 684)	(60 341)

Net present value = £266 350

The contract out option is preferred because it has the higher NPV of £45 522.

Notes:
[a] Sales revenues = 0.45 × 513.335 × £9 ×360   = £748 440
[b] Direct materials = 0.55 × £748 440   = £411 642
    Variable overhead = 0.12 × £748 440   = £89 813
    Variable costs   = £501 455
[c] Labour costs = 0.10 × £748 440 = £74 844 for year 1, Year 2 = £74 844 (1.05), Year 3 = £74 844 (1.05)^2
[d] Purchase and insurance = 0.05 × £748 440 = £37 422 (for in-house provision)
[e] Purchase and insurance = £37 422 – £21 000 = £16 422 (for contracting out)
[f] Provision of catering service by outside supplier = £250 × 360 days = £90 000
[g] Gross catering receipts are £2079 per day (£748 440/360) do not exceed £2200 so the 5% commission does not apply.
[h] Depreciation is not a cash flow and is therefore not a relevant cost.

(c) A 10% increase in sales would increase the annual contribution by £24 699 giving an increase in present value of £89 040 (£24 699 × 3.605 discount factor at 12%). The present value of the additional costs is £36 050 (£10 000 × 3.605) resulting in an increase in NPV of £52 990. This exceeds the NPV of £45 522 from changing to the contracting out alternative. However, the revised annual sales per day would be £2287 (£2079 × 1.10), thus enabling the company to receive 5% of gross sales receipts once sales exceed £2200 per day. The company would therefore receive £41 164 per annum (5% × £748 440 sales × 1.10). This would result in the contracting out alternative having the higher NPV. The choice is highly dependent on future sales being in excess of £2200 per day.

(d) The answer should draw attention to the difficulties in deriving probabilities and using past data to estimate probabilities based on the view that the past is indicative of the future. The outcome using probabilities represents an average outcome, which may be unlikely to occur. Also expected values ignore risk. For a more detailed discussion of these points you should refer to the sections on probabilities, probability distributions and expected value and measuring the amount of uncertainty in Chapter 12.

(e) The following non-financial factors need to be taken into account:
1   The loss of ability to control the quality and reliability of the service if the service is contracted out. These factors may influence the number of passengers choosing to travel with Amber plc.
2   Impact on staff morale as a result of the reduction in labour costs. Existing staff may be concerned that their jobs are under threat and may leave the company.
3   The difficulty and high costs of changing back to in-service provision once the company has contracted out the service.
4   Willingness of the supplier to respond to changes in market demand.

Question 13.9

(a) *NPV calculations*

	Cash flows (£m)	Years	Discount factor	PV (£m)
Initial outlay	(40)	t_0	1.0000	(40.000)
Disposal value	10	t_{10}	0.2472	2.472
Retraining costs[a]	(10)	$t_{0,1}$	1.8696	(18.696)
Annual cost savings	12	$t_1 - t_{10}$	5.0190	60.228
Rental income	2	t_{1-10}	5.0190	10.038
Software	(4)	t_{1-10}	5.0190	(20.076)
Reduction in working capital	5	t_0	1.0000	5.000
NPV				(1.034)

It is assumed that taxation should be ignored.

Note
[a]The question implies that retraining costs do not occur at the end of the year. It is therefore assumed that the cash flows occur at the start of years 1 and 2 (that is, t_0 and t_1).

Calculation of accounting rate of return

	(£m)
Year 1 incremental profits:	
Annual cost savings	12
Retraining costs (20m/10 years)	(2)
Rental income	2
Software	(4)
Depreciation of equipment (40 − 10)/10 years	(3)
Increase in profits	5
Year 1 incremental capital investment:	
Initial outlay	40
Capitalized retraining costs	20
Reduction in working capital	(5)
	55

It is assumed that ROI is calculated based on the opening written-down value:

$$\text{ROI} = 5/55 = 9.1\%$$

The proposed investment fails to meet either of the company's investment criteria and would be rejected.

(b) The answer should include a discussion of the following:

   (i) A theoretical explanation of the NPV rule and a justification for its use. In perfect capital markets a positive NPV reflects the increase in the market value of a company arising from acceptance of the project.

   (ii) An explanation of the impact of market imperfections on the NPV rule. For NPV to represent the increase in shareholders' value resulting from acceptance of an investment, it is necessary for investors to be aware of the project's existence and also the projected future cash flows. This implies that the efficient market hypothesis applies in its strong form and that changes in short-run reported profits do not affect market prices.

   (iii) In imperfect markets shareholders lack information regarding projected future cash flows. Consequently, they may use short-run reported profits and ROI as an indication of potential future cash flows. In such circumstances changes in reported profits will affect share prices. Hence management have reacted to this situation by considering the impact of a project's acceptance on reported ROI.

   (iv) Widespread use of ROI and payback in the UK and USA.

   (v) Shareholders and financial analysts tend to monitor short-run profits and ROI and use these measures as an input that determines their estimates of future share prices. It is therefore not surprising that companies consider the implications of their investment decisions on reported short-run profits and ROI.

(c) The answer should include a discussion of the specific problems that arise in evaluating investments in advanced manufacturing technologies (AMTs) and an explanation of why the financial appraisal might incorrectly reject such investments. In particular, it is claimed that many of the benefits from investing in AMTs are difficult to quantify and tend not to be included in the analysis (e.g. improved product quality). It is also claimed that inflation is incorrectly dealt with and that excessive discount rates are applied which overcompensate for risk.

    A further reason that has been cited why companies underinvest in AMTs is that they fail to properly evaluate the relevant alternatives. There is a danger that the investment will be compared incorrectly against an alternative that assumes a continuation of the current market share, selling prices and costs – in other words, the status quo. However, the status quo is unlikely to apply, since competitors are also likely to invest in the new technology. In this situation the investment should be compared with the alternative of not investing, based on assuming a situation of declining cash flow.

The answer should also stress that taxation has not been incorporated into the analysis. In addition, the project has been discounted at the company's normal cost of capital of 15%. This rate is only justified if the risk of the project is equivalent to the average risk of the firm's existing assets.

Capital investment decisions: the impact of capital rationing, taxation, inflation and risk

Solutions to Chapter 14 questions

(a) See 'Payback method' and 'Accounting rate of return' in Chapter 13 for the answer to this question. **Question 14.1**

(b) (i) For the answer to this question you should refer to the sections on the concept of NPV, calculating NPV's, the internal rate of return (IRR) and comparison of NPV and IRR in Chapter 13.

(b) (ii) NPV of one year replacement = £1200/1.14 − 2400 = − £1347

Equivalent annual cost of one year replacement = £1347/0.877[a] = £1535.91

NPV of two year replacement = 800/1.14^2 − 75/1.14 − 2400 = − £1850.21

Equivalent annual cost of two year replacement = 1850.21/1.647[a] = 1123.38

NPV of three year replacement = 300/1.14^3 − 150/1.14^2 − 75/1.14 − 2400 = − £2378.72

Equivalent annual cost of three year replacement = £2378.72/2.322[a] = 1024.43

Note:

[a] Annuity factors for 1, 2 or 3 years at 14%.

The three year replacement has the lowest equivalent annual cost. Therefore the three year replacement is the preferred alternative. However, the following factors should also be taken into account:

1   Likely changes in technology. If there are rapid changes in technology, the three year replacement will result in a failure to obtain the benefits of any improvement in technology.

2   Compatibility with the company's other computer systems. If the company's other computer systems are frequently updated the laptop computers may not be compatible with them.

(a) Expected value of the annual sales = (4m × 0.2) + (£5m × 0.4) + (£7m × 0.3) + (£10m × 0.1) = £5.9m **Question 14.2**

The market research survey (note vii) is a sunk cost.

Cash flows £'000s	Year						
	0	1	2	3	4	5	6
Purchase of Company	(400)						
Legal/professional		(20)	(20)	(20)	(20)	(20)	
Lease rentals		(12)	(12)	(12)	(12)	(12)	
Studio hire		(540)	(540)	(702)	(702)	(702)	
Camera hire		(120)	(120)	(120)	(120)	(120)	
Technical staff		(1560)	(1716)	(1888)	(2077)	(2285)	
Screenplay		(150)	(173)	(199)	(229)	(263)	
Actors salaries		(2100)	(2310)	(2541)	(2795)	(3074)	
Costumes/wardrobe		(180)	(180)	(180)	(180)	(180)	
Non production staff wages		(60)	(66)	(73)	(80)	(88)	
Set design		(450)	(450)	(450)	(450)	(450)	
Lost income from office accommodation		(20)	(20)	(20)	(20)	(20)	
Sales		5900	6195	6505	6830	7172	

Cash flow before tax	(400)	688	588	300	145	(42)	
Tax		–	(227)	(194)	(99)	(48)	14
Net Cash Flow	(400)	688	361	106	46	(90)	14
Disc. Factor	1	0.877	0.769	0.675	0.592	0.519	0.456
P.V. Cash Flow	(400)	603	278	72	27	(47)	6

NPV = £539 000

(b) Limitations of expected values include:
  1 Expected values represent average outcomes based on the assumption that decisions will be repeated but a specific investment decision is likely to occur once so the average outcome is unlikely to occur.
  2 Deriving probabilities is highly subjective.
  3 Expected values do not take into account the range of outcomes. A probability distribution is likely to provide more meaningful information.

For a more detailed discussion of the above points you should refer to the sections on probability distributions and expected values and measuring the amount of uncertainty in Chapter 12.

(c) (i) See 'Profitability index' in Chapter 14 for the answer to this question.

(c) (ii) Profitability index = Present value/investment outlay

Profitability index for the filmmaking acquisition $= \dfrac{\text{NPV } (£539\ 000) + \text{Investment outlay } (£400\ 000)}{\text{Investment outlay } (£400\ 000)}$

$$= 2.347$$

Investment X present value:
$(200 \times 0.877) + (200 \times 0.769) + (150 \times 0.675) + (100 \times 0.592) + (100 \times 0.519) + (100 \times 0.456) = £587$
Profitability index = £587/200 = 2.935

Investment Y present value:
$(80 \times 0.877) + (80 \times 0.769) + (40 \times 0.675) + (40 \times 0.592) + (40 \times 0.519) + (40 \times 0.456) = £221$
Profitability index = £221/100 = 2.21

Given that projects are indivisible the choice is between:
1 Investing in X and Y, yielding an NPV of £508 000 (587 + 221 – 300 investment outlay). The un-utilized funds of £100 000 can only be reinvested to obtain a zero NPV.
2 Investing all of the £400 000 in the filmmaking company yielding an NPV of £539 000.

The company should choose to invest in the filmmaking company.

(c) (iii) For a discussion of the limitations of the profitability index you should refer to the final paragraph in the section on capital rationing in Chapter 14. In addition, the answer should point out that the profitability index does not take into account:
  1 How projects interact to reduce risk or to provide a strategic alignment such as the vertical integration that may occur with the purchase of the filmmaking company.
  2 Problems can occur when projects are indivisible and the strict application of this method can result in misleading decisions. For example, investment X has the highest profitability index but it is clearly preferable to not invest in this project since it will not lead to the maximization of NPV when funds are restricted to £400 000.

(d) See 'Taxation and investment decisions' in Chapter 14 for the answer to this question.

(a) It is assumed that all of the cash flows will increase at the general rate of inflation so that estimates in current prices at the time of appraising the investment will be equal to real cash flows. Real cash flows must be discounted at a real discount rate but the question includes a nominal required rate of return (i.e. discount rate). Therefore we must convert the nominal discount rate to a real discount rate using the following formula:

1 + nominal rate = (1 + real rate) × (1 + anticipated rate of inflation)

so that (1 + real rate) = 1 + nominal rate / (1 + anticipated rate of inflation)

giving a real rate of 8% (1.14 / 1.055) = 1.08

Contribution per box sold = £20 – (£8 + £2 + £1.50 + £2) = £6.50

Allocated fixed overheads do not represent incremental cash flows and are therefore not relevant to the decision. The annual cash flows are 150 000 boxes × £6.50 × (1 – corporate tax rate (0.33)) = £653 250. The annual cash flows are constant so the cumulative discount (i.e. annuity tables) in Appendix 2 of the text can be used.

$$\text{NPV} = (£653\ 250 \times 3.993) - £2m = £608\ 428$$

IRR = (annual cash flows) × (the cumulative discount factor at $x\%$ for 5 years) – investment outlay = 0

so that IRR is where the cumulative discount factor at $x\%$ for 5 years = Investment outlay (£2m)/£653 250 = 3.062.

If you examine the five year row in Appendix 2 you will find that the figure closest to 3.062 appears between 18% and 20%. Therefore the IRR is approximately 19%.

Because the project has a positive NPV and the IRR exceeds the real cost of capital of 8% the project is acceptable.

(b) See 'Sensitivity analysis' in Chapter 14 for the answer to this question.

(c) (i) *Price (P)*

$$\begin{aligned}
\text{NPV} &= 0 = 0.15m(P - £13.50)(1 - 0.33)(AF_{8\%,\ 5}) - £2m \\
&= 0 = (0.15mP - £2025m)\ 2.675 - £2m \\
&= 0 = £0.401mP - 5.417m - 2m \\
0.401mP &= 7.417m \\
P &= £18.50
\end{aligned}$$

Therefore the price can drop by £1.50 (or 7.5%) before NPV becomes negative.

Note

$AF_{8\%,\ 5}$ = Annuity factor at 8% for 5 years

(c) (ii) *Volume (V)*

$$\begin{aligned}
\text{NPV} &= 0 = V (£20 - £13.50) (1 - 0.33) (AF_{8\%,\ 5}) - £2m \\
&= 0 = £6.50V(2.675) - £2m \\
&= 0 = £17.3875V - £2m \\
V &= £2m / 17.3875 \\
V &= 115\ 025
\end{aligned}$$

Therefore volume can drop by 34 975 boxes (150 000 – 115 025) or 23% before NPV becomes negative.

The results suggest that the NPV of the project is more sensitive to price variations than to changes in volume. The company therefore should review the estimated price to ensure that it is confident that prices will not decline by more than 7%. If prices decline by more than 7%, and the other variables remain unchanged, the project will yield a negative NPV. Consideration should be given to advertising to ensure that demand is maintained at the proposed price but it should be noted that NPV will decline by the amount spent on advertising.

Question 14.4   (a) The question indicates that a uniform inflation rate applies to all costs and revenues. Therefore, current prices will be equivalent to real cash flows. The NPV can be calculated either by discounting real cash flows at the real discount rate or discounting nominal cash flows at a nominal discount rate. If the former approach is applied, it is necessary to convert the nominal discount rate (15.5%) to a real discount rate. The calculation is as follows:

(1 + real discount rate) = (1 + nominal discount rate)/(1 + anticipated rate of inflation)
(1 + real discount rate) = (1.155)/(1.05) = 1.10
Real discount rate   = 1.10 − 1 = 0.10 = 10%
Expected value of sales = (£800 × 0.25) + (£560 × 0.50) + (£448 × 0.25) = £592 000
Contribution £325 600 (£592 000 × 0.55)
Less fixed costs £ 90 000
Taxable profits £235 600
Tax at 30% £70 680

The calculation of NPV using real cash flows and the real discount rate is as follows:

	Year 1 (£)	Year 2 (£)	Year 3 (£)	Year4 (£)	Year 5 (£)	Year 6 (£)
Contribution less fixed costs	235 600	235 600	235 600	235 600	235 600	
Scrap value					55 000	
Tax payable	(35 340)	(70 680)	(70 680)	(70 680)	(70 680)	(35 340)
Net cash flow	200 260	164 920	164 920	164 920	219 920	(35 340)
Discount factor	0.909	0.826	0.751	0.683	0.621	0.564
Present value	182 036	136 224	123 855	112 640	136 570	(19 932)

NPV = Total present value £671 393 − investment outlay (£550 000) = £121 393

The question implies that all of the above items will increase with the rate of inflation, but this is unlikely to apply to the time lag in the payment of taxation. As a result the tax payment in real terms for the delayed payment (50% × £70 680) will be slightly less than £35 340, but this will not have a significant effect and it is assumed that it is the examiner's intention for this factor not be taken into account. An alternative approach to answering the question would have been to express all of the above cash flows in nominal terms (that is, inflate them at 5% per annum) and discount them at the nominal rate of 15.5%. Given the positive NPV, the proposed expansion should be undertaken.

(b) Let x = contribution (£) after deduction of fixed costs.

The following expression indicates the point at which NPV will be zero:

$$0.85x(0.909) + 0.7x(0.826) + 0.7x(0.751) + 0.7x(0.683) + 0.7x(0.621) + £55\ 000(0.621) − 0.15x(0.564) = £550\ 000$$

In year 1 the after tax cash flows will be 85% of the contribution after deduction of fixed costs, for years 2–5 it will be 70% (1 − tax rate) and the final year represents the last instalment of the tax payment (30% × 0.15). The figures in parentheses represent the discount rates for years 1 − 6 and the £55 000 represents the disposal value at the end of year 5. The final item in the expression represents the investment outlay.

The above expression after undertaking the arithmetical calculations equals:

$$2.70475x + £34\ 155 = £550\ 000$$

$$x = £190\ 718$$

To derive the annual contribution we must add back the fixed costs of £90 000 giving £280 718. Thus, annual contribution can fall by £44 882 (£325 600 − £280 718), representing a decline of 13.78% before NPV becomes zero.

CAPITAL INVESTMENT DECISIONS: THE IMPACT OF CAPITAL RATIONING, TAXATION, INFLATION AND RISK

(c) Because the annual writing down allowances are fixed and do not increase with inflation they will decline in real terms over the years. In other words, they are already expressed in nominal terms. To express them in real terms it will be necessary to divide them by $(1 + \text{anticipated inflation rate})^n$. An alternative and easier approach to calculate their impact, after taking account of inflation, is to discount them (note they are already expressed in nominal terms) at the nominal discount rate.

The calculation of the present value of the writing down allowances is as follows:

Writing Down Allowances schedule

	(£)	Tax saved @ 30%ᵃ (£)	Year 1 (£)	Year 2 (£)	Year 3 (£)	Year 4 (£)	Year 5 (£)	Year 6 (£)
Initial expenditure	555 000							
WDA Year 1, 25%	137 500	41 250	20 625	20 625				
	412 500							
WDA Year 2, 25%	103 125	30 938		15 469	15 469			
	309 375							
WDA Year 3, 25%	77 344	23 203			11 602	11 601		
	232 031							
WDA Year 4, 25%	58 008	17 402				8701	8701	
	174 023							
Sale for scrap, year 5	70 195ᵇ							
Balancing allowance	103 828	31 148					15 574	15 574
Total tax savings			20 625	36 094	27 071	20 302	24 275	15 574
Discount factor (nominal rate)ᶜ			0.866	0.750	0.649	0.562	0.487	0.421
Present value			17 861	27 071	17 569	11 410	11 822	6557
Total present value	92 290							

The net present value for the investment will increase by £92 290 arising from the tax savings from writing down allowances.

Notes:
ᵃ Because one half of the tax payment is delayed until the following year, 50% will occur in the current year and 50% in the following year.
ᵇ The sales value must be adjusted to a nominal value so that the value equals £55 000 $(1.05)^5$ = £70 195.
ᶜ Discount factors = $£1/(1.155)^n$. For example, the discount factor for year 2 = $1/(1.155)^2$ = 0.750.

(a) The present value of the cash flows is calculated as follows:

Question 14.5

Year	0 (£m)	1 (£m)	2 (£m)	3 (£m)	4 (£m)	5 (£m)
Initial outlay	(1.000)					
EU grant		0.250				
FSL's fee		(0.050)				
Increase in costs		(0.315)	(0.331)	(0.347)	(0.365)	
Tax saving on increased costs at 33%			0.104	0.109	0.115	0.120
Tax savings on WDAsᵃ		0.083	0.062	0.047	0.035	0.104
Net cash flows	(1.000)	(0.032)	(0.165)	(0.191)	(0.215)	0.224
Discount factor at 12%	1.000	0.893	0.797	0.712	0.636	0.567
Present value of cash flows at 12%	(1.307)					
Present value of savings in finesᵇ	1.250					
NPV of project	(0.057)					

Notes
[a] The annual writing down allowances are calculated as follows:

Year	0	1	2	3	4	5
	(£m)	(£m)	(£m)	(£m)	(£m)	(£m)
Opening WDV	1.000	0.750	0.562	0.421	0.316	
Annual WDAs (Balancing allowance in year 4)	(0.250)	(0.188)	(0.141)	(0.105)	(0.316)	
Tax savings at 33% with a 1 year delay		0.083	0.062	0.047	0.035	0.104

[b] The expected value of the level of the fines = (£0.5m × 0.3) + (£1.4m × 0.5) + (£2m × 0.2) = £1.25m

(b) The following points should be incorporated in the answer:
(i) The project is not justifiable if only those items that can be expressed in financial terms are incorporated in the analysis.
(ii) The weaknesses of the expected value approach is based on it representing an average outcome. See 'Expected values' in Chapter 12 for an explanation.
(iii) The preference for examining the probability distribution of outcomes. The project has a 70% probability that the savings relating to the fines will exceed the negative present value of the net cash flows of £1.307m from the investment.
(iv) The fact that the company may not be pursuing purely financial objectives and that it may wish to pursue socially responsible objectives. The negative NPV of £0.057m indicates the cost to the shareholders of pursuing other objectives.
(v) Increased sales may result if the company is seen by customers and potential customers as being environmentally friendly.
(vi) The company has a moral responsibility to undertake such projects.

Question 14.6   (a) (i)

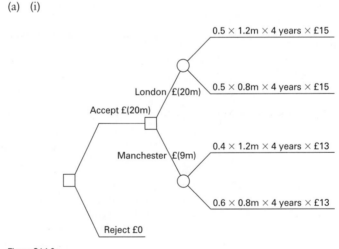

Figure Q14.6a

CAPITAL INVESTMENT DECISIONS: THE IMPACT OF CAPITAL RATIONING, TAXATION, INFLATION AND RISK

Note that the amounts of £15 and £13 relate to the contribution per visitor of £15 for London (£25 – service cost of £10) and £13 for Manchester (£23 – £10).

(a) (ii) *Expected NPV of London location*

	(£m)
0.5 × 1.2m × £15 × 3.170 (4 year cumulative discount factor at 10%)	28.53
0.5 × 0.8m × £15 × 3.170	19.02
	47.55
Less investment outlay (£20m dome + £20m land)	40.00
	7.55
Sale of land (£14m × 0.683)	9.56
NPV	17.11

Expected NPV of Manchester location

	(£m)
0.4 × 1.2m × £13 × 3.170 (4 year cumulative discount factor at 10%)	19.78
0.6 × 0.8m × £13 × 3.170	19.78
	39.56
Less investment outlay (£20m dome + £9m land)	29.00
	10.56
Sale of land (£10m × 0.683)	6.83
NPV	17.39

Manchester should be selected because its NPV is £0.28m greater than the London location.

(b) (i)

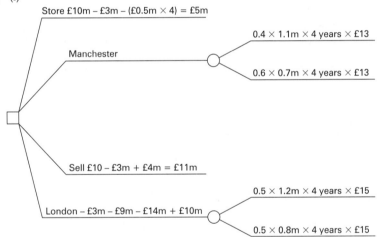

Figure Q14.6b

Note that an explanation of the meaning of each of the above figures is provided in (b) (ii).

(b) (ii) *NPV of storing the dome at Manchester*

	(£m)
Sale of the land in year 4 (£10m at year 4 discount factor of 0.683)	6.83
Dismantling cost in year 4 (£3m at year 4 discount factor of 0.683)	(2.05)
Storage costs (0.5m per annum at a cumulative discount factor of 2.165 for years 5–8)	(1.08)
NPV	3.70

	(£m)
Expected present value of annual contributions:	
(0.4 × 1.1m × £13 × 2.165 cumulative discount factor)	12.38
(0.6 × 0.7m × £13 × 2.165 cumulative discount factor)	11.82
	24.20
Dismantling cost in year 8 (£2m × 0.466)	(0.93)
Sale of land in year 8 (10m × 0.466)	4.66
NPV	27.93

Selling the dome in year 4

Sale of dome (£4m) and land (£10m) less dismantling cost (3m) = £11m
Present value (£11m × year 4 discount factor of 0.683)   = £7.51m

Transferring the dome to London

	(£m)
Expected present value of annual contributions:	
(0.5 × 1.2m × £15 × 2.165 cumulative discount factor)	19.49
(0.5 × 0.8m × £15 × 2.165 cumulative discount factor)	12.99
	32.48
Year 4: Sale of land at Manchester (£10m) – purchase of land at London (£14m) – dismantling cost (£3m) – moving cost (£9m) = – £16m discounted at 0.683	(10.93)
Sale of land in year 8 (£14m) less dismantling cost (£2m) = £12m × 0.466	5.59
NPV	27.14

The highest NPV is obtained from continuing operations at Manchester.

(c) In parts (a) and (b) the analysis was based on two separate periods rather than a single period and Manchester was the preferred option for both periods. Storing or selling the dome clearly have lower NPV's than the other alternatives over the 8 year period. Therefore the focus should be on comparing siting at London or Manchester. The relevant calculations based on the 8 year time horizon are as follows:

Manchester

	(£m)
First 4 years at Manchester (without the sale of the land)	10.56
Second 4 years	27.93
NPV	38.49

London

	(£m)
First 4 years at London without the sale of the land	7.55
Second 4 years:	
(0.5 × 1.1m × £15 × 2.165 cumulative discount factor)	17.86
(0.5 × 0.7m × £15 × 2.165 cumulative discount factor)	11.37
Dismantling and sale of land in year 8	5.59
NPV	42.37

Focusing on an 8 year horizon indicates that locating the dome and keeping it at London gives the higher expected NPV.

(d) There would appear to be little to gain from trying to assess the profitability of the individual products (i.e. individual rides or individual item of merchandise). Each of the products is likely to be complementary and so there is little point in trying to ascertain their individual profitability. Profitability analysis is likely to be more helpful in terms of customer segments (e.g. families, teenagers, parties, etc). Although insufficient information is given in the question, the data given suggest that costs are mainly direct and variable and facility sustaining. Therefore, the proportion of indirect costs that fluctuate according to the demand for them is likely to be very small. Under such circumstances ABC is unlikely to be justified and it may be preferable to adopt a direct/variable costing system for customer profitability analysis. See 'Types of costing systems' in Chapter 10 and 'Cost-benefit issues and cost systems design' in Chapter 3 for additional points that are relevant to this question.

(a) *Calculation of expected NPV (£000)*

Year	0	1	2	3	4	5	6
Investment outlay	(1500)						
Sales at £2 per unit		3000	3000	3000	3000	3000	3000
Variable costs at £1.59 per unit[a]		2385	2385	2385	2385	2385	2385
Taxable cash flows		615	615	615	615	615	615
Tax at 35%		215	215	215	215	215	215
Net cash flow[b]	(1500)	400	400	400	400	400	400

NPV at a discount rate of 8%[c] = (£400 × 4.623) − £1500 = £349 200

Question 14.7

Notes

[a]Unit variable cost = Purchase cost (£1.50 × 40%) + copyright fee (20% × £3.95) + £0.20 additional variable cost.

[b]Market research is a sunk cost.

[c]See part (b) of the answer for an explanation of why a discount rate of 8% has been used. Note that the financing costs are incorporated in the discount rate and should not be included in the cash flows as this would lead to double counting.

(b) Assuming that the company wishes to maintain its current capital structure the specific cost of financing the project should not be used as a discount rate. The project has been financed by a bank loan but this will result in less borrowing being used in the future as the company re-balances its finance to achieve the target capital structure. To reflect the company's target capital structure the weighted average cost of capital (WACC) should be used.

The money WACC should be used only if the cash flows are expressed in money/nominal terms (i.e. adjusted for inflation). Current cash flows have been used to calculate NPV. Current cash flows are equivalent to real cash flow when all cash flows increase at the general rate of inflation. This situation occurs in this question and therefore the cash flows are equivalent to real cash flows. Thus the real WACC of capital should be used to discount the cash flows.

The WACC represents the discount rate applicable for the company as a whole and reflects the average risk of all of the company's assets. If the project has a different level of risk from the average risk of the assets of the company as a whole, the existing WACC will not represent the appropriate discount rate. In this situation a separate risk adjusted discount rate should be used.

It is also assumed that all of the cash flows increase at the general rate of inflation. If the cash flows are subject to different rates of inflation it will be incorrect to use current prices. If this situation occurs the cash flows should be adjusted by their specific rates of inflation and a nominal discount rate should be used.

(c) (i) *Initial outlay*

The NPV of the project is £349 200. Therefore the investment outlay could increase by £349 200 before NPV becomes negative. This represents a percentage increase of 23.28% (£349.2/£1500 × 100).

Annual contribution

Let x = annual contribution

With a corporate tax rate of 35% the annual contribution at which NPV will be zero can be calculated from the following formula:

$$(1 - 0.35)\ 4.623x - £1500 = 0$$
$$3.005x - 1500 \qquad\qquad = 0$$
$$x = 1500/3.005 \qquad\qquad = £499.16$$

Therefore annual contribution can decline from the existing figure of £615 000 to £499 160. A percentage decrease of 18.83% (£115.84/£615 × 100). Note that 4.623 and £1500 in the above formula represents the cumulative discount factor and the investment outlay.

The life of the agreement

Let x = Annuity factor at 8%

NPV will be zero where

$$400x - £1500 = 0$$
$$x = 3.75$$

From the annuity table shown in Appendix B of the text:

PV of annuity for 4 years at 8% = 3.312

PV of annuity for 5 years at 8% = 3.993

Extrapolating, the PV annuity factor is:

$$4 \text{ years} + \frac{3.75 - 3.312}{3.993 - 3.312} \times 1 \text{ year} = 4.643 \text{ years}$$

This represents a reduction of 22.61% [(6 − 4.643)/6 years × 100]

Discount rate

Let x = PV of annuity for 6 years

NPV will be zero where:

$$400x = 1500$$
$$x = 3.75$$

From the annuity tables (Appendix B) 15% has a PV annuity factor of 3.784 and 16% is 3.685. Thus the discount rate at which NPV will be zero is approximately 15.5%. This represents an increase of 93.75% [(15.5 − 8)/8 × 100].

The above calculations indicate that the annual contribution is the most sensitive variable.

(ii) See 'Sensitivity Analysis' in Chapter 14 for an outline of the limitations of sensitivity analysis.

(d) Possible additional information includes:

    (i) Is the agreement likely to be renewed after 6 years?

    (ii) Are competitors likely to enter the market and what impact would this have on the sales volume and price?

    (iii) How accurate are the estimated cash flows?

    (iv) How reliable is the supplier who supplies microfiche readers? Can the microfiche readers be obtained from any other source or is the company dependent upon the one supplier?

The budgeting process

Solutions to Chapter 15 questions

(a) Incremental budgeting uses the previous year's budget as the starting point for the preparation of next year's budget. It is assumed that the basic structure of the budget will remain unchanged and that adjustments will be made to allow for changes in volume, efficiency and price levels. The budget is therefore concerned with increments to operations that will occur during the period and the focus is on existing use of resources rather than considering alternative strategies for the future budget period. Incremental budgeting suffers from the following weaknesses:

(i) it perpetuates past inefficiencies;
(ii) there is insufficient focus on improving efficiency and effectiveness;
(iii) the resource allocation tends to be based on existing strategies rather than considering future strategies;
(iv) it tends to focus excessively on the short term and often leads to arbitrary cuts being made in order to achieve short-term financial targets.

(b) See 'Activity-based budgeting' in Chapter 15 for the answer to this question. In particular, the answer should stress that:

(i) the focus is on managing activities;
(ii) the focus is on the resources that are required for undertaking activities and identifying those activity resources that are un-utilized or which are insufficient to meet the requirements specified in the budget;
(iii) attention is given to eliminating non-value-added activities;
(iv) the focus is on the control of the causes of costs (i.e. the cost drivers).

For a more detailed discussion of some of the above points you should also refer to 'Activity-based management' in Chapter 21.

Question 15.1

(a) *Cumbersome process*
The answer to the first comment in the question should include a very brief summary of 'Stages in the budgeting process' in Chapter 15. The process involves detailed negotiations between the budget holders and their superiors and the accountancy staff. Because the process is very time consuming it must be started well before the start of the budget year. Subsequent changes in the environment, and the fact that the outcomes reflected in the master budget may not meet financial targets, may necessitate budget revisions and a repeat of the negotiation process. The renegotiating stage may well be omitted because of time constraints. Instead, across the board cost reductions may be imposed to meet the budget targets.

Concentration on short-term financial control
Short-term financial targets are normally set for the budget year and the budget is used as the mechanism for achieving the targets. Budget adjustments are made to ensure that the targets are achieved often with little consideration being given to the impact such adjustments will have on the longer-term plans.

Undesirable motivation effects on managers
Managers are often rewarded or punished based on their budget performance in terms of achieving or exceeding the budget. There is a danger that the budget will

Question 15.2

be viewed as a punitive device rather than as an aid to managers in managing their areas of responsibility. This can result in dysfunctional consequences such as attempting to build slack into the budgeting system by overstating costs and understating revenues. Alternatively, cuts may be made in discretionary expenses which could have adverse long-term consequences. The overriding aim becomes to achieve the budget, even if this is done in a manner that is not in the organization's best interests.

Emphasizing formal organizational structure
Budgets are normally structured around functional responsibility centres, such as departments and business units. A functional structure is likely to encourage bureaucracy and slow responses to environmental and competitive changes. There is a danger that there will be a lack of goal congruence and that managers may focus on their own departments to the detriment of the organization. Also if budgets are extended to the lower levels of the organization employees will focus excessively on meeting the budget and this may constrain their activities in terms of the flexibility that is required when dealing with customers.

(b) *Cumbersome process*
Managers could be given greater flexibility on how they will meet their targets. For example, top management might agree specific targets with the managers and the managers given authority to achieve the targets in their own way. Detailed budgets are not required and the emphasis is placed on managers achieving their overall targets.

Another alternative is to reduce the budget planning period by implementing a system of continuous or rolling budgets.

Concentration on short-term financial control
This might be overcome by placing more stress on a manager's long-term performance and adopting a profit-conscious style of budget evaluation (see 'Side effects from using accounting information for performance evaluation' in Chapter 16) and also placing more emphasis on participative budgeting (see 'Participation in the budget process' in Chapter 16). Attention should also be given to widening the performance measurement system and focusing on key result areas that deal with both short-term and long-term considerations. In particular a balanced scorecard approach (see Chapter 23) might be adopted.

Undesirable motivation effects on managers
The same points as those made above (i.e. profit-conscious style of evaluation, participative budgeting and a broader range of performance measures) also apply here. In addition, the rewards and punishment system must be changed so that it is linked to a range of performance criteria rather than being dominated by short-term financial budget performance. Consideration could also be given to changing the reward system from focusing on responsibility centre performance to rewards being based on overall company performance.

Emphasizing formal organizational structure
Here the answer could discuss activity-based budgeting with the emphasis being on activity centres and business processes, rather than functional responsibility centres that normally consist of departments. For a discussion of these issues you should refer to 'Activity-based budgeting' in Chapter 15 and 'Activity-based cost management' in Chapter 21. Consideration should also be given to converting cost centres to profit centres and establishing a system of internal transfer prices. This would encourage managers to focus more widely on profits rather than just costs. Finally, budgets should not be extended to lower levels of the organization and more emphasis should be given to empowering employees to manage their own activities (see 'Employee empowerment' in Chapter 1).

(a) See 'Incremental budgeting' and 'Zero-based budgeting' in Chapter 15 for the answer to this question. Note that incremental budgeting is described within the section on activity-based budgeting.

Question 15.3

(b) The answer should draw off the material within the section on zero-based budgeting and point out that projects should be identified as decision packages and ranked on a cost versus benefits basis with resources allocated according to the ranking up to the spending cut-off level.

(c) See 'Activity-based budgeting' in Chapter 15 for the answer to this question.

Question 15.4

(a) Production budget

Product	A	B
Sales	2000	1500
Opening stock	(100)	(200)
Closing stock (10% × sales level)	200	150
	2100	1450

(b) Materials usage budget

Material type	X Kg	Y Litres
Usage		
(2100 × 2) + (1450 × 3)	8550	
(2100 × 1) + (1450 × 4)		7900

(c) Materials purchases budget

Usage	8550	7900
Opening stock	(300)	(1000)
Closing stock^a	850	800
	9100	7700
	× £10	× £7
	£91 000	£53 900

(d) Labour budget

	Skilled hours	Semi skilled hours
(2100 × 4) + (1450 × 2)	11 300	
(2100 × 2) + (1450 × 5)		11 450
	× £12	× £8
	£135 600	£91 600

Note:
aMaterial Closing Stock
Material X (2000 × 2 + 1500 × 3) × 10% = 850
Material Y (2000 × 1 + 1500 × 4) × 10% = 850

Workings

Question 15.5

Budgeted sales (units and value)

Product	Units	Price	Value (£)
F1	34 000	£50.00	1 700 000
F2	58 000	£30.00	1 740 000
			3 440 000

Budgeted production (units)

Product	Sales	Stock increase	Production
F1	34 000	1000	35 000
F2	58 000	2000	60 000

(i) Component purchase and usage budget (units and value)

Product	Component C3	Component C4	Total
F1	280 000u	140 000u	
F2	240 000u	180 000u	
	520 000u	320 000u	
Value	£650 000	£576 000	£1 226 000

(ii) Direct labour budget (hours and value)

Product	Assembly	Finishing	Total
F1	17 500 hours	7000 hours	
F2	15 000 hours	10 000 hours	
	32 500	17 000	
Value	£162 500	£102 000	£264 500

(iii) Departmental manufacturing overhead recovery rates

	Assembly	Finishing
Total overhead cost per month	£617 500	£204 000
Total direct labour hours	32 500	17 000
Overhead rate (per direct labour hour)	£19.00	£12.00

(iv) Selling overhead recovery rate

Total overhead cost per month	£344 000
Total sales value (Month 9)	£3 440 000
Selling overhead rate	10%

(v) Closing stock budget

Product	Units	Cost[a] £	Value £
F1	1000	32.80	32 800
F2	2000	19.40	38 800
			71 600

Note:
[a]See part (b) for the calculation of the cost per unit

(b) Standard unit costs for month 9

			Product		
			F1 £/unit		F2 £/unit
Material	C3	8 × £1.25	10.00	4 × £1.25	5.00
	C4	4 × £1.80	7.20	3 × £1.80	5.40
Labour	Assembly	30/60 × £5	2.50	15/60 × £5	1.25
	Finishing	12/60 × £6	1.20	10/60 × £6	1.00
M'fg. overhead	Assembly	30/60 × £19	9.50	15/60 × £19	4.75
	Finishing	12/60 × £12	2.40	10/60 × £12	2.00
Manufacturing	cost		32.80		19.40
Selling overhead (10% of selling price)			5.00		3.00
Total cost			37.80		22.40
Selling price			50.00		30.00
Profit			12.20		7.60

(c) Budgeted profit and loss account for month 9

	(£)
Components	1 226 000
Direct labour	264 500
Manufacturing overhead	821 500
Subtotal	2 312 000
Less closing stock	71 600
Cost of sales	2 240 400
Selling overhead	344 000
Total cost	2 584 400
Sales	3 440 000
Net profit	855 600

(d) The company currently uses an absorption costing system but computes predetermined overhead rates on a monthly basis. It is preferable to calculate a predetermined overhead rate at annual intervals. This is because a large amount of overheads are likely to be fixed in the short-term whereas activity will fluctuate from month to month, giving large fluctuations in overhead rates if monthly rates are used. An average, annualized rate based on the relationship of total annual overhead to total annual activity is more representative of typical relationships between total costs and volume/activity than a monthly rate. For a more detailed discussion of these issues you should refer to 'Budgeted overhead rates' in Chapter 3.

Question 15.6

(a) Raw materials:

(Units)	March	April	May	June
Opening stock	100	110	115	110
Add: Purchases	80	80	85	85
	180	190	200	195
Less: Used in production	70	75	90	90
Closing stock	110	115	110	105
(Units) *Finished production:*				
Opening stock	110	100	91	85
Add: Production	70	75	90	90
	180	175	181	175
Less: Sales	80	84	96	94
Closing stock	100	91	85	81

(b) *Sales:*

					Total
(at £219 per unit)	£17 520	£18 396	£21 024	£20 586	£77 526
Production cost:					
Raw materials (using FIFO)	3 024 (1)	3 321 (2)	4 050	4 050	14 445
Wages and variable costs	4 550	4 875	5 850	5 850	21 125
	£7 574	£8 196	£9 900	£9 900	£35 570

Debtors:
Closing debtors = May + June sales = £41 610
Creditors:
June purchases 85 units × £45   £3825

Notes:
(1) 70 units × £4320/100 units = £3024.
(2) (30 units × £4320/100 units + (45 units × £45) = £3321.

Closing stocks:
Raw materials 105 units × £45   <u>£4725</u>
Finished goods 81 units × £110⁽¹⁾ <u>£8910</u>

Note:
⁽¹⁾Materials (£45) + Labour and Variable Overhead (£65).
    It is assumed that stocks are valued on a variable costing basis.

(c) *Cash budget:*

		March (£)	April (£)	May (£)	June (£)
Balance b/fwd		6 790	4 820	5 545	132 415
Add: Receipts					
Debtors (two months' credit)		7 680	10 400	17 520	18 396
Loan		—	—	120 000	—
	(A)	<u>14 470</u>	<u>15 220</u>	<u>143 065</u>	<u>150 811</u>
Payments:					
Creditors (one month's credit)		3 900	3 600	3 600	3 825
			(80 × £45)		
Wages and variable overheads		4 550	4 875	5 850	5 850
Fixed overheads		1 200	1 200	1 200	1 200
Machinery		—	—	—	112 000
Interim dividend		—	—	—	12 500
	(B)	<u>9 650</u>	<u>9 675</u>	<u>10 650</u>	<u>135 375</u>
Balance c/fwd	(A) – (B)	<u>4 820</u>	<u>5 545</u>	<u>132 415</u>	<u>£15 436</u>

(d) *Master budget:*

Budgeted trading and profit and loss account for the four months to 30 June

	(£)	(£)
Sales		77 526
Cost of sales: Opening stock finished goods	10 450	
Add: Production cost	<u>35 570</u>	
	46 020	
Less: Closing stock finished goods	<u>8 910</u>	<u>37 110</u>
		40 416
Less: Expenses		
Fixed overheads (4 × £1200)	4 800	
Depreciation		
Machinery and equipment	15 733	
Motor vehicles	3 500	
Loan interest (2/12 × 7½% of £120 000)	<u>1 500</u>	<u>25 533</u>
		14 883
Less: Interim dividends		<u>12 500</u>
		2 383
Add: Profit and loss account balance b/fwd		<u>40 840</u>
		<u>£43 223</u>

Budgeted balance sheet as at 30 June

	Cost (£)	Depreciation to date (£)	Net (£)
Fixed assets			
Land and buildings	500 000	—	500 000
Machinery and equipment	236 000	100 233	135 767
Motor vehicles	<u>42 000</u>	<u>19 900</u>	<u>22 100</u>
	<u>778 000</u>	<u>120 133</u>	<u>657 867</u>

Current assets
Stock of raw materials		4 725
Stock of finished goods		8 910
Debtors		41 610
Cash and bank balances		15 436
		70 681

Less: Current liabilities

Creditors	3 825		
Loan interest owing	1 500	5 325	65 356
			£723 223
			(£)

Capital employed
Ordinary share capital £1 shares (fully paid)	500 000
Share premium	60 000
Profit and loss account	43 233
	603 223
Secured loan (7½%)	120 000
	£723 223

(e) See the section of cash budgets in Chapter 15 for possible ways to improve cash management.

(a) (i) *Cash budget for weeks 1–6*

Question 15.7

	Week 1 (£)	Week 2 (£)	Week 3 (£)	Week 4 (£)	Week 5 (£)	Week 6 (£)
Receipts from debtors[a]	24 000	24 000	28 200	25 800	19 800	5 400
Payments:						
To material suppliers[b]	8 000	12 500	6 000	nil	nil	nil
To direct workers[c]	3 200	4 200	2 800	nil	nil	nil
For variable overheads[d]	4 800	3 200	nil	nil	nil	nil
For fixed overhead[e]	8 300	8 300	6 800	6 800	6 800	6 800
Total payments	24 300	28 200	15 600	6 800	6 800	6 800
Net movement	(300)	(4 200)	12 600	19 000	13 000	(1 400)
Opening balance (week 1 given)	1 000	700	(3 500)	9 100	28 100	41 100
Closing balance	700	(3 500)	9 100	28 100	41 100	39 700

Notes
[a]Debtors:

	Week 1	Week 2	Week 3	Week 4	Week 5	Week 6
Units sold*	400	500	400	300	—	—
Sales (£)	24 000	30 000	24 000	18 000	—	—
Cash received (70%)		16 800	21 000	16 800	12 600	
(30%)			7 200	9 000	7 200	5 400
Given	24 000	7 200				
Total receipts (£)	24 000	24 000	28 200	25 800	19 800	5 400

*Sales in week 4 = opening stock (600 units) + production in weeks 1 and 2 (1000 units) less sales in weeks 1–3 (1300 units) = 300 units.

[b]Creditors:

	Week 1 (£)	Week 2 (£)	Week 3 (£)	Week 4	Week 5	Week 6
Materials consumed at £15	9 000	6 000	—	—	—	—
Increase in stocks	3 500	—				
Materials purchased	12 500	6 000				
Payment to suppliers (given)	8 000	12 500	6000	nil	nil	nil

^{c}Wages:

	Week 1 (£)	Week 2 (£)	Week 3 (£)	Week 4	Week 5	Week 6
Wages consumed at £7	4200	2800	nil	nil	nil	nil
Wages paid	3200 (given)	4200	2800	—	—	—

^{d}Variable overhead payment = budgeted production × budgeted cost per unit.
^{e}Fixed overhead payments for weeks 1–2 = fixed overhead per week (£9000).
less weekly depreciation (£700).
Fixed overhead payments for weeks 3–6 = £8300 normal payment less
£1500 per week.

(ii) *Comments*
1. Finance will be required to meet the cash deficit in week 2, but a lowering of the budgeted material stocks at the end of week 1 would reduce the amount of cash to be borrowed at the end of week 2.
2. The surplus cash after the end of week 2 should be invested on a short-term basis.
3. After week 6, there will be no cash receipts, but cash outflows will be £6800 per week. The closing balance of £39 700 at the end of week 6 will be sufficient to finance outflows for a further 5 or 6 weeks (£39 700/£6800 per week).

(b) The answer should include a discussion of the matching concept, emphasizing that revenues and expenses may not be attributed to the period when the associated cash inflows and outflows occur. Also, some items of expense do not affect cash outflow (e.g. depreciation).

Question 15.8

(a)
Product	V (£)	S (£)	T (£)
Contribution per unit	60	53.75	40.50
Litres of Q per unit	10	8	5
Contribution per litre of Q	6	6.72	8.10
Ranking	3	2	1

The allocation of material Q and the optimum production schedule based on the above ranking is as follows:

Product	V	S	T	Total
Minimum production (units) ^{a}	24	67	71	
Usage of Q (litres)	240	536	355	1131
Additional production		312.5^c	1353^b	
Usage of Q (litres)		2 500	6765	9265
				10 396
Production	24	379.5	1424	

Notes:
^{a} Accepted orders less stock decrease.
^{b} Maximum demand is 1450 units less stock decrease of 26 units gives a required production of 1424 units comprising of 71 units allocated to minimum production and 1353 units to additional production.
^{c} After the allocation of the minimum production and the stock decrease there are 9265 litres unused. Production of 1353 units will require 6765 litres (1353 units × 5 litres) thus leaving 2500 litres to be allocated to S. This will require 312.5 additional units of S (2500/8).

(b)

Product (units)	V	S	T
Production budget	24	379.5	1424
Add stock decrease	10	8	26
Sales	34	387.5	1450

(c) (i) *Marginal costing profit statement*

Product	V	S	T	Total
Sales (units)	34	387.5	1450	
Contribution per unit (£)	60	53.75	40.50	
Contribution (£)	2040	20 828	58 725	81 593
Less fixed overheads (£)				95 000
Loss (£)				13 407

(c) (ii) When stocks are declining, absorption costing will report a lower profit (or higher loss) compared with marginal costing due to the fixed overhead previously deferred in the stock valuation being charged as an expense against the current period. This is represented by the stock decreases for each product multiplied by the fixed overhead rate. The calculations are as follows:

$$(£)$$

V = Stock decrease of 10 units at a fixed overhead rate of £24 per unit = 240
S = Stock decrease of 8 units at a fixed overhead rate of £30 per unit   = 240
T = Stock decrease of 26 units at a fixed overhead rate of £12 per unit = 312
$$\overline{792}$$

Therefore the absorption costing loss will be £14 199 (£13 407 + £792).

For an explanation of the above issues you should refer to 'Variable costing and absorption costing: a comparison of their impact on profits' in Chapter 7.

(d) (i) Profits are based on the accruals concept to meet financial accounting reporting requirements. For example, an investment in a new asset of £100 000 involving an immediate cash payment is a cash flow but it would be recorded as a depreciation expense of £10 000 per annum (assuming a life of 10 years and no scrap value). Therefore profits are reduced by £10 000 per annum but the cash flow is £100 000.

(d) (ii) Marginal costing profits are a better indicator of cash flows because fixed overheads are recorded as an expense in the period that they are incurred whereas absorption costing includes fixed overheads in the stock valuation and records them as an expense in the period when the stocks are sold.

(a) The following points should be included in the answer:

Question 15.9

Budget preparation
A brief discussion of budget participation (see Chapter 16) and an indication that some element of participation is generally considered desirable. The lack of consultation and involvement with the departmental manager should be addressed.

Implication of the increase in volume
A fixed budget is being operated for cost control and performance evaluation but the number of visits were 12 000 compared with a budget of 10 000. For those items of expense that vary with the number of visits (such as wages, travel expenses and consumables), it is inappropriate to compare the actual costs of visiting 12 000 clients compared with a budget of 10 000 clients. The current report draws attention to this invalid comparison. There is a need to implement flexible budgets (see Chapter 16) instead of fixed budgets.

Controllability
Some of the costs in the report are not controllable by the departmental manager. Adopting the controllability principle (see Chapter 16), non-controllable costs should either be excluded from the report or shown in a separate section indicating that they are not directly controllable by the departmental manager. At present the departmental manager appears to be held accountable for expenses (e.g. allocated administrative costs) that he/she cannot directly influence.

Funding allocation
As indicated by the director it is important that the department keeps within its funding allocation to ensure that costs are controlled. For fixed expenses, such as the salary of the supervisor, managers should ensure that costs do not exceed the original (fixed) budget but for variable expenses the costs should not exceed the flexed budget for the actual level of activity. Increased expenditure should only be permitted if more funds are allocated from local or central government.

Social aspects
Social aspects generally cannot be expressed in financial terms but they must not be lost sight of in the pursuit of only those items that are incorporated in the budget. Where budget amounts are allocated to social aspects it is important that managers seek to use these funds, since underspending represents a failure to pursue objectives expressed in the budget. The main difficulty with expenses relating to social aspects is that there is not any clear input–output relationship, so it can be difficult to ascertain whether the funds are being utilized efficiently.

Other aspects
The focus of the report is entirely on financial aspects. Non-financial measures should also be incorporated such as total staff hours worked, feedback on client satisfaction on the service provided and the frequency of visits. These aspects can be vital to the success of the service and the present system does not appear to highlight them. Consideration also should be given to incorporating additional columns in the report that compare the actual against budget for the year to date so that the focus is not only on the most recent period. Also the lack of consultation and the apparent authoritarian manner in the way that the report is being used warrants attention, since this is likely to result in harmful behavioural consequences.

(b) The answer should draw off the material within the section on zero-based budgeting (ZBB), pointing out its claimed advantages. In addition, the answer should draw attention to the weaknesses of conventional budgets in the form of incremental budgets (an explanation can be found at the beginning of the section on activity-based budgeting). Finally, the problems associated with implementing ZBB should be described with an indication that for this organization it may be more appropriate to approximate the principles of ZBB using a more simplistic form of priority-based budgeting.

Question 15.10   (a) Cost driver rates:

$$W \quad \frac{£160\,000}{(20 \times 4) + (30 \times 5) + (15 \times 2) + (40 \times 3) + (25 \times 1)} = £395$$

$$X \quad \frac{£130\,000}{(20 \times 3) + (30 \times 2) + (15 \times 5) + (40 \times 1) + (25 \times 4)} = £388$$

$$Y \quad \frac{£80\,000}{(20 \times 3) + (30 \times 3) + (15 \times 2) + (40 \times 4) + (25 \times 2)} = £205$$

$$Z \quad \frac{£200\,000}{(20 \times 4) + (30 \times 6) + (15 \times 8) + (40 \times 2) + (25 \times 3)} = £374$$

Actual activities during October 2002:

W $(18 \times 4) + (33 \times 5) + (16 \times 2) + (35 \times 3) + (28 \times 1) = 402$
X $(18 \times 3) + (33 \times 2) + (16 \times 5) + (35 \times 1) + (28 \times 4) = 347$
Y $(18 \times 3) + (33 \times 3) + (16 \times 2) + (35 \times 4) + (28 \times 2) = 381$
Z $(18 \times 4) + (33 \times 6) + (16 \times 8) + (35 \times 2) + (28 \times 3) = 552$

Budget control statement

Activity	Original budget (£000)	Flexible budget (£000)	Actual costs (£000)	Variance (£000)
W	160	159 (402 × £395)	158	1F
X	130	135 (347 × £388)	139	4A
Y	80	78 (381 × £205)	73	5F
Z	200	206 (552 × £374)	206	0
	570	578	576	2F

(b) For the answer to this question see the points listed at the end of the section on the factors influencing the effectiveness of participation in Chapter 16.

(c) A fixed budget represents the original budget set at the beginning of the period based upon the planned level of activity. A flexible budget represents a budget that is adjusted to reflect what the budget would have been, based on the actual level of activity that occurred during the period. Flexible budgets are appropriate for those costs that are expected to vary with activity. Therefore actual expenditure should be compared with a flexible budget. Fixed budgets are more appropriate for controlling discretionary items of expenditure. Examples include advertising and research and development. These items do not vary with activity and there is no obvious level of optimum spending. Also the budget represents a commitment or policy decision to allocate a specific amount of funds to spend on these items. Thus underspending may be considered undesirable because it represents a failure to pursue management commitments of spending to be incurred during the budget period.

(d) y = Total cost for the period
a = Variable cost per unit of activity
b = Fixed costs for the period
x = Activity level for the period

For a more detailed explanation of the above terms you should refer to the first section in Chapter 23.

Management control systems

Solutions to Chapter 16 questions

Question 16.1

(a) See Chapter 16 for the answer to this question. In particular, your answer should stress:
  - (i) The need for a system of responsibility accounting based on a clear definition of a manager's authority and responsibility.
  - (ii) The production of performance reports at frequent intervals comparing actual and budget costs for individual expense items. Variances should be analysed according to whether they are controllable or non-controllable by the manager.
  - (iii) The managers should participate in the setting of budgets and standards.
  - (iv) The system should ensure that variances are investigated, causes found and remedial action is taken.
  - (v) An effective cost control system must not be used as a punitive device, but should be seen as a system that helps managers to control their costs more effectively.

(b) Possible problems include:
  - (i) Difficulties in setting standards for non-repetitive work.
  - (ii) Non-acceptance by budgetees if they view the system as a punitive device to judge their performance.
  - (iii) Isolating variances where interdependencies exist.

Question 16.2

(a) See 'Planning', 'Motivation' and 'Performance evaluation' in the section on the multiple functions of budgets in Chapter 15 for the answer to this question. The answer should emphasize that the role of motivation is to encourage goal congruence between the company and the employees.

(b) See 'Conflicting roles of budgets' in Chapter 15 for an explanation of how the planning and motivation roles can conflict. Prior to the commencement of the budget period, management should prepare budgets that represent targets to be achieved based upon anticipated environmental variables. It is possible that at the end of the budget period the *actual* environmental variables will be different from those envisaged when the budget was prepared. Therefore actual performance will be determined by the actual environmental variables, but the plans reflected in the budget may be based on different environmental variables. It is inappropriate to compare actual performance based on one set of environmental variables with budgeted performance based on another set of environmental variables. Consequently, a budget that is used for planning purposes will be in conflict with one that is used for performance evaluation.

   The conflict between motivation and evaluation is described by Barrett and Fraser (1977) (see Bibliography in main text) as follows:

   In many situations the budget that is most effective in the evaluation role might be called an ex-post facto budget. It is one that considers the impact of uncontrollable or unforeseeable events, and it is constructed or adjusted after the fact.
   The potential role conflict between the motivation and evaluation roles involves the impact on motivation of using an ex-post facto standard in the evaluation process. Managers are unlikely to be totally committed to achieving

the budget's objectives if they know that the performance standards by which they are to be judged may change.

In other words, for evaluation purposes the budget might be adjusted to reflect changes in environmental variables. If a manager expects that the budget will be changed for evaluation purposes, there is a danger that he or she will not be as highly motivated to achieve the original budget.

(c) (i) The planning and motivation conflict might be resolved by setting two budgets. A budget based on most likely outcomes could be set for planning purposes and a separate, more demanding budget could be used for motivation purposes.

(ii) The planning and evaluation role conflict can be resolved by comparing actual performance with an ex-post budget. See 'Ex-post variance analysis' in Chapter 18 for an illustration of how this conflict can be resolved.

(iii) Barrett and Fraser (1977) suggest the following approach for resolving the motivation and evaluation conflict:

The conflict between the motivation and evaluation roles can also be reduced by using 'adjustable budgets.' These are operational budgets whose objectives can be modified under predetermined sets of circumstances. Thus revision is possible during the operating period and the performance standard can be changed.

In one company that uses such a budgeting system, managers commit themselves to a budget with the understanding that, if there are substantial changes in any of five key economic or environmental variables, top management will revise the budget and new performance criteria will be set. This company automatically makes budget revisions whenever there are significant changes in any of these five variables. Naturally, the threshold that triggers a new budget will depend on the relative importance of each variable. With this system, managers know they are expected to meet their budgets. The budget retains its motivating characteristics because it represents objectives that are possible to achieve. Uncontrollable events are not allowed to affect budgeted objectives in such a way that they stand little chance of being met. Yet revisions that are made do not have to adversely affect commitment, since revisions are agreed to in advance and procedures for making them are structured into the overall budgeting system.

A more detailed answer to this question can be found in Barrett and Fraser (1977).

(a) The answer should include a discussion of the following points: **Question 16.3**

(i) Constant pressure from top management for greater production may result in the creation of anti-management work groups and reduced efficiency, so that budgetees can protect themselves against what they consider to be increasingly stringent targets.

(ii) Non-acceptance of budgets if the budgetees have not been allowed to participate in setting the budgets.

(iii) Negative attitudes if the budget is considered to be a punitive control device instead of a system to help managers do a better job. The negative attitudes might take the form of reducing cooperation between departments and also with the accounting department. Steps might be taken to ensure that costs do not fall below budget, so that the budget will not be reduced next year. There is a danger that data will be falsified, and more effort will be directed to finding excuses for failing to achieve the budget than trying to control or reduce costs.

(iv) Managers might try and achieve the budget at all costs even if this results in actions that are not in the best interests of the organization, e.g. delaying maintenance costs.

(v) Organizational atmosphere may become one of competition and conflict rather than one of cooperation and conciliation.

(vi) Suspicion and mistrust of top management, resulting in the whole budgeting process being undermined.

(vii) Belief that the system of evaluation is unjust and widespread worry and tension by the budgetees. Tension might be relieved by falsifying information, blaming others or absenteeism.

(b) For the answer to this question see 'Dealing with the distorting effects of uncontrollable factors before (and after) the measurement period' in Chapter 16.

Question 16.4

The answer should include a discussion of the following:

(i) The impact of targets on performance.

(ii) The use of accounting control techniques for performance evaluation.

(iii) Participation in the budgeting and standard setting process.

(iv) Bias in the budget process.

(v) Management use of budgets and the role of the accountant in the education process.

See Chapter 16 for a discussion of each of the above items.

Question 16.5

(a) See Chapter 16 for the answer to this question.

(b) For the answer to this question see 'Dealing with the distorting effects of uncontrollable factors before (and after) the measurement period', 'Participation in the budget and target setting process' and 'Side effects from using accounting information for performance evaluation' in Chapter 16.

(c) Figure 16.1 in Chapter 16 illustrates the importance of feedback (information comparing planned and actual outcomes in the control process). Feedback takes the form of control reports issued by the accountant to the managers responsible for controlling inputs. Effective control requires that corrective action be taken so that actual outputs conform to planned outputs in the future. In order to assist managers in controlling activities, the performance reports should highlight those areas that do not conform to plan. The performance reports should also provide clues as to why the actual outputs differ from the planned outputs. Feedback information is necessary to provoke corrective managerial action.

It should be noted that accounting reports of performance also have a direct effect on motivation by giving the department manager knowledge of performance. Knowledge of results has been shown in various psychological experiments to lead to improved performance. This is partly because it conveys information that can be used for acting more effectively on the next trial; but also partly because knowledge of results motivates through satisfying the achievement need. Stok (1959) investigated the effect of control systems using visual presentation of quality on workers quality performance. He found that visual presentation of quality had both an information and a motivation effect and both were instrumental in improving performance. It appears that communicating knowledge of results acts as a reward or punishment. It can serve either to reinforce or extinguish previous employee behaviours.

(d) The purpose of goal congruence is to encourage an individual manager's goals to be in agreement with the organization's goals. For a description of this process see 'Goal congruence' in Chapter 16.

Reference
Stok, T.L. (1959) *De Arbeider en de Zichbaarmaking van de Kwaliteit,* Leiden, Stenfert Kruese.

Managers may be reluctant to participate in setting budgets for the following reasons:

Question 16.6

(i) Managers may consider that they do not engage in true participation if they cannot influence the budget. They may consider the process to be one of the senior managers securing formal acceptance of previously determined target levels.

(ii) Personality of budgetees may result in authoritarian managers having authoritarian expectations of their superiors. Consequently, authoritarian budgetees may be reluctant to participate in the budget process.

(iii) The degree to which individuals have control over their own destiny (see Brownell's (1981)) appears to influence the desire for participation. Managers may believe that they cannot significantly influence results and thus consider participation to be inappropriate.

(iv) Bad management/superior relationships.

(v) Lack of understanding of the budget process or a belief by the budgetees that they will be engaging in a process that will be used in a recriminatory manner by their superiors.

The unwanted side-effects that might arise from the imposition of budgets by senior management include the following:

(i) Non-acceptance of budgets.

(ii) The budgetees might consider the method of performance evaluation to be unjust.

(iii) Creation of anti-management cohesive work groups.

(iv) Reduced efficiency by work groups so as to protect themselves against what they consider to be increasingly stringent targets.

(v) The budget system will be undermined. The real problem is the way management use the system rather than inadequacies of the budget system itself.

(vi) An increase in suspicion and mistrust, so undermining the whole budgeting process.

(vii) Encouraging budgetees to falsify and manipulate information presented to management.

(viii) Organizational atmosphere may become one of competition and conflict rather than one of cooperation and conciliation.

(ix) Managers might try to achieve the budget at all costs even if this results in actions that are not in the best interests of the organization.

Question 16.7

See 'Setting financial performance targets' in Chapter 16 for the answer to this question.

Question 16.8

(a) For the answer to this question see 'Setting financial performance targets' in Chapter 16. In particular, the answer should stress that a tight budget is preferable for motivation purposes, whereas for planning and control purposes an expected target should be set that management believes will be achieved. Consequently, a conflict occurs between the motivational and management reporting objectives.

(b) The levels of efficiency that may be incorporated in the standards used in budgetary control and/or standard costing include the following:

(i) *Perfection:* Standards based on perfection are termed 'ideal standards'. Ideal standards have no motivational advantages and are unsatisfactory for planning and control purposes.

(ii) *Tight standards:* These standards represent targets that are set at a level of performance that is difficult, but not impossible, for budgetees to achieve. Tight standards should increase aspiration levels and actual performance. Because tight standards may not be achieved, they are unsatisfactory for planning and control purposes.

(iii) *Expected performance:* Expected performance standards are based on the level of efficiency expected to be attained. One advantage of expected standards is that variances indicate deviations from management's expectations.

A further advantage is that expected standards can be used for planning purposes. Expected standards are likely to be unsatisfactory for motivational purposes, since they may not provide a challenging target.

(iv) *Loose standards:* With loose standards, the level of efficiency implied by the standard is less than expected. Loose standards are poor motivators and are unsatisfactory for planning and control purposes.

(c) See 'Participation in the budgeting and target setting process' in Chapter 16 for the answer to this question.

Question 16.9

(a) For a discussion of feedback and feedforward controls see Chapter 16. The remaining terms are also discussed in Chapter 16.

(b) For the answer to this question see 'Dealing with the distorting effects of uncontrollable factors before (and after) the measurement period', 'Participation in the budget and target setting process' and 'Side effects from using accounting information for performance evaluation' in Chapter 16.

Question 16.10

(a) For an explanation of responsibility accounting you should refer to 'The nature of management accounting control systems' in Chapter 16. Potential difficulties in operating a system of responsibility accounting include:

1 identification of specific areas of responsibility where actions can be influenced by two or more persons resulting in the problem of joint responsibility occurring. It therefore becomes difficult to ascertain which managers should be held accountable for the outcomes;

2 distinguishing between those items which managers can control and for which they should be held accountable and those items over which they have no control and for which they are not held accountable (see 'The controllability principle' in Chapter 16);

3 determining how challenging the targets should be (see 'Setting financial performance targets' in Chapter 16);

4 determining how much influence managers should have in setting financial performance targets (see 'Setting financial performance targets' in Chapter 16);

5 choosing an appropriate mix of financial and non-financial measures to be included in the performance report and seeking to avoid some of the harmful side-effects of controls (see 'Harmful side-effects of controls' in Chapter 16).

(b) See 'Feedback and feedforward controls' in Chapter 16 for the answer to this question. A diagram of feedback control is presented in Figure 16.1. This diagram can be modified to represent a feedforward control system by deleting the arrow from the output box to the regulator box. The feedforward mechanism takes place by comparing the planned inputs with the expected outcomes (the arrow from the process box to the regulator box) and taking appropriate action where plans do not meet expectations (reflected in the arrow from the regulator box to the input box).

(c) (i) The budget acts as a resource allocation device by determining the total resources available for a non-profit organization and allocating these resources within the budget process to the different programmes or activities (e.g. between spending on education, care of the elderly, or leisure provision within a municipal authority). The budget planning process specifies where and how the available funds should be spent during the current period.

(c) (ii) When the master budgets (and thus the budgets making up the master budget) have been reviewed by the appropriate top management committee, they represent the formal approval for each budget manager to carry out the plans contained in his/her budget. At the end of the appropriate budget period, actual expenditure will be compared against the budget authorization. For example, a school may be allocated with a budgeted sum to spend on part-time teaching staff. At the end of the period actual spending will be compared against the budget and the head will be held accountable for any difference.

(c) (iii) For the answer to this question see 'Control' within the section on multiple functions of budgets in Chapter 15. An example of the control process is provided in 'Line item budgets' within the section on the budgeting process in non-profit-making organizations in Chapter 15.

Question 16.11

(a) The desirable attributes of a suitable measure of activity for flexing the budget are as follows:
   (i) The selected measure should exert a major influence on the cost of the activity. The objective is to flex the budget to ascertain the costs that should be incurred for the actual level of activity. Therefore the costs of the activity and the measure selected should be highly correlated.
   (ii) The measure selected should not be affected by factors other than volume. For example, if direct labour cost is selected as the activity measure then an increase in wage rates will cause labour cost to increase even when activity remains constant.
   (iii) The measure should be easily understood. Complicated indexes are unlikely to be satisfactory.
   (iv) The measure should be easily obtainable without too much cost.
   (v) The measure should be based on output rather than input in order to ensure that managers do not obtain larger budget allowances for being inefficient.

(b) Because the activities of a service or overhead department tend not to be repetitive, it is unlikely that a system of standard costing can be justified. Output will be fairly diverse, and it may not be possible to find a single output measure that is highly correlated with costs. It might be necessary to flex the budget on inputs rather than outputs. Also, several variables are likely to cause changes in cost rather than a single measure of output, and an accurate flexible budget may require the use of multiple regression techniques. However, because multiple regression measures might not be easily obtainable and understood, a single input measure may be preferable.

   It may be necessary to use several measures of activity within a cost centre for the different costs. For example, machine maintenance costs might be flexed according to machine hours, and lighting and heating costs might be flexed according to labour hours of input.

(c) Suitable measures include the following:
   (i) *Standard hours of output:* This measure is suitable when output is sufficiently standardized to enable standard labour times to be established for each activity. It is unsatisfactory where labour efficiency is unlikely to be constant or output is too diverse to enable standard time to be established.
   (ii) *Direct labour hours of input:* This measure is suitable where costs are highly correlated with labour hours of input, output cannot be measured in standard hours and labour efficiency is fairly constant. It is unsatisfactory if these conditions do not hold, because labour hours will be an unsatisfactory guide to output.
   (iii) *Direct labour costs:* This measure is suitable where the same conditions apply as those specified in (ii) and the wage rates are not consistently changing. If these conditions do not apply then it will be unsatisfactory.

Question 16.12

(a) See 'Setting financial performance targets' in Chapter 16 for the answer to this question.

(b) See 'Participation in the budgeting and target setting process' in Chapter 16 for the answer to this question.

(c) Management by exception is based on the principle that accounting reports should highlight those activities that do not conform to plans, so that managers can devote their scarce time to focusing on these items. Effective control requires that corrective action be taken so that actual outcomes conform to planned outcomes. These principles are based on the following assumptions:

(i) Valid targets and budgets can be set.

(ii) Suitable performance measures exist that enable divergencies from plans to be correctly measured.

(iii) Plans and divergencies from plan are communicated to the individuals who are responsible for implementing the plan.

(iv) Performance reports correctly distinguish those items that are controllable by a manager from those that are non-controllable.

(v) Feedback information is translated into corrective action.

(vi) Management intervention is not required where no adverse variances exist.

(vii) Divergencies from plan can only be remedied by corrective action.

Management by exception as an effective system of routine reporting will depend on the extent to which the above conditions hold. The system will have to be supplemented by informal controls to the extent that the above conditions do not hold. Management by exception can only be a very effective means of control if behavioural factors are taken into account when interpreting the divergencies from plan. Otherwise there is a danger that other systems of control will have a greater influence on future performance.

(d) The answer should include the following:

(i) An explanation of why it is considered necessary to distinguish between controllable and uncontrollable costs at the responsibility level.

(ii) Difficulty in assigning variances to responsibility centres when dual responsibilities apply or interdependencies exist.

(iii) Possible dysfunctional consequences that might occur when a manager's performance is measured by his or her success in controlling only those items that have been designated as controllable by him or her.

(iv) Arguments for including those uncontrollable items that a manager might be able to influence in a separate section of the performance report.

The above items are discussed in 'The controllability principle' in Chapter 16.

(e) Budget statements should not be expressed only in monetary terms. This is because all aspects of performance relating to a firm's goals cannot be expressed in monetary terms. Therefore budgetary statements should be supplemented by non-monetary measures. Monetary gains can be made at the expense of items that cannot easily be measured in monetary terms but that may be critical to an organization's long-term profitability. For example, monetary gains can be made by hierarchical pressure to cut costs, but such gains might be at the expense of adverse motivational changes, increased labour turnover and reduced product quality. The long-term costs of these items might be far in excess of the cost-cutting benefits.

A range of non-monetary measures is presented in the balanced scorecard (see Chapter 22). Some qualitative variables (e.g. measurement of attitudes) are difficult to measure, but judgements based on interviews can be made. The inclusion of behavioural and qualitative factors in budget statements more accurately reflects the complexity of managerial performance in relation to a number of objectives rather than a single monetary objective. The difficulty with incorporating qualitative variables into budget statements is not sufficient grounds for expressing budget statements only in monetary terms.

Task 1
Reclamation Division Performance Report – 4 weeks to 31 May:
Original budget   250 tonnes
Actual output   200 tonnes

	Budget based on 200 tonnes	Actual	Variance	Comments
Controllable expenses:				
Wages and social security costs[a]	43 936	46 133	2197A	
Fuel[b]	15 000	15 500	500A	
Consumables[c]	2 000	2 100	100A	
Power[d]	1 500	1 590	90A	
Directly attributable overheads[e]	20 000	21 000	1000A	
	82 436	86 323	3887A	
Non-controllable expenses:				
Plant maintenance[e]	5 950	6 900	950A	
Central services[e]	6 850	7 300	450A	
	12 800	14 200	1400A	
Total	95 236	100 523	5287A	

Notes:
[a] 6 employees × 4 teams × 42 hours per week × £7.50 per hour × 4 weeks = £30 240.
[b] 200 tonnes × £75
[c] 200 tonnes × £10
[d] £500 + (£5 × 200) = £1500
[e] It is assumed that directly attributable expenses, plant maintenance and central services are non-variable expenses.

Task 2
(a)   (i)   Past knowledge can provide useful information on future outcomes but ideally budgets ought to be based on the most up-to-date information. Budgeting should be related to the current environment and the use of past information that is two years old can only be justified where the operating conditions and environment are expected to remain unchanged.
      (ii) For motivation and planning purposes budgets should represent targets based on what we are proposing to do. For control purposes budgets should be flexed based on what was actually done so that actual costs for actual output can be compared with budgeted costs for the actual output. This ensures that valid comparisons will be made.
      (iii) For variable expenses the original budget should be reduced in proportion to reduced output in order to reflect cost behaviour. Fixed costs are not adjusted since they are unaffected in the short-term by output changes. Flexible budgeting ensures that like is being compared with like so that reduced output does not increase the probability that favourable cost variances will be reported. However, if less was produced because of actual sales being less than budget this will result in an adverse sales variance and possibly an adverse profit variance.
      (iv) Plant maintenance costs are apportioned on the basis of capital values and therefore newer equipment (with higher written-down values) will be charged with a higher maintenance cost. Such an approach does not provide a meaningful estimate of maintenance resources consumed by departments since older equipment is likely to be more expensive to maintain. The method of recharging should be reviewed and ideally based on estimated usage according to maintenance records. The charging of the overspending by the maintenance

department to user departments is questionable since this masks inefficiencies. Ideally, maintenance department costs should be recharged based on actual usage at budgeted cost and the maintenance department made accountable for the adverse spending (price) variance.

(v) The comments do not explain the causes of the variances and are presented in a negative tone. No comments are made, nor is any praise given, for the favourable variances.

(vi) Not all variances should be investigated. The decision to investigate should depend on both their absolute and relative size and the likely benefits arising from an investigation.

(vii) Central service costs are not controllable by divisional managers. However, even though the divisional manager cannot control these costs there is an argument for including them as non-controllable costs in the performance report. The justification for this is that divisional managers are made aware of central service costs and may put pressure on central service staff to control such costs more effectively. It should be made clear to divisional managers that they are not accountable for any non-controllable expenses that are included in their performance reports.

Question 16.14

Task 1

(a)

	Quarter 1 units	Quarter 2 units	Quarter 3 units	Quarter 4 units
Actual sales volume	420 000	450 000	475 000	475 000
Seasonal variation	+25 000	+15 000	—	240 000
Deseasonalized sales volumes	395 000	435 000	475 000	515 000

(b) The trend is for sales volume to increase by 40 000 units each quarter:

Forecast for next year	Quarter 1 units	Quarter 2 units	Quarter 3 units	Quarter 4 units
Trend projection	555 000	595 000	635 000	675 000
Seasonal variation	+25 000	+15 000	—	−40 000
Forecast sales volumes	580 000	610 000	635 000	635 000

Task 2

(a) Seasonal variations represent consistent patterns in sales volume that occur throughout each year. For example, the seasonal variation of +25 000 for Quarter 1 indicates that sales volume in the first quarter tends to be 25 000 units higher than the underlying trend in sales. In contrast, the seasonal variation of −40 000 in Quarter 4 indicates that sales in this quarter tend to be 40 000 units lower than the underlying trend in sales.

To derive the deseasonalized data the seasonal variations must be removed so that a trend can be observed. The above figures indicate an increase of 40 000 units per quarter. This trend is concealed when the actual data is observed because of the distorting effects of seasonal variations. Observations of the actual data suggests that the rate of increase in sales is declining.

(b) Provided that the observed trend in deseasonalized data continues the deseasonalized data can be used to project the trend in future sales. The trend values are adjusted by seasonal variations in each quarter to predict actual sales.

Task 3

(a) A fixed budget is a budget for the planned level of activity and budgeted costs are not adjusted to the actual level of activity. A fixed budget is used at the planning stage because an activity level has to be initially determined so that all department activities can be coordinated to meet the planned level of activity. However, it is most unlikely that actual activity will be the same as the planned level of activity. For example, if the actual level of activity is greater than budgeted level of activity then those costs that vary with the level of activity will be greater than the budgeted costs purely because of changes in activity. It is clearly inappropriate for variable costs to compare actual costs at one level of activity with budgeted costs at another level of activity. The original fixed budget must be adjusted to reflect the budgeted expenditure at the actual level of activity. This procedure is called flexible budgeting. The resulting comparison of actual costs with a flexible budget is more meaningful for cost control because the effect of the change in the activity level has been eliminated.

(b) Possible activity indicators include number of deliveries made, miles travelled and journeys made.

(c) See 'Flexible budgets' in Chapter 16 for the answer to this question.

Task 4

(a) Production budget for product Q

	(units)
Forecast sales for year	18 135
Increase in stock (15% × 1200)	180
Finished units required	18 315
Quality control loss (1/99)	185
Total units input to production	18 500

(b) Direct labour budget for product Q

	(hours)
Active labour hours required (18 500 × 5)	92 500
Idle time allowance (7.5/92.5)	7 500
Total hours to be paid for	100 000
Standard hourly rate	£6
Budgeted labour cost	£600 000

(c) Material usage budget for material M

	(kg)
Material required for processing 18 500 units (× 9 kg)	166 500
Wastage (10/90)	18 500
Material usage for year	185 000

(d) Material purchases budget for material M

	(kg)
Material required for production input	185 000
Increase in material stocks (12%)	960
Expected loss in stores	1 000
Material purchases required	186 960

Task 5

The implications of the shortage is that the budget plans cannot be achieved and the availability of material is the limiting factor. If the limiting factor cannot be removed the materials purchase budget should be the first budget to be prepared and all the other budgets coordinated to ensure the most efficient usage of materials. The following four possible actions could be taken to overcome the problem:

(i) Seek alternative supplies for material M. Possible problems include the reliability and quality of materials delivered by new suppliers. New suppliers should be carefully vetted prior to entering into any contracts or making company plans dependent on deliveries from new suppliers.

(ii) Reduce the budgeted sales of product Q. This will lead to loss in profits and the possible permanent loss of customers to competitors if the competitors are able to meet customer demand.

(iii) Reduce the stock levels for product Q and material M. The danger with this course of action is that stocks may not be available when required which could lead to disruptions in production and lost sales.

(iv) Reduce the wastage of material M and the defective output of product Q. This course of action will cause problems if quality standards are reduced resulting in inferior quality output. This could have a harmful effect on future sales. Problems will not be caused if quality standards are maintained and improved working practices result in a reduction of waste and defective output.

Question 16.15

Task 1 (a)

Calculation of unit variable costs

	Original budget	Revised budget	Difference	Variable unit cost[a]
Units	24 000	20 000	4 000	
Variable costs				
Material	216 000	180 000	£36 000	£9
Labour	288 000	240 000	£48 000	£12
Semi-variable costs				
Heat, light and power	31 000	27 000	£4 000	£1
Analysis of heat, light and power				
Variable cost	£24 000	£20 000		
Total cost	£31 000	£27 000		
Fixed cost	£7 000	£7 000		

Note

[a]Unit variable cost = change in total cost/change in volume

Task 1 (b)

Rivermede Ltd – flexible budget statement for the year ended 31 May

	Revised budget	Actual results		Variance
Production and sales (units)	22 000	22 000		
Variable costs	(£)	(£)		(£)
Material 22 000 × £9	198 000	214 320	(£206 800 + £7520)	6320 (A)
Labour 22 000 × £12	264 000	255 200		8800 (F)
Semi-variable cost				
Heat, light and power				
(22 000 × £1) + £7000	29 000	25 880	(£33 400 − £7520)	3120 (F)
Fixed costs				
Rent, rates and depreciation	40 000	38 000		2000 (F)
	531 000	533 400		2400 (A)

Task 2 (a)

The original statement compares the actual cost of producing 22 000 units with a budget for 20 000 units. This is not comparing like with like. The flexible budget shows what budgeted costs would have been for the actual production level of 22 000 units. Because actual production was greater than budgeted production of 20 000 units variable costs are likely to be higher and this comparison will result in an adverse effect on variable cost variances. The fact that overall variances are smaller when comparisons are made with the flexible budget is due to flexing the budget and not to participative budgeting.

Task 2 (b)
The report should indicate that favourable variances may have arisen for the following reasons:
- (i) Controllable factors due to the more efficient usage of direct labour and heating, light and power.
- (ii) Budget participation may have resulted in the creation of slack through an overstatement of budgeted costs.
- (iii) Uncontrollable factors such as a reduction in the prices charged to Rivermede for rent and rates.

Task 2 (c)
The report should include the following items:
- (i) The increased sales may have been due to a general increase in demand rather than the effort of the salesforce.
- (ii) The original budget of 24 000 units may have been over-estimated or the revised budget of 20 000 units may have been understated due to the sales director creating slack by deliberately understating demand.

Question 16.16

Task 1 (a)
For 2001 x takes on a value of 9.
Therefore annual demand $(y) = 640 + (40 \times 9) = 1000$
weekly demand $= 1\,000/25 = 40$ holidays

Task 1 (b)
Weaknesses of the least squares regression formula include:
- (i) The formula assumes a linear relationship based on time but demand for holidays may not be a linear function of time.
- (ii) Seasonal variations are ignored. Demand may vary throughout the holiday season with some holiday weeks being more popular than others.
- (iii) It ignores changes in holidaymakers' tastes such as a change in demand from short haul to long haul or 10-day holidays to short-break holidays.
- (iv) Cyclical fluctuations are ignored. Demand for holidays is likely to vary depending on the state of the economy, such as boom or recession.

Linear regression is covered in Chapter 23.

Task 2 (a)

Revised cost statement 10 days ended 27 November

Flexed budget	Note	Budget (£)	Actual (£)	Variance (£)
Aircraft seats	1	18 000	18 600	600 A
Coach hire		5 000	4 700	300 F
Hotel rooms	2	14 300	14 200	100 F
Meals	3	4 560	4 600	40 A
Tour guide		1 800	1 700	100 F
Advertising		2 000	1 800	200 F
		45 660	45 600	60 F

Notes
1. £450 × 40 because purchases are in blocks of 20 seats
2. £70 × 10 days × 34 tourists × 0.5 £11 900
   £60 × 10 days × 4 tourists   £2 400
                                      £14 300

3. £12 × 10 days × 38 tourists

Task 2 (b)

The original budget is a fixed budget based on the anticipated demand when the budget was set. If actual demand is different from anticipated demand a fixed budget is inappropriate for control purposes because it does not ensure that like is compared with like. See the answer to Question 16.15 for an explanation of this point. The revised flexible budget shows what costs should have been for the volume of passengers taken on the holiday. This ensures that a more meaningful comparison of budget and actual costs is made.

Task 2 (c)

The factors to be taken into account in deciding whether or not to investigate individual variances is examined in Chapter 18. The following factors should be considered:

    (i) the absolute amount of the variance;

   (ii) the relative amount of the variance expressed as a percentage of budgeted costs;

  (iii) the trend in variances by examining the cumulative variances for the period;

  (iv) whether or not the variance is controllable;

   (v) the cost and benefits from investigating the variance.

For a more detailed discussion of the above points you should refer to Chapter 18.

Standard costing and variance analysis 1

Solutions to Chapter 17 questions

See 'Purposes of standard costing' in Chapter 17 for the answer to this question. **Question 17.1**
Additional purposes that could be added include monitoring variances through time
to ascertain the need to change the targets or changing the standard to assist in the
implementation of a continuous improvement philosophy.

(a) An explanation of the different uses of standard costing is provided in 'Purposes **Question 17.2**
of standard costing' in Chapter 17. Once standards have been set they cannot be
assumed to be valid targets over long periods of time. They should periodically be
reviewed to enable the benefits of standard costing to continue. In this respect,
standards must change with the changing practices of an organization. Some
organizations adopt a continuous improvement philosophy which reflects
improvement in methods and more efficient usage of resources. Under these
circumstances, standards need to be changed to reflect the planned improvements.
The various purposes for which standards are used will be undermined if they are
not continually reviewed. Staff will also pay little attention to standards if they do
not reflect the current circumstances.

(b) An organization may have non-financial objectives relating to:
- the welfare of employees (e.g. health and safety, the provision of adequate
  social facilities);
- the environment (e.g. avoiding pollution);
- customer satisfaction (e.g. product/service quality, reliability, on-time delivery
  and a high quality after-sales service);
- support for community services;
- meeting statutory and regulatory requirements.

Various stakeholders have a non-financial interest in organizations. They include
employees, customers, suppliers, competitors, government, regulatory authorities,
tax authorities and special interest groups (e.g. environmental protection groups).

(a) Material price $\quad = (SP - AP)AQ = (AQ \times SP) - (AQ \times AP)$
$\qquad\qquad\qquad\quad = (37\ 250\ kg \times £10) - £345\ 000 = £27\ 500F$ **Question 17.3**
Material usage $\quad = (SQ - AQ)SP = (11\ 500 \times 3\ kg = 34\ 500\ kg - 37\ 250)£10$
$\qquad\qquad\qquad\quad = £27\ 500A$
Wage rate $\qquad\quad = (SP - AP)AH = (AH \times SP) - (AH \times AP)$
$\qquad\qquad\qquad\quad = (45\ 350 \times £6 = £272\ 100) - £300\ 000 = £27\ 900A$
Labour efficiency $\ = (SH - AH)SP = (11\ 500 \times 4\ hours = 46\ 000\ hours -$
$\qquad\qquad\qquad\quad 45\ 350\ hours) \times £6 = £3900F$

Reconciliation of original budget cost with actual cost

	(£)
Original budgeted total prime cost (12 000 × (£30 +£24))	648 000
Volume prime cost variance (500 units × £54) [a]	(27 000)
Flexed budget (11 500 units × £54)	621 000
Material price variance	27 500
Material usage variance	(27 500)
Wage rate variance	(27 900)
Labour efficiency variance	3 900
Actual prime cost	645 000

Note

[a] Normally cost variances are reconciled with the flexed budget. To reflect the fact that the question requires reconciliation with the original budget, a volume variance must be extracted representing the standard prime cost of the difference between actual and budgeted production.

(b) The wage rate variance indicates that labour was paid a higher rate than the planned rate whereas the labour efficiency indicates that labour was more efficient than the standard, resulting in less hours than those specified in the standard being required for actual production. The increase in wage rate may have increased motivation and thus labour efficiency.

Question 17.4

a) *Standard cost of output produced (18 000 units)*

	(£)
Direct materials	864 000
Direct labour	630 000
Variable production overhead	180 000
Fixed production overhead	900 000
	2 574 000

(b)

	Standard cost of output (£)	Variances (£)	Actual cost (£)
Direct materials	864 000		
Price variance[a]		76 000 (F)	
Usage variance[b]		48 000 (A)	
Actual cost			836 000
Direct labour	630 000		
Rate variance[c]		16 800 (A)	
Efficiency variance[d]		42 000 (F)	
Actual cost			604 800
Variable production overhead	180 000		
Expenditure variance[e]		4 000 (A)	
Efficiency variance[f]		12 000 (F)	
Actual cost			172 000
Fixed production overhead	900 000		
Expenditure variance[g]		30 000 (A)	
Volume variance[h]		100 000 (A)	
Actual cost			1 030 000
	2 574 000	68 800 (A)	2 642 800

Notes

a (Standard price − Actual price) × Actual quantity
(£12 − £836 000/76 000) × 76 000 = £76 000 (F)

b (Standard quantity − Actual quantity) × Standard price
(18 000 × 4 kg = 72 000 − 76 000) × £12 = £48 000 (A)

c (Standard rate − Actual rate) × Actual hours
(£7 − £604 800/84 000) × 84 000 = £16 800 (A)

d (Standard hours − Actual hours) × Standard rate
(18 000 × 5 hrs = 90 000 − 84 000) × £7 = £42 000 (F)

e (Actual hours × Standard rate) − Actual cost
(84 000 × £2) = £168 000 − £172 000 = £4000 (A)

f (Standard hours − Actual hours) × Standard rate
(18 000 × 5 hrs = 90 000 − 84 000) × £2 = £12 000 (F)

g Budgeted fixed overheads − Actual fixed overheads
(20 000 × £50 = £1 000 000 − £1 030 000) = £30 000 (A)

h (Actual output − Budgeted output) × Standard rate
(18 000 − 20 000) × £50 = £100 000 (A)

(c) The statement in (b) can be used to provide a detailed explanation as to why actual cost exceeded standard cost by £68 800 for the output achieved. The statement provides attention-directing information by highlighting those areas that require further investigation. Thus management can concentrate their scarce time on focusing on those areas that are not proceeding according to plan. By investigating variances, management can pinpoint inefficiencies and take steps to avoid them re-occurring. Alternatively, the investigation may indicate that the current standards are inappropriate and need changing to take account of the changed circumstances. This may result in an alteration in the plans or more up-to-date information for decision-making.

(a) Budgeted contribution = Standard unit contribution (£1.99 − £1.39 = £0.60) × **Question 17.5**
50 000 = £30 000
Actual contribution = £96 480 − (£58 450 + £6800 + £3250) = £27 980

(b) Sales margin price = (Actual price − Standard price) × Actual sales volume
= Actual sales (£96 480) − Actual sales volume (49 700) × Standard price (£1.99)
= £2423A (note that the same answer would be obtained using contribution margins in the above formula)

Sales margin volume = (Actual volume − Budgeted volume) × Standard unit contribution
= (49 700 − 50 000) × £0.60 = £180A

Ingredients price = (SP − AP)AQ = (AQ × SP) − (AQ × AP)
= (55 000 × £1.18/1.08 = £60 093) − £58 450 = £1643F

Ingredients usage = (SQ − AQ)SP = (49 700 × 1.08 = 53 676 − 55 000)
£1.18/1.08 = £1447A

Wage rate = (SP − AP)AH = (AH × SP) − (AH × AP)
= (1200 × £6 [1] = £7200) − £6800 = £400F

Labour efficiency = (SH − AH)SP = (49 700 × 1.5 minutes = 1242.5 hours
−1200hours) × £6 = £255F

Variable conversion price = (SP − AP)AH = (AH × SP) − (AH × AP)
= 1200 × £2.40 [2] = £2880 − £3250 = £370A

Variable conversion efficiency = (SH − AH)SP = (49 700 × 1.5 minutes =
(1242.5 hours −1200 hours) × £2.40 = £102F

Notes
[1] Actual price paid for labour = £0.15/1.5 minutes = £0.10 per minute = £6 per hour
[2] Actual variable overhead price = £0.06/1.5 minutes = £0.04 per minute = £2.40 per hour

Reconciliation statement

		(£)
Budgeted contribution		30 000
Sales volume contribution variance		180 (A)
Standard contribution on actual sales		29 820
Sales price variance		2423 (A)
		27 397

Cost variances		A	F
Ingredients:	Price		1643
	Usage	1447	
Labour	Rate		400
	Efficiency		255
Conversion cost	Expenditure	370	
	Efficiency		102
Total		1817	2400	583 (F)
Actual contribution				27 980

(c) The answer should point out that in any environment fixed overhead volume variances are not particularly helpful for cost control (see 'Volume variance' in Chapter 17 for an explanation of this point). Therefore, a marginal costing variance analysis approach is preferable for most types of environment.

Question 17.6

(a) Because a JIT system is used and production is made to order it is assumed that production equals sales. The difference between marginal and absorption costing sales volume variances is that the former is valued at contribution margins and the latter at profit margins. Thus the difference in margins is due to fixed overheads being assigned to products with the absorption costing system. The budgeted fixed overhead per unit for each product is derived from dividing the difference between marginal costing and absorption costing sales volume variances by the difference between budgeted and actual production.

Alpha = (£24 000 − £18 000)/600 units = £10 per unit
Beta = (£14 175 − £11 925)/300 units = £7.50

Budgeted fixed overheads = Budgeted production × budgeted fixed overhead rate

Alpha = 2400 × £10 = £24 000
Beta = 1800 × £7.50 = £13 500
£37 500

(b) Alpha variable cost = £40 so budgeted selling price = £80 (£40 + £40 × 100%)
Beta variable cost = £47.25 so budgeted selling price = £94.50 (£47.25 + £47.25 × 100%)

Budgeted profit

	(£)
Alpha contribution (2400 × (£80 − £40))	96 000
Beta contribution (1800 × (£94.50 − £47.25))	85 050
Budgeted contribution	181 050
Less fixed overheads	37 500
Budgeted profit	143 550

(c) The £6000 adverse selling price variance is derived from multiplying the difference between the actual selling price and the budgeted price by the actual quantity. In other words, the price variance per unit is derived from dividing the total price variance by the actual sales volume. Therefore the Alpha price variance is £2 per unit adverse (£6000A/3000 units) and Beta is £3 favourable (£4500F/1500units).

Actual profit calculation

	(£)
Sales (Alpha 3000 units at (£80 – £2))	234 000
(Beta 1500 units at (£94.50 + £3))	146 250
Total sales	380 250
Actual costs	277 780
Actual profit	102 470

(d) The labour, material and variable overhead variances have been computed using the same approaches as applied to questions 17.3–17.5. Therefore the variance formulae are not repeated here. For the formulae used to calculate the fixed overhead volume efficiency and capacity variances, you should refer to Chapter 17.

Price/expenditure variances

		(£)	
Direct material:			
X	(10 150 × £5) – £48 890	1860	(F)
Y	(5290 × £8) – £44 760	2440	(A)
Z	(2790 × £10) – £29 850	1950	(A)
Direct labour:	(9140 × £7) – £67 980	4000	(A)
Variable overhead:	(8350 × £1.50) – £14 300	1775	(A)
Fixed overhead:	£37 500 – £72 000	34 500	(A)

Usage/efficiency variances

	(£)		
Direct material:			
X	{[(2 × 3000) + (2.5 × 1500)] – 10 150} @£5	2000	(A)
Y	{[(1 × 3000) + (1.5 × 1500)] – 5290} @£8	320	(A)
Z	{[(0.5 × 3000) + (1 × 1500)] – 2790} @£10	2100	(F)
Direct labour:	Idle time (9140 – 8350) @£7	5530	(A)
	Efficiency{[(2 × 3000) +(1.5 × 1500)] – 8350} @£7	700	(A)
Variable overhead:	{[(2 × 3000) + (1.5 × 1500)] – 8350} @£1.50	150	(A)
Fixed overhead efficiency:	{[(2 × 3000) + (1.5 × 1500)] – 8350} @£5	500	(A)
Fixed overhead capacity:	{[(2 × 2400) + (1.5 × 1800)] – 8350} @£5	4250	(A)

Reconcilliation statement for October 2002

	(£)	(£)	(£)	
Budgeted profit			143 550	
Sales volume variance			6075	(F)
Standard profit on actual sales			149 625	
Selling price variance			1500	(A)
			148 125	
Cost variances:	(A)	(F)		
Price/expenditure:				
Material X		1860		
Material Y	2440			
Material Z	1950			
Direct labour	4000			
Variable overhead	1775			
Fixed overhead	34 500			

Usage/efficiency:

Material X	2000	
Material Y	320	
Material Z		2100
Labour idle time	5530	
Labour efficiency	700	
Variable overhead	150	
Fixed overhead:		
Efficiency	500	
Capacity		4250
Total	53 865	8210	45 655 (A)
Actual profit			102 470

(e) Mix and yield variances are appropriate to only those processes where managers have the discretion to vary the mix of materials and deviate from engineered input–output relationships. In this question the materials input consists of metres, litres and kilogrammes which suggests that they are likely to be different and cannot be mixed. Managerial discretion to mix the material is more likely to occur where all of the materials are of a similar type, such as litres of different types of liquids. In addition, yield variances are more likely to be applicable where there is a loss inherent in the process, but managers can influence this loss by a more effective mix or usage of the materials input.

Question 17.7

(a) Wage rate variance $= (SP - AP)AH = (SP \times AH) - (AP \times AH)$
$= (£5 \times 53 \text{ workers} \times 13 \text{ weeks} \times 40 \text{ hrs}) - £138\,500$
$= £700A$

Labour efficiency $= (SH - AH)SP$
SH (Standard hours) $= (35\,000 \times 0.4 \text{ hrs}) + (25\,000 \times 0.56 \text{ hrs})$
$= 28\,000$
AH (Actual hours) $= 53 \text{ workers} \times 13 \text{ weeks} \times 40 \text{ hrs} = 27\,560$
Variance $= (28\,000 - 27\,560) \times £5 = £2200A$

(b) Material price variance $= (SP - AP)AQ$
$= (AQ \times SP) - (AQ \times AP)$
£430F (given) $= 47\,000\,SP - £85\,110$
SP (Standard price) $= \dfrac{£430 + 85\,110}{47\,000}$
$= £1.82$

Material usage variance $= (SQ - AQ)SP$
$= (SQ \times SP) - (AQ \times SP)$
£320.32A (given) $= £1.82\,SQ - (33\,426 \times £1.82)$
$- £320.32A$ $= £1.82\,SQ - £60\,835.32$
£1.82 SQ $= £60\,515$
SQ $= £60\,515/£1.82 = 33\,250$
Note that SQ $=$ Actual production (35 000 units) $\times$ Standard usage
Therefore 35 000 $\times$ Standard usage $= 33\,250$
Standard usage $= 33\,250/35\,000$
$= 0.95$ kg per unit of component X

(c) For the answer to this question you should refer to the detailed illustration of the budget process shown in Chapter 15. In particular, the answer should indicate that if sales are the limiting factor the production budget should be linked to the sales budget. Once the production budget has been established for the two components, the production quantity of each component multiplied by the standard usage of material A per unit of component output determines the required quantity of material to meet the production requirements. The budgeted purchase quantity of material A consists of the quantity to meet the production usage requirements plus or minus an adjustment to take account of any planned change in the level of raw material stock.

Question 17.8

(a) *Standard product cost for one unit of product XY*

	(£)
Direct materials (8 kg (W2) at £1.50 (W1) per kg)	12.00
Direct wages (2 hours (W4) at £4 (W3) per hour)	8.00
Variable overhead (2 hours (W4) at £1 (W5) per hour)	2.00
	22.00

Workings

(W1) Actual quantity of materials purchased at standard price is £225 000 (actual cost plus favourable material price variance).
Therefore standard price = £1.50 (£225 000/150 000 kg).

(W2) Material usage variance = 6000 kg (£9000/£1.50 standard price).
Therefore standard quantity for actual production = 144 000 kg (150 000 – 6000 kg).
Therefore standard quantity per unit = 8 kg (144 000 kg/18 000 units).

(W3) Actual hours worked at standard rate = £128 000 (£136 000 – £8000).
Therefore standard rate per hour = £4 (£128 000/32 000 hours).

(W4) Labour efficiency variance = 4000 hours (£16 000/£4).
Therefore standard hours for actual production = 36 000 hours (32 000 + 4000).
Therefore standard hours per unit = 2 hours (36 000 hours/18 000 units).

(W5) Actual hours worked at the standard variable overhead rate is £32 000 (£38 000 actual variable overheads less £6000 favourable expenditure variance).
Therefore, standard variable overhead rate = £1 (£32 000/32 000 hours).

(b) See 'Types of cost standards' in Chapter 17 for the answer to this question.

Question 17.9

(a) (i) *Sales margin volume variance (Marginal costing):*
(Actual volume − Budgeted volume) × Standard contribution margin per unit
(9500 − 10 000) × Standard margin (SM) = £7500A
500 SM = 7500
Standard margin = £15

(ii) *Sales margin volume variance (Absorption costing):*
(Actual volume − Budgeted volume) × Standard profit margin per unit
(9500 − 10 000) × Standard margin (SM) = £4500A
500 SM = £4500
Standard profit margin per unit = £9

(iii) *Fixed overhead volume variance:*
(Actual production − Budgeted production) × Standard rate
(9700 − 10 000) × Standard rate = £1800A
Standard fixed overhead rate per unit = £6
Budgeted fixed overheads = 10 000 units × £6 = £60 000
Fixed overhead expenditure variance = £2500F
Actual fixed overheads (£60 000 − £2500) = £57 500

(b) Absorption costing unitizes fixed overheads and treats them as product costs whereas marginal costing does not charge fixed overheads to products. Instead, the total amount of fixed overheads is charged as an expense (period cost) for the period. A fixed overhead volume variance only occurs with an absorption costing system. Because marginal costing does not unitize fixed costs product margins are expressed as contribution margins whereas absorption costing expresses margins as profit margins. For a more detailed answer you should refer to the section on standard absorption costing in Chapter 17.

(c) See the section on volume variance in Chapter 17 for the answer to this question.

(d) See an illustration of ABC and traditional product costing systems in Chapter 10 and the section on activity-based cost management in Chapter 21 for the answer to this question.

Question 17.10   (a) (i)

$$\text{Production volume ratio} = \frac{\text{Standard hours of actual output}}{\text{Budgeted hours of output}} \times 100$$

$$= \frac{(400 \times 5) + (300 \times 2.5) + (140 \times 1)}{(400 \times 5) + (400 \times 2.5) + (100 \times 1)} \times 100 = 93.2\%$$

$$\text{Production efficiency ratio} = \frac{\text{Standard hours of output}}{\text{Actual hours worked}} \times 100$$

$$= \frac{(400 \times 5) + (300 \times 2.5) + (140 \times 1)}{2800 \text{ hrs}} \times 100 = 103.2\%$$

(ii) The production volume ratio shows the relationship between the actual output and budgeted output (both measured in standard hours). Therefore the ratio shows the extent to which the budgeted output was met. The fixed overhead volume variance represents the monetary measure equivalent of the production volume ratio.

The production efficiency ratio represents a labour efficiency measure. During the period 2890 hours of output were produced but only 2800 hours were used thus resulting in an efficiency level in excess of 100%. The monetary equivalent variances of this ratio are the labour efficiency, volume efficiency and variable overhead efficiency variances.

(b) Practical capacity is the level of capacity at which a department can normally be expected to operate. It includes an allowance for unavoidable losses in capacity arising from such factors as planned machine maintenance and set-ups.

Budgeted capacity represents the capacity level which is planned to meet the budgeted output for the period. It is based on the budgeted level of efficiency for the period.

Full capacity represents the level of output that could be achieved without any losses or inefficiencies occurring.

Standard costing and variance analysis 2: further aspects

Solutions to Chapter 18 questions

(a) The management accountant should consider the following factors when deciding whether or not to investigate variances:

Question 18.1

 (i) *The size of the variances*: This may be expressed in terms of percentage variation from standard or budget. Alternatively, statistical techniques can be used to determine the probability of the variance occurring when it is under control. The size of the variance indicates the likelihood that the variance is due to an assignable cause.

 (ii) *Costs and benefits of investigation*: The management accountant should assess whether the costs of investigation are less than the benefits that are expected to result from the investigation.

 (iii) *Nature of the standard*: Are expected or ideal standards used? If ideal standards are used then investigation of the variances is unlikely to result in the variances being eliminated.

 (iv) *Cumulative variances*: A variance showing an increase in size over time may justify an investigation even when the variance for the particular period is not significant. Alternatively, a variance that is significant for a particular period but that is decreasing over time may be under control.

 (v) *Validity of standard or budget*: The validity of the standard will help the accountant to gauge the significance of the variance. A price variance in times of rapidly rising prices is unlikely to be due to an assignable cause.

(b) The management accountant can take the following action to improve the chances of achieving positive results from investigating variances:

 (i) *Speedy identification and reporting of variances*: Significant delays between the occurrence of a variance and its notification to managers will limit the degree of control that managers can achieve. The sooner a variance is identified, the sooner it can be investigated and acted upon.

 (ii) *Analysis of variances*: The accountant should provide clues as to the possible reasons for the variances by pinpointing where the variances have arisen. For example, the accountant might identify the reason for a direct material variance as being due to excessive usage of a certain material in a particular process. This should assist the responsibility manager in quickly identifying the cause of the excessive usage.

 (iii) *Statistical procedures*: Statistical procedures and quality control charts should be used so as to determine the probability that variances are due to an assignable cause. If managers are frequently required to investigate variances that are due to random variations then it is unlikely that they will give detailed attention to the investigation process. However, if the majority of variances reported are significant then managers will attach greater importance to the investigation process.

 (iv) *Develop a team effort approach*: The accountant should be seen by managers as supportive within the control process. If a team effort approach is developed then it is likely that managers will be more actively involved in the investigation process.

Question 18.2

(a) The following problems might occur during periods of rapid inflation:
  (i) The standards will presumably include some assumptions about inflation. If this assumption is not clearly stated then it is difficult to determine how much of a price variance is due to inflation and how much is due to buying efficiency.
  (ii) Price indices tend to reflect average price changes. Consequently, it is difficult for a company to predict future costs and interpret variances if the specific rate of inflation for its inputs is considerably different from the general rate of inflation.
  (iii) Inflation may result in relative changes in the prices of inputs. Therefore standard mixes requiring different inputs may no longer be the most efficient mix.
  (iv) If standard prices are not adjusted then the efficiency variances will be understated.
  (v) The impact of inflation will have an immediate effect on cash flows, but some delay will occur before the full extent of the variances is ascertained. Therefore management may not respond quickly enough to pricing, output and sourcing decisions in order to effectively control cash flows.
  (vi) Sharp rises in prices will raise questions as to whether unadjusted standards can be used in the decision-making process (e.g. pricing decisions).
  (vii) Administrative work in maintaining up-to-date standards when prices are constantly changing.

(b) (i) When establishing standards, the inflation factor that has been assumed should be clearly stated so that variances can be analysed by price and efficiency changes.
  (ii) Internal indices of price changes could be maintained for cost items that do not move in line with the general rate of inflation.
  (iii) Variances should be analysed by their forecasting and operational elements as indicated in Chapter 18.
  (iv) Standard mixes should be established for a range of prices for the material inputs, and management should be prepared to implement changes in the mix immediately price changes dictate that a change is necessary.

Question 18.3

(a) The sales volume variance is the difference between budgeted sales volume and actual sales volume. It can be valued at the sales revenue per unit sold, contribution margin per unit sold or the profit margin per unit sold. For an explanation of the weaknesses arising from valuing the variance using sales revenues see 'Sales variances' in Chapter 17. It is preferable to value variances at the unit contribution margin. This is because deviations from budgeted sales will result in profit changing by the amount of the unit contribution multiplied by sales volume, assuming all other factors remain unchanged. Profit margins are derived after deducting unit fixed overheads from the contribution per unit. However, in the short term, fixed overheads will remain unchanged, so changes in sales volume will not result in profit changing by the change sales volume multiplied by the profit margin per unit. As indicated above, profit will be a function of sales volume multiplied by the contribution per unit.

(b) The principle of separating variances into the planning and operational variances is explained in the section on ex post variance analysis in Chapter 18 and Learning Note 18.2. Note that in this section the terms 'efficiency' or 'controllable variances' are used to describe operational variances. The principles described in this section can be applied to sales price variances. For example, if the original budgeted selling price was £100 and the actual price was £110 the conventional method would report a price variance of £10 per unit sold. However, if the ex post efficient market price for the product is £115, it should represent the revised standard and the price variance can be separated into a favourable planning variance of £15 (£115 − £100) and an unfavourable operational price efficiency variance of £5 (£110 − £115). Future planning should be based on using the £115 standard since it reflects the most up to date standard, and investigations should be made as to why the actual selling price was less than the ex post expected market price.

(a) Because standard costs represent future target costs based on the elimination of **Question 18.4**
avoidable inefficiencies they are preferable for decision-making to estimates based
on an adjustment of past costs which may incorporate inefficiencies. For example,
where cost-plus pricing is used as an input to pricing decisions, standard costs
provide more appropriate information because efficient competitors will also base
any price bids on costs where efficiencies have been eliminated. Alternatively,
where competitive market prices exist for a firm's products so that they are price
takers, it will be necessary for such firms to periodically review the profitability of
their products to identify possible loss making activities. In such circumstances
product costs for input into the profitability analysis should be extracted from a
database of standard costs reviewed periodically. A periodic cost audit should be
undertaken to provide a strategic review of the standard costs and profitability of
a firm's products. The review provides attention-directing information for
signalling the need for more detailed studies to make cost reduction,
discontinuation, redesign and outsourcing decisions. Standard costs thus provide
the basis for such decisions and avoid the need for the detailed tracking of costs.

Standard costing can also be used with target costing for decision-making.
Target costs can be compared with costs derived from the standard costing system
to identify the estimated cost. If the estimated/standard cost exceeds the target
cost, ways are investigated of driving down the estimated cost to the target cost.
You should refer to Chapter 21 for a detailed explanation of target costing.

Finally, trends in variances can be monitored to identify the need for actions for
improvement and changes in product design, production methods, etc. Situations
where there has been a lack of improvement in the variances can be investigated
with a view to introducing alternative designs and improvements in production
methods.

(b) See 'The effect of the level of budget difficulty on motivation and performance' in
Chapter 16 for the answer to this question. In addition, the following points
should be included in the answer.

1   An over-emphasis on achieving standards and reporting variances can have
    dysfunctional effects. For example, purchasing officers might strive to achieve
    favourable price variances by purchasing inferior materials or focusing on
    prices at the expense of reliable and on-time deliveries and generally not
    fostering long-term supplier relationships.

2   Excessive focus on labour efficiency variances may encourage large
    production batches to reduce idle and set-up time but such savings may be
    outweighed by the increased costs associated with the higher stocks and work
    in progress. Also favourable volume variances may be achieved by producing
    in excess of demand and maintaining excessive stocks.

3   If overheads are absorbed on the basis of direct labour this can result in an
    over-emphasis on direct labour efficiency. However, improvements in direct
    labour will not cause overheads to reduce where there is only a weak cause-
    and-effect relationship between direct labour hours and overhead spending.

For a more detailed discussion of the above points you should refer to 'Criticisms
of standard costing' in Learning Note 18.4.

(a) *Variance analysis* **Question 18.5**
Material price = (standard price − actual price) × actual purchases
X   = (£20 − £20.50) × 9000
           = £4500A
Y   = (£6 − £5.50) × 5000
           = £2500F

Material usage = (standard usage − actual usage) × standard price
X   = (800 × 10 kg − 7800 kg) × £20
           = £4000F

$$Y \qquad = (800 \times 5 \text{ litres} - 4300 \text{ litres}) \times \pounds 6$$
$$= \pounds 1800\text{A}$$

$$\text{Wage rate} = [\text{standard rate } (\pounds 6) - \text{actual rate } (\pounds 24\ 150/4200)]$$
$$\times \text{ actual hours } (4200)$$
$$= \pounds 1050\text{F}$$

$$\text{Labour efficiency} = [\text{standard hours } (800 \times 5 \text{ hrs}) - \text{actual hours } (4200)]$$
$$\times \text{ standard rate } (\pounds 6)$$
$$= \pounds 1200\text{A}$$

$$\text{Fixed overhead expenditure} = \text{budgeted cost } (10\ 800/12 \times \pounds 50)$$
$$- \text{actual cost } (\pounds 47\ 000)$$
$$= \pounds 2000\text{A}$$

$$\text{Volume efficiency} = [\text{standard hours } (800 \times 5 \text{ hrs}) - \text{actual hours } (4200)]$$
$$\times (\pounds 50/5 \text{ hours})$$
$$= \pounds 2000\text{A}$$

$$\text{Volume capacity}^a = [\text{actual hours } (4200) - \text{budgeted hours}^b \ (4500)]$$
$$\times \text{ FOAR } (\pounds 50/5 \text{ hours})$$
$$= \pounds 3000\text{A}$$

Notes
[a] Note that the CIMA Terminology (at the time of setting the examination) described the volume variance as being equivalent to the volume capacity variance.
[b] Budgeted hours = monthly budgeted output $(10\ 800/12) \times 5$ hrs

(b)

Stores control

	(£)		(£)
K Ltd: X (AQ × SP)	180 000	WIP: (SQ × SP)	160 000
C Ltd: Y (AQ × SP)	30 000	WIP: (SQ × SP)	24 000
Material usage variance (X)	4 000	Material usage variance (Y)	1 800
		Balance	28 200
	£214 000		£214 000

Wages control account

	(£)		(£)
Cash	20 150	Wages owing b/fwd	6 000
PAYE and NI	5 000	Labour efficiency	1 200
Accrued wages	5 000	WIP (SQ × SP)	24 000
Wage rate variance	1 050		
	£31 200		£31 200

WIP control account

	(£)		(£)
Stores control: X	160 000	Finished goods control a/c	248 000
Y	24 000		
Wages control	24 000		
Fixed overhead	40 000		
	£248 000		£248 000

Fixed overhead control

	(£)		(£)
Expense creditors	33 000	WIP (SQ × SP)	40 000
Depreciation provision	14 000	Expenditure variance	2 000
		Efficiency variance	2 000
		Capacity variance	3 000
	£47 000		£47 000

Finished goods control

	(£)		(£)
WIP control	£248 000	Cost of sales	£248 000

Cost of sales

	(£)		(£)
Finished goods control	£248 000	Profit and loss (P/L)	£248 000

Material price variance

	(£)		(£)
K Ltd: X	4500	C Ltd: Y	2500
		P/L	2000
	£4500		£4500

Material usage variance

	(£)		(£)
Stores control: Y	1800	Stores control: X	4000
P/L	2200		
	£4000		£4000

Labour rate variance

	(£)		(£)
P/L	£1050	Wages control	£1050

Labour efficiency variance

	(£)		(£)
Wages control	1200	P/L	1200

Fixed overhead expenditure variance

	(£)		(£)
Overhead control	2000	P/L	2000

Fixed overhead efficiency variance

	(£)		(£)
Overhead control	2000	P/L	2000

Fixed overhead capacity variance

	(£)		(£)
Overhead control	£3000	P/L	£3000

Sales

	(£)		(£)
P/L	320 000	Debtors	320 000

K Limited

	(£)
Stores control	180 000
Price variance account	4 500

C plc

	(£)		(£)
Price variance account	2500	Stores control	30 000

Expense creditors

	(£)
Fixed overhead control	33 000

Provision for depreciation

	(£)
Fixed overhead control	14 000

Profit and loss account

	(£)	(£)	(£)
Sales			320 000
Cost of sales			248 000
			72 000
Variances	(F)	(A)	
Material price	—	2 000	
usage	2200	—	
Labour rate	1050	—	
efficiency	—	1 200	
Overhead expenditure	–	2 000	
efficiency	–	2 000	
volume	–	3 000	
	3250	10 200	6 950
Gross profit			65 050

(c) The difference of £250 in the accounts is due to the fact that the material price variance has been calculated on purchases (instead of usage) and written off as a period cost. In the question the raw material stocks are recorded at actual cost, and therefore the £250 is included in the stock valuation and will be recorded as an expense next period.

(a) *Cost variance calculations*   **Question 18.6**
Material price:

	(£)	(£)
$(SP - AP) \times AQ$		
A$(£0.30 - £0.20) \times 8000$		800 F
B$(0.70 - £0.80) \times 5000$		500 A

Material mix:
(actual wage in standard proportions − actual wage in actual proportions)
$\times$ SP

A $(6500 - 8000) \times £0.30$	450 A	
B $(6500 - 5000) \times £0.70$	1050 F	600 F

Material yield:[a]
(actual yield − standard yield)
$\times$ SC per unit of output

$(12\,000 - 13\,000) \times £0.50$		500 A

Wage rate:
$(SR - AR) \times AH$

Skilled $(£3 - £2.95) \times 6000$		300 F
Semi-skilled $(£2.50 - £2.60) \times 3150$		315 A

Labour mix:[b]
(AQ in standard and proportions
− AQ in actual proportions) $\times$ SR

Skilled $(5799 - 6000) \times £3$	603 A	
Semi-skilled $(3351 - 3150) \times £2.50$	503 F	100 A

Labour productivity:[c]
(SQ in standard and proportions
− AQ in standard proportions) $\times$ SR

Skilled $(5400 - 5799) \times £3$	1197A	
Semi-skilled $(3120 - 3351) \times £2.50$	578A	1775A

Fixed overhead spending:
$BC - AC$

$£10\,000 - £9010$		990F

Variable overhead spending:
flexed budgeted − AC

$12\,000 \times £0.50 = 6000 - £7500$		1500A

Fixed overhead volume:
(actual production − budgeted production) $\times$ FOAR

$(12\,000 - 10\,000) \times £1$		2000F
Total cost variances		Nil

Sales margin variance calculations

Sales volume variance: (£)
  (actual sales volume − budgeted volume)
  × standard margin
  (11 000 − 10 000) × £1 1000F

Sales margin price variance:
  (actual selling price − budgeted selling price)
  × actual sales volume
  (£5 − £5) × 7000 = 0
  (£4.75 − £5) × 4000 = 1000A 1000A
Total sales variances nil

The question requires the calculation of the material usage variance and the labour efficiency variance. These variances are calculated as follows:

$$\text{direct material usage variance} = \text{mix variance} + \text{yield variance}$$
$$= £600F + £500A = £100F$$

$$\text{labour efficiency variance} = \text{mix variance} + \text{productivity variance}$$

  (£)
Skilled = £603A + £1197A = 1800A
Unskilled = £503F + £578A = 75A
  1875A

Reconciliation of actual and budgeted profit
The total of the cost variances and the sales variances are zero. Therefore actual profit equals budgeted profit.

Notes
[a] Budgeted usage is 1 kg of materials for 1 unit of output. The standard yield for an input of 13 000 kg is therefore 13 000 units.
The standard material cost per unit of output is:

  (£)
A (0.5 × £0.30) =0.15
B (0.5 × £0.70) =0.35
  0.50

[b] Skilled = 9150 hrs × 4500/7100 = 5799 hrs
Semi-skilled = 9150 hrs × 2600/7100 = 3351 hrs

[c] The standard labour quantity is 0.45 skilled hours and 0.26 unskilled hours for each unit of output. For an output of 12 000 units the standard labour hours are:

skilled = 5400 (12 000 × 0.45 hrs)
semi-skilled = 3120 (12 000 × 0.26 hrs)

(b) The sales volume variance shows the effect on profit from sales volume being in excess of budget (assuming standard costs remain unchanged). The adverse sales price variance of £1000 indicates the lost profits from selling below the standard price. However, the reduction in the selling price will be partly accounted for by the increase in sales volume. An ex-post budget comparison should be used. For example, a revised target for sales that could have been obtained at the actual selling prices should be used to calculate the volume variance.

The price paid for material A is less than standard and the price paid for B is above standard. This might explain why the company has substituted material A for B during the period. The usage variance is £100 favourable, but £600 of this is due to the change in the materials mix. The difference of £500 represents the excess wage when the mix variance is not taken into account. The analysis does not indicate whether the excess usage is due to using a non-standard mix or to inefficient usage.

The wage rate variances arise because the skilled rate is below standard but the semi-skilled rate is above the standard. There is a significant adverse labour efficiency variance, which should be investigated. The mix and productivity variances are unlikely to provide any helpful clues in explaining the adverse efficiency variance.

The fixed overhead volume variance arises because output is in excess of budget but this variance is not particularly useful (see 'Volume variance' in Chapter 17 for an explanation). The variable overhead expenditure variance is partly a spending variance and a usage variance, and on its own is not very meaningful. Any meaningful analysis of this variance requires a comparison of the actual expenditure with budget for each variable cost item.

(a)

Question 18.7

	Superb	Excellent	Good	Total
1. Budget sales (units)	30 000	50 000	20 000	100 000
2. Actual sales (units) in std. proportions	28 800	48 000	19 200	96 000
3. Actual sales (units)	36 000	42 000	18 000	96 000
Standard unit valuations:				
4. Selling price (£)	100	80	70	
5. Contribution (£)	60	55	48	
6. Profit (£)	35	30	23	
Sales volume variance:				
On turnover basis				
(3–1) × 4 (£)	600 000(F)	640 000(A)	140 000(A)	180 000(A)
On contribution basis				
(3–1) × 5 (£)	360 000(F)	440 000(A)	96 000(A)	176 000(A)
On profit basis				
(3–1) × 6 (£)	210 000(F)	240 000(A)	46 000(A)	76 000(A)

Note: Fixed cost per unit = £2 500 000/100 000 units = £25

(b) The answer should:
(i) Explain the limitations of using sales revenues to value the sales variances (see 'Sales variances' in Chapter 17).
(ii) Point out the limitations of using a net profit margin derived from unitizing fixed costs. Fixed costs remain unchanged in the short term with variations in sales volumes. Therefore total profits will change by the sales volumes multiplied by the contribution per unit sold and not the net profit per unit sold.
(iii) Argue in favour of using contribution margins based on the point made in (ii) above. Contribution most closely represents the changes in cash flows. Also contribution does not involve arbitrary apportionments of fixed overheads and thus avoids the reporting of misleading sales variances.

(c) *Sales mix variance*

	Actual sales volume	Actual sales volume in budgeted proportions	Difference	Standard contribution margin (£)	Sales margin mix variance (£)
Superb	36 000	28 800 (30%)	−7200	60	+ 432 000
Excellent	42 000	48 000 (50%)	+6000	55	−330 000
Good	18 000	19 200 (20%)	+1200	48	−57 600
					+44 400F

Sales quantity variance

	Actual sales volume in budgeted proportions	Budgeted sales quantity	Difference	Standard contribution margin (£)	Sales margin quantity variance (£)
Superb	28 800 (30%)	30 000	−1200	60	−72 000
Excellent	48 000 (50%)	50 000	−2000	55	−110 000
Good	19 200 (20%)	20 000	−800	48	−38 400
					−220 000A

(d) See 'Criticisms of sales margin variances' in Chapter 18 for the answer to this question.

(e) (i)

	Original standard (£)	Revised standard (£)	Actual (£)
Selling price	100	94.00	90
Variable cost	40	38.80	38
Unit contribution	60	55.20	52

Reconciliation of actual with original budget (Ex-post variance analysis)

		£
Original budget (30 000 × £60)		1 800 000
Planning variances:		
Sales price (30 000 × £6)	180 000A	
Variable cost (30 000 × £1.20)	36 000F	144 000A
Revised ex-post budgeted contribution		1 656 000
Operational variances		
Sales volume (6000 × £55.20)	331 200F	
Sales price (36 000 × £4)	144 000A	
Variable cost (36 000 × £0.80)	28 800F	216 000F
Actual contribution (36 000 × £52)		1 872 000

(e) (ii) For the answer to this question see '*Expost* variance analysis' in Chapter 18.

Question 18.8

(a) The traditional variance analysis is as follows:

	(£)
Sales margin volume variance:	nil
(actual sales volume = budgeted sales volume)	
Sales margin price variance:	
(actual unit margin − standard unit margin)	
× actual sales volume	
(£84 − £26) × 1000	58 000F
	58 000F

		(£)
Material price:		
(standard price − actual price) × actual quantity		
(£5 − £9) × 10 800		43 200A
Material usage:		
(standard quantity − actual quantity) × standard price		
(10 000 −10 800) × £5	4 000A	47 200A

Wage rate:
  (standard rate – actual rate) × actual hours
  [£4 – (£34 800/5800)] × 5800   11 600A
Labour efficiency:
  (standard hours – actual hours) × standard rate
  [(1000 × 6 = 6000) – 5800] × £4   800F   10 800A
                     Total variances   nil
Reconciliation:
  Budgeted contribution (1000 × £26)   26 000
  Add adverse cost variances   58 000
  Less favourable sales variances   (58 000)
                 Actual contribution   26 000

(b)

	(A) Original plan		(B) Revised ex-post plan		(C) Actual results	
	(£)		(£)		(£)	
Sales (1000 × £100)	= 100 000	(1000 × £165)	= 165 000	(1000 × £158)	= 158 000	
Labour (6000 × £4)	= 24 000	(6000 × £6.25)	= 37 500	(5800 × £6)	= 34 800	
Materials:						
Aye (10 000 × £5) =	50 000	(10 000 × £8.50) =	85 000	(10 800 × £9) =	97 200	
Bee		(10 000 × £7)	= 70 000			

	(£)	
Uncontrollable planning variances (A – B)		
Sales price	65 000F	
Wage rate	13 500A	
Material price[a] (50 000 – 70 000)	20 000A	
Substitution of materials variance[a] (85 000 – 70 000)	15 000A	16 500F
Operational variances		
Sales price (B – C)	7 000A	
Wage rate (5800 × £0.25)	1 450F	
Labour efficiency (200 hrs at £6.25)	1 250F	
Material price (10 800 × £0.50)	5 400A	
Material usage (800 × £8.50)	6 800A	16 500A
Total variances		nil

Note

[a]If the purchasing officer is committed to buying Aye and it is not possible to change to Bee in
the short term then the £15 000 substitution variances is an uncontrollable price variance, and
the total planning variance will be £35 000 for materials. However, if the purchasing officer
can respond to changes in the relative prices then the £15 000 should be added to the
operational price variance.

Comment on operational variances

The operational variances are calculated on the basis of the revised *ex-post* plan. The
ex post plan represents what the target would have been, given the benefit of
hindsight. This represents a more realistic target than the original plan. For example,
given the conditions for the period, the target sales should have been £165 000. Actual
sales were £158 000. Therefore the operational sales variance is £7000 adverse. An
explanation of planning and operational variances is presented in '*Ex post* variance
analysis' in Chapter 18.

(c) *Advantages*

  (i) The traditional price variance includes unavoidable/
      uncontrollable elements due to change in environment of £20 000 or £35
      000. The revised analysis is more indicative of current purchasing efficiency.

  (ii) Traditional approach incorrectly values deviations from budgeted efficiency
      in calculating usage or efficiency variances. A better indication is provided
      by attributing the current standard cost per unit to the deviations (a variance
      of £6800 is a better indication of the excess usage of the materials than the
      £4000 under the traditional method).

Disadvantages

(i) Classification into planning (uncontrollable) and avoidable may be difficult (e.g. substitution variance) and arbitrary.

(ii) Any error in producing *ex post* standards will cause a corresponding error in the classification of the variances (for example, we could have used a £9 *ex post* standard for materials, thus affecting both the planning and operational variance).

(iii) Excessive costs compared with benefits derived.

(iv) Who sets the *ex post* standard? If the purchasing officer sets the standard then there is a danger that the standard may be biased to avoid unfavourable operational variances.

Question 18.9

(a) It is assumed that the actual selling price for the period was the same as the budgeted selling price.

$$\begin{aligned}
\text{Sale volume variance} &= (\text{Actual sales volume} - \text{Budgeted sales volume}) \\
&\quad \times \text{Standard contribution} \\
&= (2850 - 2500) \times \text{£78} \\
&= \text{£27 300F}
\end{aligned}$$

$$\begin{aligned}
\text{Material price variance} &= (\text{Standard price} - \text{Actual price}) \text{ Actual quantity} \\
&= (\text{£20} - \text{£18}) \times 12\ 450 \\
&= \text{£24 900F}
\end{aligned}$$

$$\begin{aligned}
\text{Material usage variance} &= (\text{Standard quantity} - \text{Actual quantity}) \text{ Standard price} \\
&= (2850 \times 4\ \text{kg} = 11\ 400 - 12\ 450) \times \text{£20} \\
&= \text{£21 000A}
\end{aligned}$$

$$\begin{aligned}
\text{Wage rate variance} &= (\text{Standard rate} - \text{Actual rate}) \text{ Actual hours} \\
&= (\text{£7} - \text{£8}) \times 18\ 800 \\
&= \text{£18 800A}
\end{aligned}$$

$$\begin{aligned}
\text{Labour efficiency variance} &= (\text{Standard hour} - \text{Actual hours}) \text{ Standard rate} \\
&= (2850 \times 6\ \text{hrs} = 17\ 100\ \text{hrs} - 18\ 800\ \text{hrs}) \times \text{£7} \\
&= \text{£11 900A}
\end{aligned}$$

Reconciliation statement

	(£)	(£)
Budget contribution		195 000
Sales volume variance	27 300F	
Sales price variance	–	
		27 300F
Material usage variance	21 000A	
Material price variance	24 900F	
		3 900F
Wage rate variance	18 800A	
Labour efficiency variance	11 900A	30 700A
Actual contribution		195 500

(b) (i) *Original standard*

		(£)
Materials	2500 × 4 kg × £20	=200 000
Labour	2500 × 6 hrs × £7	=105 000
		305 000
Sales	2500 × £200	=500 000
Contribution		195 000

(ii) *Revised ex post standard*

		(£)
Materials	2500 × 4.5 kg × £16.50	=185 625
Labour	2500 × 6 hrs × £6.50	= 97 500
		283 125
Sales	2500 × £200	=500 000
Contribution		216 875

(iii) *Actual*

		(£)
Materials	12 450 kg × £18	=224 100
Labour	18 800 hrs × £8	=150 400
		374 500
Sales	2850 × £200	=570 000
Contribution		195 500

The total variances consist of a favourable planning variance of £21 875 (£216 875 − £195 000) and an adverse operational variance of £21 375 (£216 875 − £195 500). The analysis of these variances is shown below.

Planning variances (1 − 2)	(£)	(£)
Material usage[a] (2500 × 0.5 kg × £20)	25 000A	
Material price[a] (£20 − £16.50) × (2500 × 4 kg)	35 000F	
Joint price/quantity variance		
(2500 × 0.50 kg) × (£20 − £16.50)	4 375F	
		14 375F
Wage rate (2500 × 6 hrs × £0.50)		7 500F
		21 875F

Operational variances		
Material usage		
(2850 × 4.5 kg = 12 825 kg − 12 450) £16.50	6 187.50F	
Material price (£16.50 − £18) × 12 450 kg	18 675.00A	
		12 487.50A
Labour efficiency		
(2850 × 6 hrs = 17 100 hrs − 18 800) × £6.50	11 050.00A	
Wage rate (£6.50 − £8) × 18 800 hrs	28 200.00A	
		39 250.00A
Sales volume (350 units at £86.75 revised unit contribution[b])		30 362.50F
		21 375.00A

Notes
[a] It is questionable whether it is meaningful to analyse the materials planning variance into its price and quantity elements because of the joint price/quantity variance. An alternative answer would be to present only the total materials planning variance of £14 375 (£200 000 − £185 625).
[b] Operational variances should be valued at the ex-post standard. The ex post unit contribution is £200 selling price − (6 hrs × £6.50 labour) − 4.5 kg × £16.50 materials) = £86.75.

Reconciliation statement

	(£)	(£)
Budgeted contribution		195 000
Planning variances:		
Materials	14 375F	
Wage rate	7 500F	
		21 875.00F
Operational variances		
Materials usage	6 187.50F	
Materials price	18 675.00A	
		12 487.50A
Labour efficiency	11 050A	
Wage rate	28 200A	
		39 250.00A
Sales volume		30 362.50F
Actual contribution		195 500.00

(c) The answer to this question should explain the meaning of planning and operational variances and why it is preferable to analyse the variances into their planning and operational elements. In particular, the answer should explain why the conventional approach reports an adverse material usage variance and a favourable price variance whereas the ex-post approach highlights a favourable usage and an adverse price variance.

Question 18.10
(a) The question relates to the role of standard costing in a modern manufacturing environment. For the answer to this question see 'The future role of standard costing' and 'The role of standard costing when ABC has been implemented' in Learning Notes 18.4 and 18.5 on the open access website.

(b) The expenditure variance is the difference between the budgeted fixed overheads (£100 000) and the actual fixed overheads (£102 300). For more detailed cost control the variance should be disaggregated by the individual categories of fixed overheads.

The budgeted capacity measured in direct labour hours of input were 10 000 but actual hours were 11 000. The extra hours of input should have enabled an extra 1000 hours of overheads to be absorbed at a budgeted rate of £10 per hour. Therefore a favourable variance of £10 000 is reported.

Budgeted standard hours for each unit of output is 0.10 hours (10 000 hours/100 000 units). Therefore for an actual output of 105 000 units the target hours are 10 500 (105 000 × 0.10 hours) but the actual hours were 11 000. This has resulted in a failure to recover £5000 overheads (500 hours × £10).

For a more detailed discussion of the above variances and a discussion of their usefulness you should refer to the sections in Chapter 17 on fixed overhead expenditure, volume capacity and volume efficiency variances.

(c) (i) It is assumed that material handling expenditure fluctuates in the longer term with the number of orders executed. The variance has been derived adopting a flexible budgeting approach using the number of orders as the cost driver as follows:

Budgeted materials handling overheads (5500 orders at a budgeted rate of £30 000/5 000)	£33 000
Actual materials handling expenditure	£30 800
Variance (favourable)	£2 200

The variance therefore indicates that the actual expenditure is £2200 less than expected for the actual level of activity. The same approach is used to calculate the expenditure variance for set ups:

Budgeted set up overheads (2600 production runs at a budgeted rate of £70 000/2800) £65 000

Actual set up expenditure £71 500

Variance (adverse) £6 500

The variance indicates that the actual expenditure is £6500 more than expected for the actual level of activity.

The efficiency variances compare the standard/budgeted cost driver usage for the actual output with the actual usage valued at the standard cost driver rate. The material handling overhead efficiency variance is calculated as follows:

Standard usage for actual output (5000/100 000 × 105 000 units = 5250 orders)

Actual number of orders (5500)

Adverse variance = 250 orders at £30 000/5000 per order = £1500 A

The variance indicates that 250 orders more than expected were executed at £6 per order.

The calculation of the set up efficiency variance is as follows:

Standard usage for actual output (2800/100 000 × 105 000 units = 2940 set ups)

Actual number of set ups (2600)

Favourable variance = 340 set ups at £70 000/2800 = £8500

The variance indicates that 340 less set ups than expected were required at £25 per set up.

(c) (ii) Presumably the company has introduced ABC because there was no cause-and-effect relationship between the previous cost drivers used by the traditional cost system and the overhead expenditure. Hence there is a need for the standard costing system to support the decision-making and cost management applications which would have been instrumental in introducing ABC. Failure to change the standard costing system to be consistent with the ABC system would have undermined the ABC system. Where reported variances prompt actions such as decisions to change the production processes/ methods it is important that decisions are based on cost driver rates that are the causes of the overheads being incurred.

For further discussion of aspects relating to (c) (i) and (c) (ii) you should refer to 'The role of standard costing when ABC has been implemented' in Chapter 18.

(a) (i) (£) **Question 18.11**

Material price variance:
(standard price − actual price) × actual quantity
[£0.05 − (£45/1000)] × 105 000   525F
Material usage variance:
(standard quantity − actual quantity) × standard price
(100 000 − 105 000) × £0.05   250A

Total variance   275F

(ii)

	Dr (£)	Cr (£)
Dr Stores ledger control account (AQ × SP)	5250	
Cr Creditors control account (AQ × AP)		4725
Cr Material price variance account		525
Dr Work in progress (SQ × SP)	5000	
Dr Material usage variance account	250	
Cr Stores ledger control account (AQ × SP)		5250

(iii) On the basis of the above calculations, the buyer would receive a bonus of £52.50 (10% × £525) and the production manager would not receive any bonus. It could be argued that the joint price/usage variance should be separated if the variances are to be used as the basis for calculating bonuses. (For a discussion of joint price/usage variances see Chapter 17.) The revised analysis would be as follows:

	(£)
Pure price variance:	
(standard price − actual price) × standard quantity	
(£0.05 − £0.045) × 100 000	500F
Joint price/usage variance:	
(standard price − actual price) × excess usage	
(£0.05 − £0.045) × 5000	25F

Buyer's viewpoint
At the purchasing stage the buyer can influence both quality and price. Consequently, the buyer can obtain favourable price variances by purchasing inferior quality materials at less than standard price. The adverse effects in terms of excess usage, because of the purchase of inferior quality of materials, are passed on to the production manager and the buyer gains from the price reduction. Indeed, if the joint price/usage is not isolated (see above), the buyer gains if production uses materials in excess of standard. Therefore the bonus system might encourage the buyer to purchase inferior quality materials, which results in an overall adverse *total* material cost variance and inferior product quality. In summary, the bonus system appears to be biased in favour of the buyer at the expense of the production manager.

Production manager's viewpoint
The isolation of the joint price/usage variance might encourage the buyer not to purchase inferior quality materials, and this will be to the production manager's advantage. Nevertheless, the problem of the control of material quality still exists. The production manager would need to ensure that the quality of material purchased is in line with the quality built into the standard. Therefore some monitoring device is necessary. If variations do occur, the quantity standard should be adjusted for the purpose of performance reporting and bonus assessment.

Company's viewpoint
The objective of the bonus system is to encourage goal congruence and increase motivation. Interdependencies exist between the two responsibility centres, and it is doubtful that the bonus system encourages goal congruence or improves motivation. If the quality of materials that can be purchased from the various suppliers does not vary then the adverse effects of the bonus system will be reduced. Nevertheless, interdependencies will still exist between the responsibility centres. One solution might be to base the bonuses of both managers on the *total* material cost variance. In addition, standards should be regularly reviewed and participation by both managers in setting the standards encouraged.

(b) (i) The minimum present value of expected savings that would have to be made in future months in order to justify making an investigation is where

$$IC + (P \times CC) = Px$$

where IC = investigation costs, P = probability that process is out of control, CC = correction cost, x = present value of expected savings if process is out of control

$$\text{Therefore } £50 + (0.5 \times £100) = 0.5x$$
$$0.5x = £100$$
$$x = £200$$

Therefore the minimum present value of expected savings that would have to be made is £200.

(ii) The standard cost will probably represent the mean value, and random variations around the mean value can be expected to occur even when the process is under control. Therefore it is unlikely that the £500 variance will be eliminated completely, because a proportion of the variance simply reflects the randomness of the variables affecting the standard. If the process is found to be out of control, the corrective action will only confine variances to the normal acceptable range of standard outcomes. If the £500 is an extreme deviation from the standard then it is likely that the potential savings from investigation will be insignificant.

(iii) Applying the notation used in (i), the firm will be indifferent about whether to conduct an investigation when the expected savings resulting from correction are equal to the expected cost of correction. That is, where

$$IC + (P \times CC) = Px$$

if $x = £600$ then

$$50 + P \times 100 = P \times 600$$
$$500P = 50$$
$$P = 10\%$$

if $x = 250$ then

$$50 + P \times 100 = P \times 250$$
$$150P = 50$$
$$P = 33\tfrac{1}{3}\%$$

Divisional financial performance measures

Solutions to Chapter 19 questions

Question 19.1

(a) If divisional budgets are set by a central planning department and imposed on divisional managers then it is true that divisional independence is pseudo-independence. However, if budget guidelines and goals are set by the central planning department and divisional managers are given a large degree of freedom in the setting of budgets and conduct of operations then it is incorrect to claim that pseudo-independence exists.

One of the reasons for creating a divisionalized organization structure is to improve motivation by the delegation of responsibility to divisional managers, thus giving them greater freedom over the control of their activities. Nevertheless, complete independence cannot be granted, since this would destroy the very idea that divisions are an integral part of a single business. The granting of freedom to divisions in conducting their operations can be allowed only if certain limits are applied within which that freedom can be exercised. This normally takes the form of the presentation of budgets by divisions to corporate management for approval. By adopting this approach, divisions pay a modest price for the extensive powers of decentralized decision-making.

As long as budgets are not imposed by the central planning department, and divisions are allowed to determine their own budgets within the guidelines set, then divisional managers will have greater independence than the managers of centralized organizations.

(b) The answer should consist of a discussion of divisional profit, return on capital employed and residual income. A discussion of each of these items is presented in Chapter 19.

Question 19.2

(a) Examples of the types of decisions that should be transferred to the new divisional managers include:
   (i) Product decisions such as product mix, promotion and pricing.
   (ii) Employment decisions, except perhaps for the appointment of senior managers.
   (iii) Short-term operating decisions of all kinds. Examples include production scheduling, subcontracting and direction of marketing effort.
   (iv) Capital expenditure and disinvestment decisions (with some constraints).
   (v) Short-term financing decisions (with some constraints).
(b) The following decisions might be retained at company head office:
   (i) Strategic investment decisions that are critical to the survival of the company as a whole.
   (ii) Certain financing decisions that require that an overall view be taken. For example, borrowing commitments and the level of financial gearing should be determined for the group as a whole.
   (iii) Appointment of top management.
   (iv) Sourcing decisions such as bulk buying of raw materials if corporate interests are best served by centralized buying.
   (v) Capital expenditure decisions above certain limits.

(vi) Common services that are required by all profit centres. Corporate interests might best be served by operating centralized service departments such as an industrial relations department. Possible benefits include reduced costs and the extra benefits of specialization.

(vii) Arbitration decisions on transfer pricing disputes.

(viii) Decisions on items which benefit the company rather than an individual division, e.g. taxation and computer applications.

(c) The answer to this question should focus on the importance of designing performance reports which encourage goal congruence. For a discussion of this topic see Chapter 19.

(a) The following factors should be considered:

Question 19.3

(i) *Definition of profit:* The question states that the measure should be used for performance measurement. It is therefore necessary to define 'controllable profit' for the companies. Clearly, apportionment of group headquarters expenditure should be excluded from the calculation of controllable profit. If investment decisions are made by the companies then depreciation should be included as a controllable expense. Otherwise, companies can increase controllable profit by substituting capital equipment for direct labour when this is not in the best interest of the group as a whole.

(ii) *Definition of capital employed:* There are many different definitions of capital employed, and it is important that the same basis of measurement be used for comparing the performance of the different companies. Capital employed might be defined as total assets or net assets. All assets that are controlled by the companies should be included in the valuation. If debtors are controlled by the companies but not included in the capital employed then there is a danger that managers might lengthen the credit period to increase sales even when this is not in the best interests of the group. The benefits from the increased credit period accrue to the companies, but the increased investment is not reflected in the capital employed.

(iii) *Valuation of capital employed:* Capital employed can be valued on an historical cost basis, or an alternative method such as replacement cost might be used. If historical cost is used then assets might be valued at written-down value or gross value. Both approaches can result in misleading comparisons. If written-down value is used then an asset that yields a constant profit will show an annual increase in ROCE because the written-down value will decline over the asset's life. Therefore those companies with old assets and low written-down values might incorrectly show higher ROCE calculations. For a more detailed discussion of this topic see 'The impact of depreciation' in Chapter 19.

(iv) *Alternative accounting methods:* For comparisons, it is important that the same accounting methods be applied to all companies within the group. For example, one company may capitalize major expense items such as advertising, lease rentals, and research and development expenditure, whereas another company might not capitalize these items. For example, if company A capitalizes lease payments and company B does not then the accounting treatment will result in the capital employed of company B being understated and consequently ROCE overstated.

(b) A single ROCE might not be an adequate measure because:

(i) Companies operate in different industries and a single ROCE measure might not give an adequate measure of performance. For example, if companies A and B have ROCEs of 20% and 10%, respectively, one might conclude that company A has produced the better performance. However, the industry ROCEs might be 25% for the industry in which A operates and 5% for the industry in which B operates. Relative to industry performance, company B has performed better than company A. The ROCE should therefore be compared with other companies and supplemented by other measures such as percentage market shares

(ii) Companies with a high existing ROCE might reject projects whose returns are in excess of the cost of capital but less than existing ROCE. Such companies might be reluctant to expand and be content with a high ROCE and low absolute profits. The ROCE should be supplemented with a measure of absolute profits (e.g. residual income) and details of investment in new projects. This would indicate whether or not the companies were restricting growth in order to preserve their existing high ROCE.

(iii) Concentration on short-run ROCE at the expense of long-run profitability. For an illustration of points that could be considered here see 'Addressing the dysfunctional consequences of short-term financial measures' in Chapter 19.

Question 19.4

(a) For cost control and performance measurement purposes it is necessary to measure performance at frequent intervals. Managers tend to be evaluated on short-term (monthly, quarterly or even yearly) performance measures such as residual income (RI) or return on investment (ROI). Such short-term performance measures focus only on the performance for the particular control period. If a great deal of stress is placed on managers meeting short-term performance measure targets, there is a danger that they will take action that will improve short-term performance but that will not maximize long-term profits. For example, by skimping on expenditure on advertising, customer services, maintenance, and training and staff development costs, it is possible to improve short-term performance. However, such actions may not maximize long-term profits.

Ideally, performance measures ought to be based on future results that can be expected from a manager's actions during a period. This would involve a comparison of the present value of future cash flows at the start and end of the period, and a manager's performance would be based on the increase in present value during the period. Such a system is not feasible, given the difficulty in predicting and measuring outcomes from current actions.

ROI and RI represent single summary measures of performance. It is virtually impossible to capture in summary financial measures all the variables that measure the success of a manager. It is therefore important that accountants broaden their reporting systems to include additional non-financial measures of performance that give clues to future outcomes from present actions.

It is probably impossible to design performance measures which will ensure that maximizing the short-run performance measure will also maximize long-term performance. Some steps, however, can be taken to improve the short-term performance measures so that they minimize the potential conflict. For example, during times of rising prices, short-term performance measures can be distorted if no attempt is made to adjust for the changing price levels. ROI has a number of deficiencies. In particular, it encourages managers to accept only those investments that are in excess of the current ROI, and this can lead to the rejection of profitable projects. Such actions can be reduced by replacing ROI with RI as the performance measure. However, merely changing from ROI to RI will not eliminate the short-run versus long-run conflicts.

(b) One suggestion that has been made to overcome the conflict between short-term and long-term measures is for accountants to broaden their reporting systems and include non-financial performance measures in the performance reports. For example, obtaining feedback from customers regarding the quality of service encourages managers not to skimp on reducing the quality of service in order to save costs in the short term. For a discussion of the potential contribution from including non-financial measures in the reporting system see 'Addressing the dysfunctional consequences of short-term financial performance measures' in Chapter 19.

Other suggestions have focused on refining the financial measures so that they will reduce the potential for conflict between actions that improve short-term performance at the expense of long-term performance. For a description of these suggestions see 'The impact of depreciation' and 'The effect of performance measurement on capital investment decisions' in Chapter 19.

(a) Current budgeted ROCE = 330/(1500 − 720) + 375 = 330/1155   = 28.57%

    (A) Profit − 8

        Current assets − 30

        Revised ROCE = 322/1125   = 28.62%

    (B) Profit + 15

        Current assets + 40

        Revised ROCE = 345/1195   = 28.87%

    (C) Loss on sale (60 WDV − 35 sale proceeds) = (25)

        Loss of profits   = (45)

        Reduced depreciation   = 60

        Net impact on profits   = (10)

Note that the above calculation assumes that the £45 000 profit contribution relates to profits before deduction of £60 000 depreciation. If the £45 000 profit is after deduction of depreciation, the £60 000 reduction in depreciation should not be included in the above calculation. It is assumed that capital employed will decline by £60 000 arising from the deletion of the £60 000 WDV of the asset. However, sale proceeds are £35 000, and it could be argued that this will increase capital employed. It is assumed that the £35 000 is remitted to group headquarters, and thus the overall impact of the transaction increases capital employed by £60 000. The revised ROCE is (330 − 10)/(1155 − 60) = 29.22%

    (D) Profit (+52.5 − 36 depreciation)   = + 16.5

        Fixed assets (+ 4/5 × 180)   = +144

        Revised ROCE = 346.5/1299   = 26.67%

An alternative assumption is that capital employed would be reduced by a further £180 000 to reflect the cash payment for the asset. It is assumed in the above calculations that group headquarters provides the cash for acquiring the asset.

    If divisional managers are evaluated on ROCE, the divisional manager would accept transactions A, B and C since they would result in an increase in ROCE. Transaction D would be rejected because it would result in a lower ROCE.

(b) (i) The evaluation should be based on NPV calculations in order to determine whether or not the non-routine transactions are in the best interests of the group as a whole. The NPV calculations are as follows:

Transaction	Year	Cash inflows (£000)	Cash outflows (£000)	Net cash flow (£000)	Discount factor (15%)	NPV (£000)
A	1	30	(8)	22	0.8696	19.131
	2–4		(8)	(8)	1.9854	(15.883)
						+3.248
B	1	15	(40)	(25)	0.8696	(21.74)
	2–4	15		15	1.9854	29.781
						+8.041
C	0	35		35	1.000	35.000
	1		(45)	(45)	0.8696	39.132

							$-(4.132)$
D	0		(180)	(180)	1.000	(180.000)	
	1–5	52.5		52.5	3.352	175.980	
							$-(4.020)$

Transactions A and B yield positive NPVs and should be undertaken, while transactions C and D should be rejected.

There is goal congruence between G Ltd and GAP Group plc in respect of transactions A, B and D, but there is no goal congruence for transaction C.

(ii) The answer should not support the proposal to substitute a ROCE investment criterion in place of DCF techniques for appraising capital projects. In particular, the answer should stress that ROCE ignores the time value of money and the opportunity cost of capital. For a discussion of the limitations of ROCE of an investment appraisal technique see 'Accounting rate of return' in Chapter 13.

Question 19.6   (a)   (i) Return on capital employed, residual income and economic value added (EVA) should be considered as potential measures. The superiority of EVA or residual income over return on capital employed (see Chapter 19) should be discussed. The objective is to select a performance measure that is consistent with the NPV rule. Residual income is the long-run counterpart of the NPV rule, but it may lead to decisions that are not consistent with the NPV rule if managers base their decisions on short-term measures. Problems occur with both return on capital employed and residual income in terms of bases that should be used for asset valuations. Current values are preferable to historical costs.

(ii) Ideally, market performance measures should indicate sales achievement in relation to the market, competitors and previous performance. Target market shares or unit sales should be established for each product or product range. Actual market shares and unit sales should be compared with targets and previous periods. Trends in market shares should be compared with overall market trends and product life cycles.

(iii) Productivity is concerned with the efficiency of converting physical inputs into physical outputs. Therefore the performance measure should be a physical one. Possible performance measures include output per direct labour hour and output per machine hour. Where divisions produce a variety of products, output could be expressed in standard hours. If monetary measures are used then changes in price levels should be eliminated. In addition to *total* measures of output for each division, performance measures should also be computed for individual products. Output measures should be compared with targets, previous periods and with other divisions.

(iv) Possible measures of the ability of divisions to offer up-to-date product ranges include:
1. number of new products launched in previous periods;
2. expenditure on product development.
Quality and reliability might be measured in terms of:
1. percentage of projects rejected;
2. comparison of target and actual market shares;
3. comparisons with competitors' products;
4. customer surveys.
The performance measures should be compared with previous periods, targets and competitors (if this is possible). Some of the measures may be difficult to express in quantitative terms, and a subjective evaluation may be necessary.

(v) Responsibility towards employees might be reflected by the following measures:

1. rate of labour turnover;
2. level of absenteeism.

Additional information is also necessary to explain the reasons for high labour turnover and absenteeism. Possible reasons might be identified by regularly undertaking attitude surveys on such issues as:

1. payment systems;
2. management style;
3. degree of participation;
4. working conditions.

Other proxy measures that might be used include:

1. number of promotions to different employee and management grades;
2. number of grievance procedures processed;
3. number of applications received per vacancy;
4. training expenditure per employee;
5. number of accidents reported per period.

The above measures should be compared with previous periods and targets.

(vi) It is extremely difficult to assess whether a firm is considered to be a socially responsible citizen within the community. Possible areas of inter-action between the firm and the local community include:

1. employment;
2. environmental effects;
3. involvement in community affairs;
4. provision of recreational and social facilities.

Surveys should be undertaken locally in order to assess the attitude of the population to each of the above areas. Possible quantitative measures include:

1. amount of financial support given to charities, sports organizations and educational establishments;
2. amounts spent on anti-pollution measures;
3. number of complaints received from members of the local community.

(vii) Possible growth measures include comparisons over time (in absolute terms and percentage changes) of the following:

1. total sales revenue;
2. profit (expressed in terms of residual income);
3. total assets;
4. total employees;
5. total market share.

Price changes should be removed where appropriate. Comparisons should be made with other divisions, comparable firms and the industry as a whole. Survival in the long term depends on an acceptable level of profitability.

Therefore appropriate profitability measures should be used. The degree of divisional autonomy might be measured in terms of an assessment of the central controls imposed by central headquarters. (For example: what are the limits on the amounts of capital expenditure decisions that divisions can determine independently?)

(b) A single performance measure underestimates the multi-faceted nature of organizational goals. It might be claimed that a profitability measure is sufficiently general to incorporate the other goals. For example, maintaining high market shares, increasing productivity, offering an up-to-date product range, being a responsible employee, and growth tend to result in increased profitability. To this extent a profitability measure might best capture the multi-faceted nature of organizational goals. Nevertheless the profitability goal alone cannot be expected to capture the complexity of organizational goals. Firms pursue a variety of goals, and for this reason there are strong arguments for using multiple performance measures when evaluating organizational performance. For a further discussion of organizational goals see 'The decision-making process' in Chapter 1.

Question 19.7

(a)
BEST OUTCOME

Year	1	2	3
	£m	£m	£m
Revenues	84.0	94.5	105
Less directed costs	45.0	54.0	63
= net cash flow	39.0	40.5	42
Less depreciation	18.0	18.0	18
= Profit	21.0	22.5	24
Less imputed interest (8%)	4.32	2.88	1.44
= Residual income	16.68	19.62	22.56
Net book value	54	36	18
ROI	39% (21/54)	62.5% (22.5/36)	133% (24/18)

The NPV calculation is as follows:

Year	Cash flow	Discount factor (8%)	DCF
0	(54)	1	(54)
1	39.0	0.926	36.1
2	40.5	0.857	34.7
3	42.0	0.794	33.3
			NPV = 50.1

WORST OUTCOME

Year	1	2	3
	£m	£m	£m
Revenues	76.0	85.5	95
Less direct costs	55.0	66.0	77
– net cash flow	21.0	19.5	18
Less depreciation	18.0	18.0	18
= Profit	3.0	1.5	0
Less imputed interest (13%)	7.02	4.68	2.34
= Residual Income	(4.02)	(3.18)	(2.34)
Net book value	54	36	18
ROI	5.6% (3/54)	4.2% (1.5/36)	0% (0/18)

The NPV calculation is as follows:

Year	Cash flow	Discount factor (13%)	DCF
0	(54)	1	(54)
1	21.0	0.885	18.6
2	19.5	0.783	15.3
3	18.0	0.693	12.5
			NPV = (7.6)

(b) The answer should point out that ROI and residual income represent performance measures that are used to measure managerial or entity performance at the end of a specific period. They can be used as a decision-making tool to measure future periodic outcomes but this is not their recommended purpose. Net present value should be used for decision-making. NPV, however, is not appropriate as an 'after-the-event' performance measure. For a description of ROI and residual income and their strengths and weaknesses you should refer to the appropriate sections in Chapter 19. A discussion of NPV is presented in Chapter 13. The major strengths are that it incorporates the time value of money and takes into account the opportunity cost of capital. The major limitations refer to the difficulties of estimating cash flows many years into the future and the difficulties in accurately determining an appropriate cost of capital.

(c) Broader issues to consider include:
- Qualitative factors as described in the section on qualitative factors in Chapter 13.
- The level of project risk
- How the project relates to existing activities in term of risk (see 'Risk reduction and diversification' in Chapter 12) and synergy?
- The strategic impact of the project on the business.

(a) *Calculation of written-down values (WDVs) and capital employed* **Question 19.8**

Year	1	2	3	4	5
	(£m)	(£m)	(£m)	(£m)	(£m)
Opening WDV	1.5	1.2	0.9	0.6	0.3
Depreciation (straight line)	0.3	0.3	0.3	0.3	0.3
Closing WDV	1.2	0.9	0.6	0.3	—
Opening capital employed (opening WDV + WC)	2.0	1.7	1.4	1.1	0.8

Calculation of residual income and ROCE

Year	1	2	3	4	5
	(£m)	(£m)	(£m)	(£m)	(£m)
Sales	2.0				
Operating costs	(1.35)				
Depreciation	(0.30)				
Net profit	0.35	0.35	0.35	0.35	0.35
Imputed interest (20%)	0.40	0.34	0.28	0.22	0.16
Residual income	(0.05)	0.01	0.07	0.13	0.19
ROCE	17.5%	20.6%	25%	31.8%	43.7%

CP's management would be unlikely to undertake the project if they are evaluated on the basis of ROCE, since it yields a return of less than 30% for each of the first three years. Consequently, the total ROCE will be less than 30% during the first three years. Residual income is negative in the first year and positive for the remaining four years. If the management of CP place more emphasis on the impact on the performance measure on the first year, they may reject the project. On the other hand, if they adopt a longer-term perspective, they will accept the project.

(b) *Calculation of annuity depreciation*

Year	(1) Annual repayment (£m)	(2) 20% interest on capital outstanding (£m)	(3) = (1) − (2) Capital repayment (£m)	(4) = (4) − (3) Capital outstanding (£m)
0				1.5
1	0.5016	0.3	0.2016	1.2984
2	0.5016	0.2597	0.2419	1.0565
3	0.5016	0.2113	0.2903	0.7662
4	0.5016	0.1532	0.3484	0.4178
5	0.5016	0.0838	0.4178	—

For an explanation of the calculations see 'Annuity depreciation' in Learning Note 19.1 on the open access website. Note that the annual repayment is determined by referring to the present value of an annuity shown in the table in Appendix B of the text for 5 years at 20%. The annual repayment of £0.5016m is calculated by dividing the investment outlay (£1.5m) by the annuity factor (2.991).

Calculation of residual income and ROCE

Year	1	2	3	4	5
	(£m)	(£m)	(£m)	(£m)	(£m)
Opening WDV	1.50	1.30	1.06	0.77	0.42
Annuity depreciation	0.20	0.24	0.29	0.35	0.42
Closing WDV	1.30	1.06	0.77	0.42	–
Total opening capital employed	2.0	1.80	1.56	1.27	0.92
Operating earnings	0.65	0.65	0.65	0.65	0.65
Depreciation	0.20	0.24	0.29	0.35	0.42
Net profit	0.45	0.41	0.36	0.30	0.23
Imputed interest	0.40	0.36	0.31	0.25	0.18
Residual income	0.05	0.05	0.05	0.05	0.05
ROCE	22.5%	22.8%	23.1%	23.6%	25%

Since the projected ROCE is less than 30%, CP's management are likely to reject the project if performance is evaluated on the basis of ROCE. If performance is evaluated on the basis of residual income, the project is likely to be accepted, since it has a positive residual income for all five years.

(c) The calculation of NPV is as follows:

	(£m)
PV of net cash inflows (£0.65m × 2.991 discount factor)	1.944
Working capital released at the end of the project (0.5m × 0.4019)	0.201
Initial outlay	(2.000)
NPV	0.145

The project should be accepted, since it has a positive NPV. The objective is to design a performance measurement system that is consistent with the NPV rule. The ROCE measure may not encourage goal congruence, because managers of divisions with a ROCE in excess of the cost of capital may incorrectly reject projects with positive NPVs. Alternatively, managers of divisions with a ROCE that is less than the cost of capital may incorrectly accept projects with negative NPVs. This situation arises because managers who are evaluated on the basis of ROCE may base their investment decisions on the impact on ROCE and use the existing ROCE as the cut-off rate.

The project outlined in the question has a positive NPV, but the ROCE is less than 30% for the first three years in (a), where straight-line depreciation is used. If annuity depreciation is used, the project has a ROCE of less than 30% for each year of the project's life. The manager is therefore unlikely to accept the investment, since it will result in a decline in the overall ROCE of the division.

In the long run, the residual income method produces a calculation that is consistent with the NPV rule. The short-term residual income calculation may not, however, motivate managers to select projects that are consistent with applying the NPV rule. In the case of constant cash flows the problem can be resolved by using the annuity method of depreciation, but when annual cash flows fluctuate, this method of depreciation does not ensure that the short-term residual income measure is consistent with the NPV rule. For a discussion of how this problem might be resolved see 'Reconciling short-term and long-term residual income/EVA measures' in Learning Note 19.1 on the open access website. You can see that, for the project outlined in the question, residual income is positive for all years where the annuity method of depreciation is used, but it is negative in the first year and positive for the remaining years where straight-line depreciation is used.

(a)   *Calculations based on best outcomes*   **Question 19.9**

	Year 1	Year 2	Year 3	Year 4
Additional capacity (standard hours) [a]	1 050	1 365	1 785	2 100
	(£)	(£)	(£)	(£)
Contribution at £1320 per hour	1 386 000	1 801 800	2 356 200	2 772 000
Less training, consultancy and salary costs	97 500	97 500	97 500	97 500
	1 288 500	1 704 300	2 258 700	2 674 500
Less depreciation	1 000 000	1 000 000	1 000 000	1 000 000
Net profit	288 500	704 300	1 258 700	1 674 500
Less imputed interest (8% × WDV)	320 000	240 000	160 000	80 000
Residual income	−31 500	464 300	1 098 700	1 594 500
ROI [b]	7.2%	23.5%	62.9%	167.5%

NPV at 8% = (£1 288 500 × 0.926) + (£1 704 300 × 0.857) + (£2 258 700 × 0.794) +
(£2 674 500 × 0.735) − £4 000 000
= £2 412 901

Notes
[a] Year 1 = 1000(1.05) with increments for years 2–4 being 300(1.05), 400(1.05) and 300(1.05)
[b] Profit/Opening WDV's of £4m, £3m, £2m and £1m.

(b)   *Bonus calculations*

	Year 1	Year 2	Year 3	Year 4	Total
	(£)	(£)	(£)	(£)	(£)
Net profit [a]	0	3150	10 350	15 750	29 250
Residual income [b]	0	0	9800	19 000	28 800
ROI basis [c]	6000	6000	6000	6000	24 000
NPV basis (£1 233 700 × 2.5%) in year 4				30 843	30 843

Notes
[a] Year 2 bonus = (£460 000 − £250 000) × 1.5% = £3150
[b] Year 3 bonus = (£740 000 − £250 000 = £490 000 = 4.9 × 5% × £40 000 = £9800)
[c] Year 1 bonus = ROI is positive for all years so the bonus is £6000 per year (15% of £40 000)

(c) The manager's choice is likely to be influenced by his/her attitude towards risk, the potential size of the bonus, the timing and ease of obtaining the bonus. The most likely outcome figures shown in (c) indicate a clear preference for (c) over the time horizon, but there is a long delay in payment. If an early receipt of the bonus is important to the manager, then ROI may be preferred since this provides a considerably higher bonus over the first two years. The manager may also find the NPV and residual income basis less attractive because both measures are influenced by the cost of capital, which is beyond the control of the manager. A risk-seeking manager is likely to find the bonus based on NPV very attractive since it yields the highest bonus if the best or most likely outcomes occur. In contrast, a risk-averse manager is likely to favour the bonus based on ROI since it produces the highest bonus for the worst outcome.

(d) The bonus system and any promotion prospects arising from the success of the programme may influence the manager's level of effort and motivation. Also, the manager's attitude to risk and the perceived extent to which he/she can influence the outcomes is likely to influence the level of effort. The level of motivation to achieve the programme will be affected by the expectation that its success will result in some benefits and the strength of preference of the manager for the benefits. The personal expectations are also important. If the manager believes in the programme he/she will be highly motivated to make it a success. Also, the expectations of success will be important. If the manager believes there is little chance of the programme being successful there may be little motivation to make an effort for it to succeed.

Question 19.10

(a) To compute EVA, adjustments must be made to the conventional after tax profit measures of $44m and $55m shown in the question. Normally an adjustment is made to convert conventional financial accounting depreciation to an estimate of economic depreciation, but the question indicates that profits have already been computed using economic depreciation. Non-cash expenses are added back since the adjusted profit attempts to approximate cash flow after taking into account economic depreciation. Net interest is also added back because the returns required by the providers of funds will be reflected in the cost of capital deduction. Note that net interest is added back because interest will have been allowed as an expense in determining the taxation payment.

The capital employed used to calculate EVA should be based on adjustments that seek to approximate book economic value at the start of each period. Because insufficient information is given, the book value of shareholders funds plus medium and long-term loans at the end of 2000 is used as the starting point to determine economic capital employed at the beginning of 2001.

	2000 ($m)	2001 ($m)
Adjusted profit	56.6 (44 + 10 + (4 × 0.65))	68.9 (55 + 10 + (6 × 0.65))
Capital employed	233 (223 + 10)	260 (250 + 10)

The weighted average cost of capital should be based on the target capital structure. The calculation is as follows:

$2000 = (15\% \times 0.6) + (9\% \times 0.65 \times 0.4) = 11.34\%$
$2001 = (17\% \times 0.6) + (10\% \times 0.65 \times 0.4) = 12.8\%$
EVA $2000 = 56.6 - (233 \times 0.1134) = \$30.18m$
EVA $2001 = 68.9 - (260 \times 0.128) = \$35.62$

The EVA measures indicate that the company has added significant value in both years and achieved a satisfactory level of performance.

(b) The present value of EVA from an investment approximates the NPV of the investment. For an explanation of this point you should refer to 'The effect of performance measurement on capital investment decisions' in Chapter 19.

(c) Advantages of EVA include:
1 because some discretionary expenses are capitalized the harmful side-effects of financial measures described in Chapters 16 and 19 are reduced;
2 EVA is consistent with maximizing shareholders funds;
3 EVA is easily understood by managers;
4 EVA can also be linked to managerial bonus schemes and motivate managers to take decisions that increase shareholder value.

Disadvantages of EVA include:
1 the EVA computation can be complicated when many adjustments are required;
2 EVA is difficult to use for inter-firm and inter-divisional comparisons because it is not a ratio measure;
3 if economic depreciation is not used, the short-term measure can conflict with the long-term measure (see 'The effect of performance measurement on capital investment decisions' in Chapter 19).
4 economic depreciation is difficult to estimate and conflicts with generally accepted accounting principles which may hinder its acceptance by financial managers.

DIVISIONAL FINANCIAL PERFORMANCE MEASURES

Transfer pricing in divisionalised companies

Solutions to Chapter 20 questions

(a) With cost-based transfer price systems, transfers are made either at actual cost or **Question 20.1** standard cost. Where actual costs are used, there is no incentive for the supplying centre to control costs because any inefficiencies arising in the supplying centre will be passed on to the receiving centre. Consequently, the receiving centre will be held accountable for the inefficiencies of the supplying division. Transfers at actual cost are therefore inappropriate for responsibility accounting.

Where cost-based transfer pricing systems are used, transfers should be at standard cost and not actual cost. This will result in the supplying centre being held accountable for the variances arising from the difference between standard and actual cost of the transfers. The managers of the supplying centres are therefore motivated to minimize their costs. When transfers are made at standard cost, any inefficiencies of the supplying centre are not passed on to the receiving centre. The receiving centre should be held accountable for usage of resources at the standard price, thus ensuring that the manager of the receiving centre is held accountable only for excessive usage of resources.

Where cost-based transfer prices are used, there is still a danger that inappropriate transfer prices are set that will not provide an appropriate basis for allocating profits between divisions. Where there is a competitive market for intermediate products, the current market price is the most suitable basis for setting the transfer price. When transfers are recorded at market prices, profit centre performance is likely to represent the real economic contribution of the profit centre to total company profits. If the supplying centre did not exist, the intermediate product would have to be purchased on the outside market at the current market price. Alternatively, if the receiving centre did not exist, the intermediate product would have to be sold on the outside market at the current market price. Responsibility centre profits are therefore likely to be similar to the profits that would be calculated if the centres were separate independent businesses. Therefore transfers based on selling prices will represent a more appropriate basis for meeting the requirements of a responsibility accounting system.

(b) When the supplying division does not have sufficient capacity to meet all the demands placed upon it, linear programming can be used to determine the optimum production level. The transfer price that will induce the supplying division to produce the optimum output level can be derived from the linear programming model. The transfer price is determined by adding the shadow prices of the scarce resources (as indicated by the output from the linear programming model) to the variable cost of the resources consumed by the intermediate product. This transfer price will result in the supplying division being credited with all of the contribution arising from the transfers and the receiving division earning a zero contribution. The allocation of zero contribution to the receiving division will have a negative motivational influence, and result in a loss of divisional autonomy and a reported performance that does not reflect the economic performance of the division.

Question 20.2

(a) (i) See 'The multiple functions of budgets' in Chapter 15 for the answer to this question.

(a) (ii) See 'Participation in the budgeting and target setting process' for the answer to this question.

(b) You should refer to each transfer pricing method in Chapter 20 for the answer to this question. Note that the marginal cost plus opportunity cost approach is the same as the opportunity cost method stated in the question. With this method the resulting transfer price will be the same as a market based transfer price where full capacity exists. Therefore the supplying and receiving divisions would incur the same costs or receive the same revenues compared with purchasing or selling from/to the external market. However, where spare capacity exists, marginal cost would represent the opportunity cost so the impact on the managers would be the same as applying marginal cost transfer prices.

(c) Where cost-based transfer prices are used, standard costs, and not actual costs, per unit of output should be used. If actual costs are used, the supplying divisions will be able to pass on the cost of any inefficiencies to the receiving divisions. Using standard costs ensures that the cost of inefficiencies are allocated to the supplying divisions.

Question 20.3

(a) DP division variable costs for October

	Budget	Actual
	(£)	(£)
Skilled labour	10 000 (£120 000/12)	11 000 (+10%)
Semi-skilled labour	8 000	8 800 (+10%)
Processing	5 000	4 750 (–5%)
Total	23 000	24 550

(i) Actual variable cost per hour = £24 550/(450 hours) = £54.555
(Note 6000/12 × 0.9 = 450)
Total charge for 200 hours = £10 911

(ii) Standard variable cost plus 40% = £23 000/450 = £51.111 × 1.4 = £71.555
Total charge for 200 hours = £14 311

(iii) Market price is based on total cost plus 40% mark-up

	(£)
Standard variable cost	51.111
Budgeted fixed cost per hour	44.444 (£240 000/5400 hours)
Total cost	95.555
Add 40% mark-up	38.222
Transfer price	133.777

Total charge for 200 hours = £26 755

(b) DP division

Transfer pricing method	Actual variable cost	Standard variable cost + 40%	Market price
	(£)	(£)	(£)
External sales (250 hours × £133.777)	33 444	33 444	33 444
Internal sales	10 911	14 311	26 755
Total revenue	44 355	47 755	60 199
Variable costs	24 550	24 550	24 550
Contribution	19 805	23 205	35 649
Fixed costs	20 000	20 000	20 000
Profit/(loss)	(195)	3 205	15 649

Consulting division

Consulting costs	2 600	2 600	2 600
Transfer price	10 911	14 311	26 755
Total cost	13 511	16 911	29 355
Project fee	15 500	15 500	15 500
Profit/(loss)	1 989	(1 411)	(13 855)

(c) Only the variable cost transfer price results in the consulting division making a profit on the project. Given that DP division has spare capacity, the opportunity cost is zero and variable cost is the relevant transfer price. Because DP should be accountable for any cost variances, standard variable cost should be used giving a transfer price of £10 222 (£51.111 × 200 hours). At the proposed transfer price, DP division will earn a zero contribution and the consulting division will obtain a contribution of £2678 [£15 500 – (£10 222 + £2600)]. The company as a whole will be better off by £2678 by accepting the project.

Question 20.4

(a) For the answer to this question see 'The role of a cost accumulation system in generating relevant cost information for decision-making' and 'Volume-based and non-volume-based cost drivers' in Chapter 10. In particular, the answer should point out that ABC ought to lead to the reporting of more accurate product costs and thus improved decision-making. In relation to M Ltd. the product profitability analysis based on the traditional costing system may be providing inaccurate information. The profitability analysis indicates that Q makes a loss although it generates a positive short-run contribution to fixed costs. Q Ltd. may choose to discontinue Q if it considers that a large proportion of the fixed costs is avoidable in the long run. However, the introduction of ABC may result in significant changes in reported product profits, such that Q makes a profit, if the traditional system inaccurately measures resources consumed by the different products.

(b) The following difficulties may be encountered:
1   identifying appropriate activity cost pools and cost drivers;
2   lack of trained staff to implement and operate the system;
3   reluctance of the staff to change to a new system;
4   the traditional system may report reasonably accurate product costs resulting in there being little difference between the reported product costs for the two systems. However, the ABC system is likely to be more costly to operate;
5   traditional systems accurately trace direct costs to cost objects and facility sustaining costs are unavoidable unless there is a dramatic change in the scale or scope of activity. Therefore the costs that can be more accurately traced to cost objects with ABC may represent only a small proportion of total costs;

(c) (i)   The supplying division has no external market for chips so the situation is very similar to that illustrated in Example 20.1. You will therefore find the criticisms of the current transfer pricing method in 'An illustration of transfer pricing' in Chapter 20. An alternative system would be for the transfer price to be based on marginal cost plus a fixed lump-sum fee. You should refer to Chapter 20 for an explanation of this method.

(c) (ii) With the introduction of an ABC, M Ltd. should continue to use the transfer pricing system recommended in (c) (i) as explained for an ABC system in the section 'Marginal cost plus a lump-sum fee' in Chapter 20.

Question 20.5   (a)

Residual income calculations

	TM division (£000)		FD division (£000)	
Sales: External	7500	(15 000 × £500)	400	(5000 × £80)
Internal			990	(15 000 × (£60 + 10%))
	7500		1390	
Less variable costs:				
Production	5490	(15 000 × £366)	800	(20 000 × £40)
Selling and distribution	375	(15 000 × £25)	20	(5000 × £4)
Contribution	1635		570	
Less: Fixed production costs	900	(15 000 × £60)	400	(20 000 × £20)
Administration costs	375	(15 000 × £25)	80	(20 000 × £4)
Net profit	360		90	
Less cost of capital charge (12%)	180		90	
Residual income	180		0	

The manager of TM has exceeded his/her target and will thus receive a bonus of £9000 whereas the manager of FD division will not receive any bonus. Given that the majority of FD's sales are internal, it is likely that the transfer price, which is currently below the external selling price, is contributing to FD's poor performance. The fact that the manager of TM receives a bonus and the manager of FD does not is likely to have an adverse motivational impact which may affect future performance.

(b) (i) The manager of TM can suffer a decline in residual income of £75 000 (£180 000 – £105 000) without losing the bonus. This represents an increase in the transfer price of £5 (£75 000/15 000 units) per unit; so at a transfer price of £71 or below a bonus will still be awarded to the manager of TM.

(b) (ii) The manager of FD requires additional residual income of £85 000 in order to receive a bonus. This represents an increase in the transfer price of £5.67 (£85 000/15 000 units) giving a minimum transfer price of £71.67.

(c) At the present level of demand, FD has 5000 units unused capacity (25 000 maximum capacity – 15 000 transfers – 5000 external sales). Therefore, transfers to TM have no opportunity cost in terms of forgone contribution as long as external demand is less than 10 000 units. Under these circumstances, theory suggests that the optimal transfer price for decision-making is the marginal/variable production cost of £40 per unit. If sales demand for the external market exceeds 10 000 units, the opportunity cost of any transfers will be represented by the lost contribution of £36 (£80 selling price – £44 variable cost) per unit on external sales. Applying the marginal cost plus opportunity cost approach described in the chapter results in an optimal transfer price of £76 (£40 variable cost of transfers + £36 opportunity cost). This is identical to the external selling price less variable costs that are specifically attributable to external sales.

Although the above transfer price is optimal for decision-making it is unsatisfactory for performance evaluation. The manager of FD will not obtain a contribution on internal sales and will not be motivated to transfer the goods to TM. Also, the transfer prices computed in (b) indicate that a conflict of interests occurs since only one of the managers can obtain the bonus. To resolve the decision-making and performance evaluation conflicts, it is recommended that a dual-rate or marginal cost plus a fixed lump-sum fee transfer pricing system be implemented. The answer should describe these methods (see Chapter 20 for a description) and show how they can resolve the conflicts.

(a) *Preliminary comments*

Question 20.6

The answer to this question requires that we compare the relevant costs for each of the three alternatives. Relevant costs will include incremental costs plus any lost contribution where a division has no spare capacity. Only RR is working at full capacity. Therefore the relevant costs are as follows:

Work undertaken by RP, RS and RT: Relevant cost equals incremental cost for the group as a whole.
Work undertaken by RR: Relevant cost equals incremental cost plus lost contribution from the displaced work. (This is equivalent to the lost sales revenue.)

Relevant cost of company A quote	£33 000
	(£)

Relevant cost of company B quote	
Cost of quote	35 000
Less benefits to group of subcontract work[a]	2 420
Relevant cost	32 580

Note

[a]It is assumed that the £13 000 RS charge to Company B includes 25% on the cost of its own work but no additional margin is added to the £7500 market price for the parts purchased from RR. Therefore the price of £13 000 by RS to Company B is assumed to include £7500 in respect of RR work plus the balance of £5500 for RS work. The total cost of RS work is £4400 (the question indicates that RS expects to earn a profit of 25% on its *own* work). Therefore the group contribution from subcontract work is as follows:

	(£)	(£)
Selling price of special unit		13 000
Less incremental cost to group of RR's own work (70% × £4400)	3080	
Relevant cost of RR's work (market price)	7500	10 580
Contribution to group		2 420

Relevant cost of RS quote

The following diagram illustrates the inter-group transfers:

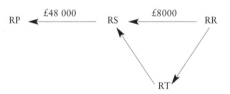

From the above information, it is necessary to ascertain the relevant cost of the *group* from producing the electronic control system. The relevant cost of RR work is the market price of £19 000 (£11 000 + £8000). The relevant cost of RS and RT work is the variable cost (excluding the cost of transfers within the group). The calculations are as follows:

	(£)
RS conversion cost:	
RS total cost	42 000
Less costs transferred from other members of the group (£30 000 + £8000)	38 000
Cost of RS conversion work	4 000
Variable cost of RS conversion work (70% of £4000)	2 800

		(£)
RT conversion cost:		
Price charged by RT to RS		30 000
Less profit margin (20% on total cost)		5 000
Total cost of RS work (including transfer from RR)		25 000
Less transfer price of parts purchased from RR		11 000
Total cost of work added by RT		14 000
Variable cost of work added by RT (65% × £14 000)		9 100

Therefore the relevant cost to the group is as follows:

	(£)
Work undertaken by RR	19 000
Variable costs of conversion work by RT	9 100
Variable costs of conversion work by RS	2 800
Relevant cost	30 900

The order should be awarded to RS because this is the lowest relevant cost alternative.

(b) The following assumptions have been made in part (a):
  (i) Incremental costs are represented by variable costs, and no additional fixed costs will be incurred for each alternative.
  (ii) Variable costs are linear with respect to output changes.
  (iii) RS and RT have sufficient spare capacity to accept the work. Hence no orders will be turned away and opportunity costs are assumed to be zero.
  (iv) RP is not free to select its own source of supply. If RP has complete independence then it is likely to accept the quote that will minimize its costs (i.e. the Company A quote).

Question 20.7

(a) (i)

Division O Budgeted profit for year ending 31 May 2005

Product	Painfree Branded	Painfree Unbranded	Digestisalve Branded	Digestisalve Unbranded	Awaysafe Branded	Total
Sales-packs (000's)	5 000	15 000	5 000	20 000	15 000	60 000
Selling price (£'s)	2.40	1.20	4.80	3.60	8.00	
	£000s	£000s	£000s	£000s	£000s	£000s
Sales revenue	12 000	18 000	24 000	72 000	120 000	246 000
Cost of sales:						
Material/conv costs	4 250	12 750	9 250	37 000	42 000	105 250
Packaging costs	750	750	1 250	3 000	6 000	11 750
Total variable costs	5 000	13 500	10 500	40 000	48 000	117 000
Contribution	7 000	4 500	13 500	32 000	72 000	129 000
Fixed costs:						
Fixed overheads						81 558
Advertising and promotion costs						17 400
Net profit						30 042
Net profit						30 042
Required return (10%)						12 000
Residual income (RI)						18 042
Invested capital (£000s)						120 000
Return on Investment (ROI)						25.04%

(a) (ii) During the years ending 31 May 2005 and 2006 capacity is restricted to 65 million packs (780 million tablets/12). Expected demand in 2005 is 65 million packs but in 2006 it is expected to increase to 66 million packs resulting in demand exceeding capacity by 1 million packs. The failure to meet customer demand in 2006 may have an adverse impact on customer goodwill which may affect future sales. Attention should now be given to ways of increasing capacity in order to satisfy customer demand.

It is possible that customers may buy more than one different type of product from the company. In other words, product sales may be interrelated. In these circumstances it is important to ensure that a full product line is maintained. There is a danger that customers will migrate to competitors that offer a full product range if they are not offered a suitable range of products to choose from.

Competitor reactions should also be considered before altering the product mix by introducing new products or redesigning existing products.

(a) (iii) See 'Residual income' in Chapter 19 for the answer to this question. In particular, the answer should point out how residual income can overcome some of the dysfunctional consequences of ROI, incorporate different cost of capital percentage rates to investments that have different levels of risk and provide a focus on utilizing capital efficiently in order to minimize the cost of capital charge.

(b) (i) The proposed transfer price is £5.60 (£8 less 30%) but since the external purchase price is £5.50 the manager of Division L will choose to purchase externally. Quotation 1 is for 5 million packs and, assuming that Division O has no alternative use for its spare capacity of 5 million packs, the incremental cost of the order is £16 million (5 million × £3.20 variable cost). If the order is obtained externally the incremental purchase costs are £27.5 million (5 million × £5.50). Therefore the group will incur £11.5 million additional costs if the order is obtained from the external supplier.

Quotation 2 is for 9 million packs and Division O can only meet this demand by utilizing the spare capacity to produce 5 million packs and reducing sales volume of one of the existing products by 4 million packs. The sales volume of unbranded 'Painfree' should be reduced because it has the lowest unit contribution (£0.30 per pack). Therefore the incremental costs of supplying 9 million packs of 'Awaysafe' are £28.8 million variable costs but the company will lose a contribution of £1.2 million (4 million × £0.30) from reduced production of unbranded Painfree, giving a total incremental cost of £30 million. The external purchase cost is £49.5 million (9 million × £5.50). As indicated above the manager of Division L will choose to purchase externally resulting in the group incurring additional costs of £19.5 million.

(b) (ii) In Chapter 20 it is pointed out that setting transfer prices at the marginal cost of the supplying division per unit transferred plus the opportunity cost per unit of the supplying division is a general rule that can be applied that should lead to optimum decisions for the company as a whole. For quotation 1 the demand can be met from existing capacity so opportunity cost is zero. Applying the general rule will result in a transfer price of £3.20 per pack or £16 million for 5 000 packs. There is an opportunity cost of £1.2 million for quotation 2 in respect of the 4 million packs lost sales of unbranded 'Painfree'. The marginal costs of producing the 9 000 packs are £28.8 million. Therefore applying the general rule the transfer price for the 9 000 packs should be £30 million (£28.8 million + £1.2 million).

(b) (iii) See 'Marginal cost plus opportunity cost' in Chapter 20 for the answer to this question. The answer should also point out that although applying the marginal cost plus opportunity cost rule meets one of the transfer pricing objectives of providing information for motivating optimal decisions it fails to meet the transfer pricing objective of providing information for evaluating the managerial and economic performance of a division. For example, with quotation 1 applying the rule leads to the Division O obtaining zero contribution on the transfers and all of the contribution from the transferred packs being allocated to Division L.

(c) (i) If Division L buys externally from a local supplier the financial implications for the group are as follows:

	£m
Contribution obtained by Division O from the sales of 15 million packs of 'Painfree' at £0.30 per pack	4.5
Taxation (40%)	1.8
After tax contribution	2.7
Division L purchases (9 million packs at £5.50)	49.50
Taxation savings (20%)	(9.90)
After tax cost of purchases	39.60
Net cost to NAW group (£39.6 – £2.7)	36.90

If Division L buys internally from Divison O the financial implications are:

	£m
Division O sales	
Contribution from 11 million packs of Painfree at £0.30 per pack	3.3
Contribution from 9 million packs of 'Awaysafe' transferred to Division L at £2.40 per pack (£5.60 – £3.20)	21.6
	24.9
Less taxation at 40%	(9.96)
After tax contribution	14.94
Division L purchases:	
Transfer costs on 9 million packs of 'Awaysafe' at £5.60 per pack	50.4
Taxation savings (20%)	(10.08)
After tax cost of purchases	40.32
Net coast to NAW group (40.32 – 14.94)	25.38

NAW group will be £11.52 million (£36.90m – £25.38m) better off if Division L purchases product 'Awaysafe' from Division O compared with purchasing it from a local supplier.

(c) (ii) See 'International transfer pricing' in Chapter 20 for the answer to this question.

(d) See 'Pricing policies' in Chapter 11 for the answer to this question.

Question 20.8

(a) *Scenario 1*

Since South has spare production capacity, the incremental cost to the company as a whole of using the internal consultant is £100 compared with £500 for the external consultant. The transfer price should encourage the use of the internal consultant. Any transfer price above the variable cost of £100 per day will enable South to obtain a contribution. North division will not be prepared to pay in excess of the external charge of £500 per day. Therefore a transfer price in excess of £100 and less than £500 will encourage both managers to make decisions that are in the best interests of the company as a whole.

Scenario 2

For the company as a whole, it is preferable to lose revenue of £400 rather than incur additional costs of £500. Therefore the transfer price should be set to encourage both managers to use the internal consultant. The transfer price should be set above £400 to encourage the manager of South division to undertake the transaction and below £500 to encourage the manager of North division to buy from South.

Scenario 3

For the company as a whole, it is preferable to earn revenues of £700 and incur external costs of £500. The transfer price should discourage the transfer between the two divisions. Therefore it should be set below £700 to encourage the manager of South division to choose to earn £700 per day and above £500 to encourage the manager of North to use the external consultant.

The above comments are based on a short-term analysis assuming the objective is to maximize short-run contribution and that the company has access to all the decision-making data that the separate divisions use.

(b) See 'The sections relating to the advantages of divisionalization, disadvantages of divisionalization and pre-requisites for successful divisionalization' in Chapter 19 for the answer to this question.

(a)

	Blackalls		Brownalls	
	(£)	(£)	(£)	(£)
Selling price		45		54
Component costs: Alpha	18 (3 × £6)		12 (2 × £6)	
Beta	8 (2 × £4)		16 (4 × £4)	
Processing cost	12	38	14	42
Contribution		7		12

Group contribution:	(£)
Blackalls 200 × £7	1400
Brownalls 300 × £12	3600
	5000

(b) Transfer price = variable cost + shadow price

Alpha	= £6	+ £0.50	= £6.50
Beta	= £4	+ £2.75	= £6.75

(i)

	Division A	Division B
	(£)	(£)
Transfer price	6.50	6.75
Variable cost	6.00	4.00
Contribution/unit	0.50	2.75

(ii)

	Black division		Brown division	
	(£)	(£)	(£)	(£)
Selling price		45		54
Component cost:				
Alpha	19.50 (3 × £6.50)		13.00 (2 × £6.50)	
Beta	13.50 (2 × £6.75)		27.00 (4 × £6.75)	
Processing cost	12.00	45	14.00	54
Contribution/unit		nil		nil

(c) When the supplying division does not have sufficient capacity to meet all the demands placed upon it, linear programming can be used to determine the optimum production level. The transfer price that will induce the supplying division to produce the optimum output level can be derived from the linear programming model. The transfer price is determined by adding the shadow prices of the scarce resources to the variable cost of the resources consumed by the intermediate product. The transfer price that induces the supplying division to transfer the optimum output to the receiving division results in the supplying division being credited with all of the contribution arising from the transfers and the receiving division earning a zero contribution. This is illustrated in part (b) of the answer.

The managers of the receiving divisions will be indifferent about producing the final products, since they yield a zero contribution, but the group as a whole will be worse off if the final products are not produced. To ensure that the optimal output of the final products is produced, it will be necessary for head office to instruct the receiving divisions to convert all the output that the supplying divisions are prepared to transfer (at the transfer prices derived from the linear programming model). This will have a negative motivational influence on the managers of the receiving division, and will result in a loss of divisional autonomy. In addition, the reported performance of the divisions will not reflect their contribution to group profits. Therefore the transfer prices will not be acceptable to the managers of the receiving divisions, whereas the managers of the supplying divisions (A and B) will be satisfied since they will be allocated with the full amount of the contribution.

(d) (i) The transfer price should reflect the opportunity cost of producing the intermediate products. The transfer prices are calculated as follows:

$$\text{variable cost} + \text{opportunity cost}$$
$$\text{Alpha} = £6 + (5\% \times £6) = £6.30$$
$$\text{Beta} = £4 + (£3.50 - £0.50) = £7$$

Note that the above transfer prices reflect the selling prices (or net sales revenue) from using the capacity of the supplying divisions to produce other products (A division) or sell the intermediate product on the external market (B division).

(ii) The contributions per unit for Blackalls and Brownalls are as follows:

	Black division		Brown division	
	(£)	(£)	(£)	(£)
Selling price		45.00		54.00
Component costs:				
Alpha (at £6.30)	18.90		12.60	
Beta (at £7)	14.00		28.00	
Processing cost	12.00	44.90	14.00	54.60
Contribution/unit		0.10		(0.60)

Brown division will not produce Brownalls, because they yield a negative contribution, but Black division will wish to maximize production of Blackalls. The production capacity of Alpha and Beta is as follows:

Alpha 2400 units (restricts maximum production of Blackalls to 800 units)
Beta 3200 units (restricts maximum production of Blackalls to 1600 units)

Production of Blackalls is therefore restricted to 800 units, thus using all of the available Alpha capacity. Production of 800 units of Blackalls requires 1600 units of Beta (800 × 2 units). The unused Beta capacity of 1600 units (3200 − 1600) will be sold on the external intermediate market. Therefore the optimal output is as follows:

Brownalls zero
Blackalls 800 units
Alpha   2400 units transferred to Black division
Beta   3200 units (1600 units transferred to Black division and 1600 units sold externally)

The resulting maximum group contribution is:

		(£)
Blackalls	(800 × £7)	5 600
Beta	[1600 × (£7 − £4)]	4 800
		10 400

Cost management

Solutions to Chapter 21 questions

Question 21.1

(a) For the answer to this section you should refer to 'Activity-based management' in Chapter 21. In this section it was pointed out that some organizations have opted for behaviourally oriented overhead allocations that aim to induce desired behavioural responses instead of seeking to accurately assign overheads to cost objects. For example, some Japanese companies have allocated overheads using direct labour as the allocation base even though there was no cause-and-effect relationship between direct labour and overheads. Their aim was, through overhead allocations, to make direct labour expensive and to encourage managers to replace labour with machinery. For a discussion of how the choice of overhead allocation bases can also be used to influence product design decisions you should refer to Chapter 21.

(b) The answer to this question should explain how absorption costing systems can encourage managers to over-produce in order to defer the allocation of fixed overheads to future accounting periods. For an explanation of this point you should refer to 'Variable costing and absorption costing: a comparison of their impact on profit' in Chapter 7. This problem can be reduced by:

1 using residual income whereby managers bear a cost of capital charge on the investment in stocks;
2 implementing a just-in-time production system;
3 reporting stock levels and monitoring their trends over time.

Question 21.2

(a) The answer to this question should point out that production will be organized based on a batch production functional layout (see Chapter 21) and materials scheduled using a material resources planning system (see Chapter 24). There will be a need for a detailed product costing system that tracks work in progress movements throughout the factory and ensures that it can be valued at various stages at frequent intervals. Standard costing is likely to be extensively used to control costs.

(b) The answer to this question should describe a just-in-time production system and just-in-time purchasing (see Chapter 21).

(c) For the answer to this question you should refer to 'JIT and management accounting' (Chapter 21), 'The future role of standard costing' in Learning Note 18.5 on the open access website and 'Backflush costing' (Chapter 4). In addition, the answer should stress the need to place greater emphasis on non-financial measures (see balanced scorecard internal business perspective in Chapter 22), activity-based cost management and various other approaches to cost management described in Chapter 21.

Question 21.3

Each of the techniques listed in the question is described in Chapter 21. You should therefore refer to Chapter 21 for the answer to this question.

Question 21.4

(a) See 'Benchmarking' in Chapter 21 for an explanation of the aims and operation. External benchmarking involves a comparison of performing activities with external organizations that are recognized as industry leaders whereas internal benchmarking involves a comparison of performing similar activities in different units within the same organization.

Activity-based-costing information can be used to compare the cost of similar activities undertaken in different business units. The information would enable apparently high cost activities that may be inefficient if targeted for benchmarking. Alternatively, a unit may have established a reputation for being a leader for performing a particular activity. This may provide the stimulus for benchmarking the activity against other similar activities performed elsewhere in the organization. External benchmarking differs in that it is more difficult to obtain access to the industry leader and may be impossible where the leader is a competitor.

A major difficulty with benchmarking is identifying a relevant benchmark and ensuring that the activities being compared are similar in terms of their objectives and the constraints that apply. If internal benchmarking is used there is no guarantee that the targeted unit for comparison represents excellent practice. Hence there will be a danger that inefficiencies will be incorporated into the new methods of undertaking the activity. A further problem is that historical data may be used to compare activity costs, inputs and outputs. Such data may be distorted by changes in technology and methods of working.

(b) Possible reasons for similar standard costs in plants with differing technology include:

(i) The investments may have been made to reduce long-term cost savings and these savings may not have been reflected in cost reductions.

(ii) Cost reduction may not have been a primary objective for investing in new technology. Improved quality, delivery and flexibility to provide product variations and obtain the benefits of economies of scope may have been the objectives of the investment. The benefits will be reflected in an increase in customer satisfaction and future sales revenues rather than cost reductions.

(iii) The new technologies may be subject to the learning curve effect that has not been incorporated into the standard costs.

(iv) Standard cost may have been computed using a traditional costing system that has failed to capture the cost benefits of the new technology. Also if the plants with the new technology are initially operating partly with the old and the new technology they will initially be under-utilized. If short-term capacity, rather than practical capacity, is used as the denominator level to set the overhead rates the new technology will be overcosted. For an explanation of this point you should refer to the sections relating to denominator levels in Chapters 7 and Learning Note 10.1 on the dedicated website.

(v) The new technology plants may have had implementation problems and the extra costs arising from such problems may have been initially incorporated into the standard costs.

(vi) Standard costs may be inappropriate benchmarks if significant variances occur. In these circumstances actual costs would be a more appropriate benchmark.

A reduction in unit costs may not have been the primary objective for investing in new technology. Therefore the focus should be on a comparison between plants of physical measures such as defect rates, cycle times, set-up times, machine efficiencies, stock levels and customer response times.

Question 21.5

(a) For an explanation of TQM you should refer to the 'Cost of quality' in Chapter 21. In addition, the answer should draw attention to the need to introduce a TQM training programme and a study of the production process to ensure that methods are in place to minimize defects and avoid scrap and rework. A 'right first time' policy should be implemented. A daily quality reporting system should also be introduced that reports defects, rework and returns from customers.

Consideration should also be given to introducing statistical quality control procedures. In addition, a six-monthly or annual cost of quality reporting system should be introduced.

(b) A JIT philosophy aims to eliminate waste and this is enhanced by the adoption of TQM. With the pull system that accompanies a JIT philosophy, defects bring the whole production process to a halt so a 'right first time' policy supports JIT production. Furthermore, the absence of stocks that is a feature of JIT means that safeguards do not exist to cope with defects, rework and returns from customers. The effects of poor quality result in costly production stoppages and a danger that customer commitments will not be met. TQM is therefore an inherent feature of JIT production.

(c) The four quality cost classifications are: prevention costs, appraisal costs, internal failure costs and external failure costs. See 'Cost of quality' in Chapter 21 for an explanation of these terms. Examples include preventive maintenance of food processing machinery (prevention cost), inspection of the output (appraisal cost), scrapping of foods because of inferior quality (external failure cost) and the cost of replacing faulty output delivered to customers and any lost profits on future sales arising from customer dissatisfaction (external failure cost).

Question 21.6

(a) The answer to this question requires a comparison of traditional production flow lines, push manufacturing and purchasing with a JIT manufacturing and purchasing policy. You will find a comparison of traditional and JIT methods in the section on just-in-time systems in Chapter 21.

(b) Cost reduction represents an attempt to reduce costs without affecting the customer's perception of the value of the product or service.

(c) Activity-based management should be introduced. This should involve identifying the product/service attributes that are valued by customers and those that are not valued (i.e. non-value-added activities). The focus should be on eliminating or reducing the cost of non-value-added activities. For a detailed description of this process you should refer to 'Activity-based management' in Chapter 21.

Question 21.7

(a) *Standard costing is a costing system whereas target costing is not a costing sytem*
Standard costing is a costing system whereby a database of estimated costs based on efficient operations is maintained. Target costing represents an approach to deriving a target cost and taking actions to achieve the target cost. It does not represent a costing system. Target costing is applied to new products, whereas standard costing is concerned with controlling the costs of existing activities. However, where a new product requires some existing operations, the cost of these operations can be derived from the standard costing system. If the estimated/standard cost exceeds the target cost, ways are investigated of driving down the estimated cost to the target cost. Thus, although standard costing is a formal costing system and target costing is not, they may be used together when adopting a target costing approach.

Proactive or not
Standard costing compares the actual cost with the target costs for different operations and provides a detailed analysis of the variances, which are used as clues to identify potential inefficiencies. It is therefore a feedback system that can be viewed as a cost containment mechanism. However, where the variance analysis identifies inefficiencies and steps are taken to avoid them reoccurring in the future, standard costing can be used in a proactive manner. Target costing is a proactive technique. A target cost is identified for a new product and this is compared with the estimated cost. Where the estimated cost exceeds the target cost, intensive efforts are made prior to the production process to drive the estimated cost down to the target cost. The fact that this process takes place

before production begins where there is an opportunity for product redesign makes the proactive nature of target costing one of its most attractive features. See 'Target costing' in Chapter 21 for a more detailed discussion of the proactive nature of target costing.

Consultation or not
There is no reason why standard costing should not involve participation of all parties involved, but since it is operated for existing products there is less need for many parties to be involved because operations can be observed when setting the standards. The comment in the question arises because a major feature of target costing is that it involves a team approach. For a description of the team approach see 'Target costing' in Chapter 21. Therefore, although standard costing can allow the same amount of consultation as target costing, in practice it is likely to involve far less participation. This is because standard costing can involve hundreds of products and operations but target costing involves an intensive study of only major new products. Therefore adopting a team approach involving consultation becomes more feasible.

(b) The answer should point out that the company should use standard costing to control the costs of existing operations and products provided that operations are of a repetitive nature to enable standards to be set. For major new products, target costing can be applied as a means of managing costs before production commences. After production commences, standard costing can be used to control the costs.

Question 21.8

(a) (i) See Figure Q21.8 for the answer to this question.

(a) (ii) Product life cycles consist of introductory, growth, maturity and decline stages. Products A and B have similar curves. Instead of an introductory stage they have a period of steady growth, a very short maturity stage followed by a period of rapid decline, but the decline phase is more rapid in B than A. Product A has a life cycle of 8 years compared to 6 years for B. Product C has more of an introductory phase and a slower rate of growth than products A and B. It also appears to have a less rapid decline stage.

(a) (iii)

Profit and loss analysis

	2001 A (£m)	2001 B (£m)	2001 C (£m)	2001 Total (£m)	2002 A (£m)	2002 B (£m)	2002 C (£m)	2002 Total (£m)
Sales revenue	3.00	9.00	6.50		2.00	3.00	7.50	
Variable costs	0.90	2.25	2.60		0.60	0.75	3.00	
Contribution	2.10	6.75	3.90		1.40	2.25	4.50	
Product specific fixed costs	2.00	4.00	2.80		1.10	1.80	3.00	
Product profits	0.10	2.75	1.10	3.95	0.30	0.45	1.50	2.25
Company fixed costs				2.50				2.50
Net profit/(loss)				1.45				(0.25)

(a) (iv) The forecasted total profit is £1.45m for 2001 and a loss of £0.25m for 2002. The total sales revenue for 2001 is £18.5m which is close to the 100% capacity level of £20m. In 2002 there has been a rapid decline in the sales revenue of product B resulting in total sales of £12.5m which represents only approximately 60% of total productive capacity. There is a need to introduce new products or increase the sales of existing products. All of the products make a positive contribution to company fixed costs.

(b) (i)

NPV calculation for product D

	2002 (£m)	2003 (£m)	2004 (£m)
Contribution at 60%	3.6	4.2	3.6
Less fixed costs	2.5	2.2	1.8
Net cash flows	1.1	2.0	1.8
Discount factor	0.909	0.826	0.751
Present value	0.9999	1.652	1.3518

NPV = Total present value (4.0037) – investment outlay (£4.5m) = –£0.4963m

(b) (ii) For product D to be viable the increase in contribution sales ratio must be sufficient to cover the negative NPV of £0.4963m.

Let x = the change in the contribution sales ratio.

$6x(0.909) + 7x(0.826) + 6x(0.751) = 0.4963$

$15.742x = 0.4963$

$x = 0.0315$

Therefore the required contribution/sales ratio would have to increase from 60% to above 63.15% for the NPV to be positive.

(b) (iii) The target variable cost for the new product exceeds the estimated cost and ways must be found to drive the estimated cost to below the target cost. For a discussion of the actions that can be taken to drive the actual cost down to the target cost, you should refer to target costing in Chapter 21.

(c) The forecasted sales for 2002–04 are respectively £18.5m, £17.5m and £13m. The company has approximately 10% unutilized capacity for the first two years and 35% in the final year. Although there is some scope for seeking methods of utilizing the spare capacity in the first two years, it is the final year where a considerable effort is required. It is important that steps are taken now to address the serious problem in the final year. Potential strategies include:

1   In the short-term make a major effort to extend the sales of products A and B. Consider product redesign to improve its marketability and developing new markets.

2   Seek to extend the maturity phase of product C and increase sales by seeking new markets and making more efforts to retain existing customers. Consider adopting new advertising strategies.

3   Investigate ways of increasing the sales of product D by extending the market and considering alternative pricing and advertising strategies.

4   Introduce a cost management programme that aims to reduce existing costs. This is particularly applicable in the first two years where only a small amount of unutilized capacity exists.

5   Take steps now to ensure that new products and markets are developed for beyond 2004.

For all of the above strategies cost/benefit principles should be applied to ensure that additional benefits exceed the additional costs.

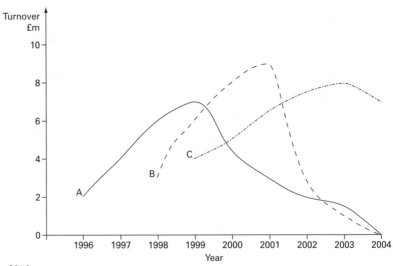

Turnover £m

Figure Q21.8

Question 21.9

(a) (i) *Total production units (pre-inspection)*

	Existing situation		Revised situation
Total sales requirements	5000		5000
Specification losses (5%)	250	(2.5%)	125
	5250		5125
Downgrading at inspection (12.5/87.5 × 5250)	750	(7.5/92.5 × 5125)	416
Total units before inspection			
(100/87.5 × 5250)	6000	(100/92.5 × 5125)	5541

(ii) *Purchase of material X (m²)*

	Existing		Revised
Materials required to meet pre-inspection			
production requirements (6000 × 8 m²)	48 000	(5541 × 8 m²)	44 328
Processing losses (4/96 × 48 000)	2 000	(2.5/97.5 × 44 328)	1 137
Input to the process (100/96 × 48 000)	50 000		45 465
Scrapped materials (5/95 × 50 000)	2 632	(3/97 × 45 465)	1 406
Total purchases (100/95 × 50 000)	52 632	(100/97 × 45 465)	46 871

(iii) *Gross machine hours*

	Existing		Revised
Initial requirements (6000 × 0.6)	3600	(5541 × 0.5 hrs)	2771
Rectification units (80% × 250 × 0.2 hrs)	40	(80% × 125 × 0.2 hrs)	20
	3640		2791
Idle time (20/80 × 3640)	910	(12.5/87.5 × 2791)	399
Gross machine hrs (100/80 × 3640)	4550	(100/87.5 × 2791)	3190

(b) *Profit and Loss Accounts*

	Existing situation (£)		Revised situation (£)
Sales revenue:			
First quality 5000 × £100	500 000	5000 × £100	500 000
Second quality 750 × £70	52 500	416 × £70	29 120
Third quality 200 × £50	10 000	100 × £50	5 000
Scrap sales 50 × £5	250	25 × £5	125
	562 750		534 245

Costs

Material X (52 632 × £4)	210 528	46 871 × £4	187 484
Insp/storage costs (52 632 × £0.10)	5 263	46 871 × £0.10	4 687
Machine costs (4550 × £40)	182 000	3190 × £40	127 600
Delivery of replacements			
(250 × £8)	2 000	125 × £8	1 000
Inspection and other costs	25 000	60% × £25 000	15 000
Product liability (3% × £500 000)	15 000	1% × 500 000	5 000
Sundry fixed costs	60 000	90% × £60 000	54 000
Prevention programme costs	20 000		60 000
	519 791		454 771
Net profit	42 959		79 474

(c) A cost of quality report is a major feature of a quality control programme. The report should indicate the total cost to the organization of producing products that do not conform to quality requirements. The cost of quality report should analyse costs by prevention costs, appraisal costs, internal failure costs and external failure costs. You should refer to Chapter 21 for a description of each of these cost categories.

The cost of quality report can be used as an attention-directing device to make top management aware of how much is being spent on quality-related costs. The report can be used to draw management's attention to the possibility of reducing total quality costs by a wiser allocation of costs among the four quality categories. For example, by spending more on prevention costs, the amount of spending in the internal and external failure categories can be substantially reduced, and therefore total spending can be lowered.

Examples of each of the four cost categories for Calton Ltd are as follows:

Internal failure costs: Incoming materials scrapped due to poor receipt and storage organization, and downgrading products at the final inspection stage.

External failure costs: Free replacement of goods, product liability claims, loss of customer goodwill.

Appraisal costs: Inspection checks of incoming materials and completed output.

Prevention costs: Training costs in quality prevention and preventative maintenance.

Strategic management accounting

Solutions to Chapter 22 questions

Question 22.1

(a) The answer to this question should draw attention to the changing manufacturing and competitive environment that occurred in the 1980s and 1990s and the failure of management accounting control systems to respond to these changes. Traditionally management accounting control systems tended to focus mainly on financial measures of performance and ignore those variables that were necessary to compete in today's competitive global environment. For a more detailed discussion of this issue you should refer to 'The balanced scorecard' in Chapter 22. The answer should also point out that traditional cost control systems have focused on cost containment rather than cost reduction (see introduction to Chapter 22) and have been applied at the later stages of the product life-cycle phases (see 'Life-cycle costing' in Chapter22).

(b) The answer to this question should draw off the content of Chapters 21 and 22. In particular, the answer should discuss how life-cycle/target costing, value chain analysis, activity-based management, linking performance measurement to strategy via the balanced scorecard and adopting a more external focus (strategic management accounting) have contributed to restoring the relevance of management accounting control systems.

Question 22.2

See 'Cost of quality' in Chapter 21 and 'Quality measures' in the section relating to the balanced scorecard in Chapter 22 for the answer to this question. The answer could also draw off some of the content relating to performance measurement in service organizations described in Learning Note 22.1 on the open access website (note in particular the determinants of quality of service in Exhibit LN22.1). The answer should also stress the need to monitor quality internally and externally. Internal controls and performance measures should be implemented as described in Chapters 21 and 22 so as to ensure that only products that meet customer quality requirements are despatched. To monitor quality externally customer feedback should be obtained and comparisons made with competitors. With service organizations the quality of the service can be assessed by using methods such as mystery shoppers. You should refer to Learning Note 22.1 for a more detailed description of how quality can be monitored in service organizations.

Question 22.3

(a) Physical measures are quantitative measures that do not use monetary measurements as a common denominator. Non-financial indices are ratios that are used to compare the trend in physical measures.

(b) (i)

$$\frac{\text{processing time}}{\text{processing time} + \text{inspection time} + \text{wait time} + \text{move time}}$$

This ratio gives an indication of the proportion of manufacturing cycle time which is engaged on value-added activities. Of the activities outlined above, only processing time adds value.

$$\text{(ii)} \quad \frac{\text{number of deliveries not on time}}{\text{total number of deliveries}}$$

This is a measure of the extent to which a company is failing to meet customer quality requirements in terms of late deliveries.

$$\text{(iii)} \quad \frac{\text{closing stocks}}{\text{average production output per day}}$$

This measure provides an indication of the average number of days production in inventory. This performance measure should be analysed by inventory category and location. It provides an indication of the extent to which the objectives of a just-in-time philosophy of minimizing stock levels is being achieved.

(c) For the answer to this question see 'Criticisms of standard costing' in Learning Note 18.4 and 'Harmful side-effects of controls' in Chapter 16 and 'JIT and management accounting' in Chapter 21.

Question 22.4

For the answer to this question you should refer to 'Benefits and limitations of the balanced scorecard approach' in Chapter 22. In addition to the points included in this section, the answer should also include the following items:
1   it integrates financial and non-financial measures of performance and identifies key performance measures that link the measurements to strategy;
2   it gives top management a fast and comprehensive view of the business unit;
3   each performance measure is part of a cause-and-effect relationship involving a linkage from strategy formulation to financial outcomes.
4   it distinguishes and links both lagging and lead measures.
See the sub-sections that relate to the four different perspectives in Chapter 22 for specific examples of quantitative measures for each aspect of the balanced scorecard.

Question 22.5

(a) Firms pursuing a cost leadership strategy aim to be the lowest cost producers or service providers in their industry. Accurate product costing and a strong focus on cost management are required. Accurate product costing is required to ensure that cost management initiatives are reflected in accurate product costs so that companies can have confidence in the bidding process when cost plus pricing is undertaken and also taking on business at prices less than competitors. Cost leadership accompanied by an accurate product costing system provides companies with the ability to lower price and compete effectively in times of severe competition.

Firms pursuing product differentiation seek to offer products or services that are considered by their customers to be superior and unique relative to their competitors. Product differentiation seeks to add attributes that are valued by the customer and which they are willing to pay for. It is therefore important that the costing system accurately assigns the costs of the resources of providing the attributes to the products requiring them. An appropriate pricing strategy (e.g. price skimming or price penetration) should be followed that ensures that the benefits of providing the attributes are reflected in long-term profits.

(b) You should refer to 'Pricing policies' in Chapter 11 for the answer to the first part of this question. For a discussion of an activity-based approach to pricing see 'A price setting firm facing long-run pricing decisions' in Chapter 11.

Question 22.6

(a) (i)

Profit and Loss Statements

	Budget (£)		Compuaid Ltd. Actual (£)		Competitors A (£)	B (£)
Revenues						
Home visits	440 000	(22 000 × £20)	464 000	(23 200 × £20)	87 500	810 000
All other advisors	1 168 000	(58 400 × £20)	1 442 000	(72 100 × £20)	756 180	1 266 000
Annual fee customers	584 000	(5840 × £100)	765 000	(7650 × £100)	495 000ᵃ	1 000 000
	2 192 000		2 671 000		1 338 680	3 076 000
Cost of sales						
Service wages	832 000	(104 000 × £8)	998 400	(124 800 × £8)	720 000	1 099 000
Sundry operating costs	950 000		1 000 000		650 000	1 250 000
Total	1 782 000		1 998 400		1 370 000	2 349 000
Profit/(loss)	410 000		672 600		(31 320)	727 000
Profit/Revenues	18.7%		25.2%		–2.3%	23.6%

Notes

ᵃ Company A = 6600 agreements at £75, Company B = 10 000 agreements at £100

(a) (ii) The figures show an improvement in net profits and net profits/sales compared with budget. The results also compare favourably with the competitor companies. The main reasons for the improvement and a better performance than the competitors include:

- Annual fee customers, other advisors and home visits revenues were respectively 30%, 23% and 5% greater than budget.
- Home visit customers were charged at a rate of £20 per hour. This is lower than the rate charged by competitors A (£87 500/3500 = £25) and B (£810 000/36 000 = £22.50).
- The rate billed for telephone and written e-mail advice was the same as company B (£1 266 000/63 300) but higher than company A (£756 180/42 010 = £18).
- The wage rate was £8 per hour compared with £9 per hour for A (£720 000/80 000 hours) and £7 per hour for B (£1 099 000/157 000 hours).
- Operating costs were budgeted at 43% of sales revenues but the actual percentage was 37%. Companies A and B had, respectively, operating costs as a percentage of sales of 49% and 41%.
- The actual hours taken up by the annual fee customers for Compuaid is significantly less than the competitors:

  Compuaid Ltd. = 2.0 Hours (15 300/7650)
  Competitor A = 4.5 hours (29 700/6600)
  Competitor C = 3.5 hours (35 000/10 000)

  Compuaid receives an annual fee of £100 per customer (the same as B but more than A) but significantly less time is required, resulting in this area of the business being far more profitable for Compuaid. This could be reflected in a lower level of customer satisfaction and future growth.

(b) (i) Competitiveness can be measured by market share or sales growth. In terms of sales growth, the annual fee customers, other advisors and home visits revenues were respectively 30%, 23% and 5% greater than budget for Compuaid. Competitiveness can also be measured by the success of the uptake of home visit enquiries received. For Compuaid the budgeted level was 67% and the actual level was 50% compared with 70% and 62% for A and B. However, competitor A had only a small number of visits so competitor B represents a more valid comparison.

(b) (ii) Quality can be measured by remedial work and customer complaints. The budgeted home visits remedial work for Compuaid was 3% but the actual level was 15%. Nevertheless, the actual percentage was significantly less than

A (400/1400 = 28%) and B (3400/15 000 = 23%). Customer complaints as a percentage of home visits were 1% for the budget and 2% for actual for Compuaid, compared with 5% for A and 1.5% for B.

(b) (iii) Resource utilization can be measured by the relationship between output to input hours and the percentage of home visit hours that are chargeable and non-chargeable. The budgeted ratio of output hours to input hours is 91.3% [(14 600 + 58 400 + 22 000)/104 000] and the actual ratio is 88.6%. The corresponding figures are 94% for A and 85.5% for B. For home visits the data can be analysed as follows:

	Compuaid (budget)	Compuaid (actual)	Company A	Company B
	%	%	%	%
Travel	9.3	14.7	5.4	8.7
Re-work	1.8	6.1	8.2	10.1
Idle time	7.4	8.0	38.4	11.6
Chargeable hours	81.5	71.2	48.0	69.6
	100.0	100.0	100.0	100.0

Note
ᵃ Home visit hours = 2500 + 2000 + 500 + 22 000 = 27 000

The above analysis shows that the percentage of chargeable hours has declined from 81.5% to 71.2% of total home visit hours and there has been a marginal increase in all three categories of non-chargeable hours. However, the actual percentage of chargeable hours is greater than both competitors.

(a) (i)   *Analysis of the total costs of the millennium proposal*

Question 22.7

	2000		2001	2002
	(£m)		(£m)	(£m)
Target cost: variable	6.000	(40% × £15m)	7.200	8.000
fixed	2.000		2.000	2.500
Internal failure cost	1.600	(20% × £8m)	0.920	0.525
External failure cost	2.000	(25% × £8m)	1.104	0.525
Appraisal costs	0.500		0.500	0.500
Prevention costs	2.000		1.000	0.500
Total cost	14.100		12.724	12.550

(a) (ii) Target costs of £8m, £7.2m and £8m in each year are significantly below the expected costs of £14.1m, £12.724m and £12.55m. The target cost represents the cost that will enable the required return on the project to be obtained. The above table shows the analysis of the gap between the target cost and the estimated cost by different categories – internal and external failure costs, appraisal costs and prevention costs. For an explanation and examples of these categories see 'Cost of quality' in Chapter 21. The answer should also point out that there appears to be a step increase in fixed costs in 2002 and a significant decline in internal and external failure costs. This may have arisen because of the large investment in prevention costs in 2000. There has also been a large decline in prevention costs over the three years possibly due to an investment in training costs in 2000 that have diminished over the years.

(b) (i)   Corporate vision seeks to define the basis on which the company will compete. The company has indicated that it will seek to identify the key competitors and compete by focusing on close cooperation with its customers by providing products to meet their specific design and quality standards. The aim is to achieve the corporate vision through focusing on internal efficiency and providing an effective after-sales service.

(b) (ii) Appropriate marketing measures indicate a projected increase in sales revenues of 20% in 2001 and 11% in 2002. The market share percentages are 12.5% (£15m/£120m) in 2000, 14.4% in 2001 and 15.4% in 2002. Net profits are expected to increase each year from £0.9m in 2000 (£15m – £14.1m) to £5.28m in 2001 and £7.45m in 2002. Net profits as a percentage of sales are respectively 6%, 29.3% and 37.25%. This may be partly due to the projected fall in quality costs.

(b) (iii) There are several measures in the schedule given in the question that contribute to customer satisfaction. The percentage of production achieving design quality standards improves over the three years from 95% to 98%. Returns from customers also declines from 3% to 0.5% and the cost of after-sales service is predicted to decline from £1.5m to £1m. Sales meeting planned delivery dates increases from 90% to 95% in 2001 and a 99% level is achieved in 2002. The cycle time from customer enquiry to delivery also declines over the three years. Therefore all of the measures support the potential for increased customer satisfaction.

(b) (iv) Decreases in cycle times and levels of waste should contribute to the long-term financial success of the proposal. The average cycle time from customer enquiry to delivery also declines over the three years being 6 weeks in 2000, 5.5 weeks in 2001 and 5 weeks in 2002. Waste, as measured by idle machine capacity, declines from 10% in 2000 to 2% in 2002 and the percentage of components scrapped in production is also expected to fall from 7.5% in 2000 to 2.5% in 2002. The latter may be attributable to the investment in prevention costs. Overall the measures support improved productivity that contribute to the improvement in financial performance.

(b) (v) Measures in (b) (iv) relate to the internal business processes of the balanced scorecard that appear to contribute to improved measures of customer satisfaction shown in (b) (iii), which in turn are assumed to contribute to improved financial performance. The answer should seek to highlight the cause-and-effect relationships that are assumed to occur from adopting a balanced scorecard approach and also show how the performance measures are linked to the mission and strategy of the organization.

Cost estimation and cost behaviour

Solutions to Chapter 23 questions

(a) Advertising expenditure is the independent variable (x) and sales revenue the dependent variable (y). **Question 23.1**

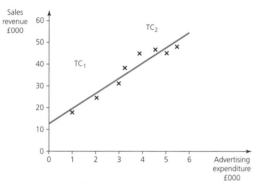

(b) Formulae 23.1 and 23.2 (see Chapter 23) were given in the examination for this question. Applying formula 23.2:

$$b = \frac{(8 \times 1055.875) - (26.35 \times 289.5)}{(8 \times 101.2625) - (26.35)^2}$$

$$= 818.675/115.7775 = 7.07$$

Applying formula 23.1
a = (289.5/8) – (7.07 × 26.35)/8 = 12.9
Therefore the regression line is y = 12.9 + 7.07x where x and y are expressed in £000s. The line of best fit is shown in the graph in (a).

(a) The first stage is to convert all costs to a 2002 basis. The calculations are as follows: **Question 23.2**

	1998 (£000)	1999 (£000)	2000 (£000)	2001 (£000)
Raw materials				
Skilled labour	$242(1.2)^4$	$344(1.2)^3$	$461(1.2)^2$	$477(1.2)$
Unskilled labour				
Factory overheads	$168(1.15)^3(1.2)$	$206(1.15)^2(1.2)$	$246(1.15)(1.2)$	$265(1.2)$
Power	$25(1.1)(1.25)^3$	$33(1.25)^3$	$47(1.25)^2$	$44(1.25)$
Raw materials				
Skilled labour	500.94	595.12	663.84	572.4
Unskilled labour				
Factory overheads	306.432	326.304	339.48	318
Power	53.625	64.35	73.32	55
Total (2002 prices)	861 000	986 000	1 077 000	945 000
Output (units)	160 000	190 000	220 000	180 000

The equation $r = a + bx$ is calculated from the above schedule of total production costs (2002 prices) and output. The calculations are as follows:

Output in units (000)	Total cost (£000)		
x	y	x^2	xy
160	861	25 600	137 760
190	986	36 100	187 340
220	1077	48 400	236 940
180	945	32 400	170 100
$\Sigma x = 750$	$\Sigma y = 3869$	$\Sigma x^2 = 142\ 500$	$\Sigma xy = 732\ 140$

Applying formula 23.2 shown in the text:

$$b = \frac{4(732\ 140) - 750\ (3\ 869)}{4\ (142\ 500) - (750)^2} = \frac{26\ 810}{7\ 500} = 3.575$$

Applying formula 23.1:

$$a = \frac{3\ 869}{4} - \frac{3.575\ (750)}{4} = 296.937$$

The relationship between total production costs and volume in 2002 is:
$y = £296\ 937 + £3.575x$

where y = total production costs (at 2002 price) and x = output level.
(b) See Chapter 23 for the answer to this question.
(c) General company overheads will still continue whether or not product LT is produced. Therefore the output of LT will not affect general production overheads. Consequently, the regression equation should not be calculated from cost data that includes general company overheads. General company overheads will not increase with increments in output of product LT. Hence short-term decisions and cost control should focus on those costs that are relevant to production of LTs. Common and unavoidable general fixed costs are not relevant to the production of LT, and should not be included in the regression equation.

Question 23.3

(a/b) See 'Cost estimation when the learning effect is present' in Chapter 23 for the answer to this question.
(c) See 'Learning-curve applications' in Chapter 23 for the answer to this question.
(d)

Cumulative production	Hours per unit of cumulative production
1	1000
2	800
4	640
8	512

The average unit costs are as follows:

4 machines	(£)	8 machines	(£)
Labour (640 × £3)	1920	Labour (512 × £3)	1536
Direct materials	1800	Direct materials	1800
Fixed costs (£8000/4)	2000	Fixed costs (£8000/8)	1000
	5720		4336

(a)

$$Y_{1000} = 18 \times 1000^{-0.1520}$$
$$Y_{1000} = 18 \times 0.3499$$
$$Y_{1000} = 6.2990 \text{ minutes}$$

The cumulative average time taken to produce 1000 units is 6.2990 minutes and the time taken to produce a total of 1000 units will therefore be 629.9 minutes (i.e. 104.98 hours).

	(£)
Standard cost of 1000 units:	
Materials (£28/0.95 × 1000)	29 474
Processing cost (104.98 hours at £25)	2625
	32 099

(b)

$$Y_{5000} = 18 \times 5000^{-0.1520}$$
$$Y_{5000} = 18 \times 0.274$$
$$Y_{5000} = 4.9321 \text{ minutes}$$

Therefore the estimated time taken to produce 5000 units is 24 660 minutes (5000 × 4.9321 minutes)

$$Y_{6000} = 18 \times 6000^{-0.1520}$$
$$Y_{6000} = 18 \times 0.2665$$
$$Y_{6000} = 4.7973 \text{ minutes}$$

Therefore the estimated time taken to produce 6000 units is 28 784 minutes (6000 × 4.7973 minutes) so the 1000 units has taken an additional 68.73 hours (28 784 minutes – 24 660 minutes) giving a standard variable processing cost of £1718 (68.73 hours × £25). Adding the direct material cost of £29 474 gives a total standard variable cost of £31 192.

(c) Revised learning curve effect:

$$Y_{1000} = 18 \times 1000^{-0.320}$$
$$Y_{1000} = 18 \times 0.1096$$
$$Y_{1000} = 1.9737 \text{ minutes}$$

The estimated total time to produce 1000 units in April is 32.89 hours (1973.7 minutes/60) giving a total standard variable processing cost of £822 (32.89 hours × £25). The standard direct material cost will remain unchanged at £29 474 giving a total standard cost of £30 296.

Original budgeted profit

	(£)
Sales	60 000
Variable costs	32 099
Contribution	27 901
Fixed costs	20 000
Profit	7 901

Actual profit

		(£)	(£)
Sales (900 × £62)			55 800
Production costs:	Direct materials	31 870	
	Variable processing	1 070	
	Fixed costs	24 840	
		57 780	

Closing stock (100 units at revised standard cost of
£30.296 per unit)   3 030   54 750
Profit   1 050

Variance calculations
Processing usage/efficiency variance (original standard of £2625 –
revised standard of £822)   £1803F
Selling price variance (£62 actual price – £60 budgeted price) ×
900 units   £1800F
Sales volume (900 actual volume – 1000 budgeted volume) × revised
stand. contrib. margin[a]   £2970A
Direct material cost (standard cost of 1000 × £29.474 – Actual cost
of £31 870)   £2396A
Variable processing expenditure (Flexed budget of 2425 minutes ×
£25/60 – actual cost)   £60A
Variable processing efficiency (1.9737 minutes revised standard ×
1000 units – actual time of 2 425 minutes) × stand. rate (£25 per hour) £188A
Fixed cost expenditure (Budgeted cost of £20 000 – Actual cost of
£24 840)   £4840A
Total variances   £6851A

Notes
[a] revised standard contribution margin = £60 selling price – revised variable cost
(£29.474 + £822/1000)   = £29.704

Reconciliation statement
Original budgeted profit   £7901
Less net variances as shown above   £6851A
Actual profit   £1050

(d) If budgets and standards are set without considering the learning effect, meaningless standards are likely to be set that are easy to attain. Therefore favourable variances would be reported that are not due to operational efficiency. Where
learning effects are expected, management should create an environment where
improvements are expected.

Question 23.5   (a)   (i) The learning curve is expressed as:

$$yx = ax^b$$

The exponent b is defined as the ratio of the logarithm of the learning curve
improvement rate divided by the logarithm of 2. For an 80% learning curve:

$$b = \log 0.8/\log 2 = -0.322$$

For an output of 14 units:

$y_{14} = 40 \times 14^{-0.322} = 17.1$ hours per unit
Time taken for 14 units = $14 \times 17.1 = 239.4$ hrs
Actual hours = 240

It would therefore appear that an 80% learning effect is a reasonable assumption.

COST ESTIMATION AND COST BEHAVIOUR

(ii) For an output of 50 units:

$$y_{50} = 40 \times 50^{-0.322} = 11.35 \text{ hours per unit}$$

Hours required for 50 units: $= 50 \times 11.35 = 567.5$ hrs
For an output of 30 units:

$$y_{30} = 40 \times 30^{-0.322} = 13.38 \text{ hours per unit}$$

Hours required for 30 units $= 30 \times 13.38 = 401.4$ hours
The time required for the additional 20 units $= 166.1$ hours $(567.5 - 401.4)$

(iii) *Estimated cost for an order of 30 units*

	(£)
Direct materials (30 × £30)	900.00
Direct labour (401.4 hrs × £6)	2408.40
Variable overhead (401.4 hrs × £0.50)	200.70
Fixed overhead (401.4 × £5)[a]	2007.00
	5516.10

The above product cost has been calculated on an absorption costing basis in accordance with the current standard absorption costing system.

Note
[a]Fixed overhead for the period $=$ £6000
Direct labour hours for the period $= 1200$ (75% × 40 hrs × 10 employees
× 4 weeks)
Fixed overhead hourly rate $=$ £5 (£6000/1200)
Where the learning effect is present, unit product costs and labour hours will not be constant per unit of output. Significant variations in product costs and labour hours per unit of output are likely to occur at lower output levels. It is therefore necessary to estimate the extent of the learning effect for standard settings, budgeting and selling price quotations. Failure to take into account the presence of the learning effect can result in significant errors in cost estimates and planned labour requirements. If standards are not adjusted, they will cease to represent meaningful targets and lead to the reporting of erroneous favourable variances.

(b) The statement refers to the fact that, with modern technology, there is a dramatic decrease in the direct labour content of most goods and services. Recent studies suggest that direct labour represents less than 10% of manufacturing cost and that overheads are more closely related to machine hours than direct labour hours. With modern technology, output tends to be determined by machine speeds rather than changes in labour efficiency. Consequently, the presence of the learning effect as workers become more familiar with new operating procedures is of considerably less importance.

The question implies that the learning curve is being replaced by an experience curve. The experience curve relates to the fact that output and efficiency are determined by manufacturing technologists such as engineers and production planners. As these groups of individuals gain experience from a range of applications of the new technology, efficiency improves and costs are minimized. It is therefore claimed that the experience curve has replaced the learning curve. However, the experience curve is extremely difficult to determine, and its impact is likely to take place over a much longer time period. It is therefore extremely difficult to capture the 'experience effect' within short-term standard setting, budgeting and cost estimation activities.

Quantitative models for the planning and control of inventories

Solutions to Chapter 24 questions

Question 24.1

$$\text{EOQ} \;=\; \sqrt{(2DO)/H} \;=\; \frac{\sqrt{[2\times(50+5)\times 4000}}{(15\times 0.1)+0.2]}$$

$$= 509 \text{ units}$$

Question 24.2

(a) TNG has a current order size of 50 000 units
Average number of orders per year = demand/order size = 255 380/50 000 = 5.11 orders
Annual ordering cost = 5.11 × £25 = £127.75
Safety stock held = 255 380 × 28/365 = 19 591 units
Average stock held = 19 591 + (50 000/^{2}) = 44 951 units
Annual holding cost = 44 591 × 0.1 = £4 459.10
Annual cost of current ordering policy = 4 459.10 + 127.75 = £4 587

(b) EOQ = $\sqrt{(2\times 255\ 380\times 25)/0.1}$ = 11 300 units
Average number or orders per year = 255 380/11 300 = 22.6 orders
Annual ordering cost = 22.6 × £25 = £565.00
Average stock held = 19 591 + (11 300/2) = 25 241 units
Annual holding cost = 25 241 × 0.1 = £2 524.10
Annual cost of EOQ ordering policy = 2 524.10 + 565.00 = £3 089
Saving compared to current policy = 4 587 – 3 089 = £1 498

(c) Annual credit purchases = 255 380 × £11 = £2 809 180
Current creditors = £2 809 180 × 60/365 = £461 783
Creditors if discount is taken = £2 809 180 × 20/365 = £153 928
Reduction in creditors = £461 783 – £153 928 = £307 855
Finance cost increase = £307 855 × 0.08 = £24 628
Discount gained = 2 809 180 × 0.01 = £28 091
Net benefit of taking discount = £28 091 – £24 628 = £3 463
The discount is therefore financially acceptable.

(d) The EOQ model assumes that demand, holding and ordering costs can be predicted with certainty and are constant for the period under consideration. In practice, demand throughout the period is likely to be uncertain and not constant. Costs are also unlikely to remain constant. The EOQ model also ignores the cost of running out of stock but the model can still be applied by ensuring that safety stocks are maintained. See 'Other factors influencing the choice of order quantity' in Chapter 24 for an explanation of how these factors might cause a firm to depart from the EOQ. Nevertheless, the EOQ model may still be useful because the model may not be significantly affected if the underlying assumptions are violated or there are variations in cost predictions. See 'Assumptions of the EOQ formula' in Chapter 24 for a more detailed discussion of these issues.

(e) See 'Just-in-time systems' in Chapter 21 for the answer to this question. In particular, the answer should discuss the elimination of waste, reduced inventories, quicker customer response times, improved longer-term relationships with suppliers and the resulting cost savings associated with these factors.

Disadvantages include greater dependence on the reliability of suppliers for adhering to quality and delivery requirements. Delay in delivery or the delivery of poor quality materials can have a dramatic detrimental impact on JIT systems in terms of production stoppages and delays in customer deliveries.

(a) *EOQ*

Question 24.3

$EOQ = \sqrt{(2DO/H)}$
where D = demand for period (43 200 units)
            O = ordering cost per unit (£900 + £750)
            H = holding cost per unit (15% × £30 + 2 × £3.25) = £11

Note that, assuming constant demand, the average stock level is one-half of the EOQ. In this question the holding costs applicable to storage space will depend upon maximum (rather than average) stock levels. It is therefore necessary to double the holding cost per unit given in the question.

$$EOQ = \sqrt{[(2 \times 43\ 200 \times £1650)/£11]} = 3600 \text{ units}$$

The EOQ is equivalent to one month's sales. Safety stocks equivalent to one month's sales are maintained. Consequently, stock levels will vary between 3600 and 7200 units.

Cash payments to trade creditors
The budgeted stock level of 21 600 units could be reduced to 7200 units. This represents stock reduction of 14 400 units, which is equivalent to 4 months' stocks. In other words, for the next four months, sales demand can be met from stocks. From month 5, purchases would be 3600 units per month.
    Budgeted monthly cost of sales = £108 000 (1296/12)

Trade creditors are therefore equivalent to 2 months' cost of sales. The schedule of payments to trade creditors would be as follows:

July and August 2000	£108 000 per month
September to December 2000	No payments made
January and February 2001	£108 000 per month

(b) (i) *Cash operating cycle at 30 June 2000*

	Months
Stockholding period (£21 600/3600)	6
Debtors average credit period [198/(2376/12)]	1
Creditors average payment period (per (a))	(2)
	5

(ii) *Cash operating cycle at 30 June 2001*

	Months
Stockholding period (7200 units)	2
Debtors (no change)	1
Creditors (no change)	(1)
	1

(c) The answer should include a discussion of the EOQ assumptions and the extent which these may be appropriate in a practical situation. The following points should be included in the answer:

(i) The formula assumes that demand can be accurately estimated and that usage is constant throughout the period. In practice, demand may be uncertain and subject to seasonal variations. Most firms hold safety stocks as a protection against variations in demand.

(ii) The ordering costs are assumed to be constant per order placed. In practice, most of the ordering costs are fixed or subject to step functions. It is therefore difficult to estimate the incremental cost per order.

(iii) Holding costs per unit are assumed to be constant. The financing charge for the investment in stocks is based on the average investment multiplied by the cost of capital. This will result in a reasonable estimate, provided that demand can be accurately estimated and that usage and the purchase price are constant throughout the period. Many holding costs are fixed throughout the period and are not relevant to the model, but other costs (e.g. store-keepers' salaries) are step fixed costs. Opportunity costs of the warehouse space and labour are other relevant holding costs that are included in the model. However, identifying lost opportunities from holding stocks is difficult to determine. Consequently, it is extremely difficult to accurately predict the holding cost for a unit in stock for one year.

(iv) Purchasing cost per unit is assumed to be constant for all purchase quantities. In practice, quantity discounts can result in purchasing economies of scale.

(v) Despite the fact that much of the data in the model represent rough approximations, the EOQ formula is likely to provide a reasonable guide of the EOQ because it is very insensitive to errors in predictions (see 'Effect of approximations' in Chapter 24). The EOQ model can also be adapted to incorporate quantity discounts. For a discussion of other issues relevant to this answer see 'Assumptions of the EOQ formula' in Chapter 24.

(d) The advantages of adopting a JIT approach include:

(i) Substantial savings in stockholding costs.

(ii) Elimination of waste.

(iii) Savings in factory and warehouse space, which can be used for other profitable activities.

(iv) Reduction in obsolete stocks.

(v) Considerable reduction in paperwork arising from a reduction in purchasing, stock and accounting transactions.

The disadvantages include:

(i) Additional investment costs in new machinery, changes in plant layout and goods inwards facilities.

(ii) Difficulty in predicting daily or weekly demand, which is a key feature of the JIT philosophy.

(iii) Increased risk due to the greater probability of stockout costs arising from strikes, or other unforeseen circumstances, that restrict production or supplies.

Question 24.4

(a) Order costs consist of variable purchasing costs (£300) plus transportation costs (£750 or £650). Note that the timing of the payments for 4200 units will be the same irrespective of the order size. Consequently, the cost of capital is omitted from the stockholding costs because it will be the same for all order quantities.

$$\text{EOQ with transportation costs of £750} = \sqrt{\left(\frac{2 \times 1050 \times 4200}{4}\right)}$$

$$= 1485 \text{ units}$$

At this level the company qualifies for the lower transport costs. Therefore the EOQ should be based on ordering costs of £950:

$$EOQ = \sqrt{\left(\frac{2 \times 950 \times 4200}{4}\right)} = 1412 \text{ units}$$

The company should therefore place orders for 1412 units.

Improvement in profit

		(£)
Gross profit (unchanged)		64 000
Purchasing department costs:		
Variable (4200/1412) × £300	(892)	
Fixed	(8400)	(9 292)
Transportation costs:		
(4200/1412) × £650		(1 933)
Insurance costs on average stockholding:		
[200 safety stock + (1412/2)] × £4		(3 624)
Warehouse fixed costs		(43 000)
Revised profit		6 151
Original profit		3 250
Improvement		2 901

(b) The re-order level should be based on the expected usage during the period plus a safety stock to provide a cushion in the event of demand being in excess of the expected usage.

Expected usage = $(500 \times 0.15) + (600 \times 0.20) + (700 \times 0.30) + (800 \times 0.20)$
$+ (900 \times 0.15) = 700$

Thus it is necessary to consider safety stocks of 0, 100 or 200 units.

Expected usage (units)	Safety stock (units)	Re-order point (units)	Stockout (units)	Annual stockout cost[a] (£18 per unit)	Probability	Annual expected stockout cost[b] (£)	Holding cost[b] (£)	Total expected cost (£)
700	0	700	200	21 600	0.15	3240		
			100	10 800	0.20	2160		
						5400	0	5400
700	100	800	100	10 800	0.15	1620	1800	3420
700	200	900	0	0		0	3600	3600

Notes
[a]Note that expected costs are calculated on an *annual* basis by multiplying 200 units × £18 × 6 (that is, six two-monthly periods).
[b]In the answer to part (a) the interest on the value of the stock was not included, because the timing of the payments for stocks was not affected by the order quantity. Consequently, the interest charge was not relevant in calculating the EOQ. The holding cost in the above calculation consists of £14 interest cost (20% of £70 purchase cost) plus £4 insurance cost. It is assumed that the safety stock represents an investment over and above the annual order quantity of 4200 units. In other words, safety stocks represent an incremental investment, and interest on safety stocks is therefore relevant to the safety stock decision.

Recommendation
Expected costs are minimized at a re-order point of 800 units (this includes a safety stock of 100 units).

(c) The answer to this question should include a discussion of the assumptions of the EOQ model (see 'Assumptions of the EOQ formula' in Chapter 24). The answer should stress that because demand is uncertain and not uniform and lead time is not constant, it is necessary to adjust the EOQ model to take account of these facts. The safety stock model applied in (b) is subject to a number of practical difficulties – for example, the difficulty of producing probability distributions for demand and lead time. In addition, stockout costs are extremely difficult to determine in practice. A further problem is that discrete distributions as estimated in (b) are unlikely to be a representation of reality because they are based on a limited number of outcomes. The answer produced represents the *expected value* of the stockholding costs, and as such represents a long-run average outcome. An alternative is to use continuous distributions, but this requires that the distribution conform to one that can easily be described mathematically (e.g. a normal distribution).

In practice, it is likely that stockout costs will be the most significant cost, and the problem is one of determining the minimum level of stock that is consistent with always satisfying demand. Most small companies are likely to concentrate on frequently reviewing stock levels and use their previous experience to subjectively determine order levels.

Question 24.5

(a) Expected annual demand = 10 000 units × 52 weeks = 520 000 units
Holding cost per unit = 18% of purchase price (£4.50) = £0.81

$$EOQ = \sqrt{\left(\frac{2 \times 520\ 000 \times £311.54}{0.81}\right)}$$

= 20 000 units

(b) The average usage during the two week lead time is 20 000 units. If sales were always 10 000 units per week, the re-order point would be 20 000 units and stocks would be replenished when the stock level had fallen to zero. No safety stocks would be required. However, if demand is in excess of 20 000 units, stockouts will occur if no safety stocks are maintained. Consideration should therefore be given to holding safety stocks.

Maintaining safety stocks reduces the probability of running out of stock and incurring stockout costs, but this policy also results in additional holding costs. The annual holding cost per unit is £0.81. Over a two-week period, the holding cost per unit is £0.031 15 (£0.81/26 weeks). Stockout costs consist of the costs associated with losing orders. The cost of losing an order is the contribution per unit of £1.50 [£6.30 − (£4.50 + £0.30)]. The lost contribution applies to 25% of the orders in any two-week period. The expected stockout cost is therefore £0.375 (0.25 × £1.50) per unit.

The expected costs for various levels of safety stocks are as follows:

Safety stock (units)	Re-order point (units)	Stockout (units)	Probability of stockout	Expected stockout cost (£)	Holding cost (£)	Total Expected cost (£)
8000	28 000	0	0	0	249[a]	249
4000	24 000	4000	0.05	75[b]	125[a]	200
0	20 000	4000	0.20	300[b]		
		8000	0.05	150[b]	0	450

Expected costs are minimized when safety stocks are 4000 units. Therefore the recommended level of safety stocks is 4000 units.

Notes
[a]Safety stocks of 8000 units = holding cost of 8000 × £0.031 15 = £249
Safety stocks of 4000 units = holding cost of 4000 × £0.031 15 = £125.
[b]Safety stocks of 4000 units: stockout of 4000 units × £0.375 × 0.05 probability = £75
Safety stocks of zero: if demand is 24 000 units (probability = 0.20), there will be a 4000 units stockout, with an expected cost of 4000 × £0.375 × 0.2 = £300. If demand is 28 000 units (probability = 0.05), there will be a stockout of 8000 units, with an expected cost of 8000 × £0.375 × 0.05 = £150.

(c) If 30 000 units are ordered instead of 20 000 units, there will be an annual purchase cost saving of £23 400 (1% × 520 000 units × £4.50) resulting from the quantity discount. The annual savings in order costs will be as follows:

$$(520\ 000/30\ 000 \times £311.54) - (520\ 000/20\ 000 \times £311.54) = £2700$$

Total annual savings are therefore £26 100 (£23 400 + £2700). The annual holding costs are as follows:

30 000 units =   18% × £4.455 revised purchase price × 15 000 units average stock = £12 028
20 000 units = 18% × £4.50 purchase price × 10 000 units average stock = £8100

Therefore the additional holding cost is £3928 (£12 028 – £8100) and the overall net saving is £22 172 (£26 100 – £3928). It would therefore be beneficial to take advantage of the quantity discount.

(d) Total relevant costs would be as follows:

50% higher (30 000 units)   = £0.81 × (30 000/2) + £311.54 × (520 000/30 000)
                              = £17 550
50% lower (10 000 units)   = £0.81 × (10 000/2) + £311.54 × (520 000/10 000)
                              = £20 250
Original EOQ (20 000 units) = £0.81 × (20 000/2) + £311.54 × (520 000/20 000)
                              = £16 200

It is assumed that this part of the question refers to the original data given and that the quantity discount is not available. Total annual costs are 8.3% higher than the original EOQ at the 30 000-units order level and 25% higher at the 10 000-units order level. Therefore stock management costs are relatively insensitive to substantial changes in the EOQ.

(e) It would be necessary to establish seasonal periods where sales are fairly constant throughout each period. A separate EOQ would then be established for each distinct season throughout the year.

(f) The EOQ model is a model that enables the costs of stock management to be minimized. The model is based on the following assumptions.
   (i) Constant purchase price per unit irrespective of the order quantity.
   (ii) Ordering costs are constant for each order placed.
   (iii) Constant lead times.
   (iv) Constant holding costs per unit.
   More sophisticated versions of the above model have been developed that are not dependent on the above assumptions. However, the EOQ is fairly insensitive to changes in the variables used in the model.

Recently, some companies have adopted just-in-time (JIT) purchasing techniques whereby they have been able to negotiate reliable and frequent deliveries. This has been accompanied by the issue of blanket long-term purchase orders and a substantial reduction in ordering costs. The overall effect of applying the EOQ formula in this situation ties in with the JIT philosophy: that is, more frequent purchases of smaller quantities.

The application of linear programming to management accounting

Solutions to Chapter 25 questions

(a) For the answer to this question you should refer to Appendix 9.1 in Chapter 9. In **Question 25.1** particular, you should point out that contribution is defined as sales revenue less short-term variable costs. In today's manufacturing environment short-term variable costs are assumed to consist of only direct materials. Direct labour is assumed to be fixed within short-term time periods and thus does not vary in the very short-term with changes in activity levels. Throughput accounting therefore focuses on short-term decision-making.

(b)

	TR (£ per batch)	PN (£ per batch)	BE (£ per batch)	Total
Selling price	340	450	270	
Ingredients	250	285	175	
Contribution	90	165	95	
Kgs of L	7	9	4	
Contributions per kg of L	12.86	18.33	23.75	
Ranking	3	2	1	
Minimum output (batches)	50	50	50	
Minimum output usage of L	350	450	200	1000
Optimum usage of L (batches)	235	350	300	
Allocation of unused L	1650	3150	1200	6000
Total output (batches)	285	400	350	

(c) The objective function value of £110 714 is the contribution from the optimal solution consisting of 500 batches of TR, 357 batches of PN and 71 batches of BE. The product slack values of 0, 43 and 279 represent the unsatisfied demand (in batches) of products TR, PN, and BE respectively.

   The slack values for ingredients L and M of £3 and £28 respectively represent the shadow prices of the scarce resources. There is no shadow price for ingredient K because there are no restrictions on the supply.

(a) **Question 25.2**

	M	F
Contribution per unit	£96	£110
Litres of material P required	8	10
Contribution per litre of material P	£12	£11
Ranking	1	2
Production/sales (units)	1000	2325[a]

Note
[a] 31 250 litres of P less (1000 × 8) for M = 23 250 litres for F giving a total production of 2325 units (23 250 litres/10)

(b)

	M (£000)	F (£000)	Total (£000)
Sales	200	488.250	688.250
Variable costs:			
Material P	20	58.125	78.125
Material Q	40	46.500	86.500
Direct labour	28	81.375	109.375
Overhead	16	46.500	62.500
	104	232.500	336.500
Contribution	96	255.750	351.750
Fixed costs (£150 000 + £57 750)			207.750
Profit			144.000

(c) Maximize Z = 96M + 110F (product contributions) subject to:

8M + 10F ≤ 31 250 (material P constraint)
10M + 5F ≤ 20 000 (material Q constraint)
4M + 5F ≤ 17 500 (direct labour constraint)
M ≤ 1 000 (maximum demand for M)
F ≤ 3 000 (maximum demand for F)

The above constraints are plotted on the graph shown in Figure Q25.2 as follows:
Material P; Line from M = 3906.25, F = 0 to F = 3125, M = 0
Material Q; Line from M = 2000, F = 0 to F = 4000, M = 0
Direct labour; Line from M = 4375, F = 0 to F = 3500, M = 0
Sales demand of M; Line from M = 1000
Sales demand of F; Line from F = 3000

The optimal solution occurs where the lines in Figure 25.2 intersect for material P and Q constraints. The point can be determined from the graph or mathematically as follows:

8M + 10F = 31 250 (material P constraint)
10M + 5F = 20 000 (material Q constraint)

multiplying the first equation by 1 and the second equation by 2:

8M + 10F = 31 250
20M + 10F = 40 000
subtracting −12M = − 8750
M = 729.166

Substituting for M in the first equation:

8(729.166) + 10F = 31 250
F = 2541.667

(d)

		(£)
Contribution:	(729 units of M at £96)	69 984
	(2542 units of F at £110)	279 620
		349 604
Less fixed costs		207 750
Profit		141 854

Moving from the solution in (c) where the lines intersect as a result of obtaining an additional litre of material Q gives the following revised equations:
8M + 10F = 31 250 (material P constraint)
10M + 5F = 20 001 (material Q constraint)

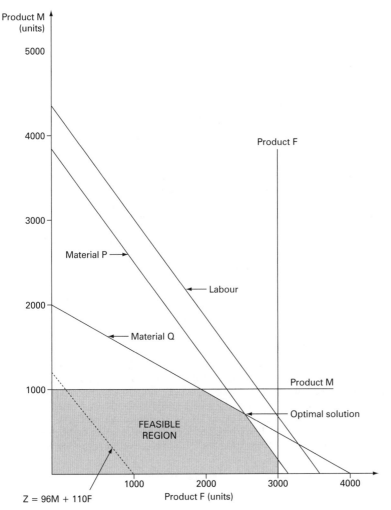

Product M
(units)

5000 —

4000 —   Product F

3000 —

Material P →

← Labour

2000 —

← Material Q

Product M

1000 —

Optimal solution

FEASIBLE
REGION

1000   2000   3000   4000

Z = 96M + 110F   Product F (units)

Figure Q25.2

The values of M and F when the above equations are solved are 729.333 and
2541.533. Therefore, M is increased by 0.167 units and F is reduced by 0.134
units giving an additional total contribution of £1.292 [0.167 × £96) – (0.134 ×
£110)] per additional litre of Q. Therefore the shadow price of Q is £1.292 per
litre.
(e) See Chapter 25 for an explanation of shadow prices.
(f) Other factors to be taken into account include the impact of failing to meet the
demand for product M, the need to examine methods of removing the
constraints by sourcing different markets for the materials and the possibility of
sub-contracting to meet the unfulfilled demand.

Question 25.3

(a) Let X = number of units of XL produced each week
Y = number of units of YM produced each week
Z = total contribution

The linear programming model is:
Maximize $Z = 40X + 30Y$ (product contributions) subject to

$$4X + 4Y \leqslant 120 \text{ (materials constraint)}$$
$$4X + 2Y \leqslant 100 \text{ (labour constraint)}$$
$$X + 2Y \leqslant 50 \text{ (plating constraint)}$$
$$X, Y \quad \geqslant 0$$

The above constraints are plotted on Figure Q25.3. The optimum output is at point C on the graph, indicating that 20 units of XL and 10 units of YM should be produced. The optimum output can be determined exactly by solving the simultaneous equations for the constraints that intersect at point C:

$$4X + 4Y = 120$$
$$4X + 2Y = 100$$

Subtracting
$$2Y = 20$$
$$Y = 10$$

Substituting for Y:
$$4X + 40 = 120$$
$$X = 20$$

The maximum weekly profit is:

$$(20 \times £40) + (10 \times £30) - £700 \text{ fixed costs} = £400$$

(b) The present objective function is $40X + 30Y$ and the gradient of this line is $-40/30$. If the selling price of YM were increased, the contribution of YM would increase and the gradient of the line ($-40/30$) would decrease. The current optimal point is C because the gradient of the objective function line is greater than the gradient of the line for the constraint of materials (the line on which the optimal point C falls). If the gradient of the objective function line were equal to

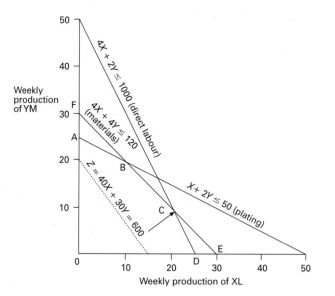

Figure Q25.3

THE APPLICATION OF LINEAR PROGRAMMING TO MANAGEMENT ACCOUNTING

the gradient of the line for the materials constraint, the optimal solution would be any point on FC. The gradient for the materials constraint line is -1. If the gradient for the objective function line were less than -1, the optimal solution would change from point C to point B. The gradient of the line for the current objective function of $40X + 30Y$ will be greater than -1 as long as the contribution from YM is less than £40. If the contribution from YM is £40 or more, the optimum solution will change. Therefore the maximum selling price for YM is £190 (£150 variable cost + £40 contribution).

(c) If plating time can be sold for £16 per hour then any hour devoted to XLs and YMs loses £16 sales revenue. The relevant cost per plating hour is now £16 opportunity cost. The contributions used in the objective function should be changed to reflect this opportunity cost. The contribution should be reduced by £4 (1 hour at £16 − £12) for XL and by £8 (2 hours at £16 −£12) for YL. The revised objective function is:

$$Z = 36X + 22Y$$

(d) The scarce resources are materials and labour. This is because these two constraints intersect at the optimal point C. Plating is not a scarce resource, and the shadow price is zero.

If we obtain an additional unit of materials the revised constraints will be:

$$4X + 4Y = 121 \text{ (materials)}$$
$$4X + 2Y = 100 \text{ (labour)}$$

The values of X and Y when the above equations are solved at 10.5 for Y and 19.75 for X. Therefore YM is increased by 0.5 units and XL is reduced by 0.25 units and the change in contribution will be as follows:

	(£)
Increase in contribution of YM (0.5 × £30)	15
Decrease in contribution of XL (0.25 × £40)	10
Increase in contribution (shadow price)	5

If we obtain one additional labour hour, the revised constraints will be:

$$4X + 4Y = 120 \text{ (materials)}$$
$$4X + 2Y = 101 \text{ (labour)}$$

The values of X and Y when the above equations are solved are 9.5 for Y and 20.5 for X. Therefore XL is increased by 0.5 units and YM is reduced by 0.5 units, and the change in contribution will be as follows:

	(£)
Increase in contribution from XL (0.5 × £40)	20
Decrease in contribution from YM (0.5 × £30)	15
Increase in contribution (shadow price)	5

The relevant cost of resources used in producing ZN consists of the acquisition cost plus the shadow price (opportunity cost). The relevant cost calculation is:

	(£)
Material A [5 kg at (£10 + £5)]	75
Labour [5 hours at (£8 + £5)]	65
Plating (1 hour at £12)	12
Other variable costs	90
	242

The selling price is less than the relevant cost. Therefore product ZN is not a profitable addition to the product range.

(e) The shadow price of labour is £5 per hour. Therefore the company should be prepared to pay up to £5 in excess of the current rate of £8 in order to remove the constraint. An overtime payment involves an extra £4 per hour, and therefore overtime working is worthwhile.

Increasing direct labour hours will result in the labour constraint shifting to the right. However, when the labour constraint line reaches point E, further increases in labour will not enable output to be expanded (this is because other constraints will be binding). The new optimal product mix will be at point E, with an output of 30 units of XL and zero of YM. This product mix requires 120 hours (30 × 4 hrs). Therefore 120 labour hours will be worked each week. Note that profit will increase by £20 [20 × (£5 – £4)].

(f) The limitations are as follows:

(i) It is assumed that the objective function and the constraints are linear functions of the two variables. In practice, stepped fixed costs might exist or resources might not be used at a constant rate throughout the entire output range. Selling prices might have to be reduced to increase sales volume.

(ii) Constraints are unlikely to be completely fixed and as precise as implied in the mathematical model. Some constraints can be removed at an additional cost.

(iii) The output of the model is dependent on the accuracy of the estimates used. In practice, it is difficult to segregate costs accurately into their fixed and variable elements.

(iv) Divisibility of output is not realistic in practice (fractions of products cannot be produced). This problem can be overcome by the use of integer programming.

(v) The graphical approach requires that only two variables (products) be considered. If several products compete for scarce resources, it will be necessary to use the Simplex method.

(vi) Qualitative factors are not considered. For example, if overtime is paid, the optimum solution is to produce zero of product YM. This will result in the demand from regular customers for YM (who might also buy XM) not being met. This harmful effect on customer goodwill is not reflected in the model.

Question 25.4

(a) The calculation of the contributions for each product is:

	X1 (£)	X2 (£)	X3 (£)
Selling price	83	81	81
Materials^a	(51)	(45)	(54)
Manufacturing costs^b	(11)	(11)	(11)
Contribution	21	25	16

Notes

^{a}The material cost per tonne for each product is:

$X1 = (0.1 \times £150) + (0.1 \times £60) + (0.2 \times £120) + (0.6 \times £10) = £51$
$X2 = (0.1 \times £150) + (0.2 \times £60) + (0.1 \times £120) + (0.6 \times £10) = £45$
$X3 = (0.2 \times £150) + (0.1 \times £60) + (0.1 \times £120) + (0.6 \times £10) = £54$

^{b}It is assumed that manufacturing costs do not include any fixed costs. The initial linear programming model is as follows:

$$\text{Maximize } Z = 21X1 + 25X2 + 16X3$$
$$\text{subject to } 0.1X1 + 0.1X2 + 0.2X3 \leqslant 1200 \text{ (nitrate)}$$
$$0.1X1 + 0.2X2 + 0.1X3 \leqslant 2000 \text{ (phosphate)}$$
$$0.2X1 + 0.1X2 + 0.1X3 \leqslant 2200 \text{ (potash)}$$
$$X1, X2, X3 \geqslant 0$$

(b) The slack variables are introduced to represent the amount of each of the scarce resources unused at the point of optimality. This enables the constraints to be expressed in equalities. The initial Simplex tableau is:

	X1	X2	X3
X4 (nitrate) = 1200	− 0.1	− 0.1	− 0.2
X5 (phosphate) = 2000	− 0.1	− 0.2	− 0.1
X6 (potash) = 2200	− 0.2	− 0.1	− 0.1
Z (contribution) = 0	21	25	16

(c) The starting point for the first iteration is to select the product with the highest contribution (that is, X2), but production of X2 is limited because of the input constraints. Nitrate (X4) limits us to a maximum production of 12 000 tonnes (1200/0.1), X5 to a maximum production of 10 000 tonnes (2000/0.2) and X6 to a maximum production of 22 000 tonnes (2200/0.1). We are therefore restricted to a maximum production of 10 000 tonnes of product X2 because of the X5 constraint. The procedure which we should follow is to rearrange the equation that results in the constraint (that is, X5) in terms of the product we have chosen to make (that is, X2). Therefore the X5 equation is re-expressed in terms of X2, and X5 will be replaced in the second iteration by X2. (Refer to Learning Note 25.1 for an explanation of this procedure.) Thus X2 is the entering variable and X5 is the leaving variable.

(d) Following the procedure outlined in Chapter 25, the final tableau given in the question can be reproduced as follow:

	Quantity	X3	X4	X5
X1	4 000	−3	−20	+10
X2	8 000	+1	+10	−10
X6	600	+0.4	+3	−1
Z	284 000	−22	−170	− 40

In Chapter 25 the approach adopted was to formulate the first tableau with positive contribution signs and negative signs for the slack variable equations. The optimal solution occurs when the signs in the contribution row are all negative. The opposite procedure has been applied with the tableau presented in the question. Therefore the signs have been reversed in the above tableau to ensure it is in the same format as that presented in Chapter 25. Note that when an entry of 1 is shown in a row or column for a particular product or slack variable then the entry does not appear in the above tableau. For example, X1 has an entry of 1 for the X1 row and X1 column. These cancel out and the entry is not made in the above tableau. Similarly, an entry of 1 is omitted in respect of X2 and X6.

The optimum solution is to produce 4000 tonnes of X1, 8000 tonnes of X2 and zero X3 each month. This gives a monthly contribution of £284 000, uses all the nitrate (X4) and phosphate (X5), but leaves 600 tonnes of potash (X6) unused. The opportunity costs of the scarce resources are:

Nitrate (X4)	£170 per tonne
Phosphate (X5)	£40 per tonne

If we can obtain an additional tonne of nitrate then output of X1 should be increased by 20 tonnes and output of X2 should be reduced by 10 tonnes.

Note that we reverse the signs when additional resources are obtained. The effect of this substitution process on each of the resources and contribution is as follows:

	Nitrate (X4) (tonnes)	Phosphate (X5) (tonnes)	Potash (X6) (tonnes)	Contribution (£)
Increase $X1$ by 20 tonnes	$-2(20 \times 0.1)$	-2	-4	$+420$
Reduce $X2$ by 10 tonnes	$+1(10 \times 0.1)$	$+2$	$+1$	-250
Net effect	-1	0	-3	$+170$

The net effect agrees with the $X4$ column in the final tableau. That is, the substitution process will use up exactly the one additional tonne of nitrate, 3 tonnes of unused resources of potash and increase contribution by £170.

To sell one unit of $X3$, we obtain the resources by reducing the output of $X1$ by 3 tonnes and increasing the output of $X2$ by 1 tonne. (Note the signs are not reversed, because we are not obtaining additional scarce resources.) The effect of this substitution process is to reduce contribution by £22 for each tonne of $X3$ produced. The calculation is as follows:

$$\text{Increase } X3 \text{ by 1 tonne} = +£16 \text{ contribution}$$
$$\text{Increase } X2 \text{ by 1 tonne} = +£25 \text{ contribution}$$

$$\text{Reduce } X1 \text{ by 3 tonnes} = -£63$$
$$\text{Loss of contribution} \quad = -£22$$

(e) (i) Using the substitution process outlined in (d), the new values if 100 extra tonnes of nitrate are obtained will be:

$$X1 \ 4000 + (20 \times 100) = 6000$$
$$X2 \ 8000 - (10 \times 100) = 7000$$
$$X6 \ \ 600 - \ \ (3 \times 100) = \ \ 300$$
$$\text{Contribution } 284\,000 + (£170 \times 100) = £301\,000$$

Hence the new optimal solution is to make 6000 tonnes of $X1$ and 7000 tonnes of $X2$ per month, and this output will yield a contribution of £301 000.

(ii) Using the substitution process outlined in (d), the new values if 200 tonnes per month of $X3$ are supplied will be:

$$X1 \ 4000 - (3 \times 200) = 3400$$
$$X2 \ 8000 + (1 \times 200) = 8200$$
$$X6 \ \ 600 + (0.4 \times 200) = \ \ 680$$
$$X3 \ \ \ \ 0 + (1 \times 200) = \ \ 200$$
$$\text{Contribution } £284\,000 - (£22 \times 200) = 279\,600$$

Hence the new optimal solution is to produce 3400 tonnes of $X1$, 8200 tonnes of $X2$ and 200 tonnes of $X3$, and this output will yield a contribution of £279 600. (Note that the signs in the final tableau are only reversed when *additional* scarce *resources* are obtained.)

THE APPLICATION OF LINEAR PROGRAMMING TO MANAGEMENT ACCOUNTING